CompTIA Network+ Certification
2005 Objectives

Student Manual

Australia • Canada • Mexico • Singapore
Spain • United Kingdom • United States

CompTIA Network+ Certification
2005 Objectives

VP and GM, Training Group: Michael Springer

Series Product Managers: Charles G. Blum and Adam A. Wilcox

Developmental Editor: Jutta VanStean

Copyeditors: Ken Maher, Robert Tillett, and Micky Markert

Series Designer: Adam A. Wilcox

Cover Designer: Abby Scholz

For more information contact:

Course Technology
25 Thomson Place
Boston, MA 02210

Or find us on the Web at: www.course.com

For permission to use material from this text or product, submit a request online at: www.thomsonrights.com

Any additional questions about permissions can be submitted by e-mail to: thomsonrights@thomson.com

Trademarks

Course ILT is a trademark of Course Technology.

Some of the product names and company names used in this book have been used for identification purposes only and may be trademarks or registered trademarks of their respective manufacturers and sellers.

Disclaimers

Course Technology reserves the right to revise this publication and make changes from time to time in its content without notice.

The logo of the CompTIA Authorized Quality Curriculum (CAQC) program and the status of this or other training material as "Authorized" under the CompTIA Authorized Quality Curriculum program signifies that, in CompTIA's opinion, such training material covers the content of CompTIA's related certification exam.

The contents of this training material were created for the CompTIA Network+ exam covering CompTIA certification objectives that were current as of December 2005.

CompTIA has not reviewed or approved the accuracy of the contents of this training material and specifically disclaims any warranties of merchantability or fitness for a particular purpose. CompTIA makes no guarantee concerning the success of persons using any such "Authorized" or other training material in order to prepare for any CompTIA certification exam.

ISBNs:

   1-4239-1443-0 = Student Manual + MeasureUp and CertBlaster
   1-4239-1445-7 = Student Manual + MeasureUp, CertBlaster, and CBT

Printed in the United States of America

  2 3 4 5 6 7 8 9 PM 08 07 06

Contents

Introduction

After reading this introduction, you will know how to:

A Use Course Technology ILT manuals in general.

B Use prerequisites, a target student description, course objectives, and a skills inventory to properly set your expectations for the course.

C Re-key this course after class.

Topic A: About the manual

Course Technology ILT philosophy

Course Technology ILT manuals facilitate your learning by providing structured interaction with the software itself. While we provide text to explain difficult concepts, the hands-on activities are the focus of our courses. By paying close attention as your instructor leads you through these activities, you will learn the skills and concepts effectively.

We believe strongly in the instructor-led classroom. During class, focus on your instructor. Our manuals are designed and written to facilitate your interaction with your instructor, and not to call attention to manuals themselves.

We believe in the basic approach of setting expectations, delivering instruction, and providing summary and review afterwards. For this reason, lessons begin with objectives and end with summaries. We also provide overall course objectives and a course summary to provide both an introduction to and closure on the entire course.

Manual components

The manuals contain these major components:

- Table of contents
- Introduction
- Units
- Appendices
- Course summary
- Glossary
- Index

Each element is described below.

Table of contents

The table of contents acts as a learning roadmap.

Introduction

The introduction contains information about our training philosophy and our manual components, features, and conventions. It contains target student, prerequisite, objective, and setup information for the specific course.

Units

Units are the largest structural component of the course content. A unit begins with a title page that lists objectives for each major subdivision, or topic, within the unit. Within each topic, conceptual and explanatory information alternates with hands-on activities. Units conclude with a summary comprising one paragraph for each topic, and an independent practice activity that gives you an opportunity to practice the skills you've learned.

The conceptual information takes the form of text paragraphs, exhibits, lists, and tables. The activities are structured in two columns, one telling you what to do, the other providing explanations, descriptions, and graphics.

Appendices

An appendix is similar to a unit in that it contains objectives and conceptual explanations. However, an appendix does not include hands-on activities, a summary, or an independent practice activity. We have also included an appendix that lists all CompTIA Network+ exam objectives with references to corresponding coverage in this manual.

Course summary

This section provides a text summary of the entire course. It is useful for providing closure at the end of the course. The course summary also indicates the next course in this series, if there is one, and lists additional resources you might find useful as you continue to learn about the software..

Glossary

The glossary provides definitions for all of the key terms used in this course.

Index

The index at the end of this manual makes it easy for you to find information about a particular software component, feature, or concept.

Manual conventions

We've tried to keep the number of elements and the types of formatting to a minimum in the manuals. This aids in clarity and makes the manuals more classically elegant looking. But there are some conventions and icons you should know about.

Convention/Icon	Description
Italic text	In conceptual text, indicates a new term or feature.
Bold text	In unit summaries, indicates a key term or concept. In an independent practice activity, indicates an explicit item that you select, choose, or type.
`Code font`	Indicates code or syntax.
Select **bold item**	In the left column of hands-on activities, bold sans-serif text indicates an explicit item that you select, choose, or type.
Keycaps like (↵ ENTER)	Indicate a key on the keyboard you must press.

Hands-on activities

The hands-on activities are the most important parts of our manuals. They are divided into two primary columns. The "Here's how" column gives short instructions to you about what to do. The "Here's why" column provides explanations, graphics, and clarifications. Here's a sample:

Do it!

A-1:   Creating a commission formula

Here's how	Here's why
1 Open Sales	This is an oversimplified sales compensation worksheet. It shows sales totals, commissions, and incentives for five sales reps.
2 Observe the contents of cell F4	F4 ▼ = =E4*C_Rate
	The commission rate formulas use the name "C_Rate" instead of a value for the commission rate.

For these activities, we have provided a collection of data files designed to help you learn each skill in a real-world business context. As you work through the activities, you will modify and update these files. Of course, you might make a mistake and, therefore, want to re-key the activity starting from scratch. To make it easy to start over, you will rename each data file at the end of the first activity in which the file is modified. Our convention for renaming files is to add the word "My" to the beginning of the file name. In the above activity, for example, a file called "Sales" is being used for the first time. At the end of this activity, you would save the file as "My sales," thus leaving the "Sales" file unchanged. If you make a mistake, you can start over using the original "Sales" file.

In some activities, however, it may not be practical to rename the data file. If you want to retry one of these activities, ask your instructor for a fresh copy of the original data file.

Topic B: Setting your expectations

Properly setting your expectations is essential to your success. This topic will help you do that by providing:

- Prerequisites for this course
- A description of the target student at whom the course is aimed
- A list of the objectives for the course
- A skills assessment for the course

Course prerequisites

Before taking this course, you should be familiar with personal computers and the use of a keyboard and a mouse. Furthermore, this course assumes that you've completed the following courses or have equivalent experience:

- *CompTIA A+ Certification: OS Technologies*

Target student

You must be a technician with 18-24 months of experience in the IT industry. This course is designed to provide you with the skills you need to plan, install, and troubleshoot a network in a corporate environment.

CompTIA certification

This course will also prepare you to pass the CompTIA Network+ exam (2005 objectives). CompTIA is a non-profit information technology (IT) trade association. CompTIA's certifications are designed by subject matter experts from across the IT industry. Each CompTIA certification is vendor-neutral, covers multiple technologies, and requires demonstration of skills and knowledge widely sought after by the IT industry.

In order to become CompTIA certified, you must:

1 Select a certification exam provider. For more information, visit www.comptia.org/certification/general_information/exam_locations.aspx.

2 Register for and schedule a time to take the CompTIA certification exam at a convenient location.

3 Read and sign the Candidate Agreement, which will be presented at the time of the exam. The text of the Candidate Agreement can be found at www.comptia.org/certification/general_information/candidate_agreement.aspx.

4 Take and pass the CompTIA certification exam(s).

For additional information about CompTIA's certifications, such as their industry acceptance, benefits, or program news, visit www.comptia.org/certification.

To contact CompTIA with any questions or comments, please call (630) 678-8300 or e-mail questions@comptia.org.

Course objectives

These overall course objectives will give you an idea about what to expect from the course. It is also possible that they will help you see that this course is not the right one for you. If you think you either lack the prerequisite knowledge or already know most of the subject matter to be covered, you should let your instructor know that you think you are misplaced in the class.

Note: In addition to the general objectives listed below, specific CompTIA Network+ exam objectives are listed at the beginning of each topic. For a complete mapping of exam objectives to course content, see Appendix C.

After completing this course, you will know how to:

- Discuss basic networking concepts, including network types, network operating systems, server types, topologies, and planning in network design.

- Explain the significance of the OSI Model, label the seven layers of the OSI Model, and describe the services provided by each layer of the OSI Model.

- Discuss network adapter configuration, NDIS and ODI models, and troubleshoot network adapter problems.

- Discuss the concept of protocols and channel access methods, and discuss transport, remote access, and security protocols.

- Illustrate the basic properties, purpose, and functionality of network cabling, identify the characteristics and appropriate implementation techniques for various types of cables and connectors, and discuss Ethernet, Token Ring, and other devices.

- Discuss internetworking, describe and contrast the functions of bridges, switches, and routers, and discuss routing protocols.

- Describe the properties, benefits, and potential issues involved with POTS, ISDN, cable modem, xDSL, satellite, and wireless remote access methods, configure Windows XP/Server 2003 with a modem, establish a dial-up network connection by using Windows XP/Server 2003, discuss Remote Access Service (RAS) and remote access clients, and discuss WAN connectivity.

- Discuss the environmental factors that affect computer networks, define physical and logical indicators of network trouble, identify the function of common network tools, and discuss the science of troubleshooting.

- Discuss the evolution of TCP/IP and the fundamentals of TCP/IP.

- Identify each networked system as a host under TCP/IP, determine the IP address class and default subnet mask, and configure TCP/IP on a Windows XP/Server 2003 computer.

- Discuss the role of the HOSTS file, DNS, NETBIOS, LMHOSTS file, and WINS.

- Discuss the purpose of firewalls and the functionality of a proxy server.

- Identify the TCP/IP troubleshooting tools, discuss the Telnet utility, its functions, the functions the File Transfer Protocol (FTP) utility, and diagnose a problem and choose the appropriate troubleshooting tools.

- Identify Network Operating Systems (NOS) features and discuss the features of Microsoft Windows, Novell NetWare, UNIX, Mac OS X Server and AppleShare IP.

- Describe the network clients that are available to connect DOS, Windows, and Macintosh based clients to a network.

- Describe Windows security models, discuss directory services planning and implementation, describe Active Directory and the new features of Active Directory in Windows Server 2003, describe the Windows NT domain model, and explain the purpose of Novell Directory Services/eDirectory and the significance of NDS/eDirectory objects and bindery emulation.

- Discuss user management and group management, identify the NTFS file system and file system security, explain shared folders and discuss Windows 2000/Server 2003 printing concepts.

- Discuss Windows 2000/Server 2003 system monitoring using Task Manager, discuss troubleshooting using Event Viewer, and describe System Monitor and Performance Logs and Alerts.

- Discuss user and group management in NetWare, describe file system security and rights and trustee assignments, discuss user account restrictions, explain NDS/eDirectory context, discuss NetWare log files, and use MONITOR.NLM, NetWare Remote Manager, as well as other utilities to monitor and manage a NetWare server and file system.

- Discuss disk configuration, Windows-based replication, and NDS partitions and replicas, backup, and UPS.

- Discuss the necessity of applying software patches and fixes, and describe viruses and anti-virus strategies.

- Describe methods to help prioritize network problems, list the basic troubleshooting steps to be followed when working on a problem, and troubleshoot various problems that might occur on the network.

Skills inventory

Use the following form to gauge your skill level entering the class. For each skill listed, rate your familiarity from 1 to 5, with five being the most familiar. *This is not a test.* Rather, it is intended to provide you with an idea of where you're starting from at the beginning of class. If you're wholly unfamiliar with all the skills, you might not be ready for the class. If you think you already understand all of the skills, you might need to move on to the next course in the series. In either case, you should let your instructor know as soon as possible.

Skill	1	2	3	4	5
Understanding network types and network operating systems					
Understanding server types, such as fax, CD, e-mail, print and other servers					
Understanding topologies, such as Bus, Star, Ring, and Mesh					
Understanding the importance of planning in network design					
Understanding the OSI Model and its layers					
Configuring a network adapter					
Understanding general network adapter troubleshooting techniques and network adapter problems					
Understanding the concept of protocols, channel access methods, transport protocols, remote access protocols and security protocols					
Understanding network cabling methods, communication methods, and twisted pair cabling					
Understanding RJ-45 Modular Plug termination (Crimping) and BNC Termination (Crimping)					
Understanding coaxial cables and fiber optic cables					
Understanding Ethernet, Token Ring and other devices					
Understanding internetworking, bridges, switches routers, brouters, and routing protocols					
Understanding the features of POTS and ISDN					

Skill	1	2	3	4	5
Understanding the features of cable modems, xDSL, satellite and wireless remote access methods					
Installing and configuring a new modem					
Understanding Remote Access Service (RAS) and remote access clients					
Understanding WAN connectivity					
Handling environmentally caused hardware problems					
Understanding the causes of network trouble					
Understanding network tools, troubleshooting techniques, troubleshooting documentation, and troubleshooting tools for hardware and software problems					
Understanding the history of TCP/IP					
Understanding RFCs, the Internet, and supported systems					
Understanding the architectural model of TCP/IP, the TCP/IP suite, ports and sockets					
Understanding IP addresses and conversions, IP address classes and subnet masks, and special addressing and private networks					
Configuring TCP/IP					
Understanding HOSTS files, Domain Name System, NETBIOS, LMHOSTS file, and WINS name resolution					
Understanding firewalls and proxy servers					
Understanding ARP, HOSTNAME, IPCONFIG, WINIPCFG, IFCONFIG, NBTSTAT, NETSTAT, NSLOOKUP, DIG, TRACERT, PING, and ROUTE					
Understanding Telnet and File Transfer Protocol (FTP)					
Understanding the basic features of Microsoft Windows NT, 2000, 2003					
Understanding the basic features of Novell NetWare					

Skill	1	2	3	4	5
Understanding the basic features of UNIX and Linux					
Understanding the basic features of Mac OS X Server and AppleShare IP					
Understanding Windows, Macintosh and Novell NetWare network clients					
Understanding Windows security models, including Workgroup and Domain					
Understanding directory services planning and implementation					
Understanding Active Directory and Active Directory naming standards and physical structure					
Installing Active Directory					
Understanding new Active Directory features in Windows Server 2003					
Understanding Windows NT domains					
Understanding Novell Directory Services (NDS)/eDirectory					
Understanding Windows user and group management					
Understanding Windows file systems and file system security					
Understanding Windows shared folder concepts					
Understanding Windows printing concepts					
Managing applications and processes with Task Manager					
Using Event Viewer to view application and system log events					
Understanding the Performance Console, System Monitor and Performance Logs and Alerts					
Understanding NetWare user and group management					
Understanding NetWare file system security					

Skill	1	2	3	4	5
Understanding NetWare rights and trustee assignments					
Understanding NetWare user account restrictions					
Understanding NDS/eDirectory context					
Understanding SYS$LOG.ERR, VOL$LOG.ERR, ABEND.LOG, and CONSOLE.LOG					
Understanding monitoring and management tools, such as MONITOR.NLM, NetWare Remote Manager and VREPAIR					
Understanding RAID					
Understanding disk duplexing, disk striping with parity, and disk configuration					
Understanding Windows-based replication					
Understanding NDS/eDirectory partitions and replicas and replica rings					
Understanding backup schemes, removable media, and backup storage					
Understanding Uninterruptable Power Supply (UPS)					
Understanding the importance of keeping NOS software up-to-date					
Understanding Windows, NetWare and other OS patches, fixes, and updates					
Identifying viruses and discussing virus protection					
Understanding methods of prioritizing network problems					
Listing basic troubleshooting steps to be followed when working on a problem					
Troubleshooting various problems that might occur on the network					

Topic C: Re-keying the course

If you have the proper hardware and software, you can re-key this course after class. This section explains what you'll need in order to do so, and how to do it.

Computer requirements

To re-key this course, your personal computer requires the following hardware and software configuration:

- A keyboard and a mouse
- Pentium II or faster processor
- At least 128 MB RAM (256 MB recommended)
- At least 2 GB of available hard-disk space
- A CD-ROM drive
- A Windows Server 2003 operating system CD
- A network card
- An SVGA or higher resolution monitor set to 1024×768 or higher

Setup instructions to re-key the course

In the classroom, students worked in pairs, but you can re-key much of this course with one machine. If you wish to set up a pair of computers on your own network, you will need to perform the following steps:

1   On one machine in each pair, install Windows Server 2003 according to the manufacturer's instructions. Accept the defaults but, at this time, don't configure the server for any roles. After the computer restarts, log in as Administrator. In the Manage Your Server dialog box, check Don't display this page at logon and close the dialog box.

2   On the other machine in each pair, Install Windows XP according to the manufacturer's instructions, accepting the default settings. For the Windows XP user name, enter the name you wish. Once Windows XP is up and running, open Windows Explorer and choose Tools, Folder Options. On the General tab, select Use Windows classic folders and click OK.

3   Adjust each computer's display properties as follows:

   a   Right-click on the desktop and choose Properties to open the Display Properties dialog box.

   b   On the Settings tab, if necessary, change the Colors setting to True Color (24 bit) and the Screen area to 1024 by 768 pixels.

   c   Click OK to save the settings.

4   On the Windows XP machines, configure Control Panel settings as follows:

   a   Choose Start, Control Panel.

   b   Click Switch to Classic View.

   c   Close Control Panel.

5 In the unit entitled "Network cabling," there are two optional activities (B-2 and C-1) that focus on crimping. If you plan to complete these activities, you'll need the following items:

- Wire cutters
- RJ-45 and BNC crimpers
- Cable testers
- Pieces of Category 5 and coaxial cable
- RJ-45 modular plugs and BNC connectors

CertBlaster test preparation for CompTIA certification

You can download CertBlaster test preparation software for the CompTIA Network+ exam from the Course ILT Web site. Here's what you do:

1 Go to www.courseilt.com/certblaster.

2 Click the link for Network+ 2005.

3 Save the .EXE file to a folder on your hard drive. (**Note**: If you skip this step, the CertBlaster software will not install correctly.)

4 Click Start and choose Run.

5 Click Browse and then navigate to the folder that contains the .EXE file.

6 Select the .EXE file and click Open.

7 Click OK and follow the on-screen instructions. When prompted for the password, enter **c_network+**.

Unit 1

Basic networking concepts

Unit time: 60 minutes

Complete this unit, and you'll know how to:

A Compare the various types of networks in use today and discuss networking fundamentals.

B Discuss types of servers found in today's networks.

C Discuss topologies used in LANs.

D Discuss the importance of planning a network design.

Topic A: Networking fundamentals

This topic covers the following CompTIA Network+ exam objectives:

#	Objective
2.14	Identify the basic characteristics (For example: speed, capacity and media) of the following WAN (Wide Area Networks) technologies: • Packet switching
3.1	Identify the basic capabilities needed for client workstations to connect to and use network resources (For example: media, network protocols and peer and server services).
3.11	Identify the purpose and characteristics of fault tolerance: • Link redundancy

Types of networks

Explanation

To start with, you need to be familiar with the common terminology associated with networking environments, as well as the different types of networks available. The types of networks available include legacy, peer-to-peer, and client/server environments.

In working with networks, you will likely encounter one or more types of networks, such as legacy networks, peer-to-peer networks, and client/server networks.

Legacy networks

You might at times encounter or want to incorporate a new computer network with a legacy network. Typically, the term *legacy* is used to define an existing mainframe or minicomputer environment.

Traditional mainframe and minicomputer operations are set up in a centralized processing environment. The features characterizing this type of environment include:

- All processing takes place at the central computer.
- Dumb terminals, or terminals having no processing power, provide user access to the mainframe/minicomputer.
- Most applications are custom-built. Therefore, there are only a limited number of off-the-shelf software products available for purchase.
- Support staff is needed for management and control.
- Incremental growth is prohibitively expensive.

Peer-to-peer networks

In a peer-to-peer environment, also referred to as a workgroup solution, systems both provide and receive services. Each workgroup member acts both like a server and a workstation. Resource and security management is handled at the individual system level. The software providing these services might run as a separate application or might be integrated into the operating system.

Features characterizing this type of environment include:

- Workstations normally store their own application and data files.
- Processing occurs at the workstation. Therefore, speed is primarily a factor of the workstation used.
- Each node on the system talks to all other nodes.
- Peer-to-peer communications make some level of file and printer sharing possible.
- No one system is in charge of the network.
- Security might be limited.
- This type of system doesn't work well with more than approximately 10 workstations or nodes because Microsoft limits most peer connectivity to 10 simultaneous connections to a drive, shared folder, printer, and so on.

Windows 95, Windows 98, Windows NT Workstation, Windows 2000 Professional, and Windows XP Professional have integrated support for peer-to-peer configurations.

Client/server networks

In a client/server environment, there are separate systems for providing resources (servers) and for accessing resources (clients). Resource and security management is fully centralized. If the servers and workstations reside within the same building or a small geographical area, this type of environment is typically referred to as a Local Area Network (LAN).

The client/server model provides distributed processing due to the following:

- Application and data files can be stored on the server.
- Files are downloaded to intelligent workstations (clients) for processing.
- Results are uploaded to the server for storage.
- The server might provide additional services, such as printing or communications support, to the client.

Most high-level network operating systems use the client/server model. Novell's NetWare and Microsoft's Windows 2000 Server and Windows Server 2003 operate in a client/server environment.

There are some similarities between mainframe, minicomputers, and LAN operations. PC LANs owe several of their features to ideas first developed in the mainframe world:

- **Multiple users.** Users are able to share data and critical resources quickly and easily.
- **Shared data.** Data files are accessed by different users on the system, making it easier for people to work together.
- **Common applications.** Applications training and support become more efficient and easier to handle.
- **Shared resources.** Selected hardware resources are made available to all (or specified groups of) network users.
- **Centralized security system.** Limits access to sensitive data. Also improves data security through password protection and central backup of all data files.

Other benefits of PC LANs include:

- **Standard PC hardware.** Typically, standard PCs are used as network servers and workstations. In some cases, Apple Macintosh and UNIX-based systems might be found in the network as well. This provides a great deal of design flexibility, relatively uncomplicated maintenance, and helps keep costs to a minimum.

- **Fault tolerance.** Usually, a number of fault tolerance features are supported and implemented, such as UPS (Uninterruptible Power Supply), RAID, and more recently, Cluster technology. This improves reliability and minimizes network downtime.

- **Communications.** In the majority of LANs, an electronic messaging or groupware system is in place, making communications between users easier and more effective.

There are significant differences between LAN and mainframe computing:

- LANs are less expensive to implement.
- LANs support a wide range of off-the-shelf products.
- LANs incorporate a modular design that makes incremental expansion possible with ease.

Note: Installation of a LAN doesn't always mean replacement of a mainframe or minicomputer system, but it might involve integration of the LAN and the legacy system.

Another aspect of a LAN is that is uses private wiring that is internal to the company in which the LAN operates.

CANs, MANs, and WANs

As networks in geographically contiguous buildings begin to be connected, a *campus area network* (CAN) is formed. As is true for multiple networks contained within a single building (still a LAN), a backbone might connect multiple buildings that are geographically contiguous. The distance, physical environment, and transmission speed requirements combine to determine the network design components.

Metropolitan area networks (MANs) connect networks that are non-contiguous, but located within a local calling area. Local telephone companies or Alternate Service Providers (ASPs) supply telecommunications facilities to link the locations together. Exhibit 1-1 shows examples of CAN and MAN.

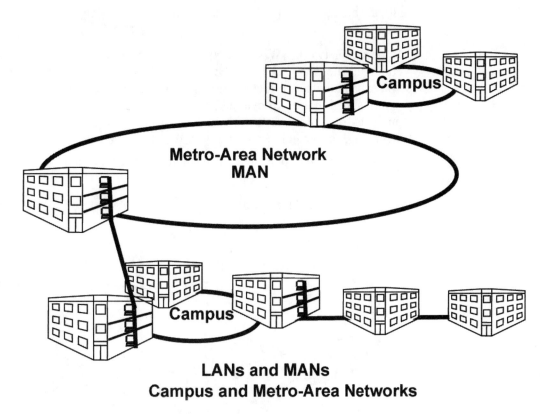

LANs and MANs
Campus and Metro-Area Networks

Exhibit 1-1: Examples of CAN and MAN

A wide area network (WAN) links networks that are located in different local calling areas, known as *Local Access Transport Areas* (LATAs).

Wide area networks (WANs) expand the basic LAN model by linking LANs to communicate with each other. By traditional definition, a LAN becomes a WAN when you expand the network configuration beyond your own premises and must lease data communication lines from a public carrier. WANs support data transmissions across public carriers by using facilities such as dial-up lines, dedicated lines, or packet switching, as shown in Exhibit 1-2. A WAN is characterized by:

- Wide geographic area, any size up to national or international
- Low- to high-speed links
- Remote links that might be operational LANs or groups of workstations only

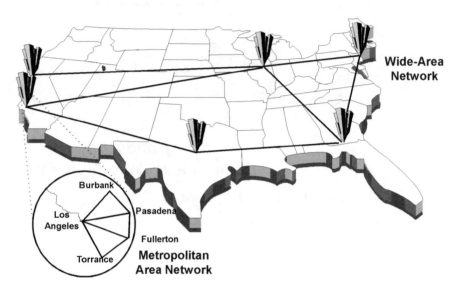

Exhibit 1-2: A wide area network (WAN)

Do it!   ## A-1:   Discussing network types

Questions and answers

1 Briefly describe the characteristics of a peer-to-peer network.

2 List two differences between LAN and mainframe computing.

3 What are the features responsible for providing distributed processing in a client/server model?

4 What is the difference between a LAN and a WAN?

5 A WAN links networks that are located in different local calling areas, known as
_____.

6 Identify the network system that connects networks in geographically adjacent buildings.

 A   Metropolitan area networks

 B   Campus area network

 C   Local Access Transport Areas

 D   Wide area network

The role of network operating systems

Explanation

A network operating system (NOS) runs on the server in a client/server network configuration and turns a PC into a network server. Examples of NOSs include Microsoft Windows NT/2000 Server/Server 2003, Novell NetWare, IBM OS/2, Banyan VINES, Mac OSX, AppleShare IP, UNIX and Linux. A LAN can support multiple types of network operating systems concurrently.

Each workstation runs software that gives it access to the network and makes it possible to use the network's shared resources. The client software is a core portion of the workstation's operating system. For example, earlier versions of Windows included compatible client software for a variety of network operating systems and in newer versions of Windows, client software is tightly integrated after installation.

The final software components are end-user applications and data files. Some applications make it possible for users to share data files and access shared data. This functionality is built into an operating system. More advanced applications take advantage of the network by making it possible for users to access shared databases, communicate with each other through electronic mail, or even collaborate in real time with video conferencing software and other advanced solutions.

Network advantages

A network has a number of advantages over stand-alone PCs. By giving users access to network services and applications, you can:

- **Reduce costs.** Cost savings come from reduced hardware requirements for each workstation. In addition, licensing for LAN applications is usually less expensive than for multiple copies of stand-alone products.
- **Streamline operations.** Files can be shared through the network instead of manually carrying copies of the file to others by using disks or other media. You can also support simultaneous multi-user access to databases.
- **Improve end-user support.** Networks make it possible for you to enforce common applications with consistent levels and versions. File support is centralized, and most file maintenance can be performed from any network location.
- **Improve security.** Data is physically protected by storing it in a central location where it is easily backed up. Access to data can be limited according to user needs.

Network pitfalls

A network doesn't, however, replace good policies and procedures, appropriate applications, or users trained to a minimum level of competency. In fact, it has some pitfalls:

- Not all applications are fully network-compatible: Some stand-alone application packages won't work on a network. Others might work but need special management.
- You must take care while setting access privileges and directory structures: Without careful planning, a network can quickly become a management nightmare if not a complete disaster.

- Multiple, competing standards are available: This can make your initial decisions about setting up a LAN confusing.
- The network needs regular, ongoing maintenance, like any other computer system: An improperly installed and managed network can be worse than a set of unconnected personal computers.

Servers, workstations, and hosts

Servers, workstations, and hosts are components of any networking environment. Servers are computers that run network operating systems, workstations are personal computers that are connected to a network, and hosts are network devices that have a TCP/IP address.

Servers

The NOS turns a personal computer into a network server. *Servers* on most networks are computers that have been optimized to run a network operating system. They might include multiple processors, redundant power supplies, and heavy-duty cooling systems, and they will have significantly more RAM and hard drive space than other machines in the office.

Some network operating systems need a dedicated server, that is, the computer running the NOS cannot be used for any other purpose. It is strictly a server. This is the case with Novell NetWare.

Other network operating systems make it possible for the server to perform other functions. For example, you can compose a letter by using a word processing application on a Microsoft Windows 2000 or Server 2003 server. However, server resources are typically best used for processing user requests; therefore, using the server for these types of tasks is not recommended.

Workstations

A *workstation* can be described as a personal computer that is connected to a network, which can perform tasks through applications or utilities. The term client or station might also be used. While a workstation can share resources such as files with other network users, this is not the workstation's primary function. A workstation must be connected to a network using some type of media, such as a cable or through a wireless connection, and it must have a networking protocol, such as TCP/IP, installed.

Hosts

A *host* is any network device that has a TCP/IP address. In the context of network operating systems, a host can be a server, a workstation, or other peripheral device, such as a printer, print server or fax server.

Do it!   ## A-2:   Discussing network operating systems

Questions and answers

1 Explain the difference between a server and a workstation.

2 A host is any network device that has a TCP/IP address. True or false?

3 Name the operating systems that have the functionality to help users share data files and access shared data.

4 List the network devices that can perform as a host.

5 Novell NetWare needs a dedicated server. True or false?

Topic B: Types of servers

This topic covers the following CompTIA Network+ exam objective:

#	Objective
3.2	Identify the basic capabilities needed for client workstations to connect to and use network resources (For example: media, network protocols and peer and server services).

Network services

Explanation

A network operating system provides basic network services, such as resource sharing and centralized management. For additional functionality, network software and peripherals can be added. While these options may or may not be included with the network operating system, many are available from the NOS (network operating system) manufacturer, as well as from third-party companies. These options supplement the network by adding additional services.

Many of these optional components do not necessarily need a dedicated server. They can be loaded as a process or service on a server you already own. If your current servers are already running at high utilizations, or the addition of the optional service will overload a marginal server, you might want to consider dedicated equipment to balance the load.

Fax servers

A *network fax* server permits users to send and, in some cases, receive facsimiles at their network workstations. Fax servers manage the re-direction of faxes to the appropriate location. There are many companies currently offering fax server products. Some fax servers are software-based products that are loaded on a server, while others are separate hardware devices.

Before selecting a product, make sure it meets your requirements. Some of the items to be considered are:

- Is it compatible with your network operating system?
- What are the hardware requirements?
- How many inbound and outbound phone lines will it support?
- Does it need any special telephone lines?
- Will it integrate with your electronic mail system?

Sending faxes

Most products permit faxes to be sent by simply selecting a special print device under Windows 95/98/NT/2000/XP. In actuality, the print device is not a printer at all, but rather a fax service that is advertised on the network in the same way as shared printers.

When the correct drivers are installed on the workstation, a user selects the fax server and merely uses the print option from any application to generate the fax. The drivers automatically prompt the user for a phone number and information for a cover page. When the information is complete, the workstation sends the fax job to the fax server, which sends the document.

Receiving faxes

Receiving faxes through a fax server is a bit more complicated. Generally, two methods are used. Each potential fax recipient is assigned an ID number. The fax sender enters this number by using the dial pad on a standard fax machine after the destination fax has answered the call. When the fax transmission is complete, the fax server uses the ID number to deliver the document to the appropriate user via e-mail or some other alert mechanism.

If the sender does not know the recipient's ID, the fax server will still receive the fax, but will not notify the recipient. Usually, the fax server will permit an administrator to view the first page of the fax, usually the cover page, to identify the recipient. The administrator will then have to manually send the document via e-mail.

The ability to route faxes to the desktop depends to some extent on the type of phone lines and modems being used. The ability to directly route faxes to a desktop based on an extension or ID number typically needs special digital phone lines and modems.

CD servers

A decline in the cost of CD-ROM readers, along with the growing popularity of CD-ROM media, has prompted an increase in CD server implementations. A CD server is usually a stand-alone device consisting of four or more, perhaps as many as 100 CD-ROM readers. These devices are frequently implemented with a runtime version of a network operating system. A runtime version is a minimal implementation of a network operating system that will provide basic file sharing and network access, along with the benefits of the NOS file caching scheme.

Installing a CD server can provide the entire enterprise with access to installation media, such as workstation applications, reference media and periodicals, or any other data needed by multiple users. The benefit of a CD server over a standard server implementation is cost. To purchase a full version of a network operating system with sufficient licenses for all users can be costly. A CD server is preconfigured with the CD-ROM drives and, with its minimal NOS, can be cost effective.

Do it!

B-1:   Discussing fax servers and CD servers

Questions and answers

1 How can a fax server identify and deliver incoming faxes?

2 If a person sending a fax does not know the recipient's fax server ID, what usually happens?

   A   The server rejects the fax.

   B   The server receives the fax then discards it.

   C   The server receives the fax, but an administrator must deliver it.

   D   The server sends a message to the sender requesting the ID.

3 Why is a CD server more cost effective than a full-function server with several CD readers?

4 You have been asked to provide access to legal reference materials to which your law firm subscribes. The reference material is provided on 10 compact disks, with replacement versions shipped monthly. Which optional network component should you suggest?

E-mail servers

Explanation
Electronic mail (e-mail) is one of the popular forms of business and personal communication. Many organizations have found that e-mail can facilitate organizational communications, reduce paper costs, and create a communications trail for future use.

In a small enterprise, the e-mail service is usually combined on the same server with file and print sharing. Due to the large volume of messages even a medium-sized network will generate, e-mail servers are frequently implemented on dedicated servers.

Many of today's e-mail packages include features such as calendars and scheduling functions, forms routing, and even document management. When an e-mail package provides more functionality than just e-mail, it is called *groupware*. Some examples of popular groupware packages are Microsoft Exchange, Novell GroupWise, and Lotus Notes.

All of these examples are designed to scale to hundreds, even thousands of users. They are best implemented on a dedicated server, as the processing needs for groupware tend to be high. When evaluating e-mail and groupware packages, the needs of your users, as well as the importance of industry standards are equally important. Your package will probably have to interface with other packages and the Internet, as e-mail is now a global business resource.

Internet gateways

For many companies, connecting to the Internet is no longer optional. The Internet is commonly used for research, advertising, customer contact, and competitor information. This, coupled with the importance of Internet e-mail, typically needs a network-oriented access solution rather than an individual user solution.

Due to market demand, hardware manufacturers have addressed this need with some specialized hardware. This hardware provides a LAN connection port, and a connection to the Internet that typically is shared by all computers on the network, using only a single IP address. This scenario cuts down on costs by permitting multiple machines to access the Internet through a single account.

Firewall protection hides the nodes within the company from the Internet by restricting or limiting incoming traffic to certain trusted systems or specific applications.

Some of the more popular products are produced by 3Com, Ascend, Nortel Networks, and Cisco Systems. Each model might vary, and you might need to test the equipment before making a commitment.

Print servers

Printers can be directly attached to workstations or servers.

Third-party alternatives

Network-direct printers feature internal network interfaces that provide a direct connection to the network cable system. In many cases, this interface also operates as a print server that is capable of polling and servicing print jobs in queues or spools.

Because data is transmitted to the printer at network speeds, network-direct printers provide the highest performance printing solution available.

Most network operating systems support the use of third-party print services such as the JetDirect series from Hewlett-Packard and the NetPort line from Intel. These connect directly to various network types and provide one or more ports for shared printer connections.

In addition, most models provide support for other client or server operating systems, including AppleTalk for Macintosh and IP for UNIX.

Implementing a third-party print solution

Most third-party print servers offer efficient and reliable operation. They typically need less administration than workstation-attached printers that need special configuration through utilities like Novell's NPRINTER or Microsoft's File and Printer Sharing.

Third-party print server devices include proprietary installation and management utilities that eliminate the need for the NOS utilities. The setup requirements of a third-party print server are typically performed by using a graphical utility. For example, Hewlett-Packard provides the JetAdmin and JetPrint utilities with all JetDirect products. When considering the use of third-party print servers in an environment, verify that the products you purchase are compatible with the NOS with which you want to use them.

Note: Some manufacturers provide an EEPROM firmware upgrade for their print servers. Check with your manufacturer if you have older print server products that will not connect with newer NOS technology.

Other types of servers

In today's network environments, you'll also encounter other types of servers such as Web servers, database servers, application servers and so on. Each provides specific functionality, and depending on the size and needs of your organization may be dedicated servers or share functionality with other servers.

Do it!   ## B-2:   Discussing e-mail, print and other servers

Questions and answers

1 Network-direct printers connect directly to the

   A   Server

   B   Gateway

   C   Client

   D   Cable system

2 E-mail servers that provide additional services such as calendaring or group
   scheduling are called _____.

3 You have been asked to implement an e-mail server for 7,000 users that will
   handle an estimated 25,000 messages each day. Will you implement this service
   on an existing file and print server, or will you recommend dedicated equipment?
   Justify your decision.

4 Network-direct printers usually need:

   A   Special management utilities

   B   No management

   C   Extra management and care

   D   Special client configurations

5 What are examples of other specialized server types you might encounter

   A   Web servers

   B   Client servers

   C   Application servers

   D   Database servers

Topic C: Topologies

This topic covers the following CompTIA Network+ exam objectives:

#	Objective
1.1	Recognize the following logical or physical network topologies given a diagram, schematic or description: • Star • Bus • Mesh • Ring
1.2	Specify the main features of 802.2 (Logical Link Control), 802.3 (Ethernet), 802.5 (token ring), 802.11 (wireless), and FDDI (Fiber Distributed Data Interface) networking technologies, including: • Topology
4.7	Given a troubleshooting scenario involving a network with a particular physical topology (For example: bus, star, mesh or ring) and including a network diagram, identify the network area affected and the cause of the stated failure.

Topology overview

Explanation

Topology defines how the physical media links the network nodes. Several methods are available, each with advantages and drawbacks.

There are four types of topologies commonly used in LANs:

- Bus
- Ring
- Star
- Mesh

Additional topologies have been developed for WAN connectivity that include point-to-point, multipoint, and clouds. Hybrid topologies are usually found in a WAN. This is simply an implementation of multiple topologies.

Bus topology

A *bus topology*, as shown in Exhibit 1-3, consists of a linear transmission medium that is terminated at both ends. Nodes attach directly to the bus, making it difficult to troubleshoot. Difficulty in troubleshooting is considered the biggest drawback for this topology.

Exhibit 1-3: A bus topology

Although a bus is normally represented as a straight line in the picture, most bus networks represent cables that snake, weave, and wrap their way through building conduits and corridors. This results in the rapid growth of the overall bus length. In addition, any break in the bus causes the entire network to become inoperable.

Bus topologies commonly use coaxial cable as their transmission medium. Traditionally, Ethernet has used a bus topology. Bus topologies are usually used for small, temporary installations.

With a bus topology, the 5-4-3 rule applies. There can be no more than five network segments and four repeaters, and only three of the five segments can be populated with hosts.

Ring topology

A *ring topology*, as shown in Exhibit 1-4, provides a closed-loop transmission medium. Repeaters at each node connection repeat the signals. This is done to minimize any signal degradation.

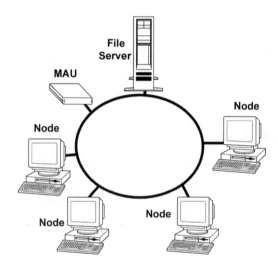

Exhibit 1-4: A ring topology

Traditional rings have the same failure risk as buses. Any break brings the entire network down. To prevent these failures, most ring implementations (such as Token Ring) are actually wired in a star topology with an out loop and a return loop from each workstation to the wiring hub.

Star topology

Star/hub networks connect the peripheral devices via point-to-point links to a central location (hub). Star topologies, as shown in Exhibit 1-5, provide architectural flexibility but need more cable than traditional bus and ring topologies.

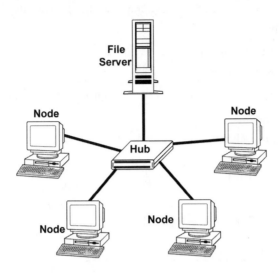

Exhibit 1-5: A star topology

Virtually all the modern data networks are configured in a star. This permits simplified adds, moves, and changes. System failure from any individual segment break is minimized.

Mesh topology

A *mesh* configuration, as shown in Exhibit 1-6, consists of a network where each device has a point-to-point connection to every other device on the network. This provides the dedicated capacity of a point-to-point link to each device and significant fault tolerance. However, the complexity and cost make this configuration impractical for networks with a large number of devices. Also, much of the bandwidth available in mesh configurations is wasted. For those reasons, mesh topologies are generally used for interconnecting only the most important sites with multiple links. This is called a *hybrid mesh* or *partial mesh*.

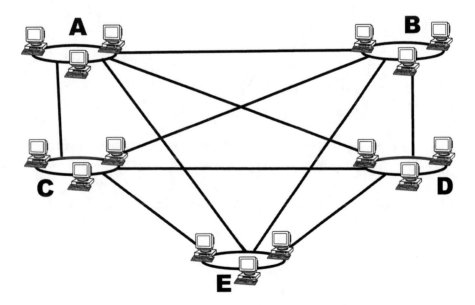

Exhibit 1-6: A mesh configuration

You can list the advantages and disadvantages of the hybrid mesh as follows:

- Advantages:
  - Troubleshooting is easy.
  - Isolation of network failures is easy.
  - Fault tolerance is maximized by rerouting traffic around failed links.
- Disadvantages:
  - Difficult to install.
  - Difficult to reconfigure.
  - Expensive because of redundant connections and wasted bandwidth.

Do it!

C-1: Discussing topologies

Questions and answers

1 A physical bus topology almost always uses

   A   Fiber optic cable

   B   Coaxial cable

   C   Twisted pair

   D   Serial cable

2 What are the advantages of a mesh topology?

3 Which of the following topologies consists of a linear transmission medium that is terminated at both ends?

   A   Ring topology

   B   Bus topology

   C   Star topology

   D   Mesh topology

4 In a ring topology, repeaters at each node connection repeat the signals. Why is this done?

Topic D: Planning in network design

Explanation

Planning is the single most critical element in any network design. Poor planning can result in a loss of productivity, revenue, and even the collapse of a company. Thus, it is important to understand planning concepts.

The purpose of a plan

A network is a complex system, and designing a network from scratch can be a daunting task. Even when planning to restructure an existing network, there are a several factors that must be considered.

Typically, there are many individuals who must have input and many variables that must be taken into account. Designing a network requires all of the necessary pieces coming together in a structured way. This necessitates a plan.

A plan provides:

- A method for verifying that all business requirements will be met prior to implementation
- A method for verifying that all technical requirements will be met prior to implementation
- A roadmap for network implementation
- A historical reference of the network design for future use

To understand the importance of planning, think of a computer network as a city. The cabling makes up the transportation infrastructure. The network resources are analogous to the community services needed by the citizens: water, sewer, and electricity. At first, there might only be a few roads and a sparse population. Without many citizens, the shortage of roads might go unnoticed. As more people move to the city, more services are needed. Without a planning commission, congestion on the roadways will ensue and citizens will get angry at the lack of services available to them.

This same scenario takes place on a new network. At first, with a small number of users, everything might seem to function properly. But as the network population increases, congestion and frustration can occur. However, a smart network designer will plan for the increased demand and would have already created the infrastructure necessary to sustain growth and productivity.

Like the city planning commission, network designers also use a solid plan to evaluate costs and benefits. If the plan incurs more cost than benefit, the design can be modified prior to implementation, thus saving the organization a great deal of time and expense.

A well-documented plan will also provide the organization two additional and valuable pieces of information, a method for implementing the design and a historical perspective on the design. The former is invaluable to the technical personnel designated to implement the design. The latter will provide the business leaders with trend information.

Creating a plan

There are several steps in creating a good plan. While your specific environment might dictate additional steps, the basic steps involved are as follows:

1 Determine what business requirements must be met.
2 Review the current infrastructure, if one exists.
3 Review new and existing technologies that can be used to meet business needs.
4 Determine the appropriate infrastructure requirements and/or changes.
5 Document the design.
6 Review the documentation with the appropriate technical personnel and business leaders and modify as necessary.

The most critical step in creating a plan involves information gathering and research. Information about business requirements, the current infrastructure, and available technologies are all necessary when planning a new network or network overhaul. Perhaps your most valuable tools for this process are your ears. Experienced network planners know that it is essential to listen carefully to both what is being said and what is not being said when gathering information.

Only after the plan has been documented, reviewed, modified, and finally accepted by all appropriate parties should implementation begin. This provides a final checklist prior to implementation.

Ongoing planning

After implementing the network design, you might be tempted to mark the planning phase as complete. The planning phase doesn't end at this point. A good network plan evolves continually as the network and the organization change. As new technologies arrive in the industry, the plan needs to be re-evaluated to see if cost savings can occur.

Furthermore, new products might mandate a change in infrastructure. Thus, the existing plan might need further analysis to see if implementation is feasible in the current environment.

Do it! ### D-1: Discussing planning in network design

Questions and answers
1 What are some problems that could result from poor planning?
2 What is the most critical step to be considered while developing a plan?
3 How does the arrival of new technologies in the industry affect planning?

Unit summary: Basic networking concepts

Topic A
In this topic, you learned about the role of **network operating systems** and their **advantages** and **pitfalls**. You also learned about **servers**. You learned that servers on most networks are computers that have been optimized to run a network operating system and that **workstations** are personal computers that are connected to a network. You also learned that a **host** is a network device that has a **TCP/IP address**. You also learned about the different types of networks, such as **legacy**, **peer-to-peer**, and **client/server**.

Topic B
In this topic, you learned about the different properties and functions of different types of servers including **Fax servers**, **CD servers**, **E-Mail servers**, **Print servers**, and others. You also learned about the different purposes and implementations of these servers.

Topic C
In this topic, you learned about the characteristics of various **topologies** used in LANs. You learned about **Bus**, **Ring**, **Star**, and **Mesh** topologies and their advantages and disadvantages.

Topic D
In this topic, you learned about the importance of **planning** in network design. You also learned why planning should be an ongoing process.

Review questions

1 Name a server on which a user can also perform word processing or similar tasks.

2 Can Windows 2000/Server 2003, NetWare, and UNIX all coexist on the same Local Area Network?

   A Yes

   B No

   C Only if all clients are dumb terminals

   D Only if each server is separated by a router

3 Define "server," "workstation," and "host."

4 What is one major advantage of using a direct print device?

5 Which device provides Network-wide Internet access?

6 A fax server advertises itself on the network in the same way as a:

A Shared Directory

B Shared Printer

C Server

D Router

7 You are consulting at a company that currently has a network configured in a bus topology. Their biggest complaint is that every time there's a physical problem at one computer, the rest of the network can no longer communicate. What would you suggest to your client to remedy this problem?

8 Why is it necessary to create a well-documented plan?

Unit 2

The OSI model

Unit time: 45 minutes

Complete this unit, and you'll know how to:

A Explain the significance of the OSI model, label the seven layers of the OSI model, and describe services provided by each layer of the OSI model.

Topic A: Introduction to the OSI model

This topic covers the following CompTIA Network+ exam objective:

#	Objective
2.2	Identify the seven layers of the OSI (Open Systems Interconnect) model and their functions.

Introducing the Open Systems Interconnection (OSI) model

Explanation

The *Open Systems Interconnection (OSI)* seven-layer model is an international standard originated to identify a common set of guidelines to facilitate communications between distinct information system components.

The benefit derived from this globally accepted communications framework is two-fold. The surface impact is that it provides a mechanism to establish a common set of protocols to support multiple-vendor solutions. Prior to the OSI model development, single-vendor solutions were the only alternative for organizations that needed to create an enterprise-wide computing strategy.

The real impact of the OSI model is found in the economic benefits derived from a common communications framework. Not only do the end-user organizations have the opportunity to research a cost-effective solution, but also the market is wide open for creative entrepreneurs to enter the computer communications industry. An innovative technology that addresses the published protocol standards can be marketed to potential buyers with the assurance of network compatibility.

Understanding the purpose and structure of the OSI model is the key to understanding the various components of a network. As you work with networking technologies, you'll realize that many problems you encounter can be more easily understood if placed in the context of the OSI model.

The OSI model

The Open Systems Interconnection (OSI) model was developed by the International Organization for Standardization (ISO) during the late 1970s. Eighty- three countries participated in the definition and acceptance of the international communications definition.

The European Community's (EC) decision to use the OSI model as a basis for integrating the information systems from each member country is an example of the economic impact that can be wielded by a technology definition.

The expansion of Internet technologies has made the global economy accessible to anyone who wants to reach out and grasp it. Understanding the connectivity issues the OSI model addresses will make you a stronger competitor because you'll be able to leverage the available tools and technologies from an end-to-end perspective.

Note: While a number of companies have endorsed and agreed to apply this model within their own products, few follow its guidelines exactly. Some use their own networking models, most of which closely parallel the OSI standard. Still, it's a tool that helps as a common point of reference for discussing network devices and concepts.

The OSI model is an open, seven-layer model (as shown in Exhibit 2-1). Each layer performs a different function in the exchange of data between different systems. It's successful because each layer builds on the activity of the preceding layers. Lower layers are considered subordinate to upper layers. Within a system, a layer can communicate only with the layer immediately above or immediately below itself (layer-to-layer handshaking). Between systems, a layer may communicate only with the same layer in another system, its peer (peer-to-peer communication).

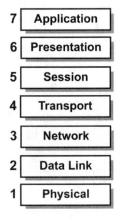

Exhibit 2-1: The OSI model

Do it!

A-1:   Introducing the OSI model

Questions and answers

1 Who developed the OSI model?

~~IOS~~ *I SO*   *International Organization for Standardization*

2 What is the purpose of the OSI model?

Common set of Purposes, Protocols
Common Communications Framework

3 What are the benefits derived by using the OSI model?

Common Communications Framework

Layers of the OSI model

Explanation

The different layers of OSI model are:

- OSI Physical layer
- OSI Data Link layer
- OSI Network layer
- OSI Transport layer
- OSI Session layer
- OSI Presentation layer
- OSI Application layer

OSI Physical layer

The *Physical layer* governs how data is transmitted across the media. It describes the cable and how it's attached to the network adapter. It defines the mechanical and electrical characteristics of the cables and connectors that link the network components. It also defines data encoding and bit synchronization, ensuring that when a transmitting host sends a 1 bit, it is received as a 1 bit, not a 0 bit.

Data networks are described as data highways. By using this analogy as an example, defining the Physical layer is much like determining if the road infrastructure will be built of concrete or asphalt.

Building a real-world implementation: Physical layer

The following table shows the traditional OSI model. The OSI layer column identifies the standard layer nomenclature. The Function column describes the communication activities assigned to the specific layer. The Examples column identifies real-world protocols or products that operate within the general description of the respective functional layer. The products listed might not be a part of the OSI protocol standards.

OSI layer	Function	Examples
Application		
Presentation		
Session		
Transport		
Network		
Data link		
Physical	Cables and connectors	Copper wire, fiber, RJ 45,RS 232-C

OSI Data Link layer

The *Data Link layer*, as shown in Exhibit 2-2, specifies how devices attached to the network gain access to the various computing resources. This layer packages data into frames that are to be sent out on the network. Some error checking and retransmission responsibilities are built into this layer. It is responsible for providing error-free transfer of frames from one computer to another through the Physical layer.

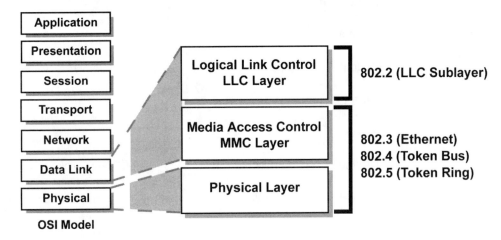

Exhibit 2-2: The Data Link layer

Continuing the data highway analogy, the Data Link layer is the entry ramp/toll booth by which you can gain access onto a highway. Similar to the traffic lights found at on-ramps for control of merging traffic, access methods are contained in the data link protocol definition to tell each node when it is its turn to transmit data.

The Institute of Electrical and Electronic Engineers (IEEE), working in conjunction with the ISO, established the IEEE 802 specification series that divides this layer into two sub-layers:

- **Logical Link Control (LLC).** The LLC sub-layer provides software controls to manage multiple protocols that are simultaneously accessing the network. The IEEE 802.2 acts like an umbrella protocol for the various MAC sublayer protocols.
- **Media Access Control (MAC).** The MAC layer physically defines how devices control access to the network. This layer defines the network adapter interface options, supported cable types, and the designated access method. There are a number of specifications defined, including 802.3 (CSMA/CD or Ethernet), 802.4 (Token Bus), and 802.5 (Token Ring).

Building a real-world implementation: Data Link layer

Because of the coordinated efforts of the IEEE and ISO organizations, the Physical and Data Link layers are implemented across the broadest number of platforms.

OSI layer	Function	Examples
Application		
Presentation		
Session		
Transport		
Network		
Data link	Access	Ethernet, Token Ring, FDDI, SDLC
Physical	Cables and connectors	Copper wire, fiber, RJ 45,RS 232-C

OSI Network layer

The *Network layer*, as shown in Exhibit 2-3, is responsible for establishing a unique network address and managing the transport of information packets between networks. The Network layer addressing function is similar to that of the area code within the domestic U.S. telephone network-addressing scheme. The area code differentiates two identical seven-digit telephone numbers by assigning a prefix unique to a specific geographical area. The Network layer bundles small data frames together for transmission across the network. Additionally, it will break larger data frames into smaller ones for transmission. If the node is receiving, it is responsible for reassembling the data. Referencing the data highway analogy and the area code metaphor, the Network layer is equivalent to the highway exit numbering scheme.

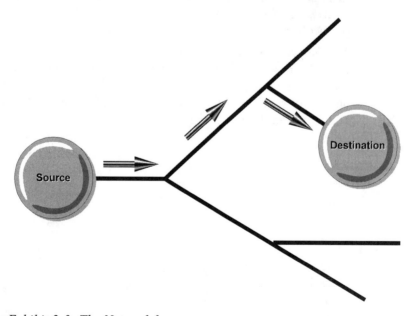

Exhibit 2-3: The Network layer

Building a real-world implementation: Network layer

The Network layer helps to coordinate the intercommunication activities between different networks. As the Internet becomes a standard resource, even stand-alone PC users will need to understand and use the IP (internet protocol) addressing schemes.

The Network layer, combined with the Transport layer, defines the full functionality of network operating systems. In the following example, IPX is the Network layer protocol associated with Novell NetWare networks. Its sole function is to establish the node presence and connection identification (virtual address) for the current user session.

OSI layer	Function	Examples
Application		
Presentation		
Session		
Transport		
Network	Address	IP, IPX
Data link	Access	Ethernet, Token Ring, FDDI, SDLC
Physical	Cables and connectors	Copper wire, fiber, RJ 45,RS 232-C

OSI Transport layer

The *Transport layer*, as shown in Exhibit 2-4, is responsible for the accuracy of the data transmission. It maintains overall management and control responsibilities. This fourth layer is what provides LAN network operating systems the intelligence to measure traffic performance that was not available with X.25 and other early packet-switching technologies. Specifically, being able to view in real-time the files a network user was accessing was a network management coup.

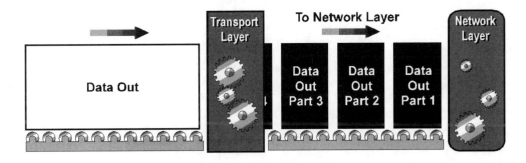

Exhibit 2-4: The Transport layer

As an extra protective measure, a copy of the original message is archived at this layer until the successful end of transmission signal is received. If data retransmission is necessary, the message is retransmitted without returning to the original application.

Referencing the data highway analogy, the Transport layer is equivalent to speed recognition devices that relay the current recorded speed of your vehicle.

Building a real-world implementation: Transport layer

TCP/IP, today's standard wide area network protocol, was initially developed to provide a management and control function for the X.25-based ARPANET network. The TCP portion of the protocol stack addressed the Transport layer's oversight functions, while IP provided an extended addressing scheme.

OSI layer	Function	Product examples
Application		
Presentation		
Session		
Transport	Management and control	TCP, SPX, NetBIOS
Network	Address	IP, IPX
Data link	Access	Ethernet, Token Ring, FDDI, SDLC
Physical	Cables and connectors	Copper wire, fiber, RJ 45,RS 232-C

OSI Session layer

The *Session layer*, as shown in Exhibit 2-5, of the OSI model is responsible for the integrity of the logical connection of the software session. In other words, this layer ensures that next month's sales forecast data does not end up in your customer database log.

By using this layer, two applications on different computers can establish, use, and end a connection called a *session*. This layer performs name recognition and by using other functions, such as security functions, two applications can communicate over the network. Finally, this layer provides synchronization between user tasks by placing checkpoints in the data stream.

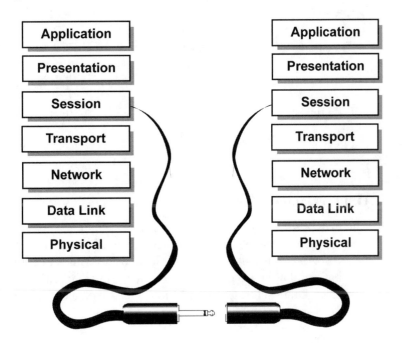

Exhibit 2-5: The Session layer

Referencing the data highway analogy, the Session layer function is equivalent to the designated traffic lanes.

Building a real-world implementation: Session layer

The Session layer currently maps to a marketed product. Two widely implemented industry protocols provide the tracking, or traffic cop, type of functions that link the software applications to the bottom four layers.

OSI layer	Function	Examples
Application		
Presentation		
Session	Traffic cop	NetBIOS, VTAM
Transport	Management and control	TCP, SPX, NetBIOS
Network	Address	IP, IPX
Data link	Access	Ethernet, Token Ring, FDDI, SDLC
Physical	Cables and connectors	Copper wire, fiber, RJ 45, RS 232-C

OSI Presentation layer

The *Presentation layer*, as shown in Exhibit 2-6, translates data into an appropriate transmission format. One function maintained at this layer is terminal emulation, which helps workstations that use different local data formats to communicate. An example of terminal emulation is the process a PC needs to communicate with a mainframe computer. Other reformatting functions include data encryption and compression.

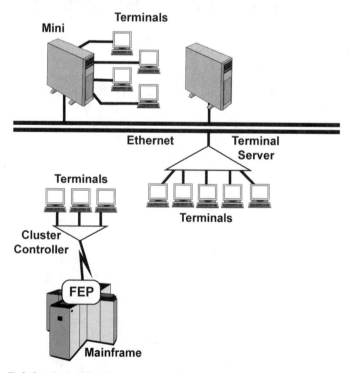

Exhibit 2-6: The Presentation layer

From a data highway perspective, the Presentation layer is similar to universal signs both on the highway and inside your vehicle. It doesn't matter what language you speak, an "X" above a traffic lane means do not traverse.

Building a real-world implementation: Presentation layer

In addition to the general terminal emulation, encryption, and compression functions, the Presentation layer functions can be related to the network shell or requester functions. For example, in a Novell NetWare environment, the NetWare Loadable Module (NLM) used to link a Macintosh to the DOS-based file server is activated at this layer.

OSI layer	Function	Examples
Application		
Presentation	Format	Terminal emulation, encryption
Session	Traffic cop	NetBios, VTAM
Transport	Management and control	TCP, SPX, NetBIOS
Network	Address	IP, IPX
Data link	Access	Ethernet, Token Ring, FDDI, SDLC
Physical	Cables and connectors	Copper wire, fiber, RJ 45,RS 232-C

OSI Application layer

The *OSI Application layer* is the layer that provides a series of definitions that are used to provide network-wide system management functions such as software for file transfers, database access, and electronic mail. It is possible to extend the definition to include the application user interface as a part of the functional definition, but the OSI specifications focus on common network services like performance management, mail, and file transfer.

Completing the data highway analogy, the Application layer is equivalent to the dashboard of your car. The different gauges make you aware of information you need to know to stay within speed limits and maintain optimal performance for your vehicle.

Building a real-world implementation: Application layer

Common Application layer support services that are defined by the ISO organization include X.400 mail services, X.500 directory services, FTP file transfer services, and Telnet terminal emulation services. TCP/IP-related services such as SNMP and SMTP function at this top layer of the OSI model.

OSI layer	Function	Examples
Application	Overall system management	SNMP, SMTP, X 400, X 500, FTP
Presentation	Format	Terminal emulation, encryption
Session	Traffic cop	NetBIOS, VTAM
Transport	Management and control	TCP, SPX, NetBIOS
Network	Address	IP, IPX
Data link	Access	Ethernet, Token Ring, FDDI, SDLC
Physical	Cables and connectors	Copper wire, fiber, RJ 45, RS 232-C

[handwritten annotations:]
logical
Physical
API - Application Programing Interface
Common transmission Format
Establishes Communication
Assemble & Disassemble
- requires alternate Addressing
- Device Driver for NIC
LLC Logical link control
MAC
NIC Card
Hubs.
Routers
— DATA is segmented
— segments are converted to Packets
- Packets are converted to Frames
- Frames are th sent out as Bits.

Do it!

A-2: Discussing the layers of the OSI model

Questions and answers

1 The ___Physical___ layer describes how cables are attached to the network interface card.

2 The Network layer of the OSI model is responsible for connecting different networks. True or false?

3 Which of the following layers of the OSI model defines how a network node accesses the LAN?

    A   Physical layer

    B   Data link layer

    C   Network layer

4 The Media Access Control layer provides software controls to manage multiple protocols that are simultaneously accessing the network. True or false?

5 Why are the Presentation layer services important for communication between diverse computing platforms? *Terminal Emulation helps workstation that use different local data formats to communicate. → also data Encryption and compression*

6 The Session layer translates data into an appropriate transmission format. True or false?

7 What is the Application layer? *Is where applications themselves reside such as FTP, TelNet, x400 mail Service*

8 Which of the following layers is responsible for the accuracy of data transmission?

   A   Transport layer

   B   Session layer

   C   Presentation layer

   D   Application layer

9 Select the OSI layer that governs how data is transmitted across the media.

   A   Network

   B   Data link

   C   Physical

   D   Transport

10 What is peer-to-peer communication? *a layer communicating with the same layer in another system*

11 Which layer governs reliability of data across the network by handling errors and recovering from them?

   A   Physical

   B   Network

   C   Transport

   D   Presentation

Unit summary: The OSI model

Topic A

In this topic, you learned about the **OSI model**. You also learned that OSI model helps as a **common point of reference** for discussing network devices and concepts. Next, you learned about the **layers** of the OSI model. You learned that there are seven layers in the OSI model: the **Physical layer**, **Data Link layer**, **Network layer**, **Transport layer**, **Session layer**, **Presentation layer**, and the **Application layer**.

Review questions

[handwritten: Application / Presentation / Session / Transport / Network / DATA / Physical]

1 What is the Open Systems Interconnection (OSI) model?

2 The most important feature of the OSI model is that it helps _____ communications components to smoothly transport information packets.

   A diverse

   B similar *(circled)*

   C expensive

   D proprietary

3 What types of components are described by the physical layer?

   [handwritten: Cables, hubs, connectors]

4 Ethernet, Token Ring, and FDDI communication protocols have one common characteristic. What is it?

   [handwritten: DATALINK   Packages Frames out in the network]

5 The table shows an expanded model of the traditional seven-layer OSI model. In the appropriate column, define the function of each layer and the protocols or products in use today that are representative of each layer's activities.

OSI layer	Function	Examples
Application		
Presentation		
Session	*Establishes communication*	*NetBios*
Transport	*Management/Control Assemble & Disassemble*	*TCP Data is segmented in proper order*
Network	*Address, reguires alternate addresses*	*IP, IPX Routers*
Data link	*Access NIC Card*	*Token Ring, 8.02 EEIE, Ethernet*
Physical	*Cables, connector, Hubs*	*RJ45, copper wire*

[handwritten margin notes: Logical; DATA; Packets; Frames — Physical; bits]

Unit 3

Network adapters

Unit time: 70 minutes

Complete this unit, and you'll know how to:

A Discuss network adapter configuration and network adapter drivers.

B Troubleshoot network adapter problems.

Topic A: Network adapter configuration

This topic covers the following CompTIA Network+ exam objectives:

#	Objective
1.6	Identify the purposes, features and functions of the following network components: • NICs (Network Interface Card)
2.1	Identify a MAC (Media Access Control) address and its parts.
2.3	Identify the OSI (Open Systems Interconnect) layers at which the following network components operate: • NICs (Network Interface Card)

NIC types

Explanation

A *network adapter*, also referred to as a network board or Network Interface Card (NIC), provides a communication channel between your computer's motherboard and the network. Understanding proper network adapter configuration is essential for configuring and supporting computers on a network.

Most of the new network adapter cards you install will be PCI Ethernet cards with an RJ-45 port to connect to unshielded twisted pair (UTP) cabling. There are also plenty of ISA cards still in use, such as the one pictured in Exhibit 3-1, which has both an RJ-45 connector and a BNC port, used to connect the PC to thinnet coaxial cable. On older machines, you may even find network adapters on an MCA or EISA bus.

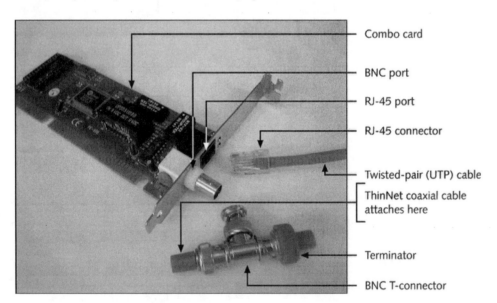

Exhibit 3-1: Ethernet combo card with BNC and RJ-45 connectors

For laptops without a built-in network adapter, PCMCIA adapters, also called PC card adapters, are most common, and they're easy to install. Usually, when a PC card NIC is inserted into the slot, the system will recognize it and load the appropriate drivers, or ask for the driver location. Most PC cards are hot-swappable.

Other easy external NIC options for both desktop and laptop PCs are parallel, USB, or Firewire (IEEE 1394) network adapters. These are plugged into the parallel, USB, or Firewire ports. USB and Firewire network adapters, like PC card adapters, are usually recognized by the system, which loads the correct drivers. With parallel network adapters, drivers must typically be loaded manually. Today, external USB or Firewire network adapters are far more frequently used than parallel adapters, but you might still find them in older installations.

Wireless

Network adapters of all current types (PCI, PC card, USB) come in wireless versions. If wireless access is available, these cards can communicate with a wireless hub or base station, allowing you to access the network without the need for cables. This is especially useful in places like libraries, where wandering around with a laptop while maintaining network access can be very convenient.

Network adapter selection criteria

Network adapter cards provide the hardware interface for the OSI Data Link layer protocols. There are several factors you need to consider before purchasing and installing these hardware components.

- **OSI Data Link layer protocol.** Each network adapter is matched to a specific OSI Data Link layer protocol and supports that low-level protocol only. If you need to support multiple access methods in your environment, you will also have to support multiple card types, such as Ethernet, Token Ring, or FDDI.

- **System bus.** The bus structure is another factor in selection. ISA bus systems support 8- and 16-bit cards, with 16-bit suggested for performance reasons. EISA-, PCI-, and MCA-based systems can support 32-bit cards.

- **Free expansion slots.** The lack of an available expansion slot in a desktop system isn't necessarily a limiting factor. Network adapters are available that plug into your system's parallel or USB ports. In addition, PC card NICs use the integrated PC card slot on the portable computer.

- **Cabling.** Select adapters that work on the type of cabling you plan to use. For example, Ethernet cards have traditionally had a BNC connector for thinnet and an AUI connector for thicknet. Many manufacturers now only make adapters with the more popular RJ-45 for twisted pair cable. NICs for fiber optic cabling are available using one of a variety of connector types. Different connectors have different characteristics, and the one chosen will depend on the type of network and installation setting. Some examples include the SC (Standard Connector), LC (Local Connector) and ST (Straight Tip) connectors. For wireless NICs, make sure the correct standard is supported (for example, 802.11b vs. 802.11g).

Care must be taken to avoid conflict with other devices during installation. Device drivers can sometimes become an issue for adapters with some network operating systems.

Network adapter settings

One of the failures after physically installing a new adapter is that it conflicts with an existing device. Conflicts can be located by checking settings for:

- **IRQ.** With some exceptions (such as COM ports and PCI adapters), each device should have a unique IRQ, or interrupt request line. An IRQ assigns a designated time slot interval on the system bus for a resource to communicate with the processor and system devices. IRQ 3, IRQ 5, and IRQ 10 are commonly used as default settings for network adapters, but others can be assigned as well.

- **I/O address.** The I/O (Input/Output) address is a memory address space used to pass commands and data between a device and the computer's microprocessor. Many devices have standard I/O addresses, such as COM ports, keyboard/mouse controllers, display adapters, and LPT ports.

- **DMA.** Some devices have the ability to directly address system memory. This process is managed through a DMA channel. ISA-, EISA-, and MCA-based systems each have eight DMA channels available.

- **ROM address.** Many adapters have their own onboard ROM BIOS, which must be given a unique memory address. Some adapters do not give you the ability to change this address, forcing you to reconfigure existing devices to make room.

IRQ, I/O address, DMA usage, and ROM addresses should be included as part of your system inventory for each computer on the network. On many networks, however, these settings are not recorded. If you can standardize how each of these is used on your system, it will make them easier to support.

Diagnostic programs, such as WinMSD (included with Windows NT/2000/XP), can provide you with information about device settings. In addition, the Device Manager within Windows can provide you with valuable information. Note, however, that some non-standard devices might generate inaccurate information.

Almost all new adapters are designed to comply with the Plug and Play standard. A Plug and Play card will be configured automatically when installed in a system that has a Plug and Play BIOS and operating system (such as Windows 2000 or XP).

Combined configuration list

The following is a combined list of common devices and the resources that adapters use. This reference might prove valuable when configuring a NIC. EGA will use IRQ 2 or none.

Device	IRQ	DMA	I/O address	Memory
System Timer	0			
Key Press	1		060-06F	
Real Time Clock	8		070-07F	
Math Coprocessor	13		0F0-0F8	
COM1	4		3F8-3FF	
COM2	3		2F8-2FF	
COM3	4		3E8-3EF	

Device	IRQ	DMA	I/O address	Memory
COM4	3		2E8-2EF	
COM5	4		2F0-2F7	
COM6	3		2E8-2EF	
COM7	4		2E0-2E7	
COM8	3		260-267	
LPT1 (LPT3 not configured)	7		378-37F	
LPT1 (LPT3 configured)	7		3BC-3BE	
LPT2 (LPT3 not configured)	5		278-27F	
LPT2 (LPT3 configured)	5		378-37A	
LPT3			278-27A	
Floppy controller	6		3F0-3F7	
XT Hard disk controller	5		320-32F	C8000-C8FFF
AT Hard disk controller	14	3	1F0-1F8	
Monochrome display adapter		0	3B0-3BF	B0000-B3FFF
CGA display adapter		0	3D0-3DF	B8000-BBFFF
EGA display adapter	2*	0	3C0-3CF	A0000-AFFFF B0000-BFFFF C0000-C3FFF
VGA display adapter	2/9	0	3C0-3DA 3C0-3BA	A0000-AFFFF C0000-C7FFF
Hercules Monochrome			3B4-3BF	B0000-B7FFF

MAC address

Any discussion of network interface adapter properties will not be complete without a brief look at the role of the Media Access Control (MAC) address.

The *MAC address* is your computer's, or more accurately, your NIC's unique hardware identifier. This address is used by the Media Access Control sub-layer of the Data Link layer within the OSI Model to control access to the network. On an Ethernet network, the MAC address is the same as the Ethernet address, and different diagnostic utilities might use one or the other name for this address.

MAC addresses are 12-digit hexadecimal numbers that are assigned to each NIC during the manufacturing process. Exhibit 3-2 shows the MAC, or Ethernet, address for a Realtek PCI Fast Ethernet NIC. Here's a sample MAC address:

```
00-A0-00-E2-8F-FA
```

The first three portions of the MAC address denote the vendor, in this case 00-A0-00. The last three are a unique hexadecimal combination, in this case E2-8F-FA.

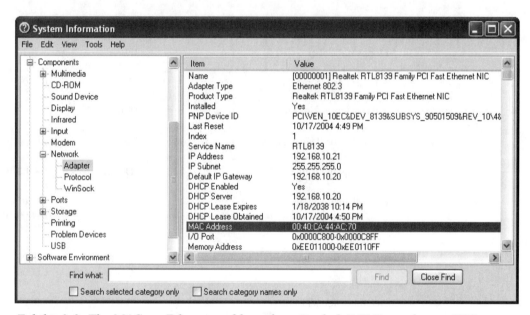

Exhibit 3-2: The MAC, or Ethernet, address for a Realtek PCI Fast ethernet NIC

Typically, it's not necessary to change this address, but situations might arise where you must. For example, if a manufacturer does not follow IEEE standards, you could have two NICs with the same MAC address. Duplicate MAC addresses on the same network cannot be used, so you must intervene if this occurs.

To override the existing MAC address of your NIC, you must consult your NIC's documentation. Some manufacturers do not provide you the capability to perform this task. You might have to physically replace the NIC as a last resort.

Boot PROMs

Another feature of network adapters that you might encounter is the use of a boot PROM (Programmable Read-Only Memory) chip. The *boot PROM chip* is an add-on item to a network adapter that helps a computer to boot entirely from a network server, therefore not needing a local hard or floppy drive.

If you examine a NIC, you'll note an empty socket, frequently marked Boot PROM. Depending on the manufacturer, this might be labeled Boot PROM, Boot ROM (Read-Only Memory), EPROM (Erasable Programmable Read-Only Memory), or EEPROM (Electrically Erasable Programmable Read-Only Memory).

Regardless of the name of this chip, it can be programmed with manufacturer-provided software to automatically boot the workstation from an operating system located on a file server. One possible use of boot PROM is to configure networked computers in a harsh environment, such as a factory floor, where hard or floppy drives will tend to fail.

Do it!

A-1: Discussing the properties of a network adapter

Questions and answers

1 What is the purpose of a network adapter?

2 What are three IRQs that are commonly used for network adapters?

3 What is a MAC address?

4 Which factors should you consider prior to purchasing and installing network adapter cards?

    A   Data Link protocol

    B   System bus

    C   Free slots

    D   All the above

5 Explain the boot PROM chip.

6 You are configuring a new network adapter that's currently configured to use IRQ 3 and I/O address 02F8. With which component could these settings conflict?

    A   LPT1

    B   COM1

    C   COM2

    D   LPT3

Configuring a network adapter

Explanation

Configuration of a NIC must be accomplished in different ways depending on the type of card in use. Below are three methods that you can use to configure a NIC:

- Jumper/switch configuration
- Software configuration
- Plug and Play (PnP)

Jumper/switch configuration

Depending on the manufacturer and model of the NIC, you might have to set switches or jumpers on the card to set the IRQ and I/O address.

Always check the documentation that was shipped with the NIC to determine the proper jumper or switch settings. For example, you might have a NIC that uses the following scheme for configuring resource settings:

Pos1 for SW1	Pos2 for SW1	IRQ
ON	ON	3
ON	OFF	5
OFF	ON	7
OFF	OFF	10

Pos1 for SW2	Pos2 for SW2	IRQ
ON	ON	270
ON	OFF	300
OFF	ON	340
OFF	OFF	360

In this case, if you were to set switch 1, position 1 to ON and position 2 to OFF, the NIC will use IRQ 5 upon installation. The I/O port address is set in a similar fashion.

Note: If the documentation for the NIC cannot be located, the manufacturer's Internet site might have information that could assist you in the configuration of the NIC.

Software configuration

Another way that a NIC can be configured is through the use of an installation disk provided by the manufacturer. Typically, this software package will not only help you to set the resource settings, but will also provide you diagnostic programs for your network adapter.

Network interface manufacturers, such as 3Com, Intel, and SMC, frequently update their software configuration programs. Therefore, you might have to frequently check your network adapter manufacturer's Web site for updates. Some models of NICs provide for both jumpered or switched resource settings, as well as software configuration. In this case, there's usually a jumper or switch setting to specify that software will be used to configure the card.

Plug and Play (PnP)

The configuration of a network adapter is done through setting physical switches on the card or by using some kind of setup configuration utility. The Plug and Play standard attempts to make this sort of configuration a thing of the past by automatically configuring the network adapter for use.

There are three components necessary for Plug and Play:

- **Plug and Play BIOS.** Almost all new computers have PnP BIOS installed. The PnP BIOS configures the PnP cards as part of the POST (Power On Self Test) process.
- **Plug and Play expansion boards.** The PnP device must minimally be able to report to the BIOS what IRQ and I/O address it is using or is able to use. The device must accept any commands from the BIOS regarding resource settings.
- **Plug and Play operating system.** This includes Microsoft Windows 95 or later desktop operating systems. Note that Windows NT 4.0 provides only limited PnP support.

This is not to say that a PnP expansion board will not work with a non-PnP system. PnP boards can be configured manually.

Currently, there are hundreds of PnP expansion boards available on the market. Compaq and other PC manufacturers have offered complete Plug and Play systems since the advent of Windows 95.

Do it!

A-2: Discussing network adapter configuration

Questions and answers
1 List three methods for configuring a network adapter.
2 List the three components necessary for Plug and Play.

Configuring basic networking components in Windows 2000/Server 2003/XP

Explanation

Once you've installed a NIC in a computer, you might also have to configure networking components in Windows 2000/Server 2003/XP. For a computer to be able to communicate with the network through the NIC, a workstation client has to be installed, file and printer sharing needs to be enabled, and a network protocol has to be installed and possibly configured.

For communicating with other computers in a small LAN, installing the NetBEUI protocol might be sufficient; otherwise, TCP/IP should be installed. In Windows 2000/Server 2003/XP, TCP/IP is installed by default. In addition, you should enable the Microsoft Client for Windows, and enable file and printer sharing. You'll also need to verify that the computer's name is correct based on the naming scheme you develop for all computers in the network (making sure there are no duplicates). For a small network that doesn't use Windows domains, you'll have to configure each computer to belong to a workgroup.

Do it!

A-3: Configuring basic network components

Here's how	Here's why
1 In Windows Server 2003, choose **Start**, **Control Panel**, **System**	To display the System Properties dialog box.
In Windows XP, choose **Start**, **Control Panel**, then double-click **System**	
2 Activate the **Hardware** tab	
3 Click **Device Manager**	
Expand the Network adapters section	Click the plus sign (+) to the left of the section name.
Right-click your network adapter	
4 Choose **Properties**	
5 Activate the **Resources** tab	
Record the IRQ and I/O settings for your network adapter	
6 Click **OK**	(On the property sheet for your network adapter.) To close the window.
7 Close the Device Manager window	
8 Click **OK**	(In the System Properties dialog box.) To close the window and return to the Control Panel.

9　In Windows Server 2003, choose **Start**,
Control Panel, **Network Connections**

In Windows XP, choose **Start**, **Control Panel**,
then double click **Network Connections**

10　Right-click **Local Area Connection**

　Select **Properties**

11	Observe the Components checked are used by this connection list	The default components include the Client for Microsoft Windows, File and Printer Sharing for Microsoft Networks and Internet Protocol (TCP/IP).
12	Click **OK**	To close the Local Area Connection Properties.
13	In Windows Server 2003, choose **Start**, **Control Panel**, **System** In Windows XP, choose **Start**, **Control Panel**, then double-click **System**	To again display the System Properties dialog box.
14	Activate the **Computer Name** tab	
15	Click **Change**	To open the Computer Name Changes dialog box.
16	Enter Student## as the Computer name, where ## is your student number.	For the Windows Server 2003 machines, enter uneven numbers for the Student##; for example, Student01, Student03, and so on. Student## for Windows XP are even numbers, for example Student02, Student04, and so on.
	In the Workgroup text box, enter your workgroup name	The naming convention for classroom purposes is Workgroup01 for lab 1 (Student01 and Student02), Workgroup02 for lab 2 (Student03 and Student04) and so on. The workgroup name helps organize groups of computers on a network into workgroups.
	Click **OK**	To save your changes.
	Click **OK**	To acknowledge the informational message that welcomes you to your workgroup.
	Click **OK**	To acknowledge the informational message that tells you that you have to reboot the computer for the changes to take effect.
17	Click **OK**	To close the System Properties dialog box.
	Restart your computer	When prompted.

The role of network adapter drivers

Explanation

Earlier network operating systems used monolithic protocols (as shown in Exhibit 3-3). *Monolithic protocols* combined the network adapter card driver, access protocol, and transport protocol into one file. These included network operating system, network adapter card, and even DOS version-specific files. This led to network management headaches.

To provide easier management, greater flexibility, and better support, the industry has moved away from this monolithic model. Instead, the elements are broken into separate segments. This is done by using a separate network adapter card driver, an interface between the MAC sub layer of the Data Link layer and the upper layers, with a separate transport protocol.

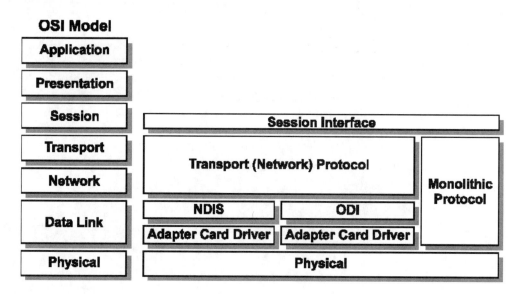

Exhibit 3-3: Monolithic Protocol networking model

There are two common implementations of this model in the industry, known by their interface names. *Network Device Interface Specification* (NDIS) is an industry standard developed by Microsoft and 3Com Corporation. NDIS has been widely implemented. *Open Datalink Interface* (ODI) is the Novell standard for the NetWare server operating system. It performs the same function as NDIS, but is used only by Novell.

NDIS and ODI

Because both are layered models, there are a number of similarities in how the NDIS and ODI models work. The primary difference is that each has a different set of specifications for compliance, so that drivers for one will not work with the other.

NDIS

- Designed by Microsoft and 3Com
- Industry standard used with Microsoft LAN Manager, Windows for Workgroups, Windows 95/98, Windows NT/2000/Server 2003/XP, IBM LAN Server, Banyan VINES, and others
- Needs an NDIS-compliant network adapter driver
- NDIS 3.0 supports unlimited network adapters and unlimited protocols bound to each adapter

- Helps network adapter drivers to communicate with upper-level protocols
- Associates NDIS-compliant protocols with the adapter through a process called binding
- Helps a single adapter to support multiple transport protocols

ODI

- Unique to Novell NetWare
- Needs an ODI-compliant network adapter driver
- Supports multiple ODI-compliant network adapters and protocols
- Helps network adapter drivers to communicate with upper-level protocols
- Associates ODI-compliant protocols with the adapter through a process called binding
- Helps a single adapter to support multiple transport protocols

Even though NDIS and ODI support the same protocols, different protocol files are needed due to differences in the interfaces. Before installing a NIC from within a Windows workstation, it is important to record the IRQ and I/O settings.

Do it!

A-4: Discussing NDIS and ODI

Questions and answers

1 NDIS drivers are used in Novell NetWare networks. True or false?

2 ODI drivers can work with what type of network adapter?

Topic B: Troubleshooting network adapter problems

This topic covers the following CompTIA Network+ exam objective:

#	Objective
4.3	Given a network scenario, interpret visual indicators (For example: link LEDs (Light Emitting Diode) and collision LEDs (Light Emitting Diode)) to determine the nature of a stated problem.

General troubleshooting tips

Explanation

Network adapter problems are common in a networked environment. Each problem should be identified correctly and potential solutions should be found to correct them.

Almost all NICs have status lights that can assist you in determining the root of a problem. For example, most have an LED labeled "Link" that should be lit when the card is properly cabled to the network. If this light is not lit, you could have problems with cabling or with network hardware in addition to, or instead of, the network adapter. In addition, you should rule out user mistakes, such as mistyping a password or username, prior to opening up the computer case to physically investigate any problems. After you've determined the problem with the NIC and resolved it, you should log onto the network and transfer a file to make sure that everything is functioning normally.

Device conflicts

Two common device conflict scenarios are provided.

Scenario one

You have just installed a PCI NIC in a Windows XP computer with a sound card, a printer, an external modem on COM2, and an IDE hard drive. When you boot the computer, you're unable to see the network, and Windows XP reports an error stating that the network cannot be browsed.

The first place to look is in the Windows Device Manager. Here, you can see if the Device Manager has detected an error with the hardware. A red "X" through the network adapter icon indicates an error. In the Properties dialog box for the network adapter, you can view the resources it has been configured to use by clicking the Resources tab.

In this case, the Resources tab indicates an IRQ conflict. You research the problem and find that the device is conflicting with COM1.

Scenario two

You have just installed an ISA NIC in a Windows 98 computer with a sound card, a printer, an external modem on COM2, a SCSI host adapter, and a SCSI hard drive. When you boot the computer, you are unable to see the network and Windows 98 reports an error stating that the network cannot be browsed. In addition, you notice that your sound card has ceased to function.

You should first go to the Device Manager to review the hardware settings, as you suspect an IRQ conflict. Investigating the properties for the network adapter, you note that the IRQ does not conflict with any devices, but the I/O address does conflict with the sound card. Viewing the properties of the Computer icon at the top of the list in Device Manager, you find that I/O address 300 is available.

As the NIC is configured through software, you restart your computer by using a boot disk and load the configuration software. You note that the NIC is set to use IRQ 10 and I/O address 220. After changing the I/O address to 300 and restarting your computer, both your network adapter and your sound card function normally.

Do it!

B-1: Discussing general troubleshooting tips

Questions and answers

1 A user comes to you with a problem logging onto the network. How should you initially approach this problem?

   A   Remove the user's network adapter and replace with a known good unit.

   B   Make sure that the user is correctly typing the username and password.

   C   Run the manufacturer's software diagnostics on the user's network adapter.

   D   Replace the network cable servicing the user's network adapter.

2 Sam, a programmer, has a problem accessing the network. When troubleshooting, where should he check first for the cause of the problem?

MAC address conflicts

Explanation
Two NICs with the same MAC address cannot be used on the same network. A situation could arise where two computers on a network have the same MAC address. This will result in only one being able to participate on the network at any time.

This could be a difficult problem to troubleshoot, but typically your network operating system, be it UNIX, Linux, NetWare, Mac OSX or Windows, could give you some information to assist in determining where the problem lies.

Scenario one

You have a small Windows Server 2003-based network consisting of one Windows Server 2003 server and Windows XP computers. After installing new NICs in all Windows 2000 computers, the Windows XP Event Log has the following entry:

```
The system detected an address conflict for IP address
0.0.0.0 with the system having network hardware address
00-E0-98-02-F0-F8. Network operations on this system
might be disrupted as a result.
```

This will most likely indicate a duplicate MAC address on the network. To troubleshoot this problem, you decide to use the network configuration software that came with each new NIC to determine which two adapters have the MAC address of 00-E0-98-02-F0-F8. After you have located one of the two computers with this address, you should change it to another address, making sure that you do not create a new conflict in the process.

Note: On larger networks where a system-by-system search for the desired MAC address will be time-prohibitive, there are available utilities, such as TCP/IP's ARP, that could help identify the target system(s).

Diagnostic software

Regardless of the manufacturer, your network adapter is shipped with some sort of diagnostic software. Diagnostics can prove invaluable when troubleshooting problems with NICs.

Exhibit 3-4 shows an example of the software diagnostics used by 3Com network adapters. This program runs several tests on the adapter to assure that it is functioning normally. It will be appropriate to run these tests after checking all cables when troubleshooting a network problem.

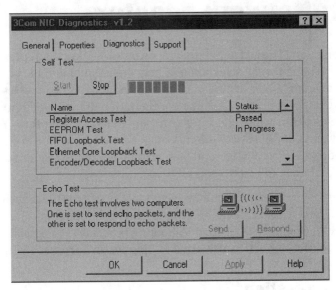

Exhibit 3-4: An example of 3Com software diagnostics

Diagnostic hardware

In addition to diagnostic software, you can use different types of diagnostic hardware to assist you in determining where a problem will be found. One type of diagnostic hardware that is most frequently used is an external loopback plug.

The purpose of using an external loopback plug is to allow the NIC to send and receive on a closed loop. This tests the integrity of the onboard transceiver and cable connectors.

After the external loopback plug is in place, use the software diagnostics provided by the manufacturer to run this test. If the test fails, the problem is most likely related to the transceiver on the NIC. The best course of action in this case will be to replace the failed network adapter.

Note: Follow all manufacturer guidelines when running an external loopback test. Failure to do so could result in damage to your NIC or to your computer.

Do it!

B-2:   Identifying network adapter problems

Questions and answers

1 Explain an external loopback plug.

2 If two computers on a network have the same MAC address, only one will be able to participate on the network at any time. True or false?

Unit summary: Network adapters

Topic A
In this topic, you learned about the properties of **network adapter cards**. You learned about the criteria for the selection of a network adapter and the procedure to install a network adapter. Additionally, you learned about **MAC addresses** and **boot PROMs**. You learned about network adapter configuration that included **jumpers, switches,** and **software configuration**, and **Plug and Play network adapters**. You also learned how to review and configure networking components from within a Windows Server 2003 and Windows XP computer. You then learned about the role of network adapter **drivers**, including the **NDIS** and **ODI** specifications.

Topic B
In this topic, you learned about the methodology of **troubleshooting** network adapter problems. You learned about the general troubleshooting tips and discussed the various scenarios that can help your troubleshooting procedures. You also learned about the importance of **diagnostic software** and **diagnostic hardware** in troubleshooting.

Review questions

1 Explain the alternative for the monolithic model to avoid network management problems.

2 You have been tasked with creating an inventory of your company's computers. What information about each network adapter's resource settings should be documented?

3 After you have replaced a network adapter card on a user's computer, what's a quick way to test if it is working normally?

   A Open the Device Manager under Windows XP and change the resource settings to IRQ 15, Port 220 and restart the machine.

   B Run an external loopback test.

   C Log on to the network and transfer a file.

   D Run an internal loopback test.

4 NDIS and ODI support the same protocols, but different protocol files are needed due to differences in the interfaces. True or false?

5 The purpose of a boot PROM or EEPROM is to:

   A Permit a computer to boot to the network without a hard or floppy drive

   B Dynamically allocate MAC addresses as needed to the network adapter

   C Store network adapter resource settings

   D Comply with the Plug and Play standard

6 You always need to manually configure MAC addresses on each new network adapter that you install. True or false?

7 Name the process by which NDIS associates NDIS-compliant protocols with the adapter.

Unit 4

Introducing protocols

Unit time: 60 minutes

Complete this unit, and you'll know how to:

A Discuss access protocols.

B Discuss channel access methods.

C Discuss transport protocols.

D Discuss remote access protocols.

E Discuss security protocols.

Topic A: Introduction to protocols

This topic covers the following CompTIA Network+ exam objective:

#	Objective
1.2	Specify the main features of 802.2 (Logical Link Control), 802.3 (Ethernet), 802.5 (token ring), 802.11 (wireless), and FDDI (Fiber Distributed Data Interface) networking technologies, including: • Speed • Access method (CSMA / CA (Carrier Sense Multiple Access/Collision Avoidance) and CSMA / CD (Carrier Sense Multiple Access / Collision Detection)) • Topology • Media

What is a protocol?

Explanation

A *protocol* is the language with which computers interact with each other. Two nodes on the same network must use the same protocol to communicate, just as two humans must speak a common language to communicate. Protocols include connectionless and connection-oriented protocols. Connectionless protocols are usually used to send small amounts of information and connection-oriented protocols are used to send large amounts of data that needs acknowledgment.

A protocol defines the way in which two (or more) computers communicate. This includes definitions of the following items:

- Identification of unique nodes (network stations)
- Addressing
- Routing between networks, if supported
- Data format and packaging
- Delivery sequencing
- Error detection and recovery

IEEE 802 series specifications

The OSI reference model does not make the actual specification of the seven layers explicit. The lower layers of the model have been standardized by organizations such as the Institute of Electrical and Electronic Engineers (IEEE) committee, which have published a series of specifications for OSI layers 1 and 2 (physical and data link), the 802 series of specifications.

The 802 series of specifications was named after the date when the IEEE Computer Society "Local Network Standards Committee," Project 802, held their first meeting, which was in February (2) of 1980(80). This committee is now called the "LAN/MAN Standards Committee (LMSC)."

The 802 series of specifications define the physical media popularly known as the following:

Specification	Media
802.3	CSMA/CD (Ethernet)
802.3z	Gigabit Ethernet
802.3ae	10 Gigabit Ethernet
802.4	Token Bus
802.5	Token Ring
802.0	Executive Committee
802.1	Higher Layer Interfaces
802.2	Logical Link Control (LLC)
802.6	Metropolitan Area Network (MAN)
802.7	Broadband LAN
802.8	Fiber Optic LAN
802.9	Integrated Voice and Data LAN
802.10	Standards for Interoperable LAN Security
802.11	Wireless networks
802.12	Demand Priority Access LAN, 100BaseVG-AnyLAN

A more advanced protocol will also define other items, sometimes unique to that protocol. The important point is that these are defined in a manner unique to the protocol. In other words, a computer, by using one protocol, cannot communicate directly with a computer that uses a different protocol. Protocols can be broadly categorized into three types:

- Access Protocols
- Transport Protocols
- Remote Access Protocols

Access protocols

The *Data Link layer* specifies how devices attached to the network gain access to network resources. The Institute of Electrical and Electronic Engineers (IEEE) modified the OSI reference model by breaking the Data Link layer into two additional layers: the Media Access Control (MAC) layer and the Logical Link Control (LLC) layer, as shown in Exhibit 4-1.

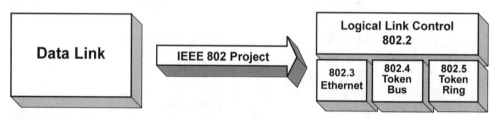

Exhibit 4-1: Modification in the Data Link layer

IEEE's Project 802 defined the MAC layer as communicating directly with the network adapter card. This layer is responsible for delivering error-free data between two computers on the network.

In the same way, Project 802 defined the LLC layer as managing data link communication. This layer also defines the use of logical interface points, called Service Access Points (SAPs) that can be referenced by other computers to transfer information from the LLC layer to the upper OSI layers.

Project 802 resulted in a number of documents, including several standards for network topologies:

- 802.3 defines standards for bus networks, such as Ethernet, that use a mechanism called Carrier Sense Multiple Access with Collision Detection (CSMA/CD) for data transmission over the media
- 802.5 defines standards for Token Ring networks, which use a mechanism called token passing for data transmission over the media
- 802.11 defines standards for wireless networks

IEEE defined functionality for the LLC layer in standard 802.2 and defined functionality for the MAC and physical layers in standards 802.3 and 802.5.

Do it!   **A-1:   Identifying protocols**

Questions and answers

1   The Institute of Electrical and Electronic Engineers (IEEE) modified the OSI reference model by breaking the Data Link layer into two additional layers. Identify the layers.

   A   Media Access Control

   B   NWLink layer

   C   Transport layer

   D   Logical Link Control

2   What is the MAC layer responsible for?

3   What is a protocol?

Topic B: Channel access methods

This topic covers the following CompTIA Network+ exam objectives:

#	Objective
1.2	Specify the main features of 802.2 (Logical Link Control), 802.3 (Ethernet), 802.5 (token ring), 802.11 (wireless), and FDDI (Fiber Distributed Data Interface) networking technologies, including: • Speed • Access method (CSMA / CA (Carrier Sense Multiple Access/Collision Avoidance) and CSMA / CD (Carrier Sense Multiple Access / Collision Detection)) • Topology • Media
1.3	Specify the characteristics (For example: speed, length, topology, and cable type) of the following cable standards: • 10BASE-T and 10BASE-FL • 100BASE-TX and 100BASE-FX • 1000BASE-TX, 1000BASE-CX, 1000BASE-SX and 1000BASE-LX • 10GBASE-SR, 10GBASE-LR and 10GBASE-ER
1.6	Identify the purposes, features and functions of the following network components: • WAPs (Wireless Access Point)
1.7	Specify the general characteristics (For example: carrier speed, frequency, transmission type and topology) of the following wireless technologies: • 802.11 (Frequency hopping spread spectrum) • 802.11x (Direct sequence spread spectrum) • Infrared • Bluetooth
1.8	Identify factors which affect the range and speed of wireless service. For example: • Interference • Antenna type • Environmental factors
2.3	Identify the OSI (Open Systems Interconnect) layers at which the following network components operate: • WAPs (Wireless Access Point)
2.14	Identify the basic characteristics (For example: speed, capacity and media) of the following WAN (Wide Area Networks) technologies: • FDDI (Fiber Distributed Data Interface)

Introducing channel access methods

Explanation
The *channel access method* determines the physical methodology by which data is sent across the transmitting media. These technologies are analogous to two of the ways that people communicate. For example, imagine that a specific problem and its possible resolutions are discussed in a meeting. This phase of the meeting is more of a free for all in which there might be moments where everyone talks and other times where most hold off speaking, yielding to only one speaker, after which everyone again attempts to communicate their thoughts.

Now, consider yourself in a departmental staff meeting discussing project status. Each member of the team waits his turn to communicate the successes and failures for the week. After completing, the next person communicates his status. This process continues in an orderly fashion until all have had a chance to speak. Today, there are various channel access methods through which conversation is made possible. The most popular network specification used today is Ethernet.

The example of several people talking at once is an example of a Carrier Sense Media Access with Collision Detection (CSMA/CD) communications methodology. CSMA/CD networks are more popularly known as Ethernet networks.

Ethernet and 802.3

The terms Ethernet and 802.3 are used interchangeably. There are some small differences, but both are CSMA/CD specifications.

Ethernet was originally developed by Xerox, Intel, and DEC in the late 1970s, with specifications first released in 1980. The IEEE 802.3 specification differs from Ethernet primarily with respect to the frame format.

An 802.3 frame contains a 2-byte length field indicating the length of the frame. An Ethernet frame is fixed in length. Short frames are padded to fill them out. In the place of a length field is information on the type of higher-layer protocol being used, such as, TCP/IP or the Xerox Network System (XNS).

Other differences involve pinouts and the Signal Quality Error (SQE) signal, also known as a heartbeat.

CSMA/CD

Carrier Sense Multiple Access with Collision Detection (CSMA/CD) is the most common implementation of contention access.

- Carrier sensing — Listens for someone talking.
- Multiple access — All have concurrent access to the media.
- Collision detection — If two or more systems transmit at once, the system realizes the message did not get through and repeats the message.

Transmission failures can be caused by:

- Bad cabling
- Improper termination
- Collisions
- Improper cable length

Collisions

Collisions slow cable throughput. At some point in its growth, an Ethernet network might encounter a reduction in performance. This will depend on the amount of traffic generated by each workstation.

A node on an Ethernet network will wait to send information to the network until it determines that no other node is transmitting information, and then begins transmitting itself. During transmission, the system also listens in on the media. If it senses that another node is also transmitting, a collision event occurs, as shown in Exhibit 4-2. When this happens, the node quits transmitting for a random period of time and then checks the media again to see if it is okay to transmit. Any station might transmit when it senses that the carrier is free. If a collision is detected, each station will wait for a randomly determined interval before retransmitting. Most network operating systems track retransmissions, which are a good indication of the number of collisions occurring on the network.

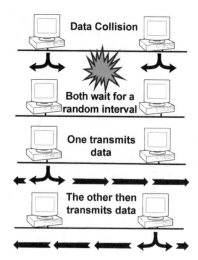

Exhibit 4-2: An example of data collision

CSMA/CA

A variation on this theme is Carrier Sense Multiple Access with Collision Avoidance (CSMA/CA). This methodology does not detect collisions as much as it attempts to avoid collisions. An alert message notifies nodes of an impending transmission. Any collisions that occur will be during this alert sequence rather than during actual data transmission. Because the alert sequence is shorter than an actual data transmission, the retransmit of lengthy data is avoided.

Ethernet topologies

Ethernet networks can be wired with different types of cable, each with its own benefits and drawbacks. Some of the specifications for Ethernet topologies are the following:

- *10Base-T* — Baseband specification that uses Category 3 or better UTP cable. This cabling medium can carry a message for 100 m (about 328 ft) between a computer and a hub. It operates at a speed of 10 Mbps and uses an RJ-45 connector.

- *10Base-FL* — Baseband specification that uses fiber optic cable. This cabling medium can carry a message for up to 2000 m between a computer and a repeater hub. It operates at a speed of 10 Mbps and can use different connectors, such as ST or SC connectors.

- *100Base-TX* — Baseband specification that uses Category 5 UTP or STP cable. This cabling medium can carry a message for 100 m (about 328 ft) between a workstation and a hub. It operates at a speed of 100 Mbps and uses an RJ-45 connector.

- *100Base-FX* — Also known as FDDI. Baseband specification that uses fiber optic cable. This cabling medium can carry a message for 2000 m between a workstation and a repeater hub. It operates at a speed of 100 Mbps.

- *1000Base-TX* — Gigabit Ethernet specification that runs over Category 5 UTP cable at 1000 Mbps with a maximum segment length of 100 meters.

- *1000Base-CX* — Gigabit Ethernet specification that runs over STP cabling at 1000 Mbps with a maximum segment length of 25 meters.

- *1000Base-SX* — Gigabit Ethernet specification that runs over fiber optic cable at 1000 Mbps with a maximum segment length of 550 meters.

- *1000Base-LX* — Gigabit Ethernet specification that runs over Category 5 UTP cable at 1000 Mbps with a maximum segment length of up to 5000 meters.

- *10Base-SR* — 10 Gigabit Ethernet specification that runs over multimode fiber optic cable at 10000 Mbps with a maximum segment length of 82 meters. Operates in full duplex mode.

- *10Base-LR* — 10 Gigabit Ethernet specification that runs over single mode fiber optic cable at 10000 Mbps with a maximum segment length of 10 kilometers.

- *10Base-ER* — 10 Gigabit Ethernet specification that runs over single mode fiber optic cable at 10000 Mbps with a maximum segment length of 40 kilometers. Operates in full duplex mode.

Note that a typical use for Gigabit Ethernet would be on a business or academic campus, where the fiber backbone would connect the buildings at 1000 or 10000 Mbps, while within the buildings copper connects individual PC's at 10 or 100 Mbps.

Do it!

B-1: Discussing Ethernet methods

Questions and answers

1 The _____ determines the physical methodology by which data is sent across the transmitting media.

2 In the term CSMA/CD, what does the CD stand for?

3 CSMA/CD networks are popularly known as _____.

4 Which type of channel access method is used by both Ethernet and 802.3?

   A   Token passing

   B   Polling

   C   CSMA/CA

   D   CSMA/CD

5 Which of the following are valid Ethernet topologies?

   A   10BASE-T

   B   1000BASE-CX

   C   10GBASE-RX

   D   100-BASE-FX

Introducing token passing/Token Ring

Explanation

This technology corresponds with the example of each person waiting his turn to speak during a meeting. In a token passing technology, a token is passed among the nodes of the network; whichever node is in possession of the token is permitted to transmit. Token Ring is an example of a popular token passing scheme.

Token Ring and 802.5

The terms Token Ring and 802.5 are frequently used interchangeably, but it is important to note that there are some subtle differences. It would be more appropriate to state that Token Ring is similar to the 802.5 standard.

Features of Token Ring include:

- Logical ring usually wired as a physical star.
- Transfer rate of 4 to 16 Mbps.
- Unshielded twisted pair, shielded twisted pair, or fiber optic cable.
- Deterministic; it is possible to predict the passage of the token.

The predictability inherent in Token Ring makes it a popular choice for timing-critical and control applications. The following statements describe token passing:

- There is only one active token on the ring at any time.
- Tokens travel at thousands of miles per second (fiber optic).
- A token (data frame) passes from system to system.
- A system can attach data to a token when the token is free (empty).
- Each system receives and regenerates the token.

With Token Ring, a token is passed around the ring to which the computers are connected. The computer that grabs the token is able to send data over the network. When the token returns to its source with an acknowledgment from the destination, the source relinquishes the token and continues passing it around the ring, permitting another workstation to send data out on the network.

Common Token Ring topologies

Computers participating on a Token Ring network are connected by shielded and/or unshielded twisted-pair cable to a wiring concentrator. Each computer can be up to 100 m (about 328 ft) from the Multistation Access Unit (MSAU) by using shielded wire or 45 m (about 148 ft) by using unshielded wire. The minimum shielded or unshielded cable length is 2.5 m (about 8 ft).

Each MSAU can support as many as 72 workstations that use unshielded wire or up to 260 workstations by using shielded wire. Each ring can have as many as 33 MSAUs.

A Token Ring is an efficient design for moving data on a network. On small- to medium-sized networks with heavy data traffic, Token Rings are more efficient compared to most Ethernet installations. On the other hand, the direct routing of data supported by Ethernet networks tends to fare better when a network includes a large number of computers with light to moderate traffic.

More about token passing

A token is a control signal that is passed from station-to-station between the transferring of data. It consists of a starting delimiter, an access control field, and an ending delimiter. The token contains a single bit (the Token Bit) that indicates that the token is ready to accept information. If the node has data to send, it appends the data to the token. The token then becomes a frame. Only one token at a time is permitted to circulate around the ring.

A *frame* is a unit of data transmission and includes delimiters, control characters, information, and checking characters.

Token passing can be viewed as a sequence of events:

1 When it wants to communicate, a station takes the token, flags it as busy (changes the token bit to 1), loads it with data, and passes it on.

2 The frame makes its way through the network to the receiving station, which takes the data, marks the frame as received (by changing 2 sets of bits in the Frame Status (FS) byte), and passes it along.

3 The frame returns to the sender, which sees the receipt (FS bits), removes the frame from the ring, and then releases a new token.

4 An option called early token release permits a transmitting station to release a token after transmitting the ending delimiter of the frame.

5 Each node acts as a repeater for the network.

6 The first station that powers on and inserts on the ring becomes the active monitor. All other stations are capable of becoming the active monitor and are called standby monitors. If the active monitor fails or is removed from the network, the standby monitor with the highest address will become the active monitor.

7 Every seven seconds or less, this active monitor will send a signal to the other nodes to identify itself as present.

The active monitor is responsible for verifying that the token is detected on the ring and generates a new token if it is missing. The active monitor will also remove continuously circulating frames.

Beaconing

When a station detects a hard error, it begins to transmit beacon frames. The beacon frame is used to define a failure domain. The failure domain includes the station reporting the failure, its nearest active upstream neighbor (NAUN), and everything in between, as shown in Exhibit 4-3. After it is identified, the NAUN removes itself from the ring and begins a self-test. If successful, the NAUN reattaches to the ring. If unsuccessful, it remains unattached. If the ring does not recover, the beaconing station assumes the NAUN has completed its self-test and the beaconing station removes itself from the ring and begins self-testing. If successful, it can reattach. If unsuccessful, it remains unattached. If the ring has not recovered at this point, manual intervention is necessary.

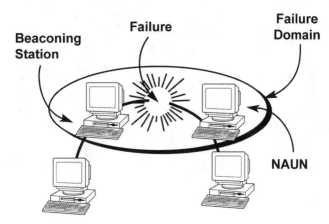

Exhibit 4-3: The failure domain

FDDI

Fiber Distributed Data Interface, or *FDDI* (pronounced "fiddy") uses a double fiber ring and runs at 100 Mbps. It is typically found as the backbone connecting buildings on a campus or wider area, as nodes can be over 60 miles apart.

FDDI uses a ring topology like Token Ring, but it uses two complete rings—the secondary ring is for redundancy, and is not used unless the primary ring experiences transmission problems.

ATM

Asynchronous Transfer Mode, or *ATM*, is a topology that can reach throughput of almost 10000 Mbps, but is more commonly implemented at 155 or 622 Mbps. ATM uses small packets, which are called cells, of a fixed size (48 bytes of data with a 5-byte header).

Although these cells are small and therefore require a lot of header information overhead, the small and predictable size allows for easier monitoring and control of traffic, resulting in greater overall throughput.

Also, ATM does not use routing like Ethernet, but uses ATM switches, which establish point-to-point connections. ATM equipment is expensive, and smaller organizations wishing to upgrade will probably go to the cheaper Gigabit Ethernet standard.

Do it!

B-2: Discussing Token Ring methods

Questions and answers

1 When a Token Ring node becomes aware of a transmission problem, what will it do?

2 A _____ is a control signal that is passed from station-to-station between the transferring of data.

3 List three features of Token Ring.

Wireless

Explanation

The most prevalent wireless access method implemented in homes, offices, and public sites (hot spots) is defined by the 802.11 family of standards. Other wireless technologies include Bluetooth and Infrared.

802.11 and 802.11x

IEEE 802.11 is a group of specifications for wireless networks. Among others, specifications include 802.11, 802.11a, 802.11b and 802.11g.

Specification	Speed	Transmission method/band
802.11	Up to 2 Mbps	FHSS or DSSS, 2.4 Ghz band
802.11a	Up to 54 Mbps	OFDM, 5 Ghz band
802.11b (also referred to as Wi-Fi)	Up to 11 Mbps	DSSS, 2.4 Ghz band
802.11g (also referred to as Wi-Fi)	Either 11 or 54 Mbps	OFDM (for backward compatibility with 802.11a) or DSSS (for backward compatibility with 802.11b), 2.4 Ghz band

802.11x wireless networks consist of Wireless Access Points (WAPs), which operate at the Physical and Media Access Control (MAC) layer of the OSI model, and wireless clients. WAPs can, on average, communicate with up to 30 clients within a 100 meter radius.

Using repeaters, reflectors, or more powerful antennae, you can, however, extend the range of the network. WAPs that are located physically next to each other cannot use the same frequency, because otherwise interference occurs.

If multiple WAPs are installed and accessible to clients, when clients try to connect to a WAP, they choose the one that provides the strongest signal and best error rate. Once connected to a WAP, the client periodically checks other WAPs to see if they can provide a stronger signal or a better error rate. If one is available, the client switches to that access point's frequency using a process that is called *reassociation*.

Transmission technologies

Different types of transmission technologies are employed for 802.11 wireless communications. Two of these are:

- Frequency Hopping Spread Spectrum (FHSS)
- Direct Sequence Spread Spectrum (DSSS)

Frequency Hopping Spread Spectrum (FHSS) uses a wide range of frequencies in the 2.4 Ghz band, where data is transmitted on a single frequency at any given time. However, the signal hops from frequency to frequency in a pseudorandom pattern.

This means that the pattern appears random, but is actually generated by a computation known to both the sender and receiver—to reduce the possibility of interference from other nearby transmissions. This transmission technology can be used by 802.11.

Direct Sequence Spread Spectrum (DSSS), which is used by 802.11b and 802.11g, also operates in the 2.4 Ghz band and employs a mechanism whereby the data being transmitted is spread over multiple frequencies, allowing for higher throughput rates.

FHSS and DSSS devices are not compatible. For example, 802.11 and 802.11b/802.11g devices cannot communicate with one another.

Interference

Both FHSS and DSSS are fairly resistant to interference from other nearby transmissions. With FHSS it's unlikely that another device is transmitting at exactly the same frequency at exactly the same time, unless there are many FHSS devices operating in close proximity. With DSSS, any interfering signal is diluted by being spread over the entire band. The more devices operate in close proximity to each other, the greater the likelihood of interference, which will negatively affect performance (speed).

Also, if devices using FHSS and DSSS are trying to transmit in close proximity to each other, problems occur. FHSS devices will have trouble finding any "free" frequencies, while DSSS—if enough FHSS devices are operating in close proximity—will eventually not have enough "free" frequencies available over which to spread its transmissions.

Further, interference can come from other devices using the 2.4 Ghz band, such as microwave ovens and cordless phones. As interference increases, transmission speeds decline. Performance and range can also degrade depending on the types of materials signals have to pass through, such as concrete walls, metal ceilings, and so on.

Orthogonal frequency division multiplexing

Another wireless transmission technology is Orthogonal Frequency Division Multiplexing (OFDM). OFDM is used by the 802.11a specification, which is not as widely implemented as the other 802.11x specifications.

With Orthogonal Frequency Division Multiplexing, the radio signal is split into multiple, smaller signals. These signals are then transmitted at the same time, but at different frequencies. OFDM operates in the 5 Ghz band, which makes it more resistant to interference than FHSS and DSSS.

However, with OFDM, distances the signal can travel are shorter, and as a result, more WAPs are needed to cover a certain area.

Other wireless technologies

Bluetooth

Bluetooth's aim is to allow the creation of small, short range, wireless networks comprised of computers, keyboards, mice, PDAs, etc., usually within a single room.

Another application is connecting two devices, such as a cell phone and its headphones, wirelessly. Bluetooth has a range of 10 meters, speeds of up to 1 Mbps and uses FHSS for its transmission method. Bluetooth and 802.11x devices cannot communicate with one another and can interfere with each other.

Infrared

Infrared (IR) allows for wireless connection of devices at very close range. For example, IR technology can be used to connect a keyboard or mouse to a computer.

Infrared is line of sight technology, meaning that the transmitting and receiving device cannot be separated by other objects. Infrared's range is up to 1 meter and speeds range from 115 Kbps to 4 Mbps.

Do it!

B-3: Discussing wireless communications

Questions and answers

1 On which standard(s) is/are wireless communication with speeds of up to 54 Mbps based?

    A   802.11a

    B   802.11b

    C   802.11g

    D   802.12

2 You want to implement a wireless 802.11g network that will be used throughout your building. The distance from one side of the building to the other is 300 meters. You install a WAP in the middle of the building to provide access to all clients. What is the problem with this configuration? What should you do to resolve the problem?

3 Which of the following wireless technologies has a range of 10 meters?

    A   Infrared

    B   802.11b

    C   802.11g

    D   Bluetooth

4 Which transmission technology employs a mechanism whereby transmitted data is spread over multiple frequencies? Name two 802.11x standards that employ this technology.

Topic C: Transport protocols

This topic covers the following CompTIA Network+ exam objectives:

#	Objective
1.2	Specify the main features of 802.2 (Logical Link Control), 802.3 (Ethernet), 802.5 (token ring), 802.11 (wireless), and FDDI (Fiber Distributed Data Interface) networking technologies, including: <ul><li>Speed</li><li>Access method (CSMA / CA (Carrier Sense Multiple Access/Collision Avoidance) and CSMA / CD (Carrier Sense Multiple Access / Collision Detection))</li><li>Topology</li><li>Media</li></ul>
1.6	Identify the purposes, features and functions of the following network components: <ul><li>Gateways</li></ul>
2.4	Differentiate between the following network protocols in terms of routing, addressing schemes, interoperability and naming conventions: <ul><li>IPX / SPX (Internetwork Packet Exchange / Sequence Packet Exchange)</li><li>NetBEUI (Network Basic Input / Output System Extended User Interface)</li><li>AppleTalk / AppleTalk over IP (Internet Protocol)</li><li>TCP / IP (Transmission Control Protocol / Internet Protocol)</li></ul>
2.10	Define the purpose, function and use of the following protocols used in the TCP / IP (Transmission Control Protocol / Internet Protocol) suite: <ul><li>TCP (Transmission Control Protocol)</li><li>UDP (User Datagram Protocol)</li></ul>
2.13	Identify the purpose of network services and protocols (For example: <ul><li>SMB (Server Message Block)</li><li>AFP (Apple File Protocol)</li></ul>

Transmission types

Explanation

Most network environments are best served by a protocol that provides both connectionless and connection-oriented services. In most cases, you'll have a protocol that can support both transmission types. This will help you to have reliable communications with a minimum of overhead traffic.

Connectionless

A connectionless protocol is used when sending small packets of data, usually less than 1 KB. Reliability improvements in current networks mean that packets are infrequently dropped, and there is usually no need for the increased overhead of acknowledging each receipt.

Connection-oriented

Acknowledgment becomes more critical when sending a large amount of information, such as a large data file that was divided into multiple packets for transmission. This is necessary because of the limits set on packet sizes by lower-level protocols.

In a large network, packets might end up taking different routes to the destination. Some might get lost in the process, or be delayed and arrive in the wrong order. A connection-oriented protocol uses packet sequence numbers to verify packet order and acknowledges the receipt of each packet. The lost or improperly delivered packets, which are not acknowledged as a successful receipt, can be retransmitted.

Transport protocols

The *transport layer* is responsible for guaranteed packet delivery and packet sequencing. Transport protocols manage network communications and determine how data moving up and down through the communications model should be presented to the next layer. The protocols responsible for transporting data are:

- NetBEUI
- IPX/SPX
- TCP/IP
- AppleTalk

NetBEUI

NetBEUI (NetBIOS Extended User Interface) is a high-speed protocol first introduced by IBM. Some facts about NetBEUI include:

- It was designed for use on small networks (20-200 nodes). NetBEUI performs well when used on small networks. This was traditionally the default protocol in older LAN Manager-based network products.
- It provides good error protection. NetBEUI has well-designed error detection and recovery routines. These are handled in the transport layer.
- Tuning parameters are available to match network and organizational requirements. Parameters are provided to match both workstation and server configurations.
- There are limited memory overhead requirements.
- Both connectionless and connection-oriented traffic are supported. NetBEUI uses either connectionless or connection-oriented methods of communication, depending on the type of data transmitted.
- It is not a routable protocol. Because NetBEUI does not function on the network layer of the OSI Model, it is not routable. Because of this, NetBEUI does not perform well on larger networks.
- NetBEUI uses the Server Message Block (SMB) protocol to allow for sharing of files, directories, and devices between clients and servers.

NetBIOS

It is common to see the term NetBIOS listed as a protocol or used in place of NetBEUI. *NetBIOS* (Network Basic Input/Output System) is an application interface operating at the session layer, rather than a protocol. Some facts about NetBIOS include:

- Applications can communicate with NetBIOS-compliant protocols by using NetBIOS. Originally, this was limited to communication over NetBEUI, but NetBIOS applications can now be supported over TCP/IP and IPX.

- You can manage communication sessions between computers by using NetBIOS. This is the session-level management needed for a two-way interchange between computers.

- You can track computers by the computer name by using NetBIOS. Under NetBIOS, each system has a unique (up to) 15-character computer name that identifies it to NetBIOS sessions.

- NetBIOS is supported over NetBEUI. It can be supported over other protocols, such as IPX/SPX and TCP/IP. Microsoft's implementation of NetBIOS over TCP/IP is called NBT. NWLINK, Microsoft's implementation of IPX/SPX, supports NetBIOS names through NWNBLink.

IPX/SPX

The *IPX/SPX protocol* suite consists of Internetwork Packet Exchange (IPX), which runs at the network layer of the OSI Model and Sequenced Packet Exchange (SPX), which runs at the transport layer. This protocol suite is commonly referred to as IPX. IPX/SPX is based on the Xerox XNS protocol.

Some facts about IPX/SPX include:

- This is a Novell proprietary protocol. IPX is owned by Novell and runs almost exclusively on NetWare networks.

- IPX/SPX is available as monolithic or ODI-compliant. You might encounter the monolithic version of IPX on older networks. All recent drivers and IPX versions are based on Novell's ODI specification.

- IPX provides connectionless service. The IPX component provides high-speed communications between stations.

- SPX provides connection-oriented services. SPX is the portion of the protocol providing error checking, windowing, and flow control.

- IPX/SPX is a routable protocol. Because IPX resides in the network layer of the OSI Model, IPX/SPX can be routed.

This is the default NetWare 3.x and 4.x protocol. It is also still supported by NetWare 5.x and 6.x; however, these network operating systems use TCP/IP as the default protocol. Its most common use is in an environment that includes older NetWare servers.

Microsoft's implementation of IPX/SPX is called NWLink. NWLink is used in a mixed Microsoft and NetWare 3.x/4.x environment.

Incorrect frame types on an IPX/SPX network

IPX/SPX uses two different frame types (802.2 and 802.3). If a workstation and a server are both running IPX/SPX but with different frame types, they will be unable to communicate.

Novell defines the following default frame types for different versions of its NetWare/IntranetWare operating system:

- 802.3 for NetWare 3.1x and earlier
- 802.2 for NetWare 4.x and later

IPX/SPX is also configurable on the Ethernet_II frame type, though it is not the default in any version.

Windows 95, Windows 98, and Windows NT/2000 will automatically configure the IPX/SPX-compatible protocol to use the frame type first received by the network adapter when the machine is booted. Most of the time this works well, especially in an environment where there is only one version of NetWare running that is using IPX/SPX.

In environments where more than one version of NetWare that is using IPX/SPX is installed, or the administrator has configured the server to use the Ethernet_II frame type, the auto-selection feature might select a frame type that will not permit communications with the user's assigned server.

An incorrect frame type selection is manifested in the following ways:

- The user is able to see some NetWare servers but not the NetWare server he or she needs to access.
- The user is unable to see any NetWare servers. However, he or she can browse other network resources.
- Occasionally, users are able to see the NetWare resource if they reboot their computers, but this might take several reboots to occur.

To remedy this problem, use the network properties sheet for the IPX/SPX protocol and manually select the correct frame type for the resources the users need to access.

Using IPX/SPX to route NetBIOS

NWLink provides Windows connectivity with IPX/SPX-based Novell NetWare networks by using the IPX/SPX transport protocol. By using NWLink Windows systems can talk with IPX/SPX-based NetWare servers, other systems running NWLink, and other computers running IPX/SPX.

NWLink also supports the transfer of Novell NetBIOS communication packets across IPX/SPX. NWNBLink (NetBIOS over IPX) can be used to communicate and share files between systems on any Windows-based network. NWNBLink is a fully routable protocol and makes a good routing mechanism for the otherwise unroutable NetBIOS traffic.

You should consider implementing NWLink in the following situations:

- When you are integrating Windows NT/2000 Server/Server 2003 into an existing Novell NetWare 3.x or 4.x network.
- When you have routing requirements.

TCP/IP

In the last few years, TCP/IP has become the protocol of choice for most medium- to large-sized networks. It is the current de facto standard for internetwork communications, a place it is likely to hold for the foreseeable future. It also provides guaranteed delivery, proper sequencing, and data integrity checks. If errors occur during transmission, TCP is responsible for retransmitting the data. The TCP/IP suite of protocols is extensive.

The Internet Protocol (IP) is an unreliable connectionless protocol. This means that the Internet Protocol does not verify that a specific packet of data has reached its destination. The sole function of the IP protocol is to transmit TCP/IP.

TCP/IP Transport layer protocols

Core protocols, utilities, and services associated with the TCP/IP suite at the transport layer include:

- **TCP/IP Transport layer protocols.** TCP provides acknowledged, connection-oriented communications and provides guaranteed delivery, proper sequencing, and data integrity checks. If errors occur during transmission, TCP is responsible for retransmitting the data. FTP (File Transfer Protocol) is an example of a TCP/IP service that depends on TCP.

- **User Datagram Protocol (UDP).** UDP is designed for connectionless, unacknowledged communications. By using IP as its underlying protocol carrier, UDP adds information about the source and destination socket identifiers. TFTP (Trivial File Transfer Protocol) is an example of a TCP/IP service that depends on UDP.

Because IP functions are at the network layer of the OSI Model, this protocol is routable. Both TCP and UDP must use IP at the network layer. TCP/IP is a connection-oriented IP transmission while UDP/IP would be a connectionless IP transmission. It is important to note that IP must have a transport layer service to either guarantee the data delivery or to not guarantee delivery.

AppleTalk

AppleTalk is a protocol suite developed by Apple Corp. in the 1980s for networks consisting of Macintosh computers. The original cabling system used in these networks is called LocalTalk. As AppleTalk became more popular, and speed became an issue, Apple Corp. designed a faster version, AppleTalk Phase 2. AppleTalk Phase 2 complies with the IEEE 802 standard and provides Ethernet support through EtherTalk.

The AppleTalk suite of protocols consists of the following protocols:

- Apple Talk Address Resolution protocol (AARP)
- Datagram Delivery Protocol (DDP)
- Routing Table Maintenance Protocol (RTMP)
- AppleTalk Echo Protocol (AEP)
- AppleTalk Transportation Protocol (ATP)
- Name-Binding Protocol (NBP)
- Zone Information Protocol (ZIP)
- AppleTalk Session Protocol (ASP)

- Printer Access Protocol (PAP)
- AppleTalk Data Stream Protocol (ADSP)
- AppleTalk Filing Protocol (AFP)

The protocols in the AppleTalk suite map to the Network through Application layers of the OSI model. At the Physical and Data Link layers are specifications that enable AppleTalk to run over a variety of different media using different media access methods:

OSI layer	Protocol/specification
Application	AFP
Presentation	AFP
Session	PAP, ASP, ZIP and ADSP
Transport	NBP, ATP, RTMP and AEP
Network	AARP and DDP
Data Link	EtherTalk, TokenTalk, FDDITalk, LocalTalk
Physical	EtherTalk, TokenTalk, FDDITalk, LocalTalk

AppleTalk uses RTMP for routing. RTMP is a distance vector routing protocol. AFP is the protocol that enables file sharing in AppleTalk networks.

AppleTalk network addresses are 24 bits in length, with 16 bits being used for the network portion of the address and 8 bits for the node's address. The node address is self-assigned. Given this setup, there can be 65,000 networks with up to 256 nodes each.

However, the limit of 256 nodes per network is eliminated in AppleTalk Phase 2, because in this version of the OS, multiple network numbers can be assigned to a single network segment. This is called an extended cable range. Further, AppleTalk networks can be divided into zones, which are logical divisions of the network that provide for easier administration.

When a computer in an AppleTalk network connects to the network, it broadcasts its self-assigned node address to see if it already exists in the network and also obtains the network address from the local router. If its self-assigned node address already exists, the computer generates a new address until a unique address is found.

It's possible to name nodes with a "friendly name" in an AppleTalk network via the NBP protocol. A node's name would consist of three parts: object name, object type, and the name of the zone to which the object belongs. For example, for a printer called Marketing3, whose object type is HPLaserjet and that's located in a zone called Headquarters, the name would be Marketing3:HPLaserjet@Headquarters.

Gateways

A *gateway* connects incompatible networks at the fourth through seventh layers of the OSI model by using protocol conversion and routing services. Gateways translate one protocol into another, so that the workstations can carry fewer protocol stacks. This simplifies routing requirements. Specialized systems are set up to act as gateways, specific to the type of network supported and the protocols needed. Gateways include both hardware and software.

Do it!

C-1: Discussing transport protocols

Questions and answers

1 NetBEUI is not suitable for

   A   Connection-oriented data

   B   Connectionless data transfer

   C   Large segmented networks

   D   Small workgroup networks

2 When does a network use connectionless protocol?

3 Why are connection-oriented protocols used when sending large data files?

4 What is the service provided by Novell's Sequenced Packet Exchange (SPX)?

   A   Connected

   B   Connection-oriented

   C   Connectionless

   D   Unconnected

5 When would you implement NWLink?

6 What is the default frame type for a NetWare 4.x network?

7 What does IPX stand for?

8 Gateways are used to connect _____ networks.

A   Incompatible

B   Similar

C   Ethernet

D   Wide Area

9 What is NetBEUI?

10 Which protocol suite is used to provide connectivity in a network of Macintosh computers

11 How is the node address for a client in an AppleTalk network assigned?

12 Which AppleTalk protocol provides the ability to name nodes with a friendly name?

A   RTMP

B   ATP

C   NBP

D   PAP

Topic D: Remote access protocols

This topic covers the following CompTIA Network+ exam objective:

#	Objective
2.16	Define the function of the following remote access protocols and services: • PPP (Point-to-Point Protocol) • SLIP (Serial Line Internet Protocol) • PPPoE (Point-to-Point Protocol over Ethernet) • PPTP (Point-to-Point Tunneling Protocol) • RDP (Remote Desktop Protocol)

Primary and other remote access protocols

Explanation

Two primary protocols exist for connecting remote devices over dial-up connections. They are Serial Line Internet Protocol (SLIP) and Point-to-Point Protocol (PPP). Other protocols include Point-to-Point Protocol over Ethernet (PPPoE) and Remote Desktop Protocol (RDP).

Serial Line Internet Protocol (SLIP)

The TCP/IP protocol can run over many differing types of media. Everything from Ethernet (IEEE 802.3) to Frame Relay has defined a methodology to encapsulate IP on the media. However, until the early 1980s there was no way to encapsulate IP over serial lines, such as the public telephone network.

The Serial Line Internet Protocol or SLIP was originally in the 3COM UNET TCP/IP implementation. *SLIP* defines a sequence of characters that frame IP packets over a serial line.

In 1984, the first widespread usage of SLIP was realized when it was incorporated in Berkeley UNIX version 4.2 and Sun Microsystems Workstations. Finally, in 1988 it was introduced by the IETF in RFC 1055 and has been a standard methodology to connect IP-based network devices over serial links. The protocol was devised to handle communications over fairly slow links (<19.2 Kbps).

Because SLIP was originally developed to frame IP packets over a serial interface, this is the only protocol it supports. Some other disadvantages of SLIP include:

- Inability to provide packet addressing
- Inability to provide any packet ID information
- Lack of error detection or error correction mechanisms
- Lack of compression mechanisms

Point-to-Point Protocol (PPP)

The current methodology for transporting multiprotocol datagrams over point-to-point links is the Point-to-Point Protocol (PPP). Definitions for the protocol can be found in IETF RFC 1661 (STD 51).

The protocol consists primarily of three main components:

- A methodology for encapsulating multiprotocol datagrams
- A Link Control Protocol (LCP) for establishing, configuring, and testing the data-link connection
- A family of Network Control Protocols (NCP) for establishing and configuring different Network layer protocols

As it was defined from its inception to be a multiprotocol transport over serial links, it can support more than just TCP/IP. It can also transport IPX, DECNet, CLNP, AppleTalk, and other protocol datagrams.

The advantages of PPP are as follows:

- Ability to employ data compression techniques
- Link quality monitoring
- Ability to support security features such as confirming the identity of users attempting to establish a connection
- Mechanisms for error detection and error correction
- Ability to provide a higher level of security through encryption

Microsoft Windows clients use PPP as the default transport protocol to connect to a Windows NT/2000/2003 network or the Internet if using a dial-up connection.

Tip: Use PPP instead of SLIP, if you're configuring a Windows-based workstation to connect to the Internet. An Internet dial-up based on SLIP might permit you to log on to your Internet Service Provider, but you might not be able to use FTP, Web browsers, SMTP/POP3 Mail Clients, and other services.

Point-to-Point Tunneling Protocol (PPTP)

The Point-to-Point Tunneling Protocol (PPTP) provides a means to secure client connections over the Internet. Through multiprotocol Virtual Private Networks (VPNs), secure communications are supported over standard Internet connections.

Many companies are looking at the Internet as a way to support some, if not all, of their communication needs between corporate locations. One of the major concerns, however, is security. A possible answer is PPTP, a way of creating multiprotocol Virtual Private Networks (VPNs) across the Internet.

In the past, a corporation would invest in communications lines, such as ISDN, to communicate between corporate sites. With PPTP, a remote client can access the corporate network across the Internet securely. You can even configure PPTP filtering on a network adapter so that only PPTP packets are permitted.

PPTP operates across PPP connections. PPTP data is encrypted and encapsulated inside PPP packets. The PPTP packets include TCP/IP, IPX, and NetBEUI packets. A session key used for the encryption is negotiated between the Remote Access Service (RAS) server and client when the initial PPP connection is made.

PPTP is supported on Windows 95/98 and Windows NT/2000/XP/2003 servers and clients. In addition, it is necessary to install the PPTP protocol on both the server and the client.

Point-to-Point Protocol over Ethernet (PPPoE)

The Point-to-Point Protocol over Ethernet (PPPoE) is derived from the PPP protocol and was designed to provide secure connectivity to the Internet for broadband connections that use an Ethernet rather than a serial connection, such as DSL and cable modem connections. PPPoE is defined in RFC 2516.

PPPoE is often used and required by ISPs that provide broadband Internet connections, particularly DLS connections. When connecting to the Internet using PPPoE, users have to provide a login name and password to connect to the ISP's PPPoE server. This enables the ISP to monitor overall traffic and traffic generated by each user.

Remote Desktop Protocol (RDP)

Remote Desktop Protocol (RDP) is part of Windows NT Terminal Server and Windows 2000/2003 Terminal Services. It's based on ITU standard T.120 (a standard for multichannel conferencing) and by default uses port 3389. RDP was designed to be able to remotely display and give input into applications running on a remote Windows computer. Supported clients include Windows 95/98/ME and Windows NT/2000/XP. RDP operates at the Application layer of the OSI model.

Do it!   **D-1:   Discussing remote access protocols**

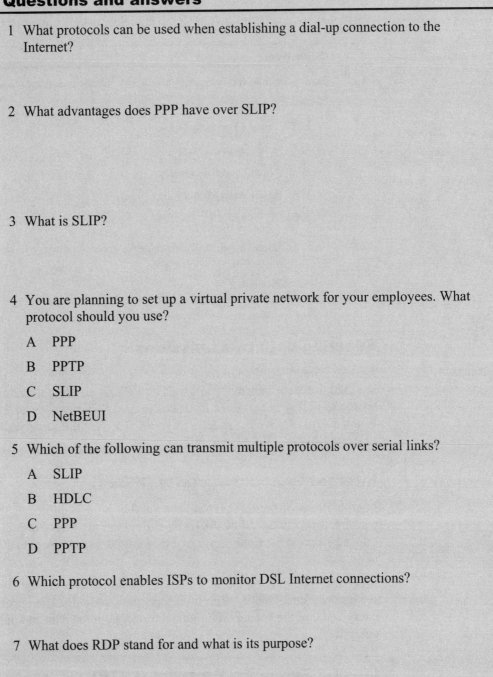

Questions and answers

1   What protocols can be used when establishing a dial-up connection to the Internet?

2   What advantages does PPP have over SLIP?

3   What is SLIP?

4   You are planning to set up a virtual private network for your employees. What protocol should you use?

   A   PPP

   B   PPTP

   C   SLIP

   D   NetBEUI

5   Which of the following can transmit multiple protocols over serial links?

   A   SLIP

   B   HDLC

   C   PPP

   D   PPTP

6   Which protocol enables ISPs to monitor DSL Internet connections?

7   What does RDP stand for and what is its purpose?

Topic E: Security protocols

This topic covers the following CompTIA Network+ exam objectives:

#	Objective
2.17	Identify the following security protocols and describe their purpose and function: • IPSec (Internet Protocol Security) • L2TP (Layer 2 Tunneling Protocol) • SSL (Secure Sockets Layer) • WEP (Wired Equivalent Privacy) • WPA (Wi-Fi Protected Access) • 802.1x
3.7	Given a connectivity scenario, determine the impact on network functionality of a particular security implementation (For example: • Authentication

Securing data transmissions

Explanation

Another category of important protocols includes a variety of security protocols. These are used to secure transmissions, such as VPN or wireless transmissions. Some of the protocols in this category are Internet Protocol Security (IPSec), Layer 2 Tunneling Protocol (L2TP), Secure Sockets Layer (SSL), Wired Equivalent Privacy (WEP), Wi-Fi Protected Access (WPA), and 802.1x.

Internet Protocol Security (IPSec)

Internet Protocol Security (IPSec) is actually a suite of protocols used to encrypt data packets. It was designed by the Internet Engineering Task Force (IETF) for secure data transmissions at the IP layer. One of its most popular implementations is in VPN networks.

IPSec uses one of two modes of encryption, transport or tunnel. Transport mode is less secure than tunnel mode. With transport mode, only the data portion of a packet is encrypted, not the header. With tunnel mode, both the data and the header are encrypted.

Layer 2 Tunneling Protocol (L2TP)

Layer 2 Tunneling Protocol (L2TP) is an extension to the PPP protocol. It is an enhanced tunneling protocol used in VPN implementations that supports multiple protocols and is also optimized to work with IPv6 and IPSec. L2TP operates at the Data Link layer of the OSI model and is defined in RFC 2661.

Secure Sockets Layer (SSL)

Secure Sockets Layer (SSL) was developed by Netscape to enable secure, reliable transmissions over the Internet. It is supported by Internet Explorer and Netscape Navigator, as well as other Web browsers, to securely obtain private information, such as credit card numbers, address information, and so on. If a URL requires an SSL connection, you'll see that the URL starts with https:// rather than http://.

With SSL, a private and public key system (RSA) is used to encrypt and decrypt data transmissions. Messages are encrypted using the receiver's public key (which the sender can look up) and then decrypted using the receiver's private key.

Wired Equivalent Privacy (WEP)

Wired Equivalent Privacy (WEP) is a security protocol designed to encrypt, and thus secure, data transmissions between clients and access points in wireless LANs (WLANs). It was intended to simulate the physical security of a wired LAN (where, for example, access to a building can be monitored and controlled); thus the term "wired equivalent privacy."

WEP uses a single, manually configured, static key for data encryption that is shared by the client and the WAP. WEP is defined as part of the 802.11b standard for wireless networks, and operates at the Physical and Data Link layers of the OSI model. Note that studies eventually showed that WEP is not as secure as originally believed.

Itroumy WPA
- can't use WEP

Wi-Fi Protected Access (WPA)

Given that WEP turned out to be less secure than originally believed, WPA was developed to improve on WEP's functionality. Improvements were made in two areas.

First, WPA provides for user authentication using the Extensible Authentication Protocol (EAP). Second, data encryption is more secure through the use of the Temporal Key Integrity Protocol (TKIP).

With TKIP, the keys are scrambled with a hashing algorithm, and an integrity checking mechanism is employed. WPA will in the future be replaced by the 802.11i standard, once this standard is completed.

802.1x

801.1x is a standard that uses EAP for user authentication in 802.11 wireless networks. With 802.1x, a supplicant (client) requests access to the wireless network from an authenticator (access point).

After receiving the request, the authenticator changes the supplicant's client software's state to unauthorized, which prohibits the supplicant from sending any messages other than EAP start messages.

Next, the authenticator requests user identification data from the supplicant. Once this information is received, the authenticator forwards it on to a central authentication server. This server then authenticates the identity of the supplicant via the use of an algorithm and returns an accept or reject message to the authenticator. The authenticator then either changes the supplicant's status to authorized (if an accept message was received) or does not authorize the supplicant (if a reject message was received).

Do it!

E-1: Discussing security protocols

Questions and answers

1 Which security protocol uses a single, static, manually configured key for data encryption?

   A   802.1x

   B   WEP

   C   SSL

   D   WPA

2 What is the term used for a wireless client in the 802.1x standard?

3 Secure data transmissions over the Internet are provided by which protocol?

   A   SSL

   B   L2TP

   C   IPSec

   D   WPA

Unit summary: Introducing protocols

Topic A   In this topic, you learned about **protocols**. You learned that protocols are the language by which computers interact with each other. You also learned about **access protocols**. You learned that the **Data Link layer** specifies how devices attached to the network gain access to the network resources. You also compared the **MAC** and **LLC Data Link** sublayers.

Topic B   In this topic, you learned about the characteristics of an **Ethernet network** and a **Token Ring network**. You also identified the differences between popular channel access methods, such as **token passing**, **CSMA/CD**, and **CSMA/CA**. You also learned about the characteristics of **wireless networks** and their channel access methods.

Topic C   In this topic, you learned about **connectionless** and **connection-oriented protocols**. You learned that a protocol, which supports both connectionless and connection-oriented protocols, would help you to have reliable communications with a minimum of overhead traffic. Then, you learned about **transport protocols**. You learned about the **NetBEUI**, **IPX/SPX** , **TCP/IP** and **AppleTalk** protocols. You also learned about **gateways**.

Topic D   In this topic, you learned about **serial protocols**, such as **Point-to-Point Protocol (PPP)**, and **Serial Line Internet Protocol (SLIP)**. You also learned about **Point-to-Point Protocol over Ethernet (PPPoE)**, **Point-to-Point Tunneling Protocol (PPTP)**, and **Remote Desktop Protocol (RDP)**.

Topic E   In this topic, you learned about **security protocols**, such as **Internet Protocol Security (IPSec)**, **Layer 2 Tunneling Protocol (L2TP)**, **Secure Sockets Layer (SSL)**, **Wired Equivalent Privacy (WEP)**, **Wi-Fi Protected Access (WPA)** and **802.1x**.

Review questions

1 When TCP is used in conjunction with IP, how is the data delivered?

   A Unacknowledged and connectionless

   B Unacknowledged and connection-oriented

   C Acknowledged and connectionless

   D Acknowledged and connection-oriented

2 What is Microsoft's implementation of Novell's IPX/SPX called?

3 What is beaconing?

4 Select the universal communications protocol suite used on the Internet.

A Ethernet

B FDDI

C Packet Switching

D TCP/IP

E OSI

5 Briefly discuss the differences between NetBEUI and IPX/SPX.

6 Which of the following is a transport layer protocol?

A IPX

B Ethernet

C IP

D SPX

7 Which protocol in the AppleTalk suite of protocols provides for routing capabilities?

A RTMP

B ZIP

C AFP

D AEP

8 What is PPTP?

9 What is PPP?

10 Which protocol provides for data encryption to protect network data?

   A PPP

   B SLIP

   C Both A and B

   D None of the above

11 Which protocol is used to be able to display applications running on a remote computer?

   A PPPoE

   B VPN

   C RDP

   D None of the above

12 What is a benefit for ISPs when using PPPoE for broadband Internet connections?

13 Which wireless network security protocol turned out to be not as secure as originally believed?

14 IPSec's transport mode is more secure than tunnel mode. True or false?

Unit 5

Network cabling and devices

Unit time: 120 minutes

Complete this unit, and you'll know how to:

A Discuss network communication methods.

B Identify the characteristics and appropriate implementation techniques of various types of cables and connectors.

C Discuss coaxial and fiber optic cables.

D Discuss Ethernet and Token Ring devices.

Topic A: Network communication methods

Explanation

When more than one computer is talking on the same cable, as is the case in a network environment, some rules of order must be established so that all transmissions can be successfully received. Some communication methods available to avoid problems that could occur in this environment include:

- Baseband
- Broadband
- Half-Duplex
- Full-Duplex

Baseband vs. broadband

Generally, network communications use baseband technology. This transmission method uses the media in such a way that the entire capacity of the cable is taken up by a single transmission. Baseband communication is much like two large ships using spotlights to transmit messages to each other at night. The computer uses the change in electrical flow to represent bits of data much the way the spotlights on the ships are switched on or off to represent a string of words.

On the other hand, in broadband communications the communicators use different frequencies to separate their messages from others by using the same media at the same time. This is similar to the way cable television works. When you turn on the TV, you only watch one program at a time. Even though all the channels are being broadcast on the same cable, your TV has a tuner that selects only the signal for the station you want to watch.

This same principle can be used in data communications. This means that several computers can transmit on the same cable simultaneously, provided the receivers are able to tune into only one signal at a time. It is important to note that each frequency in a broadband transmission can only be used for one-way communication. Another frequency must be used if a reply is needed.

The presence of a tuner and the ability to process multiple simultaneous transmissions can dramatically increase the speed at which data can be transmitted. However, the equipment needed to support this technology is costly.

Half-duplex vs. full-duplex mode

Half-duplex communications means that each participant only transmits when the other listens. Half-duplex is more than a polite conversation. In fact, there is no way for two computers to transmit at the same time.

By using full-duplex communications, both parties can transmit simultaneously. The computer can receive data while it is transmitting and vice versa.

The benefit of full-duplex mode is less delay in transmitting a message, because a computer can receive and transmit information simultaneously. The detriment is an increased cost of equipment to support the increased complexity.

Traditionally, LANs have been almost exclusively half-duplex. Recently, there has been an increase in full-duplex communications, especially for network servers.

Compatibility issues

When selecting between broadband and baseband or half-duplex and full-duplex, you need to remember that your decision is not just for an individual computer. Rather, it is a decision for all devices that will communicate on your network.

If you select a broadband full-duplex technology for one component, then all the others must be able to receive what that component transmits, as well as transmit in a fashion that the component can understand. Mixing and matching these technologies will result in a computer network that is non-functional.

Do it!

A-1:   Discussing communication methods

Questions and answers
1 Describe baseband and broadband communication technologies.
2 In _____ communications, only one participant transmits at a time.

Topic B: Cables and connectors

This topic covers the following CompTIA Network+ exam objectives:

#	Objective
1.4	Recognize the following media connectors and describe their uses:
	• RJ-11 (Registered Jack)
	• RJ-45 (Registered Jack)
	• IEEE1394 (FireWire)
1.5	Recognize the following media types and describe their uses:
	• Category 3, 5, 5e, and 6
	• UTP (Unshielded Twisted Pair)
	• STP (Shielded Twisted Pair)
3.3	Identify the appropriate tool for a given wiring task (For example: wire crimper, media tester / certifier, punch down tool or tone generator).

Cables and data transmission

Explanation

As computer networks have evolved over the last two decades, the need to connect machines miles apart has become just as important as connecting a machine to the printer down the hall. To accomplish this task, the computer industry has developed a wide array of cables, connectors, and media access protocols suited for either long distance or short run communications.

When discussing cables, it is sometimes difficult to separate the cable and its terminating connector from the media access method. Certain types of cables are suited for specific methods of data transmission.

Twisted Pair (TP) properties

Twisted-pair cable is used for both Ethernet and Token Ring networks. While there are different specifications for twisted pair, all of them include two or more pairs of wire, twisted together and housed in a single protective sheath. The installation environment and media access method will determine which type of twisted-pair cable is appropriate for each application.

Twisted pair is often used in Star topologies, although coax can also be used.

Twisted pair is made of insulated copper wires that have been twisted around each other to form wire pairs. Usually the wire is #22 to #26 gauge, and more than one pair can be carried in a single jacket or sheath. When working with twisted pair, note the difference between a wire and pair. A two-pair cable has four wires.

Because wire carrying electricity transmits and receives electromagnetic energy, nearby pairs of wires carrying signals can interfere with each other. This is called *crosstalk*. To reduce crosstalk and other EMI sources, the wires are twisted.

The number of twists and interim spacing are specified by industry standards organizations. Standard commercial-grade communications cable supports two twists per 11 inches.

Cables with a greater number of twists within the 11-inch measure can support data transmissions at higher speeds and greater distances. The exact distance specifications are dependent on the terminating equipment that is used.

Twisted-pair cabling is divided into two categories:

- Unshielded Twisted Pair (UTP)
- Shielded Twisted Pair (STP)

Unshielded Twisted Pair (UTP)

UTP, as shown in Exhibit 5-1, is a set of twisted pairs within a plastic sheath. The common use for this type of cable is telephone wiring and LAN communications.

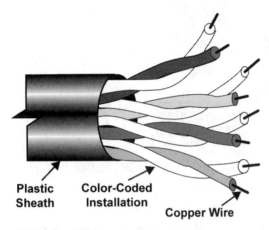

Exhibit 5-1: Unshielded Twisted Pair (UTP)

A number of wiring classification schemes are in use. The common are the levels from Underwriter's Laboratory (UL) and categories from the Electrical Industries Association.

The two older popular UTP cabling types are Category 3 and Category 5 UTP. Both cable types are designed to support #24 AWG (American Wire Gauge). Category 3 cable supports data transport rates from 10 Mbps to 100 Mbps depending on the installation. However, at 100 Mbps, imperfections in Category 3 cable can cause network problems due to EMI (Electromagnetic Interference). Category 5 cable is designed with more twists per foot and better insulation than Category 3, enabling it to more reliably support data transport rates up to 100 Mbps. Newer to the scene are Category 5e and Category 6 UTP. Both have been designed to more stringent specifications and can support transmission speeds of up to 1000 Mbps, so they can support Gigabit Ethernet. Any new installation of UTP cabling should be done with a minimum of Category 5e cable.

UTP installation

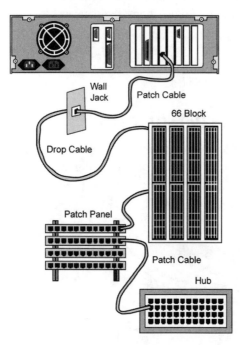

Exhibit 5-2: A typical Unshielded Twisted Pair installation

Some facts to remember about UTP include:

- **Cost.** Low cost compared to other media, typically running about 25-30 cents per foot.
- **Ease of installation.** Relatively easy to install, requiring only a few specialized tools (crimpers and a punch-down tool.)
- **Capacity.** Data transfer rates from 1 to 1000 Mbps with 10 and 100 Mbps being the most common.
- **Attenuation.** Rapid attenuation, distance limited to hundreds of meters.
- **EMI immunity.** Susceptible to EMI.

Shielded Twisted Pair (STP)

STP includes a protective sheathing around the copper wire. The twisted pair is wrapped in foil to cut down on outside interference and electromagnetic radiation. STP has many of the same characteristics of UTP. However, it is designed for #22 AWG wire, which has a thicker wire core and supports longer distances than the #24 AWG variety.

Some facts to remember about STP include:

- **Cost.** Moderate cost (approximately 20-40 cents per foot).
- **Ease of installation.** The shield in STP cable must be grounded, making installation more difficult than UTP. Special connectors and installation techniques are needed. The use of pre-configured cable and connectors makes this easier.

- **Capacity.** With the reduction of external interference, greater transmission speeds (up to 500 Mbps) can be implemented. Some 155-Mbps cabling exists, but the common transmission rate is 16 Mbps.
- **Attenuation.** Similar to UTP. Distance is limited to 100 m for 500 Mbps, longer for lower speeds.
- **EMI immunity.** The foil shielding reduces both interference and EMI emissions. STP will still suffer from outside interference, but not as much as UTP.

Twisted Pair for IEEE 802.5 (Token Ring)

IBM created and introduced Token Ring in the mid-1980s. The IEEE 802 committee later adopted it into an international standard as 802.5. Originally, it used STP and the IBM hermaphroditic connectors, but has since been adapted to use UTP and RJ-45 connectors.

Token Ring networks run at either 4 Mbps or 16 Mbps. This is a network-wide configuration. All equipment must communicate at the same rate. Mixing and matching different speeds will cause the network to fail.

Because IBM designed 802.5 Token Ring, their cabling specifications are the standard for this media access method.

Type 1

- Braided cable shield around two twisted pairs of #22 AWG (American Wire Gauge) conductors for data communication, as shown in Exhibit 5-3.
- Suitable for 16 or 4 Mbps.

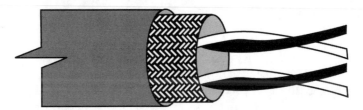

Exhibit 5-3: The type 1 model

Type 2

- Same as Type 1 cable with four twisted pairs of #22 AWG telephone conductors, as shown in Exhibit 5-4.
- Unshielded pairs are available for phone service, RS-232 data.

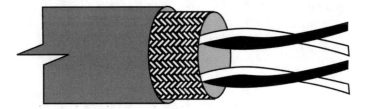

Exhibit 5-4: The type2 model

Type 3

- Four solid copper unshielded twisted pairs, #24 AWG. Simply high-quality phone wire.
- Recommended for 4 Mbps, not for all 16 Mbps rings.

Type 6

- Two shielded twisted pairs, #26 AWG, as shown in Exhibit 5-5.
- Recommended for both patch cables and adapter cables.

Exhibit 5-5: The type 6 model

Do it!

B-1: Discussing twisted pair cabling

Questions and answers

1 Shielded twisted-pair cable can run at speeds up to:

A 10 Mbps

B 100 Mbps

C 200 Mbps

D 500 Mbps

2 _____ is made of insulated copper wires that have been twisted around each other to form wire pairs.

3 What is the primary difference between UTP and STP? Which is preferred for 16-Mbps Token Ring networks?

4 Explain crosstalk.

Twisted-Pair connectors

Explanation

The RJ-45 adapter is an 8-pin modular plug and is used to terminate UTP and STP cable. This connector can be used for both Ethernet and Token Ring applications. In addition, you might see DB-9 connectors, IBM hermaphroditic data connectors, RJ-11 connectors, or RJ-14 connectors used with twisted-pair cabling.

RJ-45 connector and Ethernet

One of the major specifications in the Ethernet media access method is 10BaseT. This specification provides for a 10-Mbps-communication rate on a baseband signal by using twisted-pair cable. With 10BaseT, pins 1, 2, 3, and 6 on the RJ-45 connector are needed to transport data. The same pinout is applicable to 100BaseTX.

Pin #	Signal
1	Transmit+
2	Transmit-
3	Receive+
4	Not used
5	Not used
6	Receive-
7	Not used
8	Not used

RJ-45 connector and Token Ring

The IBM-specified twisted-pair cable for Token Ring has fewer pairs, so some of the pins in the connector will be unused. If you use standard Category 5/5e UTP or STP, the T568A wiring scheme works for both 10BaseT/100BaseT and Token Ring networks.

Many Token Ring cards have a modular connector available on the card. The active pin assignments are pins 3, 4, 5, and 6.

Pin #	Signal
1	Not used
2	Ground
3	Transmit+
4	Receive+
5	Receive-
6	Recovery
7	Ground
8	Not used but set aside for future offerings

Other uses of RJ-45 connectors

It will be difficult to determine which communications method a network is using if you were only shown an RJ-45 terminated twisted-pair cable. In fact, the RJ-45 connector is widely used for digital telephone sets, serial data transmissions, and many more applications.

Check to make sure you know what is being transmitted on a cable before plugging it in. Some specialized applications of RJ-45 connectors and UTP might damage hardware. Just because it fits does not mean it necessarily belongs there.

Other Twisted-Pair connectors

Token Ring is supported through a wide variety of connectors. The classic Token Ring cable has a DB-9 connector at one end and an IBM-style hermaphroditic data connector at the other.

DB9

Pin #	Signal
1	Receive+
2	Not used
3	Not used
4	Not used
5	Transmit-
6	Receive-
7	Not used
8	Not used
9	Transmit+

IBM Data Connector

Pin #	Signal
1	Transmit-
2	Transmit+
3	Receive-
4	Receive+

When this connector is not in use, pin 1 grounds to pin 3 and pin 2 to pin 4, creating a current loop. The connectors are termed hermaphroditic because they are genderless. Each connector is constructed the same way and will fit into another connector exactly like it.

RJ-11/RJ-14

Some manufacturers use the RJ-11 and RJ-14 modular connectors. RJ-11 is a 4-pin connector, as shown in Exhibit 5-6.

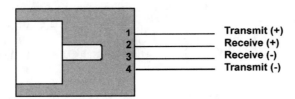

Exhibit 5-6: The RJ-11 connector

RJ-14 connectors have six pins, as shown in Exhibit 5-7.

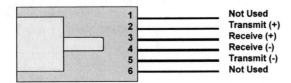

Exhibit 5-7: The RJ-14 connector

The RJ-11 and RJ-14 connectors are easily recognized as standard modular telephone connectors. The RJ-14 connector is commonly used as a two-line telephone connector, as shown in Exhibit 5-7.

Markings on the outer PVC covering are outlined in the following table.

Cable type	Description	Plenum	Riser	Commercial	Residential
OFC	Optical Fiber	FPLP	FPLR	FPL	none
CM	Communications	CMP	CMR	CM	CMX
MP	Multipurpose	MPP	MPR	MP	none
CATV	Cable TV	CATVP	CATVR	CATV	CATVX

T568A							
1	2	3	4	5	6	7	8
W/G	G	W/OR	Bl	W/Bl	OR	W/Br	BR

T568B							
1	2	3	4	5	6	7	8
W/OR	OR	W/G	Bl	W/Bl	G	W/Br	BR

Exhibit 5-8: T568A and T568B Pin-Out Configurations

Do it!

B-2: Terminating with an RJ-45 connector

Here's how	Here's why
1 Review the cable specifications	There are several different grades of cable. The markings on the outer PVC covering inform you of the exact cable grade. LAN cables that are used to connect workstations and hubs to wall jacks usually use the CM communications-grade UTP, which is found in most office buildings.
2 Using the crimper or wire cutters, carefully slice open the PVC sheath	The slit should be approximately 1.5 cm from the tip of the cable.
3 Spread the wires apart so that you can see the color assignments	This cable is engineered with the same color scheme for all eight wires: green, white/green, orange, white/orange, blue, white/blue, brown, white/brown.
4 Arrange the wires in the order shown in the table	

Pair	Color
1	Blue
2	Orange
3	Green
4	Brown

	The solid color is placed before the matching striped wire.
5 Choose one of the cabling schemes	There are several commonly used configuration schemes; however, it is essential that the scheme chosen be consistent throughout the entire implementation. Otherwise, you could run the risk of your data highway traffic lane abruptly terminating. The two most popular pin-out configurations are T568A and T568B (as shown in Exhibit 5-8).
6 Make sure that the edges of the cable are smooth, not frayed	
Strip/unsheathe the plastic casing without cutting internal wiring (1.2 cm-1.5 cm)	
Spread the cables	Pulling gently out of sheath. Then straighten the wires.
7 Organize the colors according to chosen standard scheme	Pull the wires out to verify color.
8 Position the wires as closely as possible and parallel	Clip to even out the wires.

9	Slide the wires into the module plug	Clip them on the bottom, wires 1-8, left to right.
	Verify that the copper wires are fully inserted into plug, their ends covering the metallic teeth, and their casing firmly under the crimp wedge	
10	Insert the modular plug into the crimp tool while maintaining pressure on the cable	
11	Press hard and remove the modular plug	
	Verify that the casing is firmly bit and against the wall of the chamber	All teeth should be chomped into the cable.
12	Gently tug on the cable to verify the crimp	
13	Use the tester to check continuity	

IEEE 1394 (FireWire)

Explanation

IEEE 1394 (FireWire) is an external serial bus standard with speeds of up to 400 Mbps that was developed by several companies, including Apple, Intel, Microsoft, Compaq and others. Apple Computer, Inc. trademarked the term FireWire for its 1394 products. Usually, the terms FireWire and IEEE 1394 are used interchangeably.

FireWire is most commonly used to connect peripherals to computers, such as external hard drives, video devices, printers, and so on. FireWire NICs also can be purchased, and it is possible to connect two computers together for basic file sharing using a FireWire cable.

Specifications

Each FireWire port (bus) can support up to 63 devices, either daisy chained together or connected to one or more hubs. The total number of buses that can be linked together is 1,024. FireWire data transfer speeds include 100 Mbps, 200 Mbps, and 400 Mbps; and the supported distance for FireWire devices is 15 feet.

This distance limitation can be overcome by adding repeaters every 15 feet for a maximum distance of 225 feet. Alternatively, using cabling other than the standard 28 AWG cable also lets you increase the distance.

Cables and connectors

FireWire uses the following connectors and cabling:

- 6 wire STP, which has two pairs of separately shielded twisted pairs and two power wires encased in an overall shielded cable. This uses a 6-pin connector on both ends.
- 4 wire STP, which has two pairs of separately shielded twisted pairs encased in an overall shielded cable, but no power wires. This uses a 4 pin connector on both ends.
- Another configuration uses either type of cable, with a 4-pin connector on one end and a 6-pin connector on the other.

Support for isochronous data transmissions

FireWire supports both asynchronous and isochronous data transfer. The data transfer rate in asynchronous transmissions is not steady. In isochronous data transmissions, on the other hand, data flows at a guaranteed, steady rate. This is particularly useful for audio and video devices and applications that transmit a fixed amount of data with each transmission, and transmissions are spaced in regular intervals.

Do it!   **B-3:   Discussing FireWire**

Questions and answers

1 Describe the main characteristics of isochronous data transmissions.

2 What is the maximum supported distance for FireWire devices using standard cabling without repeaters?

A   15 feet

B   10 feet

C   50 feet

D   25 feet

3 Describe the 6 wire STP cabling used with FireWire.

Topic C: Coaxial and fiber optic cables

This topic covers the following CompTIA Network+ exam objectives:

#	Objective
1.4	Recognize the following media connectors and describe their uses: • F-Type • ST (Straight Tip) • SC (Standard Connector) • LC (Local Connector) • MTRJ (Mechanical Transfer Registered Jack)
1.5	Recognize the following media types and describe their uses: • Coaxial cable • SMF (Single Mode Fiber) optic cable • MMF (Multimode Fiber) optic cable

Properties of coaxial cable

Explanation

In addition to twisted-pair cabling, you might also encounter different types of coaxial cabling on a LAN. You can also use fiber optic cable, which comprises light-conducting glass, encased in plastic fibers and surrounded by a protective cladding and a durable outer sheath.

Coaxial cable is composed of two conductors that share the same axis. The center cable is insulated by plastic foam, and then you will find a second conductor, foil wrap, and an external plastic tube.

For proper functioning, coaxial cable must always be terminated at both ends and the outer conductor grounded at only one end. Termination is achieved by connecting the inner conductor to the outer conductor by using a resistor of a specific size. Many terminators have a grounding wire, which can be connected to an earth ground, such as a water pipe.

The size of the terminating resistor is measured in ohms. By connecting the inner and outer conductors with a terminator, you complete the circuit for electrical signals to flow in the cable. When one or both ends of the cable are not terminated, there is no electrical circuit, and therefore, no data communication.

Common coaxial cable types, their properties, and purpose include the following:

Use	Cable type	Termination
10Base5 (Ethernet)	RG8 and RG11	50 ohm
10Base2 (Ethernet)	RG58	50 ohm
Cable TV	RG59	75 ohm
ARCnet	RG62	93 ohm

The type of cable you'll select to install is based largely on your data transmission method and the installation environment. In networking, coaxial cable is primarily used in Ethernet applications.

Transmissions over coaxial cable might be either baseband or broadband. With baseband, the cables carry a single high-speed signal. This is the transmission method used by Ethernet. Broadband coaxial cable carries multiple signals, each at a different frequency, as in CATV applications.

Some facts about coaxial cabling include:

- **Cost.** Moderate cost compared to other media, currently running 30-40 cents per foot.
- **Ease of installation.** Clumsy to install for individual workstations. Good choice for connecting buildings or making hub-to-hub connections.
- **Capacity.** Data transfer rates from 1 to 100 Mbps, with 10 Mbps a common rate for LAN environments.
- **Attenuation.** Moderate to low attenuation. With repeaters, distance can be extended to thousands of meters.
- **EMI immunity.** Some EMI sensitivity.

BNC cable connector

The standard BNC, or bayonet nut connector, is considered a 2-pin connector, as shown in Exhibit 5-9. Another connector type for coaxial cable is the F-type connector, often used with CATV, which works with RG 6, 7, 11 and 59 cable types.

Pin 1 is the inner wire and pin 2 is the tinned copper braid.

Pin	Signal
1	Data signal (center conductor)
2	Ground (metal sheath)

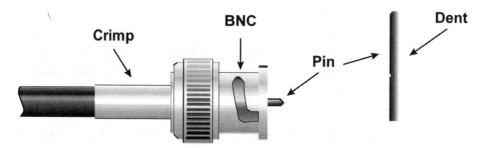

Exhibit 5-9: A BNC cable connector

Do it!

C-1:   Terminating with a BNC connector

Here's how

1 Slide the crimp onto the coaxial cable (as shown in Exhibit 5-9)

2 Strip off a section of outer sheath three-fourths the length of the crimp

3 Pull the braided outer conductor back over the stripped cable to expose the insulator surrounding the center conductor (Be sure not to cut off the braid!)

4 Observe the dent in the pin

   Remove a piece of insulator that is as long as the length of the pin from its bottom to the bottom of the dent

5 Insert the center conductor fully into the pin

6 Crimp the pin to the center conductor by using the crimp tool

7 Place the BNC over the pin and push down firmly until you feel it grab

8 Slide the crimp up over the braid and over the base of the BNC so that the braid is between the crimp and the BNC base

9 Use the crimp tool to secure the crimp to the cable

Fiber optic cable

Explanation

The bulk of the expense that characterizes fiber optic cabling systems can be attributed to the interface devices that convert computer signals to/from light pulses.

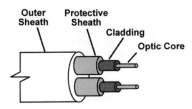

Exhibit 5-10: Fiber optic cable

Fiber optic properties

Fiber optic cable, as shown in Exhibit 5-10, can support data rates up to 4 Gbps over distances ranging from 2 to 25 km. Because it does not carry electricity, it is ideal for use in hazardous, high- voltage, or secure environments. Common fiber optic cables are classified based on the diameter of their core. Nearly all LAN fiber networks use 62.5-micron fiber cable. The outside diameter is 125 microns. This can also be expressed as 62.5/125 fiber.

Some facts about fiber optic cabling include:

- **Cost.** Moderate to expensive cost compared to other media.
- **Ease of installation.** Relatively tedious and expensive.
- **Attenuation.** Extremely low attenuation; transmission supported for distances up to 2 km.
- **EMI immunity.** EMI immune, high security.

In the IBM cabling system, fiber optic cable is referred to as Type 5.

Fiber optic cable types

Fiber optic cable can be either:

- Multimode Fiber (MMF)
- Single Mode Fiber (SMF)

MMF fiber typically has a 62.5 micron core (a 50 micron core also exists) and light travels down the core in many rays, which are also called modes (thus, the name multimode). MMF fiber works with LED light sources of different wavelengths, depending on the speed desired/required.

SMF has a very small core of about 9 microns in size, and light travels down the cable in one ray. This is optimal for very fast transmissions.

Fiber optic connectors

There are different types of fiber optic connectors. Six of the common connectors are:

- **FSD (Fixed Shroud Device).** An example will be the MIC (Media Independent Connector) dual-fiber connector.

- **ST.** This is a frequently used connector. It is a keyed BNC-style connector.

- **SC.** This is an international standard push-pull connector. The SC connector has the advantage over the ST connection because it has both transmit and receive fibers in a single duplexed clip.

- **LC**. Developed by Lucent Corporation, this is a smaller connector designed to save space on patch panels.

- **MTRJ**. Another connector designed with a small form factor to save space. Can be used with MMF or SMF fiber.

- **SMA.** A threaded connector, which is no longer used. The process of twisting the cable to connect or disconnect the fiber tends to scratch the end of the fiber strand.

It used to be a skilled art to attach a connector to fiber. This was a tedious process of cutting and polishing the end of the glass strand and then mounting it in the connector. Recently, new termination tools cut and polish in a single step, and while it still takes practice, the learning curve has been substantially shortened.

Do it!   **C-2:   Discussing fiber optic cables**

Questions and answers

1 _____ comprises light-conducting glass encased in plastic fibers surrounded by a protective cladding and a durable outer sheath.

2 _____ cables can support data rates up to 4 Gbps over distances ranging from 2 to 25 km.

  A   Coaxial

  B   Fiber optic

  C   Twisted-pair

  D   All the above

3 List six common fiber optic connectors.

4 What are the two types of fiber optic cable?

5 Why are fiber optic cables ideal for use in hazardous and high-voltage environments?

Topic D: Ethernet and Token Ring devices

This topic covers the following CompTIA Network+ exam objectives:

#	Objective
1.6	Identify the purposes, features and functions of the following network components:
	• Hubs
	• Transceivers (media converters)
2.3	Identify the OSI (Open Systems Interconnect) layers at which the following network components operate:
	• Hubs
4.3	Given a network scenario, interpret visual indicators (For example: link LEDs (Light Emitting Diode) and collision LEDs (Light Emitting Diode)) to determine the nature of a stated problem.

Ethernet devices

Explanation

To connect computers together in a network, in addition to cabling, connection devices are also necessary. These vary depending on the transport protocol used.

When wiring Ethernet in a star topology, it is necessary to use a device that will take the signal transmitted from one computer and propagate it to all the other computers on the network. This device is called an *Ethernet hub*. Hubs operate at the Physical layer of the OSI model.

There are several types of hubs on the market, of which the important ones are of four types. Each has feature of its own, but just about any combination of these feature sets can be found in a single hybrid device. When purchasing a hub, make sure to perform sufficient research to get a combination of necessary features.

Passive hubs

This is the most basic distribution device. Sometimes referred to as a concentrator, it might not even have a power source, although most do. A *passive hub* takes incoming electrical signals on one port and passes them down the cable on its other ports. In this way, all nodes see the signal just as if they were all connected on a physical bus topology.

Many passive hubs have indicator lights for power, network traffic, link state per port, and collision. Some also provide a BNC connector so that the hub can be connected to a 10Base2 backbone or an AUI port so that you can connect a transceiver of your choice.

Active hubs

Active hubs do more than simply rebroadcast incoming traffic. These hubs repair weak signals by actually retransmitting the data with proper transmission voltage and current. This essentially resets the cable length limitations for each port on the hub. For example, in a 10BaseT network the maximum transmission length is 100 m. Because the data is actually retransmitted on each port, a 100-m cable run can be attached to each port.

Other active hubs have the ability to resynchronize data that has been received from a NIC whose transmissions are not within standard timing specifications. This can help prevent data loss due to lost packets and improve the end-to-end reliability of network transmissions. Some active hubs will even alert you to this condition in a NIC so that the hardware can be replaced.

Switching hubs

A *switching hub* builds on the features of an active hub. Each port on a switching hub is isolated from the other ports. When a switching hub is first powered on, it listens to each port and makes a record of the NIC hardware address attached. A switching hub takes an incoming packet of data and actually looks inside at the destination hardware address. Then instead of rebroadcasting this packet on all the ports, the hub sends the packet out to only the port connected to the destination machine.

This is an effective method of avoiding collisions on the network. Each computer is free to transmit whenever it needs to. The switching hub will buffer the packets when more than one computer transmits simultaneously. It then propagates them as needed, giving each machine the impression that it is the only transmitter on the network.

Switching hubs can also make changes in transmission speeds. It is possible to connect both 10-Mbps and 100-Mbps NICs to the same hub. This auto-sense capability gives you flexibility to install faster 100-Mbps NICs in machines that need them and less expensive 10-Mbps NICs in those that do not. The switching hub uses its memory buffer space to hold incoming packets and then retransmits them at a slower or faster rate as needed.

Intelligent hubs

The term intelligent hub is more nebulous than the terms discussed up to this point. An intelligent hub might have management features that help it to report on traffic statistics, retransmission errors, or port connects/disconnects. It might support the TCP/IP Simple Network Management Protocol (SNMP).

You might be able to log into the hub itself and perform tasks, such as disabling/enabling ports, resetting ports, or monitoring traffic on an individual port in real-time. These hubs might have advanced features, such as built-in routing or bridging functions.

Because there is no standard definition, make sure you understand the features of a hub when it is termed intelligent.

Do it!

D-1: Discussing Ethernet devices

Questions and answers

1   Which of the following is a defining characteristic of an active hub?

   A   Retransmits lost packets

   B   Resets transmission to correct voltage and current

   C   Provides bridging functions

   D   Does not have a power source

2   You are installing a hub at a small remote office. There is no IT staff at this location. Which hub feature would you consider for this application?

3   You have a 10BaseT network node connected 97 m from a passive hub, which drops its network connection regularly. What might you do to improve performance?

4   You have a 10BaseT network node connected 90 m from the central patch panel. A patch cable of 15 m runs from the patch panel to a switching hub. The network node has frequent problems accessing the network. What is a possible cause of this problem?

Token Ring devices

Explanation   Token Ring networks have some specific devices that are analogous to Ethernet hubs—MSAUs.

Token Ring media

Token Ring can be installed by using:

- Unshielded twisted pair in star or modified star configuration at 4 Mbps
- Shielded twisted pair in star or modified star configuration at 4 or 16 Mbps

Some facts to remember about Token Ring installations include:

- Multistation Access Unit (MSAU) supports up to 8 nodes
- Maximum 12 MSAUs per ring
- Local Ring Hub permits four node connections on one MSAU port cable
- 64 - 72 (max.) nodes recommended per ring for optimal performance

Maximum distances on a Token Ring network are illustrated in the following table.

Item	Distance
Station to MSAU	45 m
MSAU to MSAU	120 m
MSAU to repeater	600 m
Maximum Network Length	750 m (Type 1 cabling)
MSAU to Fiber Optic Repeater	1.5 km (max. net. 4,000 m)

MSAUs

Even though most Token Ring networks look like a star, they work as a ring. The Multistation Access Unit (MSAU) makes this possible.

Note: Originally, a multistation access unit was abbreviated as MAU. But this became confusing as a media access unit (transceiver) was also called a MAU. It is generally accepted that a multistation access unit is now abbreviated MSAU to avoid this confusion. Be alert that you might find MAU still in use, and you'll have to make a determination of its meaning from the context of use.

When a device connects to a MSAU, a cable with two twisted pairs is used. One pair transmits from the device to the MSAU, the other from the MSAU to the device. As each device is connected and initialized, you can hear the click as the MSAU makes a physical relay connection.

In Exhibit 5-11, the MSAU is wired to provide a local loop through an internal backup path. When multiple MSAUs are used, the Ring Out of each is plugged into the Ring In of the next until the ring is completed.

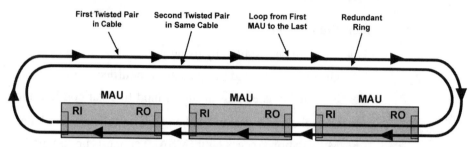

Exhibit 5-11: MSAU providing a local loop through an internal backup path

Two rings are actually completed. One is used for token passing between the devices. The second is a loop of all of the MSAU backup paths. This is known as a *redundant ring*.

The redundant ring is used when there is a break in the cable. The MSAUs on either side of the break will recognize it and set up a ring wrap connection. When the token gets to the last station in the ring, it is routed to the first station by way of the MSAU's backup path.

Miscellaneous devices

In addition to Ethernet- and Token Ring-specific hardware, there are certain devices that you might encounter regardless of the channel access method.

Network patch panels

To make a tidy termination of the entire network cabling for a star topology, the cabling is frequently terminated at a patch panel in the wiring closet. The patch panel provides a bank of network connectors representing each of the wall jacks on the premise.

Patch cables (short lengths of appropriate media) are then connected between the patch panel and a port on a hub or MSAU, thus activating the wall jack.

Remember to include the patch cable and cable from the wall jack to the computer in your calculations of network cable length. An 80-m UTP run from the patch panel to the wall jack can be extended beyond the maximum length if a 20-m patch cable is used at either end.

Transceivers

Transceivers provide a connection between one media type and another without changing the channel access method. Physically, a transceiver is usually a small box approximately $3 \times 2 \times 0.5$ in. It has an AUI port on one side and any one of a number of connectors on the other side.

A transceiver might be used to connect a 10Base5 backbone to a twisted pair hub. This is a change in media (coaxial cable to twisted pair) but not a change in access method (both are Ethernet). Transceivers are available with 10Base2, 10Base5, RJ-45, and fiber optic connections. When used in Token Ring applications, transceivers are commonly referred to as media filters.

Do it!   ## D-2:   Discussing Token Ring and other devices

Questions and answers

1 A transceiver is used to

   A   Connect segments with different network addresses

   B   Receive and transmit data on a patch panel

   C   Convert between different media types by using the same channel access method

   D   Connect a NIC to a managed hub

2 What is the maximum number of MSAUs on a single Token Ring?

3 What is a redundant ring?

Unit summary: Network cabling and devices

Topic A   In this topic, you learned that when more than one computer is talking on the same cable, there are some rules to be followed, and how they are carried out by **broadband**, **baseband**, **half-duplex**, and **full-duplex** communication methods.

Topic B   In this topic, you learned about **UTP properties**, **UTP installation**, and **STP**. Then, you learned about **RJ-45**, which is an 8-pin modular plug that is primarily used to terminate UTP and STP cables for both **Ethernet** and **Token Ring** applications. You also learned about **RJ-11**, and **RJ-14 twisted pair cable connectors**. Finally, you learned about **IEEE 1394**, commonly known as **FireWire**.

Topic C   In this topic, you learned about **coaxial cables**, which is composed of two conductors that share the same axis where the center cable is insulated by plastic foam, a second conductor, foil wrap, and an external plastic tube. Then, you learned about **BNC cable connectors**. You also learned about the **properties of fiber optic cables**, its **advantages**, **disadvantages**, and the **types** of **fiber optic cables and connectors**.

Topic D   In this topic, you learned about the various **Ethernet devices**, such as **passive hubs**, **active hubs**, **switching hubs**, and **intelligent hubs**, and the various **Token Ring devices**. You learned about the role of **Multistation Access Unit (MSAU)** that helps Token Ring networks to work as a ring. You also learned about the various miscellaneous devices, such as **network patch panels** and **transceivers**.

Review questions

1 Your 10BaseT network has been up and running over a year by using half-duplex network cards. You decide that you need more throughput from your server so you purchase a full-duplex network card. Will this work in this situation? Why or why not?

     A   Yes, because the server is the only machine that really needs the increased speed. Half-duplex cards are cheaper and sufficient for workstations.

     B   No, because all network cards in workstations are half-duplex, and will not be able to communicate with the server's full-duplex card.

     C   Yes, because the network card manufacturer has a device driver for your network operating system.

     D   No, because Token Ring does not support full-duplex.

2 When running Category 5 twisted-pair cable for a new network, which is the wiring scheme that offers maximum flexibility for RJ-45 connector termination?

     A   RJ-11

     B   T568A

     C   T586A

     D   T568B

     E   T586B

3 The network at your office is used to transmit highly confidential information between two buildings. Which of the following will provide the best security?

   A 100VG-AnyLAN

   B 100BaseTX

   C 100Base5

   D 100BaseFX

4 Why is an IBM connector referred to as hermaphroditic?

5 Which is the type of fiber optic connector that has both transmit and receive fibers in a single duplexed clip?

   A SMA

   B SC

   C ST

   D FSD

6 The RJ-45 connector is widely used for digital telephone sets and serial data transmissions. True or false?

7 What is the difference between a hub and an MSAU?

8 Working with one or more teammates, read this scenario and answer the questions that follow:

One of your clients has asked you to review her company's existing network infrastructure and determine pertinent information about network hardware components, cable types, and bus topology.

To answer the first two questions, look at the back of your computer and locate the network adapter card.

   a Which connector types can be attached to the adapter card?

   b Are there any status LEDs present?

Follow the cable from the network adapter card to the first network component.

   c What is the component?

   d What is the purpose of this component?

Continue to follow the network cable and identify components.

    e   Which cable type is in use?

    f   What are the pros and cons associated with this type of cable?

    g   What is the maximum cable length per segment?

    h   What is the maximum number of nodes per segment?

    i   What is the maximum distance between nodes?

    j   What is the minimum distance between nodes?

    k   What is the maximum length per drop cable?

Finally, answer the following questions on network topology:

    l   What network topology bus type is in use?

    m What are the pros and cons associated with this bus type?

Unit 6

Internetworking components

Unit time: 60 minutes

Complete this unit, and you'll know how to:

A Discuss basic internetworking concepts.

B Describe and contrast the functions of bridges, switches, routers and brouters, describe routing protocols, and discuss Windows 2000/Server 2003 server routing configuration.

Topic A: Introduction to internetworking

This topic covers the following CompTIA Network+ exam objective:

#	Objective
2.1	Identify a MAC (Media Access Control) address and its parts.

Internetworking devices

Explanation

Network performance is directly related to the number of computers on a cable segment and to the route data has to take to get to its destination. You use bridges, routers, and brouters to route data in a network. Before you learn more about the inner workings of bridges, routers, and brouters, you need to know about some background material to place these internetworking devices in their appropriate context.

Internetworking can be defined as the technology and devices by which computers can communicate across differing types of networks (see Exhibit 6-1).

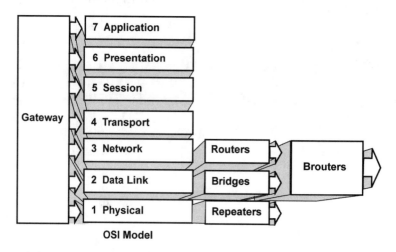

Exhibit 6-1: Internetworking devices

For example, let's say you have a computer on a Token Ring network in Washington that needs to access data on a file server resident in San Diego that participates on an Ethernet network. The two networks are tied together by WAN links maintained by a telecommunications provider. To achieve your goal, you must have a good understanding of how to internetwork the Token Ring LAN, the WAN links, and the Ethernet LAN.

Four types of devices are used to form an internetwork:

- Repeaters
- Bridges
- Routers
- Gateways

Repeaters, bridges, routers, and brouters, which combine the characteristics of bridges and routers, play an important role in network management. On a technical level, these devices are distinguished by the OSI level at which they function.

Device	Level	Layer
Repeater	1	Physical
Bridge	2	Data link
Router	3	Network
Brouter	2 & 3	Data link & Network

Segments and backbones

Large networks are frequently broken down into manageable pieces called segments. A *segment* is the portion of the network on either side of two network transmission devices, such as a router, bridge, or repeater. A network is segmented to extend the cable length, separate traffic to improve performance, or for security purposes.

Usually segments are connected directly to one another if they are in close proximity. In large buildings, or where the network spans more than one building, a backbone is constructed. The *backbone* is a high-speed network link connecting only segments (the nodes connect to the segment).

In this way, only data destined for another segment traverses the backbone. Preventing a data packet from traveling over the entire network is a key element to a well-run network. Directing data over the shortest possible route to the destination increases network availability on those segments it does not need to traverse. Exhibit 6-2 shows how segments are connected to a backbone.

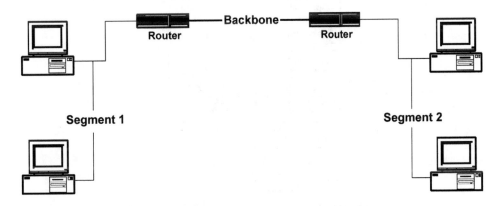

Exhibit 6-2: The segments connected to a backbone

The role of the MAC address in internetworking

The function of the MAC address in a network is to keep track of where the packet is going next on its way to a destination. Because networks have become interconnected, a mechanism to keep track of a packet's next hop towards its destination had to be designed.

The network layer of the OSI model is in charge of routing. The network layer places an address in the data packet, which is the network address of the destination machine. For example, if this were a TCP/IP data packet, the network layer will place the IP address of the final destination computer in the data packet.

However, this packet must traverse several intermediate nodes on its way to that destination. This is where the MAC address is critical. At every intermediate step, the computer must determine where to send the packet next, to the destination or to another intermediate. The network address is always a placeholder for the final destination, but the MAC address is used to specify where this packet goes next on its way to that destination. On the final hop, the network address and the MAC address indicate the same machine.

Repeaters

A *repeater* is one of the most basic internetworking components. It boosts the electronic signal from one network cable segment and passes it to another, helping you to physically extend network segments. A repeater connects network segments of similar media, as shown in Exhibit 6-3. It is not sensitive to higher-layer protocol attributes because it takes a signal from one side and amplifies it on the other side. In addition to amplifying the signal, a repeater also amplifies noise. As a result, there will be a limit to the number of repeaters that might be used in a given network segment. Intelligent repeaters regenerate the digital signal and are immune to the limitations of increasing attenuation over distance. Repeaters operate at the Physical layer of the OSI Model.

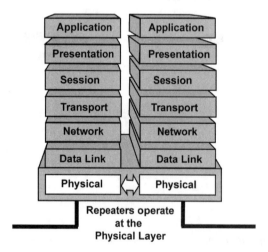

Exhibit 6-3: A repeater connecting network segments

Repeaters extend baseband networks that use one signal. Broadband networks support multiple signal transmissions simultaneously. An example of a broadband network is cable TV. Broadband networks use amplifiers to extend their signal transmissions.

Repeaters and their roles

All network media has a maximum transmission length. The earliest functional role of repeaters was to simply extend the physical length of a LAN. This is still one of the primary benefits of a repeater.

There are, however, several potential problem areas that are not addressed by repeaters. These include:

- **Signal quality.** Most repeaters do nothing to filter noise out of the line, so it is amplified and sent on with the signal.
- **Time delays**. Time delays can occur as signals are generated over greater distances. These delays might eventually generate time-out errors, keeping repeaters from being used for remote links.
- **Network traffic.** Because they do not have the capacity to filter traffic, repeaters do nothing to reduce the network traffic load.
- **Node limitations.** Repeaters are invisible to access protocols. All nodes added through a repeater count toward the total that can be supported in a subnet.

Repeaters are typically used on bus networks. To get the best signal quality, place a repeater so that the two segments connected are approximately the same length.

Do it!

A-1: Discussing internetworking basics

Questions and answers

1 Define "internetworking."

2 Name the devices used to form an internetwork.

3 What are segments?

4 A segment is a high-speed network link connecting backbones. True or false?

5 The MAC address fulfills what purpose in an interconnected network?

6 A _____ boosts the electronic signal from one network cable segment and passes it to another.

7 What is the primary benefit of a repeater?

Topic B: Introducing bridges, routers and switches

This topic covers the following CompTIA Network+ exam objectives:

#	Objective
1.6	Identify the purposes, features and functions of the following network components: <ul><li>Switches</li><li>Bridges</li><li>Routers</li></ul>
2.3	Identify the OSI (Open Systems Interconnect) layers at which the following network components operate: <ul><li>Switches</li><li>Bridges</li><li>Routers</li></ul>
3.8	Identify the main characteristics of VLANs (Virtual Local Area Networks).

The role of internetworking devices

Explanation

It's important that you understand the role of each internetworking device, including bridges, routers, and switches, to be able to select the correct device to meet network requirements. For example, bridges provide a way of segmenting network traffic and connecting different LAN types. Routers are used to build internetwork computing environments and are a key element in wide area networking. Careful planning and proper implementation of routers can help you build an efficient communications environment.

Bridges

Bridges, as shown in Exhibit 6-4, are more intelligent than repeaters. *Bridges* can read the specific physical address of devices on one network and filter information before passing it on to another network segment.

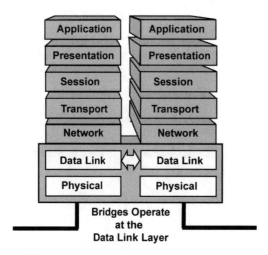

Exhibit 6-4: A bridge operating at the data link layer

Bridges operate at the data link layer, or more precisely, at the Media Access Control (MAC) sub layer. They go beyond amplifying the signal and are able to regenerate it. Rather than passing on line noise, a clean signal is sent out. Thus, bridges can expand a network beyond the normal network expansion of repeaters.

In general, bridges:

- Are transparent to higher-level protocols. Segments connected through a bridge remain part of the same logical network.

- Can filter traffic based on addresses. Thus, a bridge can reduce traffic between segments. This feature can also be used to improve security by selecting the packets that can be passed.

There are a number of other terms and concepts relating to bridges and how they operate.

Heterogeneous (translating) bridges

A bridge must read an actual MAC layer frame. Therefore, some bridges might be limited to linking similar MAC layer protocols. In special cases, where physical addressing is similar and the logical link services are identical, hybrid bridges can be developed to link between dissimilar MAC layer protocols. Because a number of the 802 series of protocols share the common 802.2 Logical Link Control (LLC) layer, it is possible for bridges to interconnect different types of networks such as Ethernet and Token Ring. One example of this is the IBM model 8209 Ethernet to Token Ring Bridge. Bridges of this type are also called *translating bridges*.

Encapsulating bridges

In *encapsulating* mode, a bridge packages frames of one format into the format of another. For example, Token Ring frames might be encapsulated in Ethernet frames and passed out onto the Ethernet network.

Presumably, there will be another Ethernet-Token Ring bridge that will de-encapsulate the packets and put them on a second Token Ring network where they will be read by a destination station. To stations on the intermediate Ethernet, these encapsulated frames will be unrecognizable because there is no lower-level address translation being performed by the bridge. Encapsulation is faster than translation.

In the example shown in Exhibit 6-5, packets from LAN A can be read by nodes on LAN C because they share a common addressing scheme. Nodes on LAN B cannot read the packets.

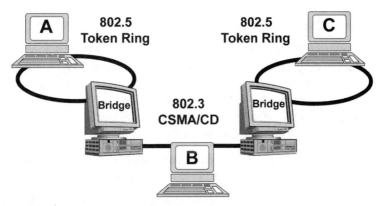

Exhibit 6-5: An example of encapsulation

Encapsulation is faster than translation. It helps the LAN to pass data quickly when the packets have to pass through multiple LANs.

Flow control in a bridge

In complex internetworks, any LAN segment might have multiple paths to reach a given destination. When such choices arise, two critical issues are confronted.

First, flow control information is necessary to know the relative capacities of each of the various bridge segments. Second, some form of routing control is necessary to make sure that segments with multiple links do not reproduce and distribute the same information. In this case, it is possible that two bridged segments will transmit the same frame, leading to a redundant message arriving at the destination node. This can cause serious operational confusion in any network system.

Flow control is especially important on large, active networks. Many studies suggest that 80% or more of the total traffic in a bridged network is local traffic. Less than 20% of the total traffic needs to be broadcast on the backbone.

Routing management for bridges

No aspect of bridging is more confusing than routing protocols that relate to bridges and not routers. The purpose of these routing protocols is to eliminate the possibility of duplicate frames that might be generated by having segments with multiple links that form loops in a bridged network. Packets can circulate within a segment of the network and ultimately clog the network by using these loops.

Spanning tree routing algorithm

Bridges that support the spanning tree algorithm are able to communicate with each other and negotiate which bridge(s) will remain in a blocking mode (not forward packets) to prevent the formation of loops in the network. The bridges in the blocking mode continue to monitor the network. When they notice that another bridge has failed, they come back online and maintain the network connections.

Source routing algorithm

Source routing is found in IBM's Token Ring networks. In this environment, a workstation determines the routes to other workstations with which it wants to communicate by transmitting an all-routes broadcast frame, which propagates throughout the network. The second station's reply to the broadcast includes the route that the original frame took, and from that point on, that route is specified by the initial station (the source) for the duration of communications between the stations.

As a result, bridges in a Token Ring environment rely on the source to supply the routing information to be able to forward frames to other networks.

Source routing transparent bridges have been proposed by IBM, which will forward other types of frames, as well as those with source routing information.

A learning (transparent) bridge

Modern bridges are usually known as learning bridges because they are capable of automatically identifying devices on the segments they connect. A *learning bridge* listens to each of the attached cable segments and creates a table of addresses originating on each segment. It does this by listening to the replies. Until it knows where a destination station is, it forwards all of the packets for that station.

In the example shown in Exhibit 6-6, A's initial message to B might go out on the backbone, but B's reply teaches the bridge not to forward packets which are sent from A to B, or B to A. In the same manner, a reply from C teaches the bridge C's location.

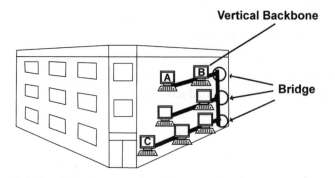

Exhibit 6-6: An example of learning bridge

When a learning bridge receives a frame from Station A, it records A's source address as a node on LAN 1. The bridge does this for all frames coming from LAN 1. For any frame that comes from LAN 1, if the destination address is one of the addresses recorded on LAN 1, the frame will simply be discarded instead of being broadcast on the backbone. Only unrecognized frames from LAN 1 will be forwarded to the backbone.

This filtering process means that all local traffic from LAN 1 remains on LAN 1 and does not hit the backbone. A learning bridge's filtering effect on local traffic can be significant.

Additional filtering and intelligence

Many vendors have realized that the processor resources necessary to read frame addresses can be put to extended use and thus have created bridge filtering. Bridge filtering consists of looking for other patterns within the frame to selectively control the frames, which will be forwarded.

This additional capability in a bridge has raised confusion over the technical definition of a bridge. The standards-oriented technicians are inclined to say that looking at information within the frame envelope for such patterns is a higher-level service, which, indeed, it is. However, these services can be layered effectively in bridge devices.

Note: Given the ability to identify patterns within the frames, bridge filtering might be deployed to selectively bridge only certain protocols.

Local and remote bridges

In addition to filtering and learning capabilities, bridges can also be categorized based on the linkage between the two network segments.

When a bridge has a LAN link directly attached on each side, it is known as a *local bridge*. Local bridges are characterized by comparable input and output channel capacities.

When a bridge must link a local network across a wide area segment, it is known as a *remote bridge*. The output channel from the remote bridge is usually of dramatically lower bandwidth capacity.

This difference in relative bandwidth capacity on the input and output channels makes remote bridges significantly more complex to design and manage. They must be able to buffer inbound traffic and manage time-out errors. It is also necessary to design your network to keep traffic requirements over the remote link to a minimum.

Layer 2 switches

The term Layer 2 switch (also known as a data switch or just switch) is generally a more modern term for multiport bridge. Like bridges, switches operate at the data link layer of the OSI model. However, although their basic functionality is the same, switches implement some more advanced filtering techniques to optimize performance. These filtering techniques are called *Virtual LAN* (*VLAN*) features and enable the implementation of a VLAN. In a VLAN, computers that are connected to separate segments appear and behave as if they're on the same segment. Although most VLAN filtering techniques have no universally accepted standard, they tend to fall into a few categories:

- **Port-based grouping.** Certain ports can be assigned to a specific VLAN. Packets will be kept local to the VLAN.

- **Address-based grouping.** Certain addresses can also be assigned to a specific VLAN. Packets will be forwarded only to the appropriate VLAN.

- **Protocol-based grouping.** The switch can examine the access protocol and forward the packet accordingly. This is Level 3 switching.

- **Subnet-based grouping.** If you are using TCP/IP, some switches might be able to identify the appropriate subnet and forward the packet accordingly. This is Level 3 switching.

Do it!   **B-1:   Identifying types of bridges and switches**

Questions and answers

1 A bridge operates at which layer of the OSI model?

2 What is a defining characteristic of a heterogeneous bridge?

3 You have two Ethernet networks connected by an intermediate Token Ring segment. The computers on the Ethernet segment need to communicate with each other. However, they do not need to communicate with computers on the Token Ring network. Which device is the best choice for connecting the three segments?

   A   Router

   B   Translating bridge

   C   Transparent bridge

   D   Encapsulating bridge

4 What is a translating bridge?

5 What is a learning bridge?

6 What is a switch?

7 What is one of the differences between a bridge and a switch?

Routers and routing

Explanation   As networks become more complex, simple bridging does not provide enough control of the flow of traffic. For example, broadcasts in a bridged network might propagate unnecessarily throughout the network. You can segment an extended internetwork into manageable, logical subnets by using routers.

Routers, as shown in Exhibit 6-7, are fundamentally different from bridges because they operate at the network layer. This means that a router opens the MAC (Media Access Control) layer envelope and looks at the contents of the packet delivered at the MAC layer. The contents of the MAC layer envelope are used to make routing decisions. This also means that protocols must have network layer addressing to be routable.

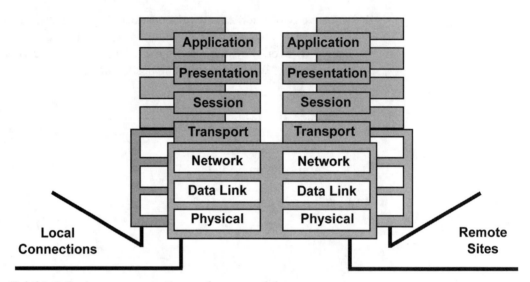

Exhibit 6-7: A router operating at the network layer

Routers might not match the throughput of bridges. A router activity needs more processor time, more memory, and multiple network connections. Current routers have enough speed to handle Ethernet and Token Ring traffic without dropping packets.

About routers

Early routers supported a single protocol, such as TCP/IP or XNS. Today, multiple-protocol routers might support 15 to 20 protocols simultaneously. The rise of networks running multiple protocols on the same wire is leading to the increased use of third-party multiple-protocol routers.

When a router receives a packet, it will generally forward it to the appropriate network based on a table maintained in the router. These tables might be either static or dynamic.

A *static table* is maintained by a system manager and is updated manually as the network is modified. A *dynamic table* is updated automatically as routers converse among themselves, by using a common routing protocol.

Bandwidth is cheaper on the LAN. Modern backbone networks are now migrating to 100-megabit speeds and above. The need for flow control, multiple-path management, and routing decision rules arises primarily in wide area links.

A wide area connection generally needs a routable protocol, such as TCP/IP or IPX. That is, the protocol must add information to the packet that differentiates between a destination on the local network and one on a different network. Microsoft's NetBEUI protocol is an example of a non-routable protocol. Each network segment is a separate logical network and might be administered independently. This also provides easier fault isolation.

The additional intelligence of routers provides for multiple (redundant) paths between locations, which provide both backup and the ability to do load balancing, and makes full use of available bandwidth. With bridges, multiple paths have to be avoided. Spanning tree, for example, shuts down redundant links until they are needed.

Offsetting the higher cost of managing and coordinating these more complex connections is the increased functionality that includes the ability to isolate individual workgroup networks as unique subnets. The router provides a port of entry that can control entrance and exit of traffic to and from the subnet. This segmentation is vital in organizations that rely on department-level network management. It also improves security and reduces congestion across the internetwork.

The programmable features of routers provide for effective management of remote links. Because these wide area connections are the most expensive components of the network, proper management and prioritization of traffic on these links is a vital concern for multi-site organizations.

Router features

The features of a router are:

- Processor/memory/storage
- Physical interfaces (ports) supported
- Protocols supported
- Configuration/management (open/proprietary)

Processor/memory/storage

Routers are actually specialized microcomputers with highly tailored I/O capabilities. Memory is especially important because it is used to buffer packets in times of congestion.

Routers are contained in a box about the size of a PC. In some cases they might be an actual PC, such as a NetWare or Windows 2000/2003 server configured as a router. There is also a trend toward router cards used in hubs or wiring concentrators.

Physical interfaces (ports) supported

These might vary considerably from vendor to vendor. In some cases, the router might be a simple box with multiple ports from which two or three specific ports might be selected. Other boxes might be expanded through the addition of cards supporting specific interfaces.

On the LAN side, there might be the common Ethernet, Token Ring, or ARCnet interfaces. Connections to the wide area (telecommunications) network might include RS-232, V.35, and RS-442 interfaces. Other possible interfaces include FDDI and broadband.

Because hardware is similar for bridges, routers, and brouters, upgrades might need new software.

Protocols supported

Multiprotocol routers support most of the common network protocols including, but not limited to, TCP/IP, Xerox XNS, other XNS-based protocols such as Ungermann-Bass, Banyan VINES, Novell's IPX, the ISO CLNS, DECnet, HP Advancenet, SDLC, and AppleTalk.

In the wide area, protocols to consider include X.25, Frame Relay, and Switched Multimegabit Data Services (SMDS), in addition to dedicated lines ranging up to 56 Kb or T3 speeds.

Protocols used between routers to communicate routing table information include Routing Information Protocol (RIP), Open Shortest Path First (OSPF), the End System-Intermediate System protocol (OSI ES-IS), and the Intermediate System-Intermediate System protocol (OSI IS-IS), as well as proprietary vendor protocols.

LAN protocols	Router protocols	WAN protocols
TCP/IP	RIP	ATM
XNS	OSPF	X-25
IPX	OSI-ES-IS	Frame relay
Apple Talk	OSI-IS-IS	SMDS

Configuration/management (open/proprietary)

Most routers will have a simple (RS-232) serial port to provide terminal access to the router, either directly or by modem. This provides a simple, generally character-oriented interface for configuring and managing the router. There might also be the possibility of connecting across the network to manage the router remotely.

Security with respect to managing the router might consist of simple password protection, but it might be possible to restrict access to specific network addresses or only the serial port. Many routers help in the use of filters or access lists to limit access to or from a specific router. This feature makes it possible to isolate specific subnets or to restrict access to the wider network to specific users or stations.

Simple Network Management Protocol (SNMP) is a TCP/IP-based management protocol that might be implemented on routers. With SNMP, it might be possible to show or set various characteristics of a router to an SNMP-based management station. The difficulty with SNMP is that it does not provide for security, so the ability to set the parameters of routers by using SNMP is avoided.

OSI standards for network management are expected to provide more in the way of security. *Common Management Information Protocol (CMIP)* is the OSI-based protocol expected to provide standard management of network devices in general. CMOT (CMIP over TCP/IP) is an implementation of CMIP by using TCP/IP as a transport for use in managing TCP/IP networks specifically. Until CMIP is widely available, proprietary offerings might be the best alternatives where security is an issue.

Types of routers

Some key points to remember about routers include:

- A router connects two or more subnetworks.
- A router might be configured to support a single protocol or multiple protocols.
- A router will only process packets specifically addressing it as a destination.
- Packets destined for a locally connected subnetwork are passed to that network.
- Packets destined for a remote subnetwork are passed to the next router in the path.
- A router that exists in the same subnet as a host can be configured as a default gateway.

Note: The term "gateway" is also used to refer to a network device used to connect dissimilar systems or protocols.

Routers are intelligent devices. Many can dynamically determine the best route to a destination subnetwork. They can also inform the originating host if any problems occur during transmission.

Static routers

While still used in some situations, most static routers have been replaced by dynamic routers. Static routers are more difficult to manage and less efficient than their dynamic counterparts, for several reasons:

- **Manual configuration.** Each entry in the routing table must be made manually. In a large network, this can be a time-consuming process.
- **Manual updates.** If there are changes to the network, such as subnets added or removed or other router configurations changed, these must be entered into the routing table manually. The more dynamic the network, the more time that must be spent configuring routers.
- **Changing environments.** A static router cannot compensate for a failed route or high levels of traffic on a primary route. This means that data might be lost, or might be delayed over an inefficient route.

Static routers might provide an inexpensive solution on small networks, but it can become difficult to manage them efficiently on a larger network. Use of default routers is also critical to avoid losing packets whose destination has not been configured on the router.

Dynamic routers

Dynamic routers use an Interior Gateway Protocol (IGP) to communicate with each other. The two most common Interior Gateway protocols are:

- **Routing Information Protocol (RIP).** Routers use RIP to keep each other informed about routing destinations. It is based on a Distance Vector algorithm that normally uses the fewest hops (router transversals) to determine the best path.
- **Open Shortest Path First (OSPF).** OSPF uses a Link State algorithm that provides for configuration of hierarchical topologies and helps quick response to changing network conditions.

In a network connected to the Internet, it would clearly be impossible for any routing table to contain a list of all the available networks. Only information about networks on the network's own side of the Internet gateway is exchanged by using the IGP.

Default gateway

Gateway-to-Gateway Protocol is used to update the massive routing tables maintained on routers within the Internet. To access the Internet, routers are configured with a default gateway (or smart gateway). Any requests for networks to which a route is not known are forwarded to the default gateway.

Routing tables

Both static and dynamic routers use routing tables to pass packets on to remote subnetworks. The only difference is whether the table is created manually or automatically. In either case, the routing table will contain the same information such as:

- The destination network IP address
- The destination network subnet mask
- The router interface used to get to the network
- The IP address of the next router in the path to the destination
- The number of hops to the destination

The number of hops refers to the number of intermediate networks (other routers) that must be crossed to reach the destination. Each packet will have a Time to Live (TTL) value that is decremented with each hop. When TTL reaches zero, the packet is dropped.

An IP address of 0.0.0.0 refers to a default router. A default router intercepts all packets destined for networks not specifically designated in the routing table (as shown in Exhibit 6-8).

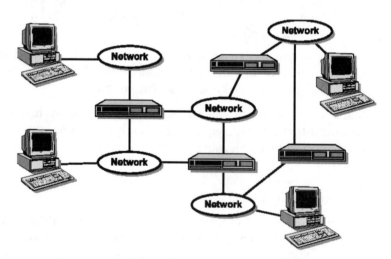

Exhibit 6-8: A sample routing table

Routing examples

Some specific situations are handled as follows:

- **Local destination.** The packet will be addressed for the destination host. Any other systems, including routers, will ignore the packet.

- **Remote destination, next hop known.** The source host will place the IP address for the next router as the immediate destination. That router will then pass the packet on to the following hop, if known. If not known, the router will pass the packet to its default gateway.

- **Remote destination, next hop unknown.** The source host will place the IP address for the default gateway as the immediate destination. That router will then pass the packet on to the following hop, if known. If not known, the router will pass the packet to its default gateway.

If a packet reaches a point where no routing is available to the next hop, the packet is destroyed and an ICMP message returned. ICMP (Internet Control Message Protocol) provides error reporting during datagram processing. This is a means by which dynamic routers can update their routing tables. If the TTL value reaches zero, indicating that the packet is likely lost and being bounced between default gateways, the packet is destroyed and an ICMP message generated.

Brouters

Brouters operate at both the network layer for routable protocols and at the data link layer for non-routable protocols.

As networks continue to become more complex, a mix of routable and non-routable protocols has led to the need for the combined features of bridges and routers. Brouters handle both routable and non-routable features by acting as routers for routable protocols and bridges for non-routable protocols. Bridged protocols might propagate throughout the network, but techniques such as filtering and learning might be used to reduce potential congestion.

Bridges vs. routers

Routers should be given preference over bridges when designing and configuring WANs. Bridges, by design, can escalate a transient reliability problem into a serious network failure.

Frequently, a host will use broadcast transmissions if there is an unexplained loss of contact with another host. Routers do not propagate these broadcasts.

Remote bridges, on the other hand, pass on all broadcasts. Every host receiving the broadcast must process it, if only to reject it. As broadcasts go above a certain level, the performance loss due to broadcast can lead to further broadcasts. This can lead to a broadcast storm, which can result in a complete breakdown of network communications.

Do it!

B-2:   Discussing routers and brouters

Questions and answers

1 Static routers are more efficient than their dynamic counterparts. True or false?

2 What is the basic difference between static and dynamic routers?

3 Name a non-routable protocol.

4 List three features of routers.

5 Define the purpose of a router.

6 Name the protocol used to update the massive routing tables maintained on routers within the Internet.

7 Only dynamic routers use routing tables to pass packets on to remote subnetworks. True or false?

8 A device that can handle both routable and non-routable protocols is called a _____ .

A   Bridge

B   Repeater

C   Brouter

D   Router

9 A router operates at which layer of the OSI Model?

   A   LLC

   B   Data link

   C   Network

   D   Physical

   E   B, C, and D

10 What is Common Management Information Protocol (CMIP)?

Understanding the routing protocols

Explanation

There are two basic types of routing algorithms: distance vector and link state.

In *distance vector* algorithms, each node (or router in this discussion) maintains the distance from itself to each possible destination. The distance is computed by using information obtained from neighboring nodes. RIP is a distance vector routing protocol.

For example, imagine that you are a student cartographer. As a test, you and your fellow classmates have been given the task of mapping a town. To complicate the matter, you are all blindfolded and each student is dropped off at a major intersection in the town. After your placement, you can remove the blindfold and begin the mapping. However, you can only physically proceed to the next set of intersections.

You begin by marking the distance to the intersection you are at as zero miles. Next you measure the distance to the adjacent intersections. Meanwhile, your fellow students do the same. After completing the map, any student can determine the route to any intersection by summing the distance information they have.

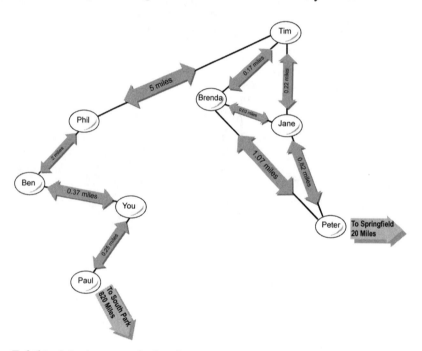

Exhibit 6-9: An example for distance vector algorithms

Consider another example. You need to figure out how to get to Jane's house, using Exhibit 6-9. You know the distance to your neighbors, Ben and Paul, as 0.37 miles and 0.25 miles. Therefore, you ask them how to get to Jane's. Paul replies that his shortest path is 1,500 miles and Ben says his is 7.20 miles. Therefore, the total distance to Jane is 7.57 miles. How did Ben and Paul know the distance?

They followed the same process you did—they asked their neighbor. Examine this through Ben's intersection. As Ben's only neighbor (besides you) is Phil, he asks Phil (which tacks on 2 miles to your computation). Phil's only other neighbor is Tim. So Phil asks Tim (this adds another 5 miles to your computation). Tim is directly connected to Jane at 0.22 miles. Tim also asks Brenda who is 0.17 miles away. Brenda says Jane is only 0.03 miles from her. Tim realizes that the route through Brenda's intersection is 0.20 miles while the direct route is 0.22 miles. So Tim tells Phil that the best route from him to Jane is 0.20 miles going through Brenda's intersection. Thus, Phil knows it's 5.20 miles from him to Jane. Ben, therefore, knows it's 7.2 miles from him to Jane, and this is what he tells you. Exhibit 6-9 shows the distance vector algorithms for this example.

Link state routing algorithms, used for example by the OSPF routing protocol, work differently. The following four steps illustrate the basic concepts driving this algorithm:

- Each router is responsible for meeting its neighbors and learning their names.
- Each router constructs a packet known as a link state packet (LSP), which contains a list of names and the distance to each of its neighbors.
- The LSP is transmitted to every other router. Every router stores the most recent LSP from every other router.
- Each router, now armed with a complete map of the topology, computes the route to every destination.

RIP

When a router comes online, Routing Information Protocol (RIP) broadcasts a request for routing table information from all other routers it can see. The information passed through RIP includes a destination, routing metric, and hop count for each known route. The information received is used by the router to determine the shortest path to each destination. The route information is then entered into the local routing table. After the table is built, the router sends a RIP broadcast every 30 seconds. This broadcast contains its known destinations and the cost (in hops) to get to each.

While effective, RIP is not without its drawbacks:

- **Maximum fifteen hops.** This path limit is too restrictive to support some larger internetworks.
- **Routing loops.** Because of time delays in the transmission of updated routing table information, routing loops might occur in large internetworks.
- **Network conditions.** Fixed metrics are used to determine routing paths. Because of this, there is no permission for dynamic conditions such as changes in traffic load or transmission delays.

RIP assumes that all devices keep their own routing tables.

OSPF

Rather than a separate protocol, Open Shortest Path First (OSPF) packets are carried within IP datagrams. Its Link State algorithm provides several enhancements over RIP, including:

- Hierarchical topology configuration
- Support for large internetworks
- Adaptation to changing conditions
- Traffic-balancing over multiple paths
- Authentication of router table information exchange

ICMP

Internet Control Message Protocol (ICMP) is a module of IP that provides error reporting during datagram processing. A common use is passing error information between host and router. This error data provides dynamic routing table updates.

- A packet cannot reach its destination.
- A packet's Time to Live (TTL) expires.
- An error is detected in IP header parameter data.
- A router cannot buffer an incoming packet.
- A router cannot keep up with an incoming stream of packets.
- A router sends a message to a host advising of a shorter route to a destination.
- A host sends an echo packet to determine if another host is alive.
- A host needs to determine to which network it is attached.

ICMP helps keep the network running smoothly when hardware problems occur, such as a router going offline.

Routing support in Windows

Windows 2000 Server and Windows Server 2003 support both RIP and OSPF. To configure a Windows Server 20003 server as a router, you have to configure routing in the Routing and Remote Access Service (RRAS). RRAS is installed by default, but not enabled or configured.

To access RRAS on a Windows 2000/Server 2003 server, choose Start, (Programs), Administrative Tools, Routing and Remote Access. Then, to configure the server as a router, select the server in the left pane and choose Action, Configure and Enable Routing and Remote Access. Then, follow the Routing and Remote Access Server Setup Wizard, specifying a custom configuration in which you want to configure LAN routing. After the Wizard has finished, you can see that the server has been configured as a router by viewing the General tab in the server's properties (right-click the server and choose Properties) as shown in Exhibit 6-10. You can use the remaining tabs to further configure the Windows router.

Also, when you're done with the Wizard, you have to configure routing protocols for each network interface. To do so, expand the server in the console tree, then expand IP Routing. Right-click General, choose New Routing Protocol and select the appropriate protocol. Then, right-click the protocol in the console tree, and select New Interface. Next, select the appropriate interface, click OK and then configure the Properties of the protocol.

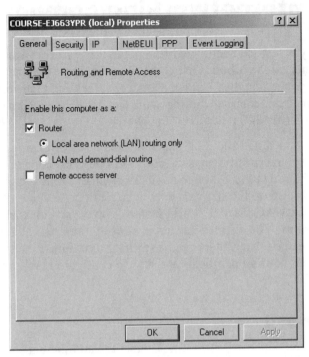

Exhibit 6-10: The General tab of a Windows 2000/Server 2003 server that has been configured as a router in RRAS

Do it!

B-3: Understanding routing protocols

Questions and answers

1 What are the two types of routing algorithms?

2 Which routing protocols does Windows 2000/Server 2003 support?

3 What is the maximum number of hops allowed by RIP?

4 Which protocol is used for error reporting during datagram processing?

Unit summary: Internetworking components

Topic A   In this topic, you learned about the different types of **internetworking devices** and about **segments** and **backbones**. Next, you learned about the role of the **MAC address** in internetworking. You then learned about **repeaters** and their role in internetworking. You also learned that internetworking is the technology by which computers communicate across different types of networks.

Topic B   In this topic, you learned about the functions and types of **bridges**. You also learned that bridges read the specific physical address of devices on one network and **filter information** before passing it on to another network segment. You also learned about **routers**, and **brouters**. Further, you compared a bridge with a router and learned that a router opens the **MAC** (Media Access Control) **layer envelope** and then uses it to make **routing decisions**. You also learned about **routing tables** and the different the types of routers. You learned that routers can be **static** or **dynamic**. Finally, you learned how to describe various **routing protocols** and how to configure LAN routing on a Windows 2000/Server 2003 server.

Review questions

1 You need to connect a Token Ring segment to an Ethernet segment. Would you use a router, a brouter, or a bridge? Explain your answer.

2 Is the network layer address important to a transparent learning bridge? Why or why not?

3 What is source routing used for in an Ethernet network?

4 Your network uses both IPX and NetBEUI. Which device would provide the best connectivity if you have many (more than 10) segments?

5 How does a link state routing protocol help routers?

6 Is the MAC layer address important to a router? Why or why not?

7 What is a default gateway?

8 Which of the following are router protocols?

   A RIP

   B IANA

   C Ethernet

   D IPX/SPX

   E OSPF

9 Your IP address is 128.0.1.2. You want to contact a host at 130.120.10.2. Two
   routers reside between you and the destination. Their IP addresses are 128.0.1.1 and
   130.120.1.1. With the help of the Exhibit 6-11, determine which router will act as
   your default gateway. Explain how you came up with your answer.

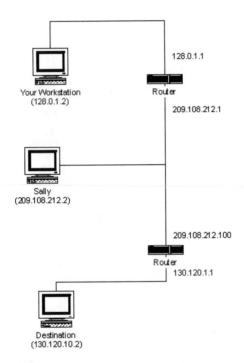

Exhibit 6-11: A representation of the network setup

10 Only dynamic routers use routing tables to pass packets on to remote subnetworks.
    True or false?

11 What does the TTL value zero indicate?

Unit 7

Remote and WAN connectivity

Unit time: 120 minutes

Complete this unit, and you'll know how to:

A Describe the properties, benefits, and potential issues involved with POTS and ISDN circuits, and describe other remote access options such as cable, xDSL, satellite, and wireless access.

B Configure Windows Server 2003/XP with a modem and establish a dial-up network connection by using Windows Server 2003/XP.

C Discuss Remote Access Services (RAS).

D Describe WAN connectivity options.

Topic A: Introduction to remote connectivity

This topic covers the following CompTIA Network+ exam objectives:

#	Objective
1.6	Identify the purposes, features and functions of the following network components: • ISDN (Integrated Services Digital Network) adapters
2.14	Identify the basic characteristics (For example: speed, capacity and media) of the following WAN (Wide Area Networks) technologies: • ISDN (Integrated Services Digital Network)
2.15	Identify the basic characteristics of the following internet access technologies: • xDSL (Digital Subscriber Line) • Broadband Cable (Cable modem) • POTS / PSTN (Plain Old Telephone Service / Public Switched Telephone Network) • Satellite • Wireless
4.4	Given a troubleshooting scenario involving a client accessing remote network services, identify the cause of the problem (For example: file services, print services, authentication failure, protocol configuration, physical connectivity and SOHO (Small Office / Home Office) router).

Remote and Internet connectivity

Explanation

Most network clients are connected directly to the network. In some cases, however, you'll need to provide remote connectivity for your users. Remote connectivity can be made possible by using POTS and ISDN circuits.

A local connection to the network can be made from a remote site. However, any type of data transfer runs significantly slower in this case. Therefore, it is important to select connection options appropriate to your access needs, available support, and budgetary constraints. Several options are available to establish remote connectivity whether it is connecting remote workstations to your network or the Internet. They are:

- **Modem via POTS.** A modem provides a connection over a standard phone line. Although transfer rates are limited, this provides connections for nearly any type of client and from nearly any location.

- **ISDN.** Integrated Services Digital Network provides a connection of moderate speed (typically 64 Kbps to 128 Kbps) between stationary remote sites. ISDN needs special digital telephone lines and connection equipment.

- **Cable modem.** Provides high-speed access through a cable company's TV cable. Typically, cable modem service provides 1 to 10 Mbps download speed and up to 2 Mbps upload speed.

- **xDSL.** Digitial Subscriber Line groups several technologies under the term xDSL, such as ADSL, HDSL and others. Used to provide high speed access through regular copper telephone lines or over fiber optic cable, xDSL can provide speeds of up to 8 Mbps downstream and 1 Mbps upstream.

- **Satellite**. Satellite services provide fairly high speed access to the Internet using satellites and local equipment for users who aren't close enough to a telephone company for DSL service and who don't have access to Cable TV.
- **Wireless**. Wireless services provide high speed access to the Internet at what are called "hot spots" located at airports, hotels, coffee shops, and so on. They're available throughout the US and are aimed at users that travel a lot and need Internet access without the hassle of having to connect via a cable connection.

POTS

POTS stands for Plain Old Telephone Service and is the standard telephone service you subscribe to for making voice calls. POTS runs on the copper telephone wire network whose installation began in the late 1800s. The design of this network was based around people talking to each other. It was not designed for data communications but has been adapted to this purpose over the last 20 to 25 years.

A POTS circuit is frequently referred to as a local loop. The circuit is made with two wires from the premise equipment (telephone) to the switch (phone company). One wire is called the TIP and the other is called the RING. These are named for the two connectors on a cord from a manual switchboard.

When you pick up your telephone, a connection is made between the TIP and the RING; this is interpreted by the phone company as a request for service. The dial tone is presented to the caller telling them that the phone is ready for use.

A POTS line is completely analog. It will not accept digital data directly. Instead, a modem (derived from MOdulator-DEModulator) must convert, or modulate, the digital data in a computer to an analog signal that the Public Switched Telephone Network (PTSN) can accept. Another modem is used to convert, or demodulate, the analog signal back to digital at the destination computer.

POTS circuits are frequently used for remote access to computer resources because they are inexpensive and available everywhere. Every day, millions of people telecommute to work, connect to the Internet, and perform bank transactions by using modems and POTS lines.

However, the maximum transmission rate for POTS circuits has already been reached. The current V.90 standard, which provides 56-Kbps throughput, actually exceeds the POTS line's capacity. In fact, the fastest a V.90 modem can transmit data on a POTS circuit is 53 Kbps. The switches on the telecommunications side of the network were not designed to handle 56 Kbps. Therefore, the FCC has limited the maximum speed.

Additionally, POTS circuits can only handle a single session at a time. That is, when the line is busy, it cannot be used to establish another connection for data or voice. This is a limitation that has no solution. If you need multiple simultaneous sessions, you'll need multiple POTS circuits.

Advantages of POTS

POTS has several benefits and these are as follows:
- Available everywhere
- Reliable connectivity
- Low cost
- Easy setup

Disadvantages of POTS

POTS also has several disadvantages:
- Only one session per circuit
- FCC limited transmission speed at 53 Kbps
- Most circuits will only reach 44 Kbps due to line noise
- Analog transmissions only

ISDN

An attractive alternative to POTS is Integrated Services Digital Network (ISDN) service.

ISDN properties

Integrated Services Digital Network (ISDN) is a digital telephone service that works over copper telephone wiring. ISDN Basic Rate Interface (BRI) is most commonly used for individual computer users.

Over the telephone line, BRI is divided into three digital channels. This includes two B channels and one D channel. Each of these can be used simultaneously.

- **B channel.** B channels transmit data at the rate of 64 Kbps to 56 Kbps. The rate is dependent on your telephone company. You can use the two B channels to make two calls simultaneously.

- **D channel.** The D channel communicates with the telephone network to perform functions such as setting up and canceling a call.

Primary Rate Interface, or PRI, uses 23 B channels and one D channel. The B channels can carry voice or data, independently or working in groups. The maximum transfer rate for PRI is 1.544 Mbps, the same as a T1 line (discussed below).

Most of the world's telephone networks are digital. Typically, only the section that runs from the local exchange to your home or office is not digital. ISDN makes that final connection to the home or office digital, thereby providing a complete digital path to remote systems.

Availability

ISDN service is not universally available. The central office that serves you must have the necessary equipment installed. This can be difficult for some service providers and carries a significant investment. For example, ISDN is sensitive to outside interference. This means that the telephone company equipment that serves you must be within a given distance, typically within 18,000 feet. There should be no anomalies near the wiring, which might interfere with the transmission.

Note: You should contact your telephone company to find out what services they have available. If they support ISDN lines, schedule a line qualification check for your immediate area.

Provisioning

Provisioning is a term used by the telecommunication industry to describe the configuration of your telephone line. ISDN lines have many options and choices that must be defined for the line to function. A flexible service, ISDN can provide support for solutions such as PC connectivity, intrusion or fire alarm monitoring, and virtual PBX telephone services.

There are three pieces of information you must collect from your telephone company to make your ISDN work with your Windows-based PC:

- **Switch type.** Switch type refers to the brand of equipment and software version that your telecommunications provider uses to provide the ISDN service. This is needed for most types of ISDN hardware adapters.

- **Phone numbers.** Depending on the B channel that your telecommunications provider has given you, you might have a separate phone number for each ISDN line. In some cases, the B channels might be sharing a phone number. Having separate phone numbers on the ISDN can be of use if you plan to take incoming calls for the ISDN.

  Note: If you have a choice, you need to make sure that your telecommunications provider is clear on which one you plan to use.

- **Service Profile Identifier (SPID).** SPID usually consists of additional digits added to the beginning and end of the phone number and might be 10 to 14 digits in total length. SPIDs are unique within each telco switch and can be considered similar to a network address. Switches can understand what kind of equipment is attached to the line by using the SPIDs. When multiple devices are attached, SPID routes calls to the appropriate device.

  Note: SPIDs are used only in the United States and Canada.

You should communicate to your telecommunications provider that you'll need all provisioning information at or before installation of the ISDN line.

ISDN hardware

ISDN can be used with either of two types of hardware adapters:

- **Internal.** An ISDN terminal adapter that is put inside the PC.

- **External.** An ISDN terminal adapter that connects to a serial or parallel port, usually at the back of your PC.

There are drawbacks to using an external adapter:

- Most PC serial ports do not transmit more than 115 Kbps. ISDN's maximum speed is 128 Kbps.
- The serial port usage imposes overhead between the PC and the external adapter, further slowing the data speed.
- The external adapter places heavy requirements on the CPU. This would impact the overall performance of your system.

However, available expansion slots, adapter availability, and cost will be additional deciding factors between an internal or external adapter.

U and Subscriber/Termination (S/T) interfaces

Your equipment will accept one of two ISDN interfaces. They are:

- **U Interface.** This is for carrying ISDN signals over a single pair of wires for long distances, such as between your location and the central office. Most ISDN adapters sold today have a U Interface. Make sure that you obtain the appropriate interface needed for your specific implementation.
- **S/T Interface.** Subscriber/Termination Interface uses two pairs of wires for shorter distances, for example, from the wall jack to your ISDN equipment.

If your equipment supports the S/T Interface, another device, called a Network Termination 1 (NT-1), is also needed. This device converts between the U Interface and the S/T Interface. Some ISDN adapters connect directly to the U Interface. At the time of this writing, adapters of this type are only sold in North America.

Do it!

A-1:   Discussing the features of POTS and ISDN

Questions and answers

1   Name the two options available to establish remote connectivity.

2   Name the standard service you subscribe to for making voice calls.

3   A POTS circuit is made with two wires from the premise equipment (telephone) to the switch (phone company). Name them.

4   POTS circuits can handle multiple sessions at the same time. True or false?

5   What is the maximum data transmission rate for a POTS line?

   A   56 Kbps

   B   53 Kbps

   C   33.6 Kbps

   D   28.8 Kbps

6 What does BRI stand for with regard to ISDN?

   A   Baseband Redundant Interface

   B   Basic Refractive Integration

   C   Basic Rate Interface

   D   Balun Reduction Initiative

7 BRI ISDN is divided into three channels. Two B channels and one D channel. What is the function of each?

8 Name the term used by the telecommunication industry to describe the configuration of your telephone line.

9 List the three pieces of information you must collect from your telephone company to ensure that your ISDN will work with your Windows-based PC.

10 Name the ISDN interface used for carrying ISDN signals over a single pair of wires for long distances.

Cable modems

While ISDN is delivered over copper cabling provided by the phone company, users can also get high-speed access through the cable company's coaxial TV cable. Given the need for sharing and other bottlenecks, a typical cable modem service will offer 1 to 10 Mbps download speeds and up to 2 Mbps upload speeds, even though the technical maximum is much higher.

Usually, the cable connects to a cable modem, which has an RJ-45 port that can connect directly via UTP to an Ethernet NIC in the customer's PC. Addressing is typically via DHCP from the cable company, and many users connect a router to the cable modem to provide access to several PC's or other network devices.

xDSL

xDSL is the term used to group together a family of technologies used for high speed, digital access over regular, copper telephone lines. DSL stands for Digital Subscriber Line, and the x denotes one or more letters used for the different technologies available, such as ADSL and HDSL. Access speeds range from 1.544 to 8 Mbps for downstream data transfers and are around 1.5 Mbps for upstream data transfers. Actual speed is influenced, however, by how far away the connecting user is from the telephone company's central office (CO). The further away, the slower the speed.

The way DSL works is that the regular phone line is split into two frequencies, one for upstream data transfers and one for downstream data transfers. Typically, a dedicated phone line is not required, although this does depend on the DSL technology used and the service offered by the telephone company. With ADSL, for example, only one phone line (usually existing) is required, and regular phone service is not affected. That is, a DSL user can make or receive a phone call while being connected to the Internet or corporate network. Available bandwidth for the DSL access also is not affected by simultaneous telephone use. Some telephone companies don't offer POTS service and DSL service on the same line, in which case a dedicated p hone line would have to be installed for DSL access.

The setup for DSL is fairly straightforward. A DSL modem is required at the end user's home. The modem plugs into the telephone line for access to the line, and an Ethernet cable runs between the modem and the computer's Ethernet NIC, a router or a hub. If the DSL line is to also be used for regular telephone and fax service, a POTS splitter box is also required. The following table outlines some of the xDSL technologies in use today.

Technology	Description
ADSL	Asymmetric Digital Subscriber Line. Has higher downstream data transfer rates (1.544 Mbps to 8 Mbps) than upstream data transfer rates (1.5 44Mbps). Can share the line with telephone equipment.
HDSL	High Bit Rate Digital Subscriber Line. A symmetrical implementation of DSL that requires two or three cable pairs for upstream and downstream speeds of up to 2.048 Mbps. HDSL-2 requires only a single cable pair for speeds of 1.544 Mbps. Can't share the line with telephone equipment; a dedicated line is required.
SDSL	Symmetric Digital Subscriber Line. Has equal upstream data transfer rates (up to 2.048 Mbps) and downstream data transfer rates (up to 2.048 Mbps). Can't share the line with telephone equipment.

Satellite

Satellite access is another option for establishing a high-speed connection to the Internet. It is most practical for people who live in or travel to rural areas where cable or DSL connections aren't available. Satellite access requires a dish mounted on the outside of a building through which to exchange data via the satellite.

Usually, a clear view of the southern sky is also required. Speeds aren't as high as with cable or DSL access, but higher than with modem access. Also, with satellite connections, weather and other atmospheric conditions can affect performance or cause interference.

Wireless

Wireless communications and access is becoming more prevalent. It enables users to make a connection to the Internet while traveling, or to the Internet or a LAN while freely moving about their house or office. Wireless access also helps eliminate cable clutter in an office environment. It can be configured for a single machine or network within a building. For travel, users can connect to the Internet via hot spots (public areas in which a connection to the Internet can be established wirelessly).

Implementing wireless access in a home or office is not exorbitantly expensive either. All that's required is a wireless network card in the PC and a WAP (wireless access point) to connect computers together or to connect to the Internet. Wireless capability is built into many newer laptops as standard equipment and can easily be added to laptops using wireless PC Card or USB NICs. For desktop PCs, wireless NICs can be installed into an available PCI slot or plugged into a USB port.

Do it!

A-2: Discussing cable modem, xDSL, satellite and wireless access methods

Questions and answers

1 What is the typical maximum download speed available through a cable modem connection to the Internet?

2 What does DSL stand for?

3 Which of the following are xDSL specifications?

   A ADSL

   B DDSL

   C SDSL

   D PDSL

4 HDSL is an asymmetrical implementation of DSL. True or false?

5 What are typical downstream xDSL access rates?

6 What is required at the user's site for satellite Internet access?

Topic B: Installing and configuring a modem

This topic covers the following CompTIA Network+ exam objectives:

#	Objective
1.6	Identify the purposes, features and functions of the following network components: • Modems
4.4	Given a troubleshooting scenario involving a client accessing remote network services, identify the cause of the problem (For example: file services, print services, authentication failure, protocol configuration, physical connectivity and SOHO (Small Office / Home Office) router).

Installing an external modem

Explanation

A new modem can be installed and configured by using the Windows Server 2000/2003/ XP Phone and Modem Options utility. You can also configure a Windows 2000/2003/XP remote access client by first creating a dial-up connection using the New Connection Wizard in the Control Panel's Network Connections area. After a dial-up connection has been established, users can access resources and work as if they were connected directly to the remote network. After establishing a dial-up connection, you can also connect to a remote server.

Before a modem can be used in a dial-up network or to access the Internet, it must be installed. Under Windows 2000/Server 2003/XP, internal modems installed in an available slot are typically detected and configured through PnP. External modems are plugged into the computer's serial port and are installed by using the Phone and Modem Options utility in the Control Panel. Typically, they will be assigned to port COM1. Both internal and external modems are managed through the Phone and Modem Options utility.

To install a new modem by allowing Windows to detect the modem:

1   From the Control Panel, open the Phone and Modem Options utility.
2   If this is the first time you're using the Phone and Modem Options utility, specify the country/region you are in. In the US, enter the area code for your area and, if you need to dial a number to access an outside line, enter that number into the respective field. Finally, specify whether you use tone or pulse dialing. Click OK. You're taken to the Phone And Modem Options window.
3   Activate the Modems tab.
4   Click Add to start the Install New Modem Wizard.
5   Click Next for Windows 2000/Server 2003/XP to locate your modem. Click Finish to return to the Phone And Modem Options window. Your new modem is listed in the list of modems.

To install a new modem by manually selecting from the list:

1 From the Control Panel, open the Phone and Modem Options utility. Activate the Modems tab and click Add to start the Install New Modem Wizard.

2 Check Don't detect my modem; I will select it from a list. Click Next.

3 From the list of Manufacturers, select the manufacturer. If no manufacturers are shown, you can choose from one of the listed standard modem types.

4 From the list of Models, select the modem. You can also insert the manufacturer's installation disk and click Have Disk, browse to the installation source, and click OK.

5 Click Next.

6 From the list of ports, select the modem port and click Next. The modem is added. Click Finish to return to the Phone And Modem Options dialog box.

Configuring general modem settings

You can use the Phone and Modem Options utility from the Control Panel to configure general modem settings and modems. Note that the available modem settings will vary, depending on the modem you've installed.

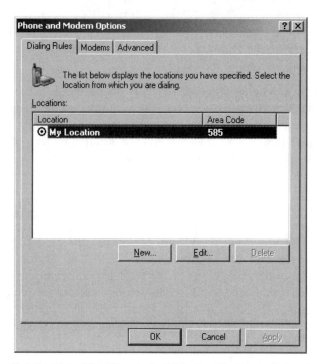

Exhibit 7-1: The Phone And Modem Options dialog box

After you open the Phone And Modem Options dialog box, as shown in Exhibit 7-1, three tabs are available, Dialing Rules, Modems and Advanced. Dialing Rules lets you add and edit locations. To edit a location, select it in the list and click Edit. This opens the Edit Location dialog box for that location, as shown in Exhibit 7-2. This dialog box has three tabs available, General, Area Code Rules and Calling Card.

The General tab lets you configure your location. You can specify a name for the location, the country/region the location is in, and what special rules apply to dialing from this location, such as numbers to access an outside line, how to handle call waiting, and so on. Any changes you make in this dialog box will apply to all modems installed in the computer when this location is selected.

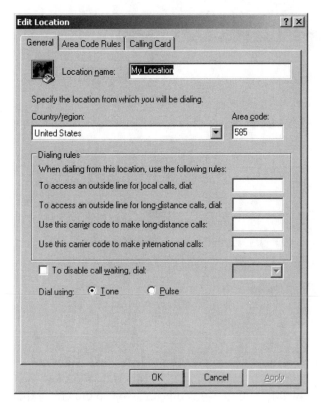

Exhibit 7-2: The Edit Location dialog box

The Area Code Rules tab lets you configure settings for calls made to specific area codes. For example, you can specify prefixes to be used for the area code, and whether to include the area code when dialing.

The Calling Card tab lets you configure using a calling card for making calls from your modem, so that the card is charged rather than the line you're using. On this tab, you can configure settings such as your card's account number, PIN, and so on.

Configuring a modem

The Modems tab in the Phone And Modem Options dialog box contains a listing of the modems currently installed on the computer, as shown in Exhibit 7-3. To add a new modem, click Add. To remove an installed modem, select the modem to be removed and click Remove.

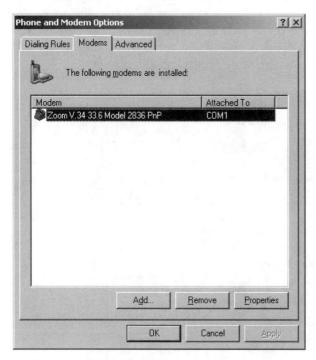

Exhibit 7-3: The Modems tab

The General tab

To view general information about the modem, such as device type, manufacturer, and status, select the modem in the list, click Properties and view the General tab that displays, as shown in Exhibit 7-4. You can also use the General tab to disable or enable the modem.

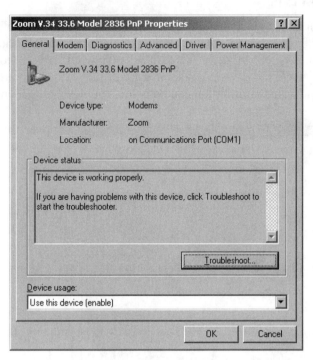

Exhibit 7-4: The General tab of a modem's properties

The Modem tab

To edit and configure a modem's properties related to port speed, speaker volume, and waiting for a dial tone, activate the Modem tab, as shown in Exhibit 7-5.

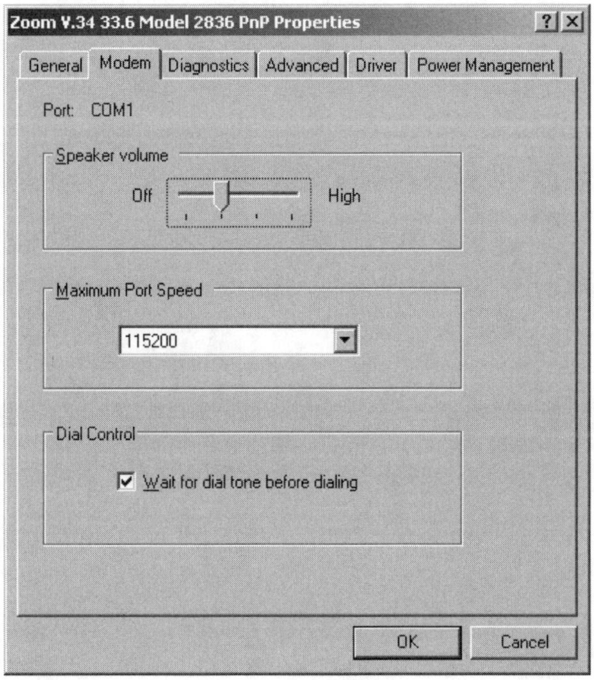

Exhibit 7-5: The Modem tab of a modem's properties

The Diagnostics tab

To enable logging, view the log or query the modem to determine if the modem is properly configured and responding, select the Diagnostics tab, shown in Exhibit 7-6. When you click Query Modem, standard AT commands are sent to the modem. Each command sent and the modem's response are displayed in the bottom portion of the diagnostics tab. This information can help you troubleshoot modem problems.

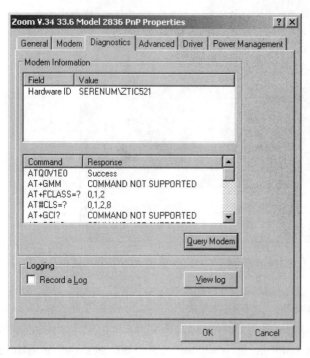

Exhibit 7-6: The Diagnostics tab after a modem has been queried

Changing default preferences

For configuration of connection time, compression, and flow control and other data connection preferences, select the Advanced tab and then click Change Default Preferences. You'll find these settings on the General tab that displays, shown in Exhibit 7-7. Finally, for settings related to data bits, parity, stop bits, or modulation, select the Advanced tab.

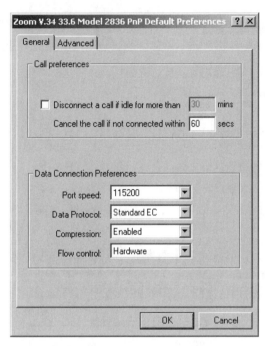

Exhibit 7-7: The General tab for configuring default preferences

Other configuration options

Depending on the modem you have installed, you may see additional tabs for configuring your modem. For example, you may see a driver tab, which you can use to view current driver information and update the modem driver. You may also see a Power Management tab on which you can specify how the modem affects power settings for your computer.

Logging and viewing modem errors

Capturing a log of the communications session might be helpful in diagnosing modem problems. The log can be viewed by clicking View Log on the Diagnostics tab in the modem's Properties dialog box. The log showing modem errors appears (as shown in Exhibit 7-8). This log file contains commands that were sent to the modem and modem settings sent by the modem, as well as errors encountered.

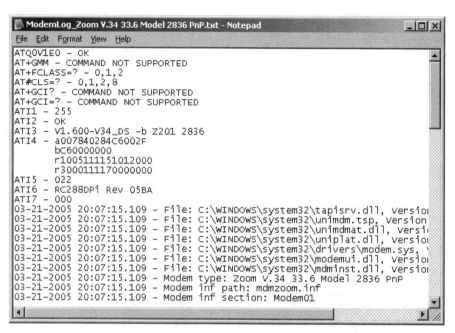

Exhibit 7-8: A log of modem diagnostic information

Do it!

B-1: Installing and configuring a new modem

Here's how	Here's why
1 From the Control Panel, open the Phone and Modem Options utility	
2 Select your country from the Country/Region dropdown list	If prompted. You're only prompted if this is the first time Phone and Modem Options has been opened.
3 Enter the area code for your area in the Area code field and make any other changes	You can make other changes, such as country, number to dial to get an outside line, Tone or Pulse dialing.
4 Click **OK**	You're taken to the Phone And Modem Options
5 Activate the Modems tab and click **Add**	To start the Install New Modem Wizard.

6 Check **Don't detect my modem; I will select it from a list**

   Click **Next**   To go to the next step in the wizard. You'll select a modem from a list.

7 From the list of manufacturers, select **(Standard Modem Types)**

   From the list of models, select **Standard 56000 bps Modem**

   Click **Next**

8 Select **COM2**

   Click **Next**

   Click **Finish**   To return to the Modems tab in the Phone And Modem Options dialog box.

9 Select **Standard 56000 bps Modem**

   Click **Properties**

10 Navigate the available tabs and options   You'll see the modem and connection settings and preferences.

11 Click **OK**   To close the Standard 56000 bps V90 Modem Properties dialog box.

12 Activate the **Dialing Rules** tab

13 Click **New**

   In the Location name box, enter **St. Louis office**

   In the Area Code box, enter **314**

14 Click **OK**   To close the New Location dialog box. On the Dialing Rules tab, the new location is now automatically selected, which means it's the default location.

15 Click **OK**   To close the Phone and Modem Options dialog box.

Topic C: Remote Access Service (RAS) and remote access clients

This topic covers the following CompTIA Network+ exam objectives:

#	Objective
2.13	Identify the purpose of network services and protocols (For example: • ICS (Internet Connection Sharing)
2.16	Define the function of the following remote access protocols and services: • RAS (Remote Access Service) • PPP (Point-to-Point Protocol) • SLIP (Serial Line Internet Protocol) • VPN (Virtual Private Network)
2.18	Identify authentication protocols: • CHAP (Challenge Handshake Authentication Protocol) • MS-CHAP (Microsoft Challenge Handshake Authentication Protocol) • PAP (Password Authentication Protocol) • RADIUS (Remote Authentication Dial-In User Service)
3.4	Given a remote connectivity scenario comprised of a protocol, an authentication scheme, and physical connectivity, configure the connection. Includes connection to the following servers: • Windows
3.7	Given a connectivity scenario, determine the impact on network functionality of a particular security implementation (For example: • Authentication and encryption
4.4	Given a troubleshooting scenario involving a client accessing remote network services, identify the cause of the problem (For example: file services, print services, authentication failure, protocol configuration, physical connectivity and SOHO (Small Office / Home Office) router).

Using RRAS for dial-up connections

Explanation

Windows 2000/Server 2003 uses the *Routing and Remote Access Service (RRAS)* to act as a dial-up server. This service is always installed, but is not configured by default. Using the Routing and Remote Access Setup Wizard you can configure RRAS as a dial-up server, a VPN server, a router, or other service.

Management of RRAS is done with the Routing and Remote Access console available from the Administrative Tools menu. When the Routing and Remote Access console is started for the first time, you notice a red arrow pointing down beside the name of your server, as shown in Exhibit 7-9. This indicates that RRAS is not started. In this case, it is because RRAS has not yet been configured.

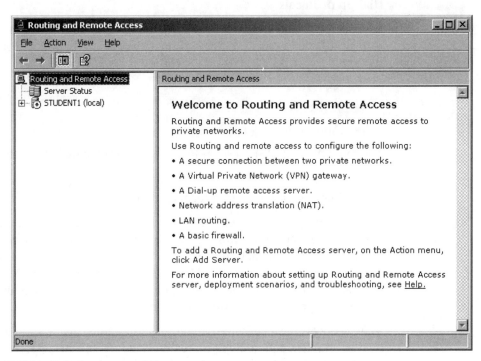

Exhibit 7-9: Routing and Remote Access console

You use the Routing and Remote Access Wizard to enable and configure RRAS for the first time. After you have completed the wizard and RRAS is started, the arrow beside your server in the Routing and Remote Access console will point up and be green, as shown in Exhibit 7-10.

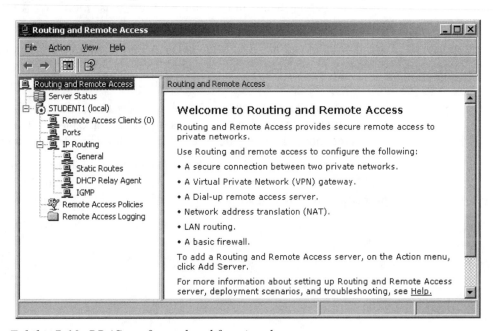

Exhibit 7-10: RRAS configured and functional

Dial-up protocols

LAN protocols and *remote access protocols* need to be considered when configuring Windows 2000/Server 2003 for dial-up networking. The following LAN protocols are supported by RRAS for dial-up networking:

- TCP/IP
- IPX/SPX
- AppleTalk

The following remote access protocols are supported by RRAS for dial-up networking:

- Point-to-Point protocol (PPP)
- Serial Line Internet Protocol (SLIP)

When a dial-up client is connected to the dial-up server, it has access to the resources on the LAN. The same protocols required by client computers to access resources on the LAN are required by dial-up clients to access resources on the LAN through the dial-up server. Most dial-up clients use TCP/IP, but support for IPX/SPX is included to support older applications, and support for AppleTalk is included to support Macintosh clients. These LAN protocols can also be used for VPN connections.

Remote access protocols are used only for dial-up connections, not VPN connections. SLIP is an older, and rarely used, remote access protocol supported only when Windows Server 2003 is acting as a dial-up client. SLIP cannot be used when Windows Server 2003 is a dial-up server. The only time SLIP is used is when dialing up to older UNIX remote access servers, and TCP/IP is the only LAN protocol supported.

PPP is a newer remote access protocol that is commonly in use. Windows Server 2003 can use PPP when acting as a dial-up client or server. PPP has a number of advantages over SLIP, including the ability to automatically configure clients with IP configuration information, wide availability, and the ability to use multiple LAN protocols.

Two remote access protocols supported in Windows 2000 Server have been removed in Windows Server 2003. The Microsoft RAS protocol used to support older Microsoft clients using the NetBEUI protocol has been removed. As well, the AppleTalk Remote Access Protocol used to support older Macintosh clients has been removed.

The selection of a remote access protocol when using Windows 2000/Server 2003 as a dial-up client is made in the properties of the dial-up connection on the Networking tab. PPP is the most commonly used remote access protocol for dial-up connections.

PPP has several options that can be enabled to enhance performance. These options are enabled using the Routing and Remote Access console on the PPP tab of the server properties, as shown in Exhibit 7-11.

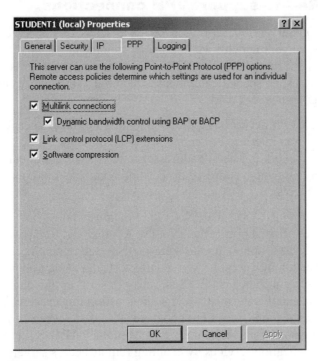

Exhibit 7-11: PPP tab of RRAS server properties

When Multilink connections are enabled, Windows 2000/Server 2003 can combine multiple dial-up connections into a single logical connection to speed up data transfer. For example, a client computer with two modems can dial-up to the remote access server and connect to two modems on the remote access server. When data is transferred between the client and the server, the speed of the connection is the aggregated speed of the two connections. To use two modems, there must be two phone lines.

If the Dynamic bandwidth control using BAP or BACP option is enabled, it allows the multilink connection to dynamically add and drop modems from a dial-up connection as the amount of data transferred varies. This is very useful for long-term connections between physical locations, particularly if long distance charges are incurred, because phone line use is minimized. The criteria used for controlling the addition or removal of modems from the multilink connection are set in remote access policies.

If you enable Link control protocol (LCP) extensions, then the dial-in server can use enhancements to *Link Control Protocol (LCP)* that control *callbacks* and other options. LCP is a protocol that controls the establishment of PPP sessions. If this option is disabled, then using callback is not possible.

If the Software compression option is enabled, then data transferred on this connection is compressed using Microsoft Point-to-Point Compression Protocol.

Using RRAS to support VPN connections

Windows 2000/Server 2003 also uses RRAS to act as a VPN server to provide secure remote access to your network via the Internet. In many ways, VPN connections behave like dial-up connections; however, when a remote access server is configured to provide VPN connections, no special equipment is required. All connectivity is accomplished through a regular network card.

Notice that if a VPN server has multiple network interfaces, then VPN clients receive an IP address from an interface not connected to the Internet. Also, if you use a DHCP server on the network to lease IP addresses to remote access clients, ensure that the DHCP server has enough addresses to accommodate the remote access clients as well as local DHCP clients.

When configuring RRAS as a VPN server, you must choose how authentication is performed. Your first choice is the "No, use Routing and Remote Access to authenticate connection requests" option, and this means that each remote access server performs its own authentication by querying Active Directory and using policies that exist on that server. Your second choice is the "Yes, set up this server to work with a RADIUS server" option, and this means that all authentication requests are forwarded to a Remote Authentication Dial-In User Service (RADIUS) server, and the remote access server allows connections based on results from the RADIUS server. A RADIUS server provides authentication services by enabling remote access servers to communicate with a single, central server that holds all authentication information in a central database.

Do it!

C-1:   Discussing RRAS

Questions and answers

1 Which utility is used to configure a Windows 2000/Server 2003 computer as a dial-in server and where do you access this utility?

2 Which LAN protocols are supported by RRAS on a Windows 2000 and a Windows 2003 server?

   A   IPX/SPX

   B   NetBEUI

   C   AppleTalk

   D   TCP/IP

3 Which is the more commonly used remote access protocol for dial-in connections?

4 You're configuring a Windows Server 2003 server as a VPN server. You want to have authentication handled by a dedicated server that holds authentication information in a central database. Which configuration option will you choose?

Configuring remote access clients

Explanation

To configure a Windows 2000/Server 2003/XP remote access client, you must first create a dial-up connection by using the New Connection Wizard in Network Connections (accessible in the Control Panel). Users can create dial-up connections to remote servers, such as ISPs or perhaps a server on a network at work.

A dial-up connection gives mobile users the opportunity to work as if they were connected directly to the remote network. After a network connection has been established by using a dial-up connection, you'll be able to access resources just as you would from a local network connection. However, the speed of a dial-up connection will be much slower than a direct network connection. Word processing and spreadsheet applications can still be accessed remotely but will function much more slowly. It's best to install and run applications from the local machine, accessing primarily data files on the remote network.

Creating new dial-up connections

To set up a dial-up connection to a private network (not the Internet) from a Windows Server 2003/XP computer:

1 In Windows Server 2003, choose Start, Control Panel, Network Connections, New Connection Wizard. In Windows XP, choose Start, Control Panel, and open Network Connections. In the Network Connections dialog box, double-click New Connection Wizard.

2 In the Welcome screen, click Next.

3 Select Connect to the network at my workplace and click Next.

4 Select Dial-up connection and click Next.

5 Enter a name for Company Name and click Next

6 Enter the phone number of the computer you will be dialing and click Next.

7 Specify whether this connection should be available for all users (Anyone's use) or only the current user (My use only) and click Next.

8 Click Finish. The dial-up connection you created automatically starts and you can click Dial to connect to the remote server. Click Cancel to see the new connection as an icon in the Network Connections window, as shown in Exhibit 7-12.

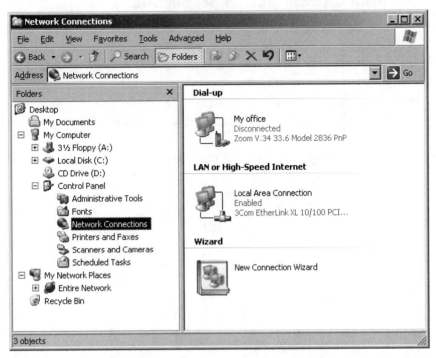

Exhibit 7-12: The Network Connections window in Windows Server 2003 after creating a new dial-up connection

Dial-up connection properties

To view and configure a connection's properties, shown in Exhibit 7-13, right-click the connection and choose Properties. There are several connection properties, such as dialing and redialing options, security options, and server type and protocol options.

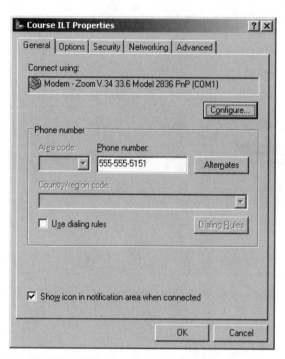

Exhibit 7-13: The General properties tab of a connection

General tab

On the General tab, you can configure which device is used to establish the connection, the phone number for the connection, whether to use dialing rules, and whether to show an icon in the taskbar while connected.

Options tab

On the Options tab, you can specify dialing options such as whether to prompt for the name, password, certificate, and phone number for the connection and whether to display progress while connecting. You can also use this tab to configure redial options, such as how many redial attempts to make, the time that should elapse between redial attempts, and how long the connection has to be idle before the call is hung up.

Security tab

On the Security tab, you can specify security options, such as whether to allow unsecured passwords, and whether and what authentication protocols to allow. To configure encryption and authentication protocols, select Advanced (custom settings) and then click Settings. This brings up the Advanced Security Settings dialog box shown in Exhibit 7-14.

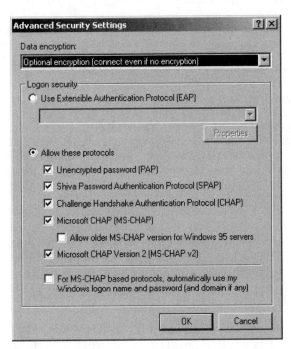

Exhibit 7-14: The Advanced Security Settings dialog box

In addition to specifying whether to require encryption for the connection, on this tab, you can also specify the authentication scheme/protocol you want to use for the connection. You can use Extensible Authentication Protocol (EAP) for authentication with the computer to which you're connecting, or allow one or more other authentication protocols.

The following table lists the function of the various authentication protocols from which you can choose.

Name	Description
EAP	**Extensible Authentication Protocol**. Is an extension to the PPP protocol (PPP is used for establishing remote access connections). It supports a variety of methods for authentication, such as smart cards, certificates, Kerberos, one-time passwords and so on.
PAP	**Password Authentication Protocol**. Provides basic and not very secure authentication. Both the username and password of a connecting computer are transmitted and compared to a table which lists authorized usernames and passwords in pairs. The passwords in this table are typically encrypted, but the transmission of the username and password is not.
CHAP	**Challenge Handshake Authentication Protocol**. A much more secure authentication protocol than PAP, it uses a fairly complex procedure for authentication. With CHAP, both computers share a previously set secret. When a connection is attempted, the computer to which another computer is trying to connect (often a server in a network) sends an ID value and a random value to the connecting machine. This machine in turn calculates a hash value (a number derived out of a string of text) out of the secret, the ID value and the random value and returns this hash to the authenticating computer. This machine in turn performs the same calculation. If the result of its own calculation matches that of the connecting computer, the connecting computer is authenticated.
MS-CHAP	**Microsoft Challenge Handshake Authentication Protocol**. Derived from CHAP, this authentication protocol uses Windows-based encryption and hashing algorithms.
SPAP	**Shiva Password Authentication Protocol**. Shiva proprietary authentication protocol for PPP connections.

Finally, on the Security tab, you can also specify whether to display a terminal window once the remote computer connects, as some remote access servers require logon information to be provided through a terminal window. You can also specify whether and what script to run once a connection is established. Both displaying a terminal window and running a script is supported only by serial modems.

Networking tab

On the Networking tab, shown in Exhibit 7-15, you can specify the type of dial-up servers you are calling with this connection. The following table lists the available dial-up servers:

Server type	Allowed protocols
PPP: Windows 95/98/NT4/2000, Internet	NetBEUI IPX/SPX Compatible TCP/IP
SLIP: UNIX Connection	TCP/IP

On this tab, you can also view and configure the components that are used for the connection, such as the protocol and client.

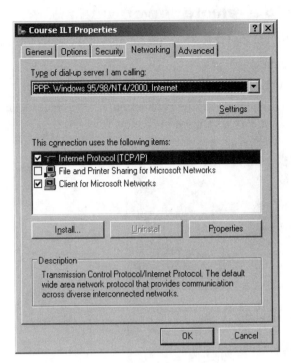

Exhibit 7-15: The Networking tab

Advanced tab

On the Advanced tab, you can enable and configure an Internet Connection Firewall and Internet Connection Sharing. Internet Connection Sharing allows other clients in the network to access the Internet through this connection. This can be a cost-effective and useful strategy in smaller networks, where only one account for a connection to the Internet may be available. If configured, you can also enable on-demand dialing. This means that if the connection to the Internet is not active when another computer tries to access an Internet resource through this connection, the connection automatically dials out at that point.

Connecting to a remote server

After the connection entry is created, you can use it to connect to a remote server.

To connect to a remote server:

1 Open Network and Dial-up Connections.

2 Double-click the icon for the connection. The Connect *<connection name>* dialog box appears, as shown in Exhibit 7-16.

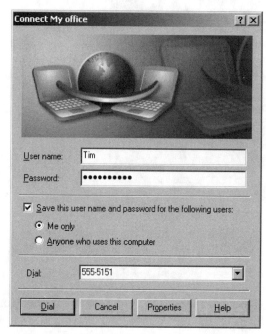

Exhibit 7-16: The Connect <connection name> dialog box

3 If necessary, type in the User name and Password, check Save password (if you want the password for the user saved on this computer), verify the phone number, and click Dial. The Connecting to My Office dialog box appears, as shown in Exhibit 7-17.

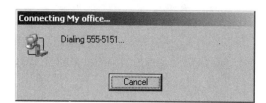

Exhibit 7-17: The Connecting My office dialog box

4 After you're connected, depending on the connection you're establishing (to the Internet or a private network) you may have to provide logon information, such as a logon name and password.

Connection information

Once you're connected, you can view connection information by double-clicking the dial-up icon on the taskbar. You'll see information such as the status of the connection, the connection duration and speed, as well as the number of bytes sent and received, compression information and errors.

Do it!   **C-2:   Discussing remote access clients**

Questions and answers

1 By using a dial-up connection, you can access resources just as you would from a local network connection. What are the disadvantages of using this utility?

2 A programmer your company has just hired will be telecommuting from his home office. You have a remote access server set up in your network. Which utility do you use to configure the programmer's laptop as a remote client, and where do you access this utility?

3 Which authentication protocol uses a secret, random value and ID value?

   A   PAP

   B   DAP

   C   CHAP

   D   EAP

4 A user tells you that she can't connect to the Unix-based remote access server she's connected to successfully in the past. You determine that no hardware issues are involved. What else can you check to identify the possible problem?

Topic D: WAN connectivity

This topic covers the following CompTIA Network+ exam objectives:

#	Objective
1.6	Identify the purposes, features and functions of the following network components:
	• CSU / DSU (Channel Service Unit / Data Service Unit)
2.14	Identify the basic characteristics (For example: speed, capacity and media) of the following WAN (Wide Area Networks) technologies:
	• Packet switching
	• Circuit switching
	• T1 (T Carrier level 1) / E1 / J1
	• T3 (T Carrier level 3) / E3 / J3
	• OCx (Optical Carrier)
	• X.25
4.4	Given a troubleshooting scenario involving a client accessing remote network services, identify the cause of the problem (For example: file services, print services, authentication failure, protocol configuration, physical connectivity and SOHO (Small Office / Home Office) router).

Creating WANs

Explanation

A wide area network (WAN) is more than a really big LAN. Connections between computers and LANs that are geographically remote need to make use of high-speed, long-distance connections, often provided by a third-party.

T-carriers

The most common T-carrier connections used for colleges and businesses are T1 and T3. A T1 line has a maximum throughput of 1.544 Mbps, while a T3 has a throughput of 44.736 Mbps

An organization that wants a constant connection but does not need 1.544 Mbps might lease a fractional T1 – or just some of the channels in a T1 line. Like PRI ISDN, a T1 line has 24 channels of 64 Kbps each, so a company could lease as many of these channels as necessary, and be billed accordingly.

On the other hand, a company that needs more bandwidth than 1.544 Mbps might want to lease multiple T1 lines. There's a big difference between a T1 and a T3, both in bandwidth and in leasing cost, and only an organization that moves around huge amounts of data, such as a data warehousing company, needs a full T3 or more.

Comparable carrier connections in Europe are termed E1 (2.048 Mbps) and E3 (34.368 Mbps) and in Japan they are termed J1 (1.544 Mbps) and J3 (32.064 Mbps).

CSU/DSU

A CSU/DSU forms the connection point between a T1 line and the customer's internal network. The CSU (channel service unit) and the DSU (data service unit) are two separate devices that are normally contained in one box. The T1 line terminates at the CSU, which monitors the connection for integrity and provides error correction. The DSU converts the signal used by internal bridges and routers into a signal that can be sent over the T1.

SONET

SONET (Synchronous Optical Network) is a fiber optic standard, and typically uses a double ring topology like FDDI, with one ring acting as the primary and the other for backup.

The transfer speed of SONET is measured by its Optical Carrier level, or OCx level. OC1 is about 51.8 Mbps, with subsequent levels being multiples of that rate. Thus, OC3 is 155.5 Mbps, OC12 is 622 Mbps, and OC48 is 2480 Mbps. SONET can be used for ATM or to carry multiple T1 or T3 lines.

SDH

SONET is the American version of SDH, or Synchronous Digital Hierarchy, an international standard for transmission of fiber optic cable. Because it integrates well with different standards and carriers, and has large throughput, SDH is used to link WANs spanning continents.

To add to the confusion, the SDH transfer rates are measured with the STS level, which is the same as the OC level of SONET. So, OC1 = STS-1 = 51.8 Mbps. Because STS-3, or 155.5 Mbps, is the lowest rate expected to transmit ATM traffic, this rate is referred to as STM-1, or Synchronous Transport Module, level 1.

X.25 packet switched networks

X.25 networks provide a connection between remote computers over private virtual circuits without the need to lease individual lines. The X.25 standard describes a packet switched network where data transmissions are broken down into individual packets and addressing information inside of each packet is used to route packets to their destination.

In packet switched networks, a physical dedicated circuit between the sender and the receiver is not necessary; logical (virtual) dedicated circuits are used instead. As a result, the same data path can be shared by multiple users in the network. In an X.25 network, end user equipment is called DTE (Data Terminal Equipment) and the equipment at the carrier is called Data Circuit-Terminating Equipment (DCE). The X.25 protocol operates at the Physical, Data Link, and Network layers of the OSI model.

In contrast to packet-switched networks are circuit-switched networks, where the data path is established exclusively for use between two communicating devices. For example, when you make a telephone call using a standard telephone network, a dedicated path (circuit) between the callers is established for the duration of the call. No other users can share this circuit.

Do it!

D-1: Discussing WAN connectivity

Questions and answers

1 What's the transfer rate of a T1 line? A T3?

2 Your company needs a constant WAN connection, but doesn't quite need a T1. What can you do to resolve the problem?

3 A company needs more than a T1, but can't afford a T3 – what might they do?

4 What device connects a T1 line to a private LAN?

5 What fiber optic standard is typically used to connect WANs that span several countries?

6 What is the least SONET/SDH transfer rate expected to transfer ATM traffic?

7 Explain packet switching.

Unit summary: Remote and WAN connectivity

Topic A   In this topic, you learned that **remote connectivity** means establishing a local connection to the network from a remote site. You learned that a **modem** provides connection over a standard phone line and that **Integrated Services Digital Network (ISDN)** provides a moderate-speed connection between stationary remote sites. You also learned that **POTS** stands for Plain Old Telephone Service and is the standard telephone service you subscribe to for making voice calls. You learned about the properties, hardware, interfaces, and provisioning related to ISDN. Further, you learned about other remote access options, including **cable modem** access, **xDSL**, **satellite**, and **wireless**.

Topic B   In this topic, you learned how to install and configure a modem to be used by a remote access client or a remote access server. You also learned how to configure general and specific modem settings.

Topic C   In this topic, you learned about the Windows 2000/Server 2003 **Routing and Remote Access Service (RRAS)**. You learned that you can configure Windows 2000/Server 2003 as a **dial-in** or **VPN server**, among others. You then learned that to configure a Windows 2000/Server 2003/XP **remote access client**, you must create a **dial-up connection** using the **New Connection Wizard** in **Network Connections**. You learned that users can create dial-up connections to remote servers, such as ISPs or perhaps a server on a network at work. You also learned that through a dial-up connection, mobile users have the opportunity to work as if they were connected directly to the remote network. You also learned how to create and configure a dial-up connection and how to connect to a remote server.

Topic D   In this topic, you learned that the most common **T-carrier** lines are **T1** and **T3**, which have transfer rates of 1.544 Mbps and 44.736 Mbps, respectively. You also learned that a **CSU/DSU** connects a T1 line to a LAN. You learned that **SONET** is the American implementation of **SDH**, and both are a fiber optic standard with very high bandwidth. Finally, you learned about **X.25 packet-switched** networks and you also learned about **circuit-switched** networks.

Review questions

1 What is the function of a modem?

2 What is the maximum throughput you can achieve on a PRI ISDN line by using an external ISDN adapter?

3 The ISDN interface using two pairs of wires for short distance transmission is called:

A SD Interface

B External Interface

C S/T Interface

D Internal Interface

4 What are some benefits of ISDN that might make it more attractive to a particular business?

5 You have a remote user who needs Internet access in a small town that doesn't provide cable or DSL access? What option is available for this user? What are the drawbacks?

6 You want to provide remote access to your network for your offsite workers via the Internet. What type of server do you have to configure to accomplish this?

7 You have just connected a new external modem to a serial port. The port is labeled "SERIAL 1." Which COM port is most likely to have the correct port setting when configuring the modem under Windows 2000?

A COM1

B COM2

C COMA

D PORT1

8 Where do you configure a modem under Windows 2000/Server 2003/XP?

9 You are connecting a small business network to the Internet. Only one person will be using the connection. Would you select BRI ISDN or analog modem? Explain your answer.

10 What are the European and Japanese "equivalents" of T1 and T3 lines?

11 In an X.25 network, what is end user equipment called?

Unit 8

Troubleshooting hardware components

Unit time: 60 minutes

Complete this unit, and you'll know how to:

A Discuss the environmental factors that affect computer networks and define physical and logical indicators of network trouble.

B Identify the function of common network tools.

C Discuss the science of troubleshooting.

Topic A: Introduction to troubleshooting

This topic covers the following CompTIA Network+ exam objective:

#	Objective
4.8	Given a network troubleshooting scenario involving an infrastructure (For example: wired or wireless) problem, identify the cause of a stated problem (For example: bad media, interference, network hardware or environment).

Effective troubleshooting

Explanation

Troubleshooting is a complex topic because problems can have a variety of causes. In addition to configuration errors, hardware failure and user errors, there are also various environmental factors that have an adverse impact on computer networks.

You can resolve most network difficulties if you are able to identify both physical and logical indicators of network trouble. Error messages also play an important role in troubleshooting network difficulties. For computer networks to work faultlessly, you need to be able to troubleshoot, isolate, and eliminate network problems. To do so, you should adopt a methodical approach to identifying potential causes of a problem.

Effects of environmental factors on networks

When choosing a location for a networked computer, you need to find a place that can provide the proper environmental conditions. The computer's environment helps determine the network's overall reliability. The environment for the individual network devices and associated cabling must also be suitable.

Room conditions

Room conditions take into account a wide array of external influences that can have a dramatic effect on the performance, reliability, and longevity of any computer network. Sometimes, the surroundings in the network location will substantially impact how that network performs. You can prevent several difficulties by being observant. You can contribute to the optimization of your network by following these environmental guidelines:

- **Avoid harsh environments.** Find a place where the temperature and humidity stay relatively stable. A cool environment with about 60% relative humidity is best. High humidity can cause condensation. Low humidity increases the possibility of static problems. If you must place a workstation by a window, make sure it is not exposed to direct sunlight. Sunlight contributes to heat buildup and heat-related problems.
- **Make sure all power supplies are properly grounded and the polarity is correct.** Wall sockets use surge protectors to protect electronic equipment from overvoltages.
- **Look for sources of magnetic fields.** Magnetic fields can cause electromagnetic interference with respect to network cabling, as well as data loss and corruption to sensitive read-only memory circuitry.
- **Avoid static electricity.** In many areas, static is the number one avoidable cause of hardware failures. Proper grounding, anti-static mats, anti-static treatment for carpets, and proper humidity levels will all help reduce static-related failures.

- **Keep network components out of locations that might flood.** Large amounts of water and computer equipment do not mix.

- **Choose correct fire extinguishers.** Make sure you have electronics-rated fire extinguishers, rather than water extinguishers, strategically placed near network hardware.

- **Avoid cigarette smoke.** Smoke can bond to components, causing them to overheat. It can also leave a conductive residue on components, leading to intermittent failures.

Placement of building contents and personal effects

When looking for possible sources of problems, pay special attention to the placement of building contents and individuals' personal effects. You can save yourself countless hours of troubleshooting phantom problems by paying attention to the placement of everyday items. Some items might be obvious while others might be so obvious as to go undetected.

- **Ensure that network cabling systems remain clear of electrical power lines**: If a network cable must cross a power cable, it should do so at a 90-degree angle to minimize the amount of electromagnetic interference (EMI).

- **Heat can be destructive in any environment where there are electronic components**: Make certain that office personnel do not use portable space heaters, hotplates, coffee warmers, and similar devices in close proximity to network components. The potential for accidents is greater when these items are present in the immediate work area.

- **Electromagnetic Interference (EMI) can cause network data problems**: Be sure you do not place cables near anything that can generate EMI. Common sources of electromagnetic interference include fluorescent lights, anything with a motor (such as, fans, generators, and air conditioners), and anything with a magnet (such as, telephones and speakers). EMI is also caused by radio transmitters and portable televisions.

- **Computer terminals themselves can be a cause of network trouble**: Ensure that your network cabling is routed cleanly away from backup power supply units and monitors.

- **How and where the office personnel sit at their desks**: Try to relocate network cable connectors away from where they might be constantly brushed by an errant foot or knee. Constant friction on a connection will eventually cause the connection to degrade.

In addition to these items, it is important to review the local fire and electrical codes prior to cable installation. Inspectors will not hesitate to remove non-code adherent cable configurations. Most jurisdictions inspect all cable media installation to ensure that all codes have been met. Typically, the cable media codes need the cable to be encased in fireproof conduits. Cable media that have a plenum fireproof coating sealed onto the outer PVC jacket can be placed in open airways.

Computer equipment

Computer equipment refers to the hardware that physically handles data on the network. This hardware can be made up of servers, workstations, network cards, cabling, hubs, routers, and interconnecting devices of all types. It is important to pay close attention to each device in turn because of the sheer number of hardware devices involved in any given network.

- As with any electronic equipment, computer equipment is susceptible to damage from extremes in temperature, dust, liquids, and other foreign bodies. A well-maintained environment can significantly increase the longevity of your computer equipment. Make it a practice to perform routine user maintenance on the systems in your charge.

- Avoid temperature extremes. It is always preferable for equipment to be cooler rather than warmer, within reason. Check the CPU fan, power supply fan, and case fans with regularity.

- See to it that the equipment is protected if it must be exposed to a harsh environment, such as in the production line of a manufacturing facility. Extra care must be exercised in these situations if the equipment is to perform reliably.

- Coffee, soft drinks, and other liquids spell trouble if spilled. Avoid all liquids at the workstation.

Do it!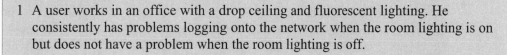

A-1:   Handling environmentally caused problems

Questions and answers

1   A user works in an office with a drop ceiling and fluorescent lighting. He
    consistently has problems logging onto the network when the room lighting is on
    but does not have a problem when the room lighting is off.

    What could be the source of this problem and what could be done to prevent it?

2   You have been called to a temporary construction site where several computers
    re-boot themselves sporadically and seemingly without warning. As you
    investigate the surroundings, you notice several strategically placed electric space
    heaters throughout the area. They are all thermostat-controlled units.

    What could be a possible reason for the computers to re-boot?

3   You are called to a site where the server room is adjacent to the building's boiler
    room. Conditions in the server room are 95 degrees with 95% humidity. The
    servers are randomly restarting themselves.

    What could be causing these problems?

Physical and logical indicators of network trouble

Explanation
Resolving a network difficulty depends on troubleshooting, isolating, and eliminating a problem or series of problems. Take a methodical approach to identify potential causes of a problem. Make a list of potential causes. After this, start eliminating them one by one. Start with the most obvious, least intrusive causes and then work your way down your list. By starting with the most likely causes, you stand a better chance of a quick resolution. A good place to begin your list is with:

- Network hardware
- Error messages

Network hardware

Computer equipment refers to the hardware physically tasked with handling data on the network. This hardware can be made up of servers, workstations, network cards, cabling, hubs, routers, and internetworking devices of all types. Because of the sheer number of hardware devices involved in any given network, it is important to pay close attention to each device in turn.

Workstations and servers

The workstation and server should be made up of quality hardware with enough processor power, RAM, and bus speed to accommodate the flow of data they need to handle. Network bottlenecks can and do occur as a result of undersized servers and workstations. It is not a rare occurrence to come upon a network that was planned for 25 users but has expanded to 50 users without any significant hardware upgrades. Be aware of what was initially installed as opposed to what is currently onsite.

Network adapters

Network adapter cards provide the hardware interface for the Data Link protocols. Following are several factors to consider when troubleshooting or installing network adapters:

- **Data Link protocol.** Each network adapter is matched to a specific Data Link protocol and supports that low-level protocol only. If supporting multiple access methods, you'll have to install multiple card types (For example, Ethernet and Token Ring).

- **System bus.** The bus structure is another factor. ISA bus systems support 8-bit and 16-bit cards. Both EISA- and MCA-based computers can support 32-bit cards. Today, PCI bus cards are most commonly used, which provide a 32-bit (and sometimes a 64-bit) interface.

- **Connectors.** Select adapters that work on the type of cabling you plan to use. For example, Ethernet cards have traditionally had a BNC connector for Thinnet and an AUI connector for Thicknet. Many manufacturers now only make adapters with the more popular RJ-45 for twisted pair. Most NIC cards also provide an LED display that makes it possible for a technician to tell at a glance if the card is on and processing data.

Cabling

Cabling is the arterial system of any network and carries within it the data that is the lifeblood of your network. Crimps in a cable, gouges, breaks, and other inconsistencies can damage network throughput.

When installing cables, be certain not to fight the lay of the wire. The lay is determined by the way in which individual conductors are wrapped at the time of manufacturing. Working with the natural direction a piece of cable coils will not only save you time and frustration, but you'll not run the risk of introducing tiny fractures into the conductors themselves.

Install cabling in protected troughs whenever possible. When adding connectors to a piece of cable, be slow and deliberate no matter how many times you have done it in the past. One miscrimped piece of cable in an otherwise clean installation will force you to verify each piece of hardware already in place.

When working with Category 5 cable with RJ-45 connectors, pay specific attention to the difference between a patch cable and a crossover cable. When working with fiber optic cable, be especially careful as it's quite easy to damage the cable and connectors.

Hubs

Hubs are centralized connecting points for network wiring. They provide an excellent point to begin troubleshooting efforts.

Typically, hubs are used to link workstations to servers. If you are certain that the hardware in your workstation is intact and error free, the hub provides an isolating point in the wiring plan of the network. Visually observe the LEDs on the hub for indications of data flow and proceed accordingly. Be certain to notice any data collision errors that might be occurring.

Routers

Routers are used to link dissimilar networks together. This feature provides an excellent nexus for troubleshooting. You can also determine whether the problem is internal to your LAN or external to it by using routers. As with all internetworking devices, care should be taken to prevent environmental factors from impacting the router's performance.

Error messages

Error messages will generally manifest themselves in one of two ways, either at the server or at the workstation. These messages are typically either hardware related or software related.

Hardware error messages

Hardware error messages are usually indicative of a misconfiguration. They indicate whether the settings for the hardware component, such as the NIC, are correct and whether they have the proper IRQ and I/O addressing. They can also indicate whether a card is seated well in its socket on the motherboard and whether it was working previously and whether something has changed. These are some of the factors you must consider when troubleshooting hardware problems.

Software error messages

Software error messages might not be clear at times. These messages indicate whether the error occurs only in certain applications and whether all resident software packages are configured correctly. They also indicate whether any software was installed recently and whether all necessary protocols are loaded and available to the hardware. Other factors considered include whether the hardware is installed correctly. The more sophisticated your network configurations are, the easier it is to overlook a seemingly insignificant setting.

Do it!

A-2: Discussing causes of network trouble

Questions and answers
1 You receive a call that a user is unable to log into the network. You check the NIC card and find that the link light is lit. Proceeding to the hub, you notice that the port link light is not lit, however. You move the patch cable to a different port on the hub and the problem is resolved. What was the problem?
2 You are confronted by a user who is not able to connect to the network. You check his NIC link lights, and they are not lit. You check the hub and notice the port link lights are not lit. You move the patch cable to a new port on the hub but nothing changes. What would be your next troubleshooting step?

Topic B: Introduction to common network tools

This topic covers the following CompTIA Network+ exam objective:

#	Objective
3.3	Identify the appropriate tool for a given wiring task (For example: wire crimper, media tester / certifier, punch down tool or tone generator).

Troubleshooting tools

Explanation

Several tools are available for use in troubleshooting network problems. These tools include crossover cables, devices such as tone generators, cable testers, Fox and Hound, multimeters, time domain reflectometers, and diagnostic tests such as a hardware loopback test.

Crossover cable

A *crossover cable* refers to a length of network cable that has been wired to provide a connection from one hub to another, or alternatively, from one network interface card to another, alleviating the need for an Ethernet hub. You can purchase an Ethernet crossover cable inexpensively from any good computer supply store. You can also create one with ease.

To create a crossover cable for a 10BaseT network, you need a length of Category 5 cable and two RJ-45 connectors. In crimping RJ-45 connectors, there are two prevalent pin-out configurations, T568A and T568B. The following table presents these standards:

Configuration	1	2	3	4	5	6	7	8
T568A	W/G	G	W/OR	Bl	W/Bl	OR	W/Br	Br
T568B	W/OR	OR	W/G	Bl	W/Bl	G	W/ Br	Br

To create crossover cables, you'll first crimp an RJ-45 connector onto one end by using either the T568A or T568B pin-out configuration. When you prepare to crimp the other end, however, you'll use a slightly different scheme:

Configuration	1	2	3	4	5	6	7	8
T568A Crossover	W/OR	OR	W/G	Bl	W/Bl	G	W/Br	Br
T568B Crossover	W/G	G	W/OR	Bl	W/Bl	OR	W/ Br	Br

From these tables, you can see that position 1 has been switched with position 3 and position 2 with position 6, effectively crossing over the signals.

A crossover cable is a useful tool to have on hand when confronted with a symptom such as the loss of connectivity for a block of workstations all connected to the same hub. In many instances, a normal patch cable has been substituted for a crossover cable at the hub. This can result in the isolation of the hub. This symptom could be easily misdiagnosed as a faulty hub if the crossover connection is not verified.

An example

A new Ethernet hub has been installed. The users connected to the hub can all see each other, but they are unable to see anyone else on the network. Upon investigation, you notice that the port labeled UPLINK (MDI-X) on the new hub has been connected to the existing hub by using a standard patch cable. You need to identify the procedure you would use to resolve this issue and ensure that all users are available to each other on the network.

You can resolve the problem by replacing the standard patch cable with a crossover cable. Communication between the two hubs is made possible by using the crossover cable, and all users can see each other on the network.

Tone generator

A *tone generator* is a device that emits an audible tone to test primarily for continuity. An example of this type of circuit is the continuity function on your digital multimeter. A tone is sent through a medium and can be heard at the remote end if the medium maintains continuity.

Cable tester

Cable testers come in a variety of types and are readily available through numerous electronics distributors. In most instances, an effective cable tester performs two functions, namely checking continuity and also the exact wiring order of a piece of cable. It does this order checking conductor by conductor. This is useful in that the master of the unit can be placed at one end of the cable and the slave unit can be placed at the other. An indicator shows the exact wiring order of the cable. This helps ascertain whether the cable is a normal patch cable or a crossover cable. It is also instrumental in identifying unknown cables across a distance.

Fox and Hound

Fox and Hound is made up of two individual units. The Fox sends a signal down the cable, and the Hound hunts down that signal. This provides a means of checking continuity, as well as troubleshooting for cable integrity.

Multimeter

Multimeters come in two varieties, analog and digital. Digital multimeters feature an audible continuity tester while analog meters do not. The significant advantage that multimeters have over other types of network tools is their ability to measure resistance. This is paramount when knowing the value of terminating resistors is a requirement.

Time domain reflectometer

A *time domain reflectometer (TDR)* is a sophisticated tool used to find a break in the middle of a cable. A time domain reflectometer calculates the length of a cable by measuring the time a reflected pulse takes to return to the TDR and multiplying that measurement by the Nominal Velocity of Propagation. They are used in network environments where cables are long and replacement costly.

Hardware loopback

A *hardware loopback* test is a diagnostic test that transmits a signal across a medium, while the sending device waits for the return of the signal. Hardware loopback tests help to determine the operational capability of individual hardware components, as well as the interconnecting medium.

Do it!

B-1:   Identifying network tools

Questions and answers

1 What does TDR stand for?

2 You have been asked to troubleshoot a workstation that is connecting to the network intermittently. You notice that the patch cable for the workstation is plugged in directly under the desk. What tool would you use to verify the integrity of the patch cable?

3 Name the network tool that provides connection from one hub to another, or alternatively, from one network interface card to another.

4 Name the two prevalent pin-out configurations used in crimping RJ-45 connectors.

5 Name the devices that can be used to check continuity.

Topic C: The science of troubleshooting

This topic covers the following CompTIA Network+ exam objective:

#	Objective
4.8	Given a network troubleshooting scenario involving an infrastructure (For example: wired or wireless) problem, identify the cause of a stated problem (For example: bad media, interference, network hardware or environment).

Introducing troubleshooting

Explanation

Troubleshooting is more of an art than a science. The DIReCtional troubleshooting model is aimed at increasing your level of troubleshooting expertise. This model breaks down troubleshooting into a series of logical steps.

Troubleshooting hardware and software problems can be a daunting experience. You need to learn as much as you can about the equipment you'll be servicing. If you have a thorough understanding of how the system works, you'll be more prepared to fix it when it does not. Approach the situation in a straightforward, logical manner, and keep the following information in mind when problems occur.

Troubleshooting is just another word for problem solving. Problem solving is a process of logically evaluating the symptoms, analyzing possible solutions, and eliminating improbable factors until a resolution is reached.

Unfortunately, system repair is usually a process of putting out fires, and it seems like you never make any headway. All that is needed is to put a formal troubleshooting system in place. You need to:

- Streamline the reporting process
- Repair problems quickly and accurately
- Find, track, and resolve any ongoing problems
- Perform trend analyses on system failures

The right system can move you from crisis management to managing and avoiding a crisis.

Efficient troubleshooting

There are a number of things you can do to improve the efficiency and effectiveness of your system troubleshooting:

- **Basic troubleshooting skills.** Developing basic skills is more of an organization process than anything else. This will help you find and repair problems quickly.
- **Documentation.** Having the right documentation on hand is vital. This goes far beyond manuals and other references and includes documentation you should be generating. Complete system inventories and failure histories are necessary tools.
- **Tools.** Proper troubleshooting needs proper tools, both hardware and software. Software tools can repair data-related problems or help diagnose hardware problems. Hardware tools are necessary when you finally have to open the machine.

Building troubleshooting skills

You need to know how much effort is needed to build your troubleshooting skills. Some of the factors involved in this decision include:

- **Systems.** A key factor is the age of your systems. If the majority of your systems are still under warranty, your responsibilities on those systems might be limited. You'll need to verify that it is a system failure, but repair should be left to an authorized warranty service provider. Most systems now carry at least a one-year warranty.

- **Service options.** If you are going to be the primary service provider, then obviously you need to develop a high level of troubleshooting expertise. Even if most service is provided by a third party, you still have some responsibilities. You need to verify the problem and will be taken through basic troubleshooting by a third-party technician.

- **Responsibilities.** Though the exception rather than the rule, your troubleshooting responsibilities might be spelled out in your job description. Mostly, you'll find all problems coming your way. It is up to you to determine whether you feel competent to make the repair.

- **Available resources.** If you do not have the proper tools, hardware and software, you'll be limited in what you can do. When planning to make your own repairs, you'll need either spare parts on hand or a ready and reliable source.

The DIReCtional troubleshooting model

DIReCtional troubleshooting model is a troubleshooting model that will help you increase your level of troubleshooting expertise. While troubleshooting is sometimes called an art more than a science, it is possible to quantify this process by using a model. In this model, troubleshooting is described as a series of logical steps, as shown in Exhibit 8-1.

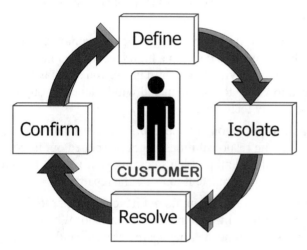

Exhibit 8-1: Troubleshooting as a series of logical steps

- **Define the problem.** You have to be able to describe what type of problem it is, what conditions are present, and whether there is a quick fix that you can try. Make sure to document all information as it is collected. In addition, set the expectations of the user at this time.

- **Isolate the occurrence.** To determine the exact cause of the problem, you need to isolate it. Classify the problem as a hardware-related or software-related problem. Re-create the problem by using technical documentation and your notes. Reconfirm that the problem exists. Be sure to document all results.

- **Resolve the problem.** After you find the problem, you have to fix it. Use technical documentation, your notes, and the Internet to research the problem. Identify likely causes and eliminate unlikely causes. Solve the problem and repeat your solution to assure that it is correct. Document the steps that you took to resolve the malfunction.

- **Confirm the resolution and expectations.** Now that everything is fixed, confirm whether it will stay that way. Review the case history of the problem to ensure that no steps were missed. Find out whether the customers or users are happy with the solution. Broadcast the solution to all concerned parties. Confirm these items before considering the matter closed. Document the final status of the problem.

The importance of documenting each step as you go through the process cannot be over emphasized. In this way, you can organize your thoughts, avoid repeating the same steps, and have access to the basis for preparing your service records.

The following table explains the concepts introduced and breaks them into the following steps:

Step	Activities
Define the problem	Describe the problem Determine the problem type Specify the conditions Try an immediate solution Document everything pertaining to the problem Set expectations
Isolate the occurrence	Reproduce the problem Classify the problem Reconfirm the problem Document
Resolve the problem	Research the problem Identify potential causes Eliminate unlikely causes Solve the problem Repeat the solution Document the resolution
Confirm the resolution and expectations	Review case history Confirm with your customer Broadcast the solution Document final findings

Each component of the DIReCtional troubleshooting model is discussed in detail below.

Define the problem

Before any repairs can be made, you must identify that a problem exists. This might be through trouble reports from users, error messages on the screen, or observations made during preventive maintenance. You should supply your users with some type of trouble reporting form, giving you a way of tracking the problem through to its resolution.

Part of the problem is information. Sometimes you have too much, not all of it easily understood, and some of it contradictory. It is important to look at the source of the information and give it appropriate weight. Users will add their own observations with their own interpretations when reporting a problem. These interpretations might not be completely accurate. Error messages can be misleading if you do not understand what they are telling you. Learn to recognize the relevant information and discard the rest.

Another problem is that all errors might not be reported. This is especially true if users have reported minor problems in the past and never received any type of response or follow-up. These small difficulties might, however, have led to a major failure.

While defining a potential problem, you might realize that there could be a quick solution to the malfunction. Try these quick fixes before proceeding. They might save you time by immediately resolving the problem.

Ensure that you speak to users in a professional manner. Do not become impatient or condescending. Many support professionals work from a script or checklist when speaking with users to remind themselves of relevant and appropriate areas of inquiry. Make sure that you set expectations with the users, providing them with a timeline for correction.

It is to your advantage to supply your users with a trouble reporting form. This will help them organize their thoughts, ensure that you get the information you need, and give you a way of starting documentation of the problem.

You should also train the users to fill out the form properly, emphasizing the information you need, such as:

- **User contact.** You need to know who has first-hand information regarding the failure.
- **System description.** The level of description detail you need will depend on how well your system inventory has been documented.
- **Failure information.** You need to know what the user was doing when the error occurred and any error messages or other symptoms that might have occurred. It is also helpful to know if the error can be repeated and if any changes have been made to the system.

While users are your first step in troubleshooting, you have to consider the source of trouble reports. You might have some users who are unable to accurately report the problem due to limited computer experience or other reasons.

Isolate the occurrence

You need to isolate the cause of the failure, classify the problem, and if possible, consistently re-create the failure. In this way, you can verify that you have found the cause and know when it is repaired.

To isolate the cause of failures, you must be familiar with the following components:

- Workstation hardware
- Server hardware
- Network hardware
- Workstation operating systems
- Network operating systems
- Workstation applications
- Cabling

Complicating the process is the fact that components might work properly when tested separately or fail only in certain specific combinations. In addition, it is seldom possible to isolate all components that you want to test. It is necessary to isolate as much as possible, keeping variables to a minimum.

By recreating a problem, you are able to verify that it does exist and determine when it has been corrected. It is important to document the process, listing all involved variables.

Repeat the factors involved in the original occurrence as closely as possible. Keep variables to a minimum while you are working.

You'll not be able to recreate the problem in all situations. If the problem is physical or data damaging, you'll not want to. If intermittent, you might not be able to. In situations such as this, you must depend heavily on intuitive logical processes.

Resolve the problem

After you have found the problem, you must fix it. Bear in mind that solving the problem does not always determine the cause. You need to look at underlying factors, such as system environment and correct these as well. An important part of this process is a regular preventive maintenance schedule.

An important point that is missed in the rush to repair the hardware (or software) is that you need to fix the business problem first. Ensure that the operational requirements of your business are met. This might mean having the user work at a different system while repairs are being made. The first priority is to keep the user productive while you fix the problem.

It might be necessary to bring in a third-party service provider to assist with the repair. You'll find that any background work you have done, including documentation, isolation, and re-creation, will help streamline the process. This will also help reduce repair costs.

Confirm the resolution and expectations

When you have resolved the problem, make sure that the resolution does not create additional problems. Verify the stability of the computing environment through follow up with the users. Talk to the users and find out whether they are happy with your resolution of the problem. Document the information you obtain. Broadcast the results to your peers and other interested parties. Do not consider your job done until you complete this step.

Troubleshooting tips

Before you open the case of a computer and begin removing and/or replacing components, consider the following:

- **Make sure the problem is not being caused by the operator**: You need to find out whether the programs and peripherals are being used correctly. If you are on the telephone, you might ask the person to tell you what he/she was doing when the error occurred. If you are on-site, have the person show you how the machine failed. Many malfunctions are caused by the operator doing something wrong, rather than by a real system error. It is cheaper to check to see that the operator is not making a mistake than to take the computer apart and replace boards.

- **Check to see that all the devices are plugged in and switched on and that the wall outlet is supplying power**: Another cheap fix for broken equipment is plugging it into the wall. A laser printer on a network that is not by the user's desk could be unplugged, generating a message that the laser printer could not be found. Having the client check to see that the printer is plugged in and online could save a service call. Check to see that the cables are attached at both ends and secured by using the restraint devices installed. Cable connectors can slide out of place if they are not securely attached. A person stretching his legs under the desk could accidentally knock them loose.

- **Check to see that the problem is not caused by software**: Sometimes software can cause a machine to crash. You need to find out whether the machine crashes when one specific software package is running and whether the PC has terminate and stay resident (TSR) programs loaded. Try deactivating the TSR programs and running the troublesome program. It might be a conflict between a TSR and the troublesome software. Extensions such as TSRs are loaded into memory and can cause conflicts with some software packages.

- **Check to see that the correct device drivers are being used**: For example, problems with a digitizing tablet could be due to a mouse driver being installed rather than the digitizer's driver. When working on a computer on the network, make sure the external devices the user thinks are being used are selected in the setup. It is possible that someone else borrowed the system and changed the destination of printed output.

- **Check to see that external indicators show peripherals are ready**: You need to check whether the printer is online and whether the paper out lamp on the printer is lit. An indicator lamp on a peripheral device such as an online lamp on a printer points to a state of readiness.

- **Run diagnostic programs**: Diagnostic programs can be run that exercise portions of the PC. Most PCs are supplied with a diagnostic program. If you cannot find the diagnostic program that came with the PC, you can use one that is commercially available. These programs do not necessarily locate errors on system boards. However, the inventory these programs make can be useful.

- **Remove the case and re-seat the boards**: If these steps do not provide you with a solution to your problem, it is time to open up the PC. Look for loose connections or dust in the connections between the daughter boards and the motherboard that can cause PCs to malfunction. Look for chips that are socketed. Chips generate heat when the computer is turned on. According to the laws of physics, chips expand when heated and contract when cooled. The board they are mounted on might not expand at the same rate. This difference of expansion rates can lead to socketed chips creeping out of their sockets over time. This phenomenon, thermal cycling, is known as *socket creep*. Boards can appear to be bad because a socketed chip has become loose. You can bring these boards back to life by re-seating these chips. To re-seat a socketed chip, gently press the chip back into its socket while supporting the backside of the board.

Troubleshooting software

One of the hardest parts of system troubleshooting is determining whether the problem is hardware or software related. While each can be taken as the other, there are some hints that will help you isolate software-related problems:

- **Check whether the application or operating system has been recently upgraded**: If you have made recent changes to either the operating system or the application, one of these is the most likely problem.

- **Check whether you have made any hardware changes recently**: While this would imply the problem is hardware-related, it might be that there is a software problem that only appears on certain hardware configurations.

- **Check whether the problem is common to all your systems**: If the problem is showing up on all your systems, you can be relatively sure it is software-related. This is especially true if you are running different hardware configurations.

- **Check whether the problem is limited to one type of system**: If the problem not only shows up on one system, but on all the systems of that type, it is still most likely software-related. It might be that the problem occurs only on certain hardware configurations.

- **Check whether the problem is limited to one system**: When a problem is limited to only one system and cannot be reproduced on any other system, then you are most likely looking at some type of hardware failure.

Do it!

C-1: Discussing troubleshooting techniques

Questions and answers

1 What are the four steps of the DIReCtional troubleshooting model?

2 Name the factors needed to improve the efficiency and effectiveness of your system troubleshooting.

3 List the steps in the problem solving process.

4 Define thermal cycling.

5 How do you identify that a problem exists?

Troubleshooting documentation

Explanation

An essential part of your system troubleshooting is your documentation. The better you document both your systems and the process, the easier troubleshooting will become. There are several ways of documenting troubleshooting systems.

System inventory

You need to thoroughly document all of your systems, including:

- Manufacturer and model
- Any expansion boards, including type and manufacturer
- Floppy drive(s)
- Hard disk drive, if any
- Display
- Keyboard
- Any additional peripherals
- Operating system type and version
- Applications

You might want to keep a brief record of service information on the same form:

- Service performed
- Service date
- Any parts replaced

Problem resolution reports

Depending upon how you manage the support process, trouble report forms can be filled out by the user or by support personnel over the telephone. Minimally, you should have the following data:

Data	Description
Date	This is important for tracking and follow-up purposes.
User contact	This is the person experiencing the problem.
System description	This might not be necessary if you have a complete and accurate system inventory.
Symptoms	This is a description of the problem, including what the user was doing when the problem occurred and any error messages.
Priority	This will normally be set by the service technician but might be an area where the user can describe the seriousness of the problem, such as nuisance or system down.
Problem	This is what you determined to actually be wrong with the system.
Status	This indicates whether the problem has been fixed. If not repaired, explain why, such as awaiting parts. The status should be dated separately.
Resolution	This is what you did to fix the system. Include a list of any spare parts that were used.

A sample problem resolution report is shown in Exhibit 8-2.

Date			
Time			
User			
Hardware Involved			
Scope of Problem			
Evidence of Problem			
Person Contacted			
Person Reporting Problem			
Notes			

Exhibit 8-2: A sample problem resolution report

Electronic documentation

You should keep system inventory and resolution report information in some type of electronic format, such as a database. Some reasons for this include:

- **Easy access.** This makes information easily and readily available to those who need it.
- **Simplified reporting.** You can generate reports on the data collected. This can be used as a basis for performing an annual inventory, documenting repair time and costs, or for generating restocking orders for spare parts.
- **Trend analysis.** Most failure trends are never seen or are seen only after many occurrences. The data you have in your database can be analyzed for failure trends, helping isolate where you might have environmental concerns.

There are both commercial and shareware products available that you can use to set up your database and collect information. You can start by setting up a flat file database and collecting the most vital information.

Do it!

C-2: Discussing troubleshooting documentation

Questions and answers
1 List the minimum information needed for trouble report forms.
2 Which columns will you fill in the Problem resolution reports to indicate the actions taken to rectify the problem?

Troubleshooting tools

Explanation

Troubleshooting tools refer to anything you use to help you in your troubleshooting. You need to gather the tools best matched to your specific troubleshooting needs before you can put them to use. Troubleshooting tools belong to several categories: traditional tools, various commercial publications, and vendor-supplied hardware diagnostics.

Traditional tools

Screwdrivers and pliers are what most people think of when they hear the word "tools." You can service most of your systems by using a few simple tools, as described in the following table.

Tools	Use
Screwdrivers	Helpful in opening systems, removing and replacing boards, and attaching cables.
Standard pliers	Necessary for certain types of clips.
Long-nose (needle-nose) pliers	Helpful when pulling or replacing jumpers and also used for straightening bent pins on DIP packages.
Nut drivers (or a small socket set)	Necessary for hex-topped screws.
Tweezers	One of the best tools available for picking up small items that you have dropped.
Torx (spline) drivers	Necessary to get into some system enclosures, including many Macintosh and some Compaq systems.
Small flashlights	Helpful when system enclosures are not in well-lit areas.
Time-Domain Reflectometer (Cable tester)	Can be used to test network cabling for breaks. Especially useful for testing long cables.
Tone generators	Useful for testing cables for breaks as well as other problem types.
Multimeters or Volt-Ohm-Meters (VOMs)	Useful for checking power supply voltages.

The need for information

When troubleshooting, information is a vital tool. Whether from commercial publications, your own database, or gathered by talking with others, a good reference base can mean the difference between success and failure.

It is not what you know but what you know how to look up that makes the difference in performance. There are a number of sources available to help you in your troubleshooting.

- **In-house documentation.** Probably the best source of information about your specific system is the information you have collected. By reviewing your trouble reports and repair information, you can find the fix you need already documented.

- **Vendor manuals.** Vendor software and hardware manuals are usually the best source for information on configuration, setup, installation, and possible conflicts. Unfortunately, most of these are user's manuals that do not contain a great deal of technical information.

- **Commercial publications.** Both books and magazines can be a great source of information. Publications such as PC Week give you the latest in PC news, and publications such as Network Magazine help keep you abreast of networking technologies. A number of good books on PC configuration and repair are available, but you should take time to look through any book before buying. Each author sees different aspects as important, and some books might not meet your specific needs. There are several database programs that contain jumper settings, installation instructions, CMOS settings for motherboards, I/O boards, modems, network adapters, and hard drives. Probably, the most widely used program of this type is the Micro House Technical Library. One of the benefits found with this type of program is that they are updated regularly, usually quarterly, as new devices are added to the database. Several of these programs also provide Internet Web sites where you can search for new devices, which were not included in the latest update.

- **Bulletin boards and online services.** A number of vendors run their own bulletin boards to make it easier to download updated, installable driver files. Some user groups and computer clubs also run bulletin boards. Their general forums can be a good source of information. Online services, such as America Online and similar forums, deal with different aspects of networking and include a large number of vendor-specific forums.

- **The Internet.** The Internet is an excellent resource for computer technicians. You can use the various search engines to search for a specific item on the World Wide Web or Usenet Newsgroups. The following table provides a brief listing of PC hardware vendors, software vendors, and other resources, along with their URLs.

- **Associates and co-workers.** On-the-job technical experience can help fine-tune troubleshooting skills and sometimes the best information is spread by word-of-mouth. Network with those around you who might have tips and techniques to share with you.

URL	Company
www.microsoft.com	Microsoft Corporation
www.intel.com	Intel Corporation
www.mot.com	Motorola Corporation
www.sun.com	Sun Microsystems
www.ibm.com	IBM Corporation
www.apple.com	Apple Corporation
www.novell.com	Novell, Inc.
www.seagate.com	Seagate Technology
www.hp.com	Hewlett-Packard Corporation
www.3com.com	3Com/US Robotics
www.zdnet.com	Ziff-Davis Publishing
www.packardbell.com	Packard-Bell Corporation
www.wavetech.com	Wave Technologies
www.comptia.org	CompTIA

System diagnostics

Vendor-supplied hardware diagnostics are matched to a specific piece of hardware. That means they are designed to test that hardware and will probably give it the best check.

There are some problems, however, with vendor diagnostics:

- **Availability.** Some vendors supply basic diagnostic sets with their systems. To get more advanced diagnostics, you might have to go through an authorized service training course. Many manufacturers of compatible systems do not have system-specific diagnostics available but might be able to suggest a third-party diagnostics package. Many suppliers of expansion cards also supply diagnostics for their specific cards. The same is true of some peripheral manufacturers.

- **Range of tests.** With vendor diagnostics, you are limited to the tests that the vendor feels you should be able to run. In some cases, this might be limited.

- **Expansion hardware.** Vendor system diagnostics are limited to that specific system. That means they most likely will not be able to test any of your expansion hardware. For this, you'll need diagnostics supplied by the expansion hardware vendor or third-party diagnostics that can test that type of device.

Third-party diagnostics and utilities

There is a wide assortment of commercial diagnostics packages available. There are some definite advantages to packages of this type:

- **Range of support.** One advantage of third-party diagnostics is that they are not tied to any specific system. They usually cover a wide range of system types so that one package should cover most of your PCs. You need to read the licensing information carefully because many are licensed for use on a single machine and might require the purchase of a site license.

- **Available tests.** Third-party diagnostics usually have a wide range of tests covering all your system hardware. You can test the system board, parallel and serial ports, memory, keyboard, and even mouse operation and video display.

- **Customized testing procedures.** You can usually choose not only the tests that run but also the order in which they run and the number of times that they repeat. Some packages make it possible for you to build your own custom test sets and then call these up by name.

- **Other utilities.** The basic diagnostics are much the same on all the packages. Therefore, each attempts to stand out by the extras they offer. These include reporting DMA and IRQ usage, testing hard disk and system performance, and providing automated procedures for setting up a new hard disk.

Selecting a diagnostic software package

When selecting a diagnostics package, there are some factors you need to keep in mind.

- **Systems supported.** Make sure your specific systems are supported. If it is not specified on the package, you should contact the vendor and find out if your systems are supported.

- **Available tests.** Any diagnostic package you buy should provide a full set of hardware tests.

- **Testing procedures.** Verify that the package provides flexible testing procedures. You need to be able to select the tests that run, the order in which they run, and the number of times to loop through each test. It is important that tests can loop, unattended, overnight. This might be the only way to check for intermittent failures.

- **Reporting capabilities.** It is best to have the option of either logging test results to a file or printing them directly. Either way, you need a way to make a copy of the test results so you can refer back to them later, if necessary.

- **Destructive tests.** Many disk and hard disk tests are destructive, writing over the data on the disk. Make sure you are aware of any destructive tests and use extreme caution when running them. It is strongly suggested that you back up your hard disk before running any hard disk tests.

Do it!

C-3: Identifying troubleshooting tools

Questions and answers

1 Name the traditional tool that can be used for pulling or replacing jumpers and straightening bent pins on DIP packages.

2 Which is the device that will help you in checking for power supply voltages?

3 What kind of information can you get from vendor software and hardware manuals?

4 List the problems faced when using vendor diagnostics.

Unit summary: Troubleshooting hardware components

Topic A

In this topic, you learned about various **environmental factors** that affect the **performance**, **reliability**, and **longevity** of networks. You learned that resolving a network difficulty depends on **troubleshooting, isolating,** and **eliminating** a problem. You also discussed **error messages** and **scenarios** pertaining to **physical** and **logical** causes of network trouble.

Topic B

In this topic, you learned about **tools** that are used for troubleshooting network problems. You learned that a **crossover cable** refers to a length of network cable that has been wired to provide a connection from one hub to another or from one network interface card to another. You also learned that a **tone generator** is a device that emits an audible tone to test primarily for continuity and that a **time domain reflectometer** is a sophisticated tool used to find a break in the middle of a cable.

Topic C

In this topic, you learned that **problem solving** is a process of **logically evaluating** the symptoms, **analyzing possible solutions**, and **eliminating improbable factors** until a resolution is reached. You also looked at **DIReCtional troubleshooting model**. You learned that **documentation** forms an essential part of your system troubleshooting and also about various **troubleshooting tools**.

Review questions

1 You are called to a site to investigate a workstation that cannot log onto the network. Upon investigating, you notice there is no traffic indicated on the workstation's NIC. What is your first course of action?

2 What could an electrical motor in the vicinity of your network cables cause?

3 Ideally, network cables should never cross power lines. If they must, at what angle should they cross?

4 Which of the following increases the possibility of static problems?

A Magnetic fields

B Low humidity

C Cool environments

D Dust, liquids, and other foreign bodies

5 Name the steps and devices that will help reduce static-related failures.

6 Name one cause of a network bottleneck.

7 What kind of environment is the best to improve computer network performance?

8 You must determine why a working network has suddenly lost eight workstations. They are all on the same hub. They can see each other, but no one else on the network. What is the probable cause?

9 Name the tool that can be used for opening systems, removing and replacing boards, and attaching cables.

10 List the reasons why it is recommended that you keep system inventory and resolution report information in an electronic format, such as a database.

Unit 9

TCP/IP fundamentals

Unit time: 45 minutes

Complete this unit, and you'll know how to:

A Discuss the evolution of TCP/IP.

B Discuss TCP/IP fundamentals, including protocols and ports.

Topic A: Evolution of TCP/IP

Explanation   Over time, TCP/IP has moved from being a specialty protocol used predominantly on UNIX-based minicomputers to the protocol of choice for many desktop computers. Its wide-spread support and flexible architecture were significant factors that made TCP/IP the universal default protocol to link dissimilar computer platforms such as UNIX, NetWare, OS/2, and Windows. TCP/IP is the current de facto standard for internetwork communications, a place it's likely to hold for the foreseeable future.

A brief history

TCP/IP's roots reach back into the Cold War and the USSR's launch of Sputnik 1 in 1957. Concerned about a perceived loss of ground in defense research, the U.S. Government set up the Advanced Research Projects Agency (ARPA). ARPA projects involved major universities throughout the United States, and in the summer of 1968 a plan was developed to link four of the sites together in an experimental computer network.

A technology called packet switching was selected. This was to become the most ambitious packet-switched network. A unique nature of the network was that computers at each site were of different types (IBM, DEC, and SDS), running different operating systems. The experiment proved a success, and by 1972 the ARPANET, as it was then known, linked most major U.S. universities.

Basic real-world requirements, such as remote logon capabilities and file transfer between computers, drove early development efforts. This led to the initial development of three main protocols for the ARPANET:

- **NCP.** This protocol provided host-to-host communications through routers, originally called Interface Message Processors (IMPs) and later known as Packet Switch Nodes (PSNs).
- **FTP.** This is a file transfer protocol developed for sending files between computers.
- **Telnet.** This was designed to support remote logon requirements.

The U.S. Government officially adopted ARPANET as the Defense Data Network (DDN) in 1982. The next year, NCP was replaced by a new layered protocol stack, including TCP and IP. Needed by Military Standard 1777 for all nodes on ARPANET, TCP/IP became an immediate standard. It was distributed with all versions of Berkeley UNIX and became the University Science Center's protocol of choice. In 1985, the National Science Foundation adopted TCP/IP as the protocol necessary for connection to their new NSFnet network.

Do it!   ## A-1:   Discussing the history of TCP/IP

Questions and answers

1 List the main protocols for the ARPANET.

2 In 1985, the National Science Foundation adopted the _____ protocol to connect to their NSFnet network.

RFCs

Explanation
Graduate students at four pilot universities were asked to define the original ARPANET protocols. When they learned that a group of professionals might take over the project at any time, they were careful not to be assertive in their early specifications, for fear of offending the professionals. With this in mind, the early documents were labeled *RFC* (Request for Comments) indicating that anybody could contribute anything and that nothing was official.

When it became obvious that no professional team was taking over, *RFCs* became the defining documents that set the standards for the Internet protocol suite. TCP and IP are both defined by RFCs. RFCs are also used for information and guidance notes. There are even April fool's RFCs created on a regular basis as Internet comic relief.

Unlike most documents defining protocol standards, for example those created by the ITU-T (International Telecommunications Union-Telecommunications Standardization Sector, formerly the CCITT, Comite Consultatif Internationale de Telegraphique et Telephonique or Consultative Committee on International Telephone and Telegraphy), you can read and understand RFCs with ease. This is due to the fact that they were designed to provoke comments from the widest possible audience. RFCs can be obtained by FTP or HTTP from a number of servers on the Internet, including www.faqs.org/rfcs and www.rfc-editor.org/rfc.html.

You might also request RFCs by standard mail from:

```
DDN Network Information Center
SRI International
Room EJ291
333 Ravenswood Avenue
Menlo Park, CA 94024
```

It is RFCs, and the culture that underlies them, that are TCP/IP's real strength. When new modifications or additions to TCP/IP are needed, someone will create a new RFC. After it's been published and any amendments or suggestions incorporated, it becomes an official protocol standard. This mechanism helps in making changes. Upgrades and improvements can be incorporated rapidly, so that quick adaptation can be made to meet changing requirements.

Do it!

A-2: Discussing RFCs

Questions and answers

1 What is the name given to the documents that define TCP/IP?

2 When does an RFC become an official standard protocol?

The Internet

Explanation

The Internet evolved from ARPANET. Today, the *Internet* is a public network that consists of a collection of diverse networks, each connecting a range of systems together for a distinct purpose. Included in the Internet are NSFnet, MILNET (which replaced ARPANET), and networks outside the U.S., such as JANET (the Joint Academic Network in the UK) and EUnet, the European commercial network. There is now an ever-expanding list of systems connected to the Internet, including most major academic institutions throughout the world, the U.S. defense establishment, and a rapidly growing number of commercial organizations and individuals.

The common denominator between these networks is the use of TCP/IP. By using TCP/IP, you can communicate between different computer systems, even those that use different communication methods. TCP/IP hides the computer types and communication methods from users on the Internet, so that they can communicate on a peer-to-peer basis.

Each Internet user has access to a wealth of information, most supplied free by Internet subscribers. TCP/IP shields users from the mechanics involved in providing the information. Users can communicate seamlessly with available computer systems regardless of their type.

Supported systems

TCP/IP isn't owned by any one organization or corporation, but accepted by almost all computer systems, and therefore it has value beyond the Internet. TCP/IP has become the obvious first choice for interconnectivity. The following is a partial list of supported systems:

- MS-DOS PCs and compatibles
- Microsoft Windows-family PCs and compatibles
- OS/2 PCs and compatibles
- Apple Macintosh
- Novell NetWare
- Banyan VINES
- DEC VAX VMS and ULTRIX
- IBM AS/400
- IBM VM or MVS mainframes
- UNIX-based systems

Though TCP/IP might not meet all networking needs, it fills the communication and connectivity requirements of most organizations.

Do it!   **A-3:   Discussing the Internet and supported systems**

Questions and answers

1 What is the Internet?

2 Name any five systems that support TCP/IP.

Topic B: TCP/IP fundamentals

This topic covers the following CompTIA Network+ exam objectives:

#	Objective
2.4	Differentiate between the following network protocols in terms of routing, addressing schemes, interoperability and naming conventions: • TCP / IP (Transmission Control Protocol / Internet Protocol)
2.10	Define the purpose, function and use of the following protocols used in the TCP / IP (Transmission Control Protocol / Internet Protocol) suite: • TCP (Transmission Control Protocol) • UDP (User Datagram Protocol) • FTP (File Transfer Protocol) • SFTP (Secure File Transfer Protocol) • TFTP (Trivial File Transfer Protocol) • SMTP (Simple Mail Transfer Protocol) HTTP (Hypertext Transfer Protocol) • HTTPS (Hypertext Transfer Protocol Secure) • POP3 / IMAP4 (Post Office Protocol version 3 / Internet Message Access Protocol version 4) • Telnet • SSH (Secure Shell) • ICMP (Internet Control Message Protocol) • ARP / RARP (Address Resolution Protocol / Reverse Address Resolution Protocol) • NTP (Network Time Protocol) • NNTP (Network News Transport Protocol) • SCP (Secure Copy Protocol) • LDAP (Lightweight Directory Access Protocol) • IGMP (Internet Group Multicast Protocol) • LPR (Line Printer Remote)
2.11	Define the function of TCP / UDP (Transmission Control Protocol / User Datagram Protocol) ports.

#	Objective
2.12	Identify the well-known ports associated with the following commonly used services and protocols:
	• 20 FTP (File Transfer Protocol)
	• 21 FTP (File Transfer Protocol)
	• 22 SSH (Secure Shell)
	• 23 Telnet
	• 25 SMTP (Simple Mail Transfer Protocol)
	• 53 DNS (Domain Name Server)
	• 69 TFTP (Trivial File Transfer Protocol)
	• 80 HTTP (Hypertext Transfer Protocol)
	• 110 POP3 (Post Office Protocol version 3)
	• 119 NNTP (Network News Transport Protocol)
	• 123 NTP (Network Time Protocol)
	• 143 IMAP4 (Internet Message Access Protocol version 4)
	• 443 HTTPS (Hypertext Transfer Protocol Secure)
2.13	Identify the purpose of network services and protocols (For example:
	• SNMP (Simple Network Management Protocol)
	• Zeroconf (Zero configuration)
	• LPD (Line Printer Daemon)

TCP/IP and OSI

Explanation   TCP/IP is a term used in the industry to refer to the Internet family of protocols. It is the default protocol for UNIX and has become a de facto standard for wide area networking. It is fully routable and is available on most system platforms. It provides utilities to facilitate communications and information sharing between dissimilar hardware platforms. Interest in the Internet and in setting up corporate intranets has helped fuel TCP/IP's growth.

TCP/IP is based on a five-layer architectural model, as shown in Exhibit 9-1. A similar approach is used in the *DoD (Department of Defense) reference model*, which uses four layers. With the DoD model, the Hardware and Network Interface layers of the TCP/IP model are combined into the Network Access layer. Some of the functionality that the OSI model defines as taking place in the session layer is described by the TCP/IP model as occurring at the transport layer. The rest of the session layer and presentation layer functionality is incorporated into the TCP/IP application layer.

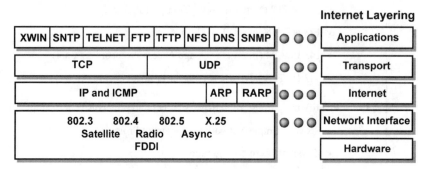

Exhibit 9-1: The five-layer architectural model of TCP/IP.

The five layers of the TCP/IP model are:

- **Hardware (Layer 1).** This layer is equivalent to the OSI physical layer. This is where physical aspects of transmitting and receiving packets are defined. Also sometimes referred to as the Physical layer. In the DoD model, this layer together with the Network interface layer make up the Network Access layer.

- **Network interface (Layer 2).** This layer describes the physical connection medium between hosts. It's responsible for packet frame content over different interfaces and low-level protocols. Protocols fall into two distinct categories, those associated with LANs and those associated with WANs. Common LAN protocols include Ethernet, Token Ring, and Token Bus. Common WAN protocols include Serial Line Internet Protocol (SLIP), Point-to-Point Protocol (PPP), X.25, Integrated Digital Services Network (ISDN), and Fast Packet Systems. Also sometimes referred to as the Data Link layer. In the DoD model, this layer together with the Hardware layer make up the Network Access layer.

- **Internet (Layer 3).** This layer works like the OSI network layer and is responsible for routing packets between different hosts and networks. Protocols included in this layer are Internet Protocol (IP), the Internet Control Message Protocol (ICMP), Address Resolution Protocol (ARP), and the Reverse Address Resolution Protocol (RARP). Routing protocols also reside at this layer. Two significant examples are Routing Information Protocol (RIP) and Open Shortest Path First (OSPF).

- **Transport (Layer 4).** In the DoD model, this layer is also called the host-to-host or Service layer. It is equivalent to the OSI transport layer, with some features of the session layer included. There are two protocols at this layer, Transmission Control Protocol (TCP) and User Datagram Protocol (UDP). They are responsible for end-to-end integrity of data packets transmitted across the network, supporting options for both connection-oriented and connectionless communication. They also provide communication with the higher-level application protocols.

- **Application (Layer 5).** This layer, also called the Process layer, is equivalent to OSI model layers 5 through 7. An ever-increasing number of protocols have been defined at this layer. Each of these is designed to support a specific application requirement. Significant applications, which were part of the original design goals, include File Transfer Protocol (FTP), Terminal network emulation (Telnet), and the Simple Mail Transfer Protocol (SMTP). Additional applications include Simple Network Management Protocol (SNMP), Domain Name System (DNS), and Network File Services (NFS).

TCP/IP applications usually conform to the client/server model. For that reason they come in two parts, a client application and a server application, commonly known as a daemon. Application protocols define the communication format between the client and server processes.

Do it!

B-1:   Discussing the architectural model of TCP/IP

Questions and answers

1 The four-layer model known as the _____ is sometimes used to represent the TCP/IP architecture.

2 Which layers of the DoD model contain the same functionalities that are incorporated in the session and presentation layers of OSI model?

3 What are the different layers of the DoD model?

TCP/IP suite

Explanation

All TCP/IP protocols are defined through RFCs. The specification documents are part of the public domain. They might be acquired and reproduced free of charge.

Core protocols, utilities, and services associated with the TCP/IP suite include:

- **IP (Internet Protocol).** It provides packet routing and delivery between computer systems. Because it is a connectionless protocol, there is no guarantee of proper sequencing or even arrival at the destination. Higher-level protocols should ensure data integrity and proper sequencing.

- **TCP (Transmission Control Protocol).** It provides acknowledged, connection-oriented communications. It includes fields for packet sequencing and acknowledgment, as well as source and destination socket identifiers so that you can communicate with higher-level protocols. Through these, TCP provides guaranteed delivery, proper sequencing, and data integrity checks. If errors occur during transmission, TCP is responsible for re-transmitting the data.

- **ICMP (Internet Control Message Protocol).** It is used to control and manage information transmitted by using TCP/IP. By using ICMP, nodes can share status and error information. This information can be passed to higher-level protocols, informing transmitting stations of unreachable hosts and providing insight into the detection and resolution of transmission problems. ICMP also helps re-route messages when a route is busy or has failed.

- **ARP/RARP (Address Resolution Protocol/Reverse Address Resolution Protocol).** ARP and RARP are maintenance protocols. They are used on local area networks so that hosts can translate IP addresses to the low-level MAC addresses that are needed to communicate at the data link layer. ARP is used to request a station's MAC address when only its IP address is known. After obtaining the MAC address, this information is stored in the requesting system's ARP cache for later use. Because the information can be broadcasted, it can also be used to update other systems. RARP is used when the MAC address is known, but not the IP address. Updated information, when received, is also cached.

- **UDP (User Datagram Protocol).** UDP is designed for connectionless, unacknowledged communications. By using IP as its underlying protocol carrier, UDP adds information about the source and the destination socket identifiers. UDP also supports optional checksums for verifying header and data integrity.

- **Telnet.** Telnet might be more accurately described as a connectivity utility. It is a simple remote terminal emulation application by which one host can connect and run a session on another. Variants have been implemented to handle different terminal data streams. For example, there are 3270 and 5250 variants for communications with IBM mainframe and minicomputers. Telnet uses TCP for acknowledged communications.

- **HTTP (Hyper Text Transfer Protocol).** HTTP provides the framework for exchanging text, images, sound, and video on the World Wide Web. HTTP servers, more frequently known as web servers, have an HTTP daemon that handles all HTTP requests as they arrive and delivers the content to the requesting host.

- **FTP (File Transfer Protocol).** FTP supports file transport between dissimilar systems. Telnet is used for initial user authentication. FTP supports interactive use assuming sufficient rights, directory searches and file operations are supported, as well as file format and character conversion.

- **SFTP (Secure File Transfer Protocol).** SFTP is similar to FTP, but is used for secure, encrypted file transfer. File transfers can be accomplished between similar and dissimilar systems.

- **TFTP (Trivial File Transfer Protocol).** TFTP is also similar to FTP in that it is a method to transfer files between dissimilar systems. However, TFTP doesn't support interactive use and is a bare-bones file transfer protocol used for special purposes.

- **SMTP (Simple Mail Transfer Protocol).** SMTP provides a mechanism for the exchange of mail information between systems. It is not concerned with the mail format, just the means by which it is transferred. SMTP is the most widely used service on the Internet.

- **POP3 (Post Office Protocol 3).** POP3 is a component of the TCP/IP suite that receives and holds e-mail for you at your Internet mail server. POP3 deals with the receiving of e-mail, while SMTP is responsible for transferring mail across the Internet.

- **IMAP (Internet Mail Access Protocol).** IMAP is an improvement over POP in some ways. The current version, IMAP4, allows the users to store, read, and organize messages on the server, allowing them to access mail from any computer. This, of course, uses more storage space on the server. Also, IMAP4 supports authentication, making it more secure than POP.

- **SNMP (Simple Network Management Protocol).** SNMP uses UDP to send control and management information between TCP/IP hosts. SNMP can collect management statistics and trap error events from a wide selection of devices on a TCP/IP network. An SNMP management station gives you the capabilities of remote device control and parameter management.

- **DNS (Domain Name System).** Through DNS, a common naming convention is provided throughout the Internet. It is implemented as a distributed database supporting a hierarchical naming system. DNS should have a static name to IP address mapping.

- **NFS (Network File Services).** NFS is the industry standard for UNIX-environment distributed file systems. It provides a common, transparent environment in which users can share files, regardless of their hardware platform.

- **NNTP (Network News Transport Protocol).** NNTP is the main protocol used for the management of the information posted on Usenet newsgroups. NNTP clients are typically included as part of a web browser suite, such as Netscape or Internet Explorer.

- **NTP (Network Time Protocol).** Used to synchronize computer clocks on a network.

- **SSH (Secure Shell or Secure Socket Shell).** Used for accessing a remote computer securely. When connecting to a remote computer using SSH, passwords and all data are encrypted, and authentication is accomplished via a digital certificate.

- **SCP (Secure Copy Protocol).** SCP is used to securely copy data from one network computer to another. It uses SSH for data encryption and authentication.

- **LDAP (Lightweight Directory Access Protocol).** LDAP is a protocol suite used to enable applications to access information stored in X.500-compatible directories. Information stored in these directories includes user names, email addresses, and so on. LDAP is based on the X.500 standard, but is much simpler in its implementation. LDAP is defined in RFC 1777 and 1778.

- **IGMP (Internet Group Multicast Protocol).** IGMP is the standard for Internet IP multicasting. IP multicasting enables messages to be sent to multiple hosts simultaneously. Through IGMP, a host machine communicates to a router that it needs to receive messages sent to a particular multicast group (of which the host is a member).

- **LPD/LPR (Line Printer Daemon/Line Printer Remote).** LPD/LPR enables the transfer of print jobs between networked workstations and printers. The LPD portion of the software typically resides in the printer; the LPR portion on the workstation.

HTTPS

Sometimes you'll see a Web URL that starts with HTTPS. This is a secure HTTP connection. Seeing HTTPS in a URL implies that the Web page requires data to and from the server to be encrypted. This secure connection uses Secure Sockets Layer (SSL) to encrypt TCP/IP transmissions. Most browsers display a closed padlock icon to indicate that a secure connection has been established between the client and server.

Zero configuration IP networking (zeroconf)

Zero configuration IP networking (zeroconf) enables sharing of files and resources in a TCP/IP network without manual (or dynamic) configuration. For example, with zeroconf, IP addresses are assigned automatically without the need of a DHCP server, name resolution is provided without requiring a DNS server, and resources in the network can be located without requiring a directory service.

Zeroconf is primarily used to create small home networks, or to create small networks on the fly, for example, during a business meeting.

Do it!

B-2:   Discussing the TCP/IP suite

Questions and answers

1 Which three protocols in the TCP/IP protocol suite support file transfers between dissimilar systems?

2 Which of the following TCP/IP protocols is a simple remote terminal emulation application by which one host can connect and run a session on another?

   A   SMTP

   B   NNTP

   C   Telnet

   D   SNMP

3 Which protocol is the standard for multicasting?

4 What is POP3 (Post Office Protocol 3)?

5 Zeroconf requires a DHCP server for IP address assignment. True or false?

Ports and sockets

Explanation

A common use of networks is the implementation of client/server applications, as shown in Exhibit 9-2. In these, the application is divided into two parts. The server performs background functions in response to client requests. The client provides an end user interface and a means of communicating with the server. Internetwork addresses are used to direct service requests to the appropriate server and return responses to the requesting client.

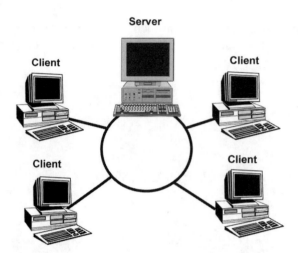

Exhibit 9-2: A representation of the Client/server environment

This process becomes more complicated when you consider that both the client and the server are likely to be running several simultaneous processes. Network packets need to contain not only the source and destination addresses, but the destination processes as well. In TCP / UDP, these are indicated by port identifiers.

How ports are used

Some ports are called well-known ports. These ports are the ports at which an application listens for a request by default. One example of a well-known port is port 80. This is the port on which the HTTP service listens. Another example is port 21. This is the port on which the FTP service listens.

When a computer receives a packet destined for port 21, that packet is given to the application running the FTP service. The FTP server then opens a private port for communication between itself and the client that sent the packet. This keeps their conversation distinct from other conversations the FTP service is having with other clients and thereby many FTP conversations can occur simultaneously.

The IP header takes care of getting data to the right destination host. TCP makes sure that the packet gets to the correct application on the receiving host by using its port address. The table shows examples of some well-known port addresses.

Port address	Application
20	FTP (File Transfer Protocol, data)
21	FTP (File Transfer Protocol, control)
22	SSH (Secure Shell)
23	Telnet
25	SMTP (Simple Mail Transfer Protocol)
53	DNS (Domain Name Server)
69	TFTP (Trivial File Transfer Protocol)
79	FINGER
80	HTTP (Hypertext Transfer Protocol)
110	POP3 (Post Office Protocol version 3)
119	NNTP (Network News Transport Protocol)
123	NTP (Network Time Protocol)
137	NNS
143	IMAP4 (Internet Message Access Protocol version 4)
161	SNMP (Simple Network Management Protocol)
443	HTTPS (Hypertext Transfer Protocol Secure)
1512	WINS
1701	L2TP
1723	PPTP

For an exhaustive list of well-known port addresses, see RFC 1700 "Assigned Numbers," October 1994. You can also check the IANA's Web site at www.iana.org/assignments/port-numbers for an updated list of common port assignments.

Windows sockets

Windows sockets, or Winsock, is a standard application interface defining communications between Windows and the underlying protocol stack. It provides a layer of abstraction, which can be used by applications on different computers to communicate with each other, without knowing the details of the underlying protocol. As long as the application and the protocol stack both comply with the Windows sockets standard, they should be able to communicate. Although originally designed for use over TCP/IP, other protocol stacks provide their own Winsock.

Before the introduction of this standard, there was a chance that applications and protocol stacks coming from different vendors would not work together. In 1992, work began on defining a standard for communication between a Microsoft Windows application and the underlying protocol stack by using a universal service-addressing scheme. This address was based on the protocol id, host address, and port/socket id.

There are two types of sockets available:

- **Stream.** This is used for reliable, two-way sequenced flow. It is used with TCP.
- **Datagram.** Less reliable, this supports unsequenced two-way flow. It is used with UDP.

Do it!

B-3: Discussing ports and sockets

Questions and answers

1 FTP uses port _____ and _____, and NNTP uses port _____.

   A   20 and 21,119

   B   21 and 25,79

   C   23 and 25,119

   D   21 and 22,121

2 What is a well-known port?

3 What is the port address of TFTP?

4 What is Winsock?

5 Distinguish between the stream and datagram sockets.

Unit summary: TCP/IP fundamentals

Topic A   In this topic, you learned about the history of **TCP/IP** and about **RFCs**, the **Internet**, and **supported systems**. You learned that TCP/IP is the current de facto standard for internetwork communications.

Topic B   In this topic, you learned about **TCP/IP** and **OSI**. You also learned about the **TCP/IP suite**, and **ports** and **sockets**. You learned that TCP/IP provides utilities to facilitate communications and information sharing between dissimilar hardware platforms.

Review questions

1 Your organization currently has a Windows 2000 network and a separate UNIX network. It's your responsibility to determine the most appropriate way to connect these two networks. Based solely on this information, select the correct statement from those shown.

   A TCP/IP can't be used because it's not a routable protocol.

   B TCP/IP should be used on the UNIX side, but not on the Windows 2000 side because it is an unsupported protocol.

   C TCP/IP is the most obvious choice because it's supported by both systems.

   D NetBEUI is the most obvious choice because it's supported by both systems.

2 Each system on a TCP/IP network is referred to as a:

   A Device

   B Client

   C Host

   D Port

3 Port 143 is what kind of a port for the IMAP4 protocol?

   A Often-used

   B Well-known

   C Secure

   D Private

4 Which of the following items must be installed on a Windows 2000 workstation to provide basic TCP/IP connectivity on a local area network?

   A Network Adapter

   B TCP/IP protocol

   C Client for Microsoft Networks

   D POP3 Client

   E SMTP Client

5 What is FTP?

6 Zeroconf is usually used to create what type of network?

Unit 10

TCP/IP addressing and subnetting

Unit time: 90 minutes

Complete this unit, and you'll know how to:

A Discuss TCP/IP addressing, and determine the IP address class and default subnet mask.

B Discuss subnetting and special addressing.

C Discuss the installation and configuration of TCP/IP.

Topic A: IP addressing

This topic covers the following CompTIA Network+ exam objectives:

#	Objective
2.4	Differentiate between the following network protocols in terms of routing, addressing schemes, interoperability and naming conventions: • TCP / IP (Transmission Control Protocol / Internet Protocol)
2.5	Identify the components and structure of IP (Internet Protocol) addresses (IPv4, IPv6) and the required setting for connections across the Internet.
2.6	Identify classful IP (Internet Protocol) ranges and their subnet masks (For example: Class A, B and C).
2.8	Identify the differences between private and public network addressing schemes.
2.9	Identify and differentiate between the following IP (Internet Protocol) addressing methods: • Static • Dynamic • Self-assigned (APIPA (Automatic Private Internet Protocol Addressing))
4.6	Given a scenario, determine the impact of modifying, adding or removing network services for network resources and users. (For example: • DHCP (Dynamic Host Configuration Protocol)

IP addresses

Explanation

Each networked system, known as a host under TCP/IP, must be identified as unique. One way of accomplishing this is through the machine's MAC address, the address encoded in each network adapter. Each machine must also have a unique IP address that identifies it for TCP/IP communication purposes.

To communicate on a network or on the Internet, computers must have unique identifiers to differentiate one computer from another. This is accomplished through IP addresses. An *IP address* is made up of a 32-bit address, or four-octet address. An IP address, also called a dotted quad, consists of four parts separated by decimal points.

Examples are:
- 199.250.196.1
- 128.30.3.10
- 127.0.0.1

IP addresses are similar to telephone numbers. When you call an IP address, through a variety of connection methods such as HTTP and FTP, you get connected to the computer to which that IP address is assigned. Every host has at least one unique IP address. In addition, every router has a unique IP address for every network adapter it possesses.

Address conversion

An IP address is typically referred to as a decimal representation of a binary number. For example, the IP address of 195.143.67.2 is actually 11000011.10001111.01000011.00000010 in binary. This way of representing an IP address is also known as *dotted decimal notation*.

Binary numbers and IP addresses are related to each other. For this, it is important to understand the conversions from binary to decimal and decimal to binary.

A *binary number* is made up of a series of bits or binary digits. Each bit can be set to either 0 or 1. Bit values are based on powers of 2 and on the digit position, as shown in Exhibit 10-1. As IP addresses are grouped in octets, sets of eight bits, you'll look at the position values for an octet.

Position	8	7	6	5	4	3	2	1
Power of 2	2^7	2^6	2^5	2^4	2^3	2^2	2^1	2^0
Decimal Value	128	64	32	16	8	4	2	1

Exhibit 10-1: A sample of binary numbers

Binary-to-decimal conversion

To convert binary to decimal, determine the decimal value for each of the bits, as shown in Exhibit 10-2 and Exhibit 10-3. Add up the bit values and you have the decimal number. Following are some examples:

11000000	11011010	10011101	00000011

Exhibit 10-2: A sample binary to decimal conversion

1	1	0	0	0	0	0	0
128	64	32	16	8	4	2	1
128	64	0	0	0	0	0	0

Exhibit 10-3: A sample binary to decimal conversion

The decimal value is 128+64, or 192, as shown in Exhibit 10-3.

1	1	0	1	1	0	1	0
128	64	32	16	8	4	2	1
128	64	0	16	8	0	2	0

Exhibit 10-4: A sample binary to decimal conversion

The decimal value is 128+64+16+8+2, or 218, as shown in Exhibit 10-4.

1	0	0	1	1	1	0	1
128	64	32	16	8	4	2	1
128	0	0	16	8	4	0	1

Exhibit 10-5: A sample binary to decimal conversion

The decimal value is 128+16+8+4+1, or 157, as shown in Exhibit 10-5.

0	0	0	0	0	0	1	1
128	64	32	16	8	4	2	1
0	0	0	0	0	0	2	1

Exhibit 10-6: A sample binary to decimal conversion

The decimal value is 2+1, or 3, as shown in Exhibit 10-6. Therefore, the binary number 11000000.11011010.10011101.00000011 is equal to decimal number 192.218.157.3.

Decimal-to-binary conversion

There are different methods you can use to convert decimal into binary. One is to set up a table, as shown in Exhibit 10-7.

128	goes into	----------	----------	times, leaving	
64	goes into	----------	----------	times, leaving	
32	goes into	----------	----------	times, leaving	
16	goes into	----------	----------	times, leaving	
8	goes into	----------	----------	times, leaving	
4	goes into	----------	----------	times, leaving	
2	goes into	----------	----------	times, leaving	
1	goes into	----------	----------	times, leaving	

Exhibit 10-7: A sample decimal to binary conversion

The fourth column provides bit values as shown in Exhibit 10-8 and Exhibit 10-9.

128	goes into	157	1	times, leaving	29
64	goes into	29	0	times, leaving	29
32	goes into	29	0	times, leaving	29
16	goes into	29	1	times, leaving	13
8	goes into	13	1	times, leaving	5
4	goes into	5	1	times, leaving	1
2	goes into	1	0	times, leaving	1
1	goes into	1	1	times, leaving	0

Exhibit 10-8: A sample decimal to binary conversion

2	goes into	1	0	times, leaving	1
1	goes into	1	1	times, leaving	0

Exhibit 10-9: A sample decimal to binary conversion

This gives a value, reading top to bottom, of 10011101 and agrees with the earlier example.

Do it!

A-1: Discussing IP addresses and conversions

Questions and answers
1 _____ is typically referred to as a decimal representation of a binary number.
2 What is a MAC address?
3 Bit values are based on powers of 3. True or false?
4 How do you convert a binary to a decimal?

The IP address classes

Explanation

IP addresses are grouped in different classes. Five address classes are supported by TCP/IP–these are named A, B, C, D, and E. Only Classes A, B, and C are assigned to the general Internet user community. Class D addresses are reserved for multicasting, and Class E addresses are reserved for experimental purposes. A value of 127 in the first octet is reserved for loopback testing.

A class can be determined from the first three bits, with the first two being sufficient to distinguish among the three primary classes.

The Class A network

In a Class A network, the first octet defines the network portion of the address. The last three octets are used for host addresses and subnet masking.

In the first octet, the first bit, also called the most significant or high order bit, must be set to zero. Only the seven least significant bits are used for addressing and might be set to either zero or one. This defines 128 Class A networks with network addresses ranging from 0 to 127. Out of these, only 126 are usable. Addresses 0 and 127 are reserved.

Class A networks support up to 16,777,214 (2^{24}-2) hosts. You can't use .0.0.0 or .255.255.255 as the host portion of the address.

Note: A host address of all 0s means "this network" and a host address of all 1s means "broadcast to all nodes." This is true for any host address regardless of address class.

The Class B network

In a Class B network, the first two octets are used for the network address. The last two octets are used for host addresses and subnetting.

The most significant bit of the first octet must be set to one. The second most significant bit must be set to zero. The next 14 bits are used for addressing purposes. This gives us 16,384 Class B networks, ranging from 128.0.0.0 to 191.255.0.0.

Class B networks support 65,534 (2^{16}-2) hosts. A Class B address is often used when setting up a moderate- to large-sized network. You can do this as long as you are not directly connecting to the Internet, if you are connecting through a firewall or some other means of isolating your network, or already have a Class B address assigned by InterNIC.

The Class C network

In a Class C network, the first three octets are used for the network address. The last octet is used for subnetting and host addresses.

The first 2 bits of the first octet must be set to one, and the following bit must be set to zero. The following 5 bits in the first octet, plus the following 16 bits from the next two octets are used to determine the network address. This provides 2,097,152 Class C networks, ranging from 192.0.0.0 to 223.255.255.0.

The following table provides a summary, showing each address class, the IP address range for each class, the number of networks possible within the class, and the number of hosts per network.

Class	Network range	# of networks	# of hosts per network
A	1.0.0.0-126.0.0.0	126	16,777,214
B	128.0.0.0-191.255.0.0	16,384	65,534
C	192.0.0.0-223.255.255.0	2,097,152	254
D	224.0.0.0-239.0.0.0	N/A	N/A
E	240.0.0.0-255.0.0.0	N/A	N/A

All Class A addresses are already allocated, and Class B addresses are difficult to obtain. New connections to the Internet are assigned Class C addresses. If this does not meet an organization's needs, multiple Class C addresses are assigned.

Note: All hosts on the same physical network must have the same network prefix. Hosts with dissimilar network prefixes must communicate through a router.

IPv6

Most of the IP subjects in this book deal with IPv4, which has 32-bit addresses made up of four 8-bit fields. The next generation of addressing, IPv6, allows for the growth that the inventors of the current system did not envision. Addresses in IPv6 are 128 bits, made up of eight 16-bit fields, allowing for a total of 2^{96} addresses.

The fields in an IPv6 address are represented by 16-bit hexadecimal numbers. So, each field can be from 0 to FFFF (65535 in decimal).

Aside from a larger number of addresses, IPv6 includes built-in features for better security, automatic addressing, and routing. For instance, IPSec (Internet Security Protocol), a security protocol for TCP/IP transmissions, is part if IPv6, but can be added as an enhancement to IPv4. To use IPv6 on a Windows Server 2003 or Windows XP machine, you need to install the Microsoft TCP/IP version 6 protocol in the Properties of a local area connection.

Do it!

A-2: Discussing IP addressing

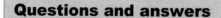

Questions and answers

1 How many IP address classes exist? What are they?

2 What does the first octet in a Class A network define?

3 How many hosts can a Class B address support?

   A   16,777,214

   B   2,097,152

   C   65,534

   D   254

   E   126

4 An IP address of 220.29.14.10 would be an example of a Class _____ address.

Managing addresses

Explanation TCP/IP is accepted as the standard for internetwork communications. Its popularity at the desktop continues to grow. However, TCP/IP was not designed for use with PCs. In fact, PCs did not exist when TCP/IP was developed. This has led to some potential problems:

- **Population size.** TCP/IP was designed for use with a limited population of mainframes and minicomputers. The large number of PCs in modern networks leads to problems in allocating unique IP addresses and has created an address shortage.

- **Portability.** PCs, by design, are portable. They can move easily between different physical locations. This means that they can be moved between logical subnets. Thus, PCs should have reconfigured IP addresses, or the need for dynamic address management.

- **End users.** The average PC user lacks the sophistication to fully understand IP address and subnetting concerns. This can sometimes lead to errors in address and configuration parameters.

Manufacturers, including Microsoft, have developed products and procedures to help work around these problems and simplify TCP/IP management. One standard that has emerged to assist in managing TCP/IP addresses is DHCP.

Dynamic Host Configuration Protocol (DHCP)

By using Dynamic Host Configuration Protocol (DHCP), TCP/IP systems configured as DHCP clients can automatically receive TCP/IP address configuration parameters. This is called *dynamic* addressing. *DHCP* is an open standard that is defined within RFC 2131, Dynamic Host Configuration Protocol. Microsoft was the first manufacturer to implement DHCP, but other companies have since then introduced both clients that use DHCP and servers that implement it.

DHCP provides an automated means of managing host IP addresses. The DHCP server is configured with IP address information, including a range of valid addresses and a lease period for those addresses. The range of valid addresses is called a *scope*.

It's important to note that two DHCP servers on the same network should never have scopes that overlap. Overlapping scopes would lead to address conflicts on the network as two different clients could receive the same IP address. In addition, any addresses that are within a scope should never be assigned manually to a host. This could easily cause address conflicts on the network.

DHCP clients can query the server for an IP address when they start up. The DHCP server then provides the DHCP client with a valid address for the network. In addition, you can configure the DHCP server to provide the client with appropriate default gateway addresses, WINS server addresses, and many other options.

An example

This example shows an implementation of DHCP on a small network.

You are the network administrator of a small local area network consisting of one Novell NetWare 6 server and 25 Windows 2000 workstations. You want to use TCP/IP as your network protocol and have IP addresses dynamically assigned to each computer. You do not have any external connectivity issues.

To meet this requirement, you decide to use the private Class C network address of 192.168.200.0 on your network and assign the address of 192.168.200.1 to your NetWare server. You then install the DHCP server component of NetWare 6 on the server and configure it with a pool of addresses in the range of 192.168.200.10 through 192.168.200.100. As each DHCP-enabled Windows 2000 client starts up on the network, the NetWare DHCP server will allocate a unique address to the client.

BOOTP

BOOTP (Bootstrap protocol) was an earlier solution to centralizing IP address management. When a machine using BOOTP is turned on, it broadcasts a request for an address to the network. The BOOTP server then sends back an address based on the requesting machine's MAC address. This protocol differs from DHCP in that the address for each machine is maintained in a static table, a configuration file, rather than being taken from a dynamic range. This configuration file allows an administrator to centrally manage the IP addresses for machines on the network – changing a machine's IP address requires only that the configuration file be edited.

Other IP addressing methods

In addition to IP addresses being assigned dynamically using DHCP, you can also assign them in one of two other ways:

- Statically
- Through self-assignment

These two address assignment methods differ greatly from dynamic address assignment and are usually used under specific circumstances.

Static addressing

With static IP addressing, you configure each host to always use a specific IP address. In Windows 2000/Server 2003/XP, you can assign IP addresses statically through the properties of the TCP/IP protocol. If you're not connected to the Internet or any other network—that is, if you're on a private network—it doesn't in theory really matter which addresses you assign, as long as they all have the same network prefix.

Typically, in this scenario, you would use a class C address for the network, and one of the available 254 host addresses for each host's static IP address. If, however, there is even a remote chance you might at some point connect your network to the Internet, you should choose the IP address range you're using very carefully, because you'll otherwise likely have to reassign IP addresses to all of the hosts in your network at that time to avoid addressing conflicts.

Self-assigned addressing (APIPA)

Another IP address assignment scheme involves Automatic Private Internet Protocol Addressing (APIPA). With APIPA, a client running Windows 98, ME, 2000, or XP that is configured to use DHCP for IP address assignment can assign an IP address to itself in the event that a DHCP server isn't available. The IP addresses used by APIPA clients are from a range of address reserved for this purpose (169.254.0.0 through 169.254.255.255).

In addition, the client also automatically configures the default class B subnet mask (255.255.0.0) for itself. The client checks for a DHCP server at regular intervals and continues to use the self-assigned IP address and subnet mask until a DHCP server becomes available. APIPA was designed with small, private networks in mind to make use of the ease of DHCP even if no DHCP server is configured or if a DHCP server may occasionally not be available.

Choosing an IP addressing method

Which method you end up using depends on your network environment. In a small network that's not connected to the Internet, static addressing is an easy way to get users connected quickly, without the need to set up and configure DHCP.

In larger networks, or networks that are connected to the Internet, dynamic addressing makes more sense because it reduces or removes the likelihood of IP address conflicts, reduces administrative overhead, and, if you're connected to the Internet, makes better use of the IP addresses assigned to your organization. APIPA is usually used by small organizations whose networks consist of fewer than 25 clients without routers.

Do it!
A-3: Discussing IP addressing methods

Questions and answers
1 What network service is used to automatically assign IP addresses?
2 What is a scope?
3 In the properties of a workstation's TCP/IP protocol, you specify that the host should use the IP address 192.168.200.15. Which addressing method are you employing?
4 Which protocol is used by workstations that self-assign IP addresses?
5 Though TCP/IP is accepted as the standard for internetwork communications, what are the different problems that arise while implementing TCP/IP?

Topic B: Subnetting and special addressing

This topic covers the following CompTIA Network+ exam objectives:

#	Objective
2.4	Differentiate between the following network protocols in terms of routing, addressing schemes, interoperability and naming conventions: • TCP / IP (Transmission Control Protocol / Internet Protocol)
2.6	Identify classful IP (Internet Protocol) ranges and their subnet masks (For example: Class A, B and C).
2.7	Identify the purpose of subnetting.
2.8	Identify the differences between private and public network addressing schemes.
2.13	Identify the purpose of network services and protocols (For example: • NAT (Network Address Translation) • NFS (Network File System)
3.7	Given a connectivity scenario, determine the impact on network functionality of a particular security implementation (For example: • Port blocking / filtering
3.9	Identify the main characteristics and purpose of extranets and intranets.

Subnetting

Explanation

The primary reason for subnetting relates to network performance and available bandwidth (as shown in Exhibit 10-10). Without separate networks, each transmission would be broadcast across the internetwork, waiting for the destination system to respond. As the network grows, traffic increases until it exceeds the available bandwidth.

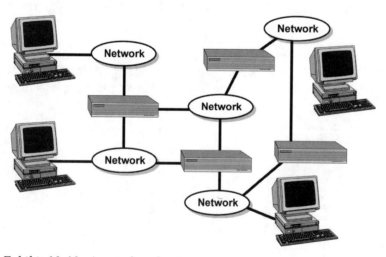

Exhibit 10-10: A sample subnet

Subnet masks

Each IP address will have an associated default subnet mask dividing the address into its network prefix and host suffix. Different IP address classes use a certain number of octets for the network prefix and a certain number of octets for the host address. For example, the default subnet mask for a Class C address, such as 221.20.53.89, would be 255.255.255.0. This indicates that the first three octets, 221.20.53, indicate the network prefix and the last octet, 89, the host address.

The network portion identifies where the host is located, and the host portion identifies the device connected to that network.

The default subnet masks for Class A, B, and C addresses are:

- **Class A**: 255.0.0.0.
- **Class B**: 255.255.0.0
- **Class C**: 255.255.255

Your subnet mask is restricted by your choice of network ID. With a Class A network, your subnet mask must be at least 8 bits long. A Class B subnet mask must be at least 16 bits long, and a Class C address must be at least 24 bits long.

Creating a custom subnet mask

Fortunately, TCP/IP helps you to divide a network into subnets by creating a custom subnet mask that tells TCP/IP to consider some of the bits, which by default would identify a host, as part of the network address. For example, the Class C network of 204.32.23.0 could use a subnet mask of 255.255.255.224 instead of the default mask of 255.255.255.0 if you wanted the first 3 bits of the last octet to be used to identify the network the host resides on. This effectively helps you to subdivide the assigned network address into multiple subnets.

When a network is divided into subnets, all members of that subnet will have the same network prefix. Routers divide the networks and provide communication between them. Packets bound for a destination within the local network are kept local. Only packets bound for other networks are propagated across the router, moving from router to router. Thus, overall traffic levels are reduced by subnetting.

Do it!

B-1:   Discussing subnet masks

Questions and answers

1   What is the default subnet mask for a Class C TCP/IP address?

   A   255.0.0.0

   B   255.255.0.0

   C   255.255.255.0

   D   255.255.255.255

2   Given the default subnet mask for a Class C address, how would you identify the network and host portions of the address?

3   Consider the IP address 192.168.1.43 with the subnet mask of 255.255.255.0. What are the network and host IDs for this address?

Special addressing

Explanation

There are several special addressing structures, as shown in the following table. These fall under the guidelines of generally accepted principles. These conventions are documented and used on the Internet and are part of the Internet Protocol.

Destination	Network	Host
Host on this Net	All Zeros	Host ID
Local Broadcast	All Ones	All Ones
Directed Broadcast	Network ID	All Ones
Loopback	127	Anything

As these addresses are defined as having a special use, they are not available as host addresses. Some problems with IP addresses include:

- Addresses with an inappropriate subnet mask
- Class D addresses
- Class E addresses
- Duplicate addresses on the same network
- Two systems, separated by a router, with the same network address
- Two systems on the same physical network with different network addresses

A valid address will be unique, will have a network address falling in the defined class range, and will have an appropriate subnet mask.

Private networks

A *private network* is one that will not be connecting directly to the Internet. The term *intranet* is commonly being used to refer to internetwork environments of this type. The two most common intranet examples are:

- Networks with no need to connect to the Internet
- Networks connecting to the Internet through an application gateway (such as Microsoft's Proxy Server) that remaps IP addresses

The Internet Assigned Numbers Authority (IANA) has set aside three sets of addresses for use on intranets:

- 10.0.0.0 - 10.255.255.255
- 172.16.0.0 - 172.31.255.255
- 192.168.0.0 - 192.168.255.255

There are some obvious disadvantages to using these addresses. The foremost disadvantage is that it will be impossible to connect directly to the Internet or reference these addresses from the Internet; they have no meaning in the global Internet community. Routers connecting to the Internet typically filter out any reference to these addresses.

Note: A private network is the opposite of a public network, such as the Internet.

NAT (network address translation)

Network address translation (NAT) refers to an IP gateway's translating private network addresses into valid Internet addresses.

For example, a small college has about 1,000 computers on campus, but typically only 100-200 users access the Internet at any given time. In this case, administrators can address machines on the private campus network according to any scheme they see fit, and have only a class C address range for external access. When a machine attempts to access the Internet, the IP gateway, using NAT, translates between the internal private address and the valid external address for both incoming and outgoing traffic. This has the added security advantage of effectively hiding internal machines from the Internet.

Do it!

B-2: Discussing special addressing and private networks

Question and answers
1 What are the features of a valid address?
2 What is the disadvantage of private network addresses?
3 What is the purpose of NAT?

Topic C: TCP/IP configuration

This topic covers the following CompTIA Network+ exam objective:

#	Objective
4.6	Given a scenario, determine the impact of modifying, adding or removing network services for network resources and users. (For example:
	• DNS (Domain Name Service)
	• WINS (Windows Internet Name Server)

Using TCP/IP

Explanation

The TCP/IP protocol is installed by default on Windows 2000/Server 2003/XP computers. You can disable it, but you cannot remove it. Using TCP/IP makes sense in many different situations and it is the de facto standard for network communications today.

As a general guideline, use TCP/IP:

- When you have significant routing requirements
- When you need UNIX connectivity
- If you want to employ TCP/IP utilities in network management
- In environments where TCP/IP is already in use
- In Internet/Intranet environments

Requirements for a flexible communications protocol will continue to grow as intelligent devices, including home appliances, become the rule. In addition, home networks will soon become as common as business networks.

Note that if your network has a DHCP server present or if you select automatic private addressing, computers in the network will dynamically receive an IP address when it starts up. If your network uses a static addressing scheme where each computer has an IP address manually assigned, you'll need to perform some additional configuration prior to participating as a host on your TCP/IP network.

TCP/IP configuration

To configure TCP/IP on a Windows Server 2003/XP computer, open the properties of the Local Area Connection. Then select Internet Protocol (TCP/IP), as shown in Exhibit 10-11.

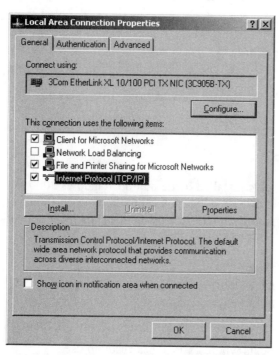

Exhibit 10-11: The Local Area Connection dialog box on a Windows Server 2003 computer.

Click Properties to display the Properties dialog box for this protocol. You can also double-click Internet Protocol (TCP/IP) from the Network dialog box to display the same Properties dialog box. On the Internet Protocol (TCP/IP) Properties dialog box, you can access two properties sheets, General and Alternate Configuration.

General

By using the General tab, as shown in Exhibit 10-12, you can either specify an IP address, subnet mask, and default gateway for the computer or have the computer obtain the information automatically by using a DHCP server. The same holds true for DNS server address information.

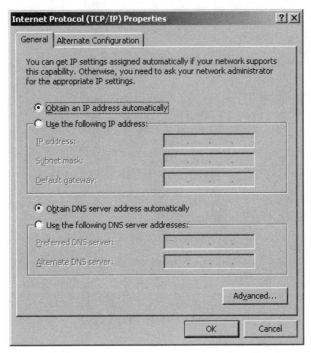

Exhibit 10-12: The Internet Protocol (TCP/IP) Properties dialog box showing the General tab

An important consideration is that two computers on the same network (private or public) can't have the same IP address. DHCP servers help eliminate duplicate IP addresses by automatically configuring TCP/IP on client machines.

To assign a static IP address, select Use the following IP address and enter the IP address. Then, place the cursor into the Subnet mask field and the subnet mask field will be automatically populated with the default subnet mask for the class into which the IP address falls. If you're subnetting, adjust the subnet mask as appropriate.

If you're configuring IP address information manually, and the computer needs to communicate with other hosts in a different subnet or if it needs to connect to the Internet, you'll also need to define a default gateway. To add a gateway, enter the appropriate IP address in the Default gateway field.

Alternate Configuration

The Alternate Configuration tab, shown in Exhibit 10-13, lets you specify alternate settings for IP address assignment in the event that the machine belongs to more than one network. Note that if you specify a manual IP address on the General tab, the Alternate Configuration tab no longer displays.

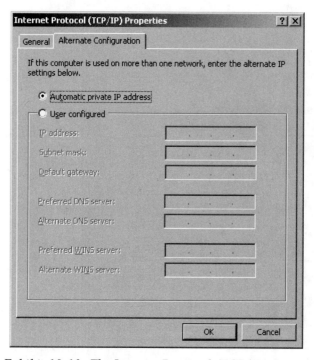

Exhibit 10-13: The Internet Protocol (TCP/IP) Properties dialog box showing the Alternate Configuration tab

Back on the General tab, click Advanced to access four additional properties sheets, as outlined below. Note that in Windows 2000, you'll find these sheets on the Internet Protocol (TCP/IP) Properties dialog box.

- IP Settings
- DNS
- WINS
- Options

IP Settings

To access the IP Settings tab, shown in Exhibit 10-14, click Advanced. On this tab, if you have previously configured an IP address manually on the General tab, you can configure additional IP addresses and subnet masks to be used by this machine. To do so, click Add and enter the appropriate IP address and Subnet mask information. If you have DHCP enabled, the Add button will be unavailable. Further, if the computer needs to communicate with other hosts in a different subnet or if it needs to connect to the Internet, you can also define a default gateway. To add a gateway, enter the appropriate IP address in the Default gateway field.

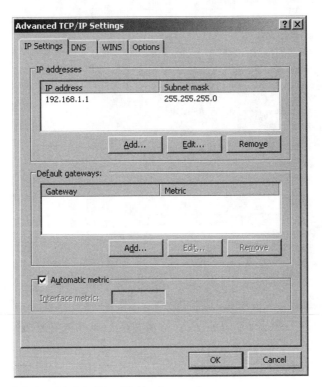

Exhibit 10-14: The IP Settings tab

DNS

You can configure Domain Name System parameters on your workstation by using the DNS tab, as shown in Exhibit 10-15. A DHCP server might automatically configure your workstation with DNS information and any manual changes on this tab might result in an inability to resolve names on the network.

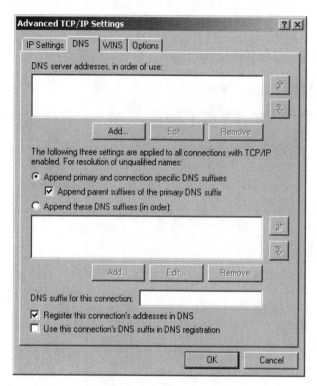

Exhibit 10-15: The Advanced TCP/IP Settings dialog box with the DNS tab activated

WINS

You can enable or disable Windows Internet Name Services (WINS) resolution for your workstation by using the WINS Configuration tab, as shown in Exhibit 10-16. A DHCP server might automatically configure your workstation for WINS. Any manual changes on this tab might result in an inability to resolve names on the network. You can also enable or disable support for NetBIOS over TCP/IP, or specify that NetBIOS information is provided by a DHCP server. If you have an LMHOSTS file with NetBIOS information for NetBIOS name resolution, you can also specify on this tab to use this file. You'll have to import the file by clicking on Import LMHOSTS.

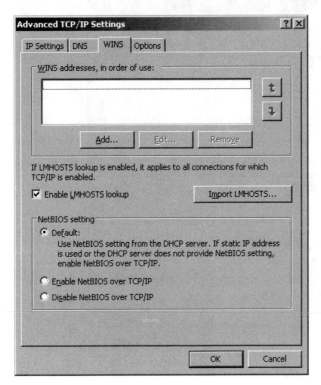

Exhibit 10-16: The WINS tab

Options

The Options tab, shown in Exhibit 10-17 lets you configure IP security (IPSec) and TCP/IP filtering settings. To configure these settings, select the appropriate setting and click Properties. By default, IPSec and TCP/IP filtering are disabled. IPsec is a set of protocols often used as part of implementing virtual private networks (VPNs), which enables secure data transmission over a public network (the Internet). TCP/IP filtering is used to provide inbound access control. With TCP/IP filtering enabled, you can specify which TCP UDP ports and which IP protocols to allow.

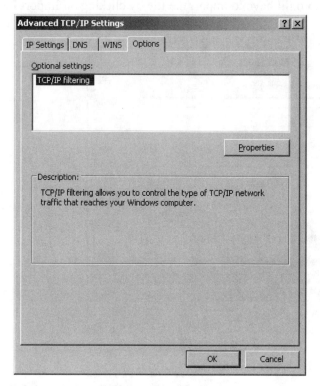

Exhibit 10-17: The Options dialog box

Do it!

C-1: Configuring TCP/IP

Here's how

1 In Windows Server 2003, choose **Start**, **Control Panel**, **Network Connections**

   In Windows XP, choose **Start**, **Control Panel**, then double-click **Network Connections**

2 Right-click **Local Area Connection** and select **Properties**

3 Select **Internet Protocol (TCP/IP)** and click **Properties**

4 Select **Use the following IP address**

   Enter the IP address and the subnet mask information as outlined in Exhibit 10-18

5 Verify that Use the following DNS server addreses is selected

6 Enter the DNS server address for the Preferred DNS server, as outlined in Exhibit 10-18.

7 Click **OK**

8 Click **Close**

9 Note the IP address specified by your instructor

10 Close any open dialog boxes

Student#	IP address	Subnet mask	Preferred DNS server
Student01	192.168.1.1	255.255.255.0	192.168.1.1
Student02	192.168.1.2	255.255.255.0	192.168.1.1
Student03	192.168.1.3	255.255.255.0	192.168.1.3
Student04	192.168.1.4	255.255.255.0	192.168.1.3
Student05	192.168.1.5	255.255.255.0	192.168.1.5
Student06	192.168.1.6	255.255.255.0	192.168.1.5
Student07	192.168.1.7	255.255.255.0	192.168.1.7
Student08	192.168.1.8	255.255.255.0	192.168.1.7
Student09	192.168.1.9	255.255.255.0	192.168.1.9
Student10	192.168.1.10	255.255.255.0	192.168.1.9
Student11	192.168.1.11	255.255.255.0	192.168.1.11
Student12	192.168.1.12	255.255.255.0	192.168.1.11
Student13	192.168.1.13	255.255.255.0	192.168.1.13
Student14	192.168.1.14	255.255.255.0	192.168.1.13
Student15	192.168.1.15	255.255.255.0	192.168.1.15
Student16	192.168.1.16	255.255.255.0	192.168.1.15
Student17	192.168.1.17	255.255.255.0	192.168.1.17
Student18	192.168.1.18	255.255.255.0	192.168.1.17
Student19	192.168.1.19	255.255.255.0	192.168.1.19
Student20	192.168.1.20	255.255.255.0	192.168.1.19
Student21	192.168.1.21	255.255.255.0	192.168.1.21
Student22	192.168.1.22	255.255.255.0	192.168.1.21
Student23	192.168.1.23	255.255.255.0	192.168.1.23
Student24	192.168.1.24	255.255.255.0	192.168.1.23

Exhibit 10-18: Network information table

Unit summary: TCP/IP addressing and subnetting

Topic A   In this topic, you learned about **IP addresses**. You also learned how to convert **binary to decimal** and **decimal to binary**. You learned five address classes are supported by TCP/IP: Classes A, B, C, D, and E. You also learned about **Dynamic Host Configuration Protocol (DHCP)**. You learned how a DHCP server reduces the amount of administration necessary on a TCP/IP-based network.

Topic B   In this topic, you learned about the role of **subnets** and you learned how **subnetting** works. You also learned about **special addressing** and **private** networks.

Topic C   In this topic, you learned how to use **TCP/IP**. You learned about the procedures necessary to **configure TCP/IP protocol support** on a Windows Server 2003 and Windows XP computer.

Review questions

1 Define subnetting.

2 As a network administrator, you have configured your workstations to run TCP/IP. To make IP address management easier, what would you implement to help TCP/IP clients to automatically receive configuration parameters?

   A SMTP

   B DHCP

   C SNMP

   D NNTP

3 You are the network administrator for a medium-sized law firm. A new application you're planning to implement should have the TCP/IP protocol be installed on each of your 45 Windows XP workstations and your single Windows Server 2003 server. You don't have any other internetworking requirements. What would be the best way to implement TCP/IP on your network?

4 DHCP only provides clients with an IP address. True or false?

5 Is the IP address 242.1.2.254 a valid address for a host on a TCP/IP network? Why or why not?

6 What is the purpose of having various classes of IP addresses?

Unit 11

Name resolution

Unit time: 45 minutes

Complete this unit, and you'll know how to:

A Discuss the role of the HOSTS file and DNS.

B Discuss the role of NETBIOS, LMHOSTS file, and WINS.

Topic A: The HOSTS file and Domain Name System

This topic covers the following CompTIA Network+ exam objectives:

#	Objective
2.13	Identify the purpose of network services and protocols (For example:
	• DNS (Domain Name Service)
4.6	Given a scenario, determine the impact of modifying, adding or removing network services for network resources and users. (For example:
	• DNS (Domain Name Service)

Introducing name resolution

Explanation

It's easier to remember a host name that is in a friendly format as opposed to its IP address. That is, it's easier for a user on the network to search for files on a server called FRODO than to remember that the server's IP address is 192.168.200.2. While surfing the World Wide Web, it would be easier for you to go to www.cnn.com for your daily news than to remember to go to 207.25.71.23.

However, computers need the IP address to converse with each other. *Name resolution* is the process of converting the friendly name to its IP address. For this reason, name resolution is a vital part of network configuration and management.

Name resolution in Windows is handled through four different methods:

- HOSTS files
- LMHOSTS files
- WINS servers
- DNS servers

On most UNIX platforms, name resolution is handled through the use of:

- HOSTS files
- DNS servers

Note: An additional service called Samba is available that provides NetBIOS over TCP/IP communications in Windows systems. This will give UNIX systems access to WINS servers and NetBIOS name resolution methodologies.

Novell NetWare uses:

- HOSTS files
- DNS servers

Host name resolution

It's important to have a method of mapping IP addresses to friendly names. There are two methods you can use to accomplish this on a TCP/IP network: through the use of a HOSTS File or through Domain Name System (DNS). It is important to note that both HOSTS and DNS can be used by any host on a TCP/IP network, regardless of the operating system. Windows 95/98, Windows NT/2000/Server 2003/XP, and UNIX workstations can all resolve names by using either of these methods.

Name resolution using a HOSTS file uses a locally stored ASCII text file. The file is named HOSTS and is stored in different places on different operating systems:

- Windows 95/98 machines store HOSTS in the \WINDOWS directory.
- Windows NT/2000 systems store HOSTS in the \WINNT\SYSTEM32\DRIVERS\ETC directory.
- Windows Server 2003/XP systems store HOSTS in the \WINDOWS\SYSTEM32\DRIVERS\ETC directory.
- NetWare servers store HOSTS in the SYS\ETC directory.
- UNIX-based systems store HOSTS in the \ETC directory.

As this is an ASCII text file, it can be edited by using any ASCII text editor, but you might need administrative rights on the specific system to make any changes.

Each HOSTS file entry will contain an IP address, a TAB or SPACE, and one or more symbolic name(s). A TAB is the preferred delimiter. The IP address maps to the symbolic name next to it.

```
193.121.98.65 mainserver.wavetech.com
193.121.98.78 wavesite WAVESITE wavesite.wavetech.com
#194.150.30.30 oldserver.wavetech.com OLDSERVER oldserver
```

Each IP address should appear only once in the HOSTS file. A HOSTS file with duplicate IP entries will not resolve names correctly. Any number of aliases, each separated by a TAB, might be included in the line. Host names are case-sensitive, so host names are entered as both lowercase and uppercase. Fully Qualified Domain Names (FQDN), in the format of servername.domain.organizational_domain can be used in the HOSTS file as well.

If you decide to use HOSTS name resolution, edit the sample HOSTS file. Include the IP addresses and host names with which you need to communicate. The number symbol (#) is used to designate a line as a comment. A line that begins with this symbol will not be processed.

If a HOSTS file exists, it will be parsed by TCP/IP when a command is issued with a symbolic name. Depending on how your system is configured, other methods, such as DNS, might first be consulted for name resolution.

HOSTS name resolution does not support net use or other Microsoft network-style commands. These must be managed through NetBIOS name resolution.

Do it!

A-1: Discussing HOSTS files

Questions and answers

1 Assuming Windows Server 2003 was installed in the directory C:\WINDOWS, where would the HOSTS file be located?

2 What line or lines would you add to a HOSTS file to have IP address 192.121.98.67 map to the names wave, Wave, and WAVE?

Domain Name System

Explanation   Imagine that you are the administrator of a large LAN with approximately 250 hosts that are running UNIX, Windows 2000, and Windows XP. Each of these machines has a HOSTS file that must be maintained to provide name resolution. But if you need to change the HOSTS file on every machine on your network, it could be a time-consuming process.

An alternative to using HOSTS files for name resolution is the Domain Name System, or DNS (as shown in Exhibit 11-1). All major network operating system families, including Windows 2000 Server/Windows Server 2003, Novell NetWare, and UNIX/Linux provide DNS server software that can store hostname-to-IP address resolution data in a centralized database that DNS clients can access. This alleviates the necessity of maintaining separate HOSTS files on each host.

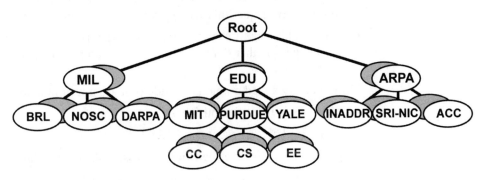

Exhibit 11-1: The Domain Name System

DNS is a hierarchical naming system for identifying hosts on a private network or on the Internet in the format *somewhere.domain*, for example, wavetech.com. The format is sometimes described as *host.subnet.domain*. The hierarchical structure identifying domain names is called the *domain name space*. Each domain can be divided into subdomains, and these into host names, with a period acting as a delimiter between each portion of the name.

Domains are the root level of the DNS identifiers and include organization types and countries. Each domain name is unique. This root is managed by the Internet Corporation for Assigned Names and Numbers (ICANN). Each domain is managed by a different organization, which administers its own subdomain. Each subdomain must be unique to the domain, and administration of that subdomain is normally assigned to the organization it represents.

DNS domains

The following are some DNS domains you might encounter.

Organizational domains:

- **com** — Usually a company, commercial institution, or an organization. For example, the DNS name for Wave Technologies International is wavetech.com.
- **edu** — This identifies educational institutions. For example, mit.edu is the name of Massachusetts Institute of Technology.
- **gov** — These are government organizations, such as nasa.gov for the National Aeronautic and Space Administration.
- **mil** — This represents a military site, such as af.mil for the United States Air Force.
- **net** — This is used for Internet gateways and administrative hosts, such as internic.net for the Internet Network Information Center.
- **org** — This identifies noncommercial organizations or organizations that don't fit easily into other domain classes. For example, the address for National Public Radio is npr.org.

More recently added domains include (but are not limited to):

- **biz** — This identifies businesses.
- **name** — This represents individuals.
- **pro** — This identifies certified professionals and affiliated bodies.

Some country domains are given in the following table.

Domain	Country
us	United States
au	Australia
ca	Canada
fr	France
de	Germany
uk	United Kingdom

Country domains also support subdomains. For example, the United States has a subdomain for each of the 50 states. The United Kingdom supports subdomains, such as co.uk for commercial organizations and ac.uk for educational institutions.

DNS name resolution

DNS names are maintained and managed through DNS servers. Each top-level domain, such as com, will have one or more DNS servers. It contains information about all of the domains that it supports. DNS servers are also supported at the subdomain level, which will contain the host name information. Subdomains can be further divided into logical zones, with a server managing all of the hosts for that zone.

When name resolution is needed, the request is handled through name servers. A name server interprets the FQDN it receives to determine its specific address. If the local name server does not contain the requested information, the request is passed on to other name servers that are likely to contain the information. The query continues until the name and IP address are located.

Name servers will locally cache domain name space information learned during the query process. The information then becomes locally available to the local hosts.

DNS resolution example

You are a Web developer for Alphahost, Inc. (alphahost.com) and you have a friend who is located in London, England. He has developed a Web site for his company, Python Co. that he has asked you to critique. It is located at www.pythonco.uk. When you type www.pythonco.uk in your Web browser, the Web page loads. Your browser resolves www.pythonco.uk to its IP address.

A simplified view of the process that takes place to resolve the domain name is illustrated in Exhibit 11-2 and Exhibit 11-3.

The example used in this book is oversimplified. However, the important thing to remember is that the domain name resolution takes the path of ALPHAHOST.COM, COM, UK, and PYTHONCO.UK.

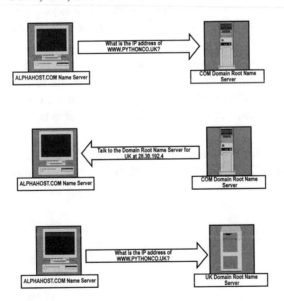

Exhibit 11-2: A representation of the process that resolves the domain name

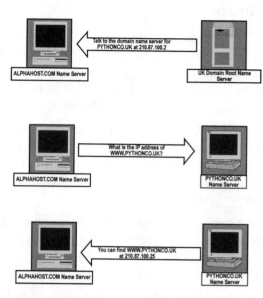

Exhibit 11-3: A representation of the process that resolves the domain name

DNS client configuration

You can use the DNS tab, shown in Exhibit 11-4, in the Advanced TCP/IP Settings of a Local Area Connection's TCP/IP Properties through the Control Panel's Network Connections utility to configure a Windows 2000/Server 2003/XP computer. You can use DNS to resolve the names of Internet or UNIX computer(s). The specifications in the DNS tab are:

- **DNS Server addresses, in order of use.** This lets you specify the IP addresses of DNS servers you want to use. The query is done in the order in which the server's IP addresses are listed.

- **Append primary and connection specific DNS suffixes.** Specifies that only the primary domain suffix is appended during name resolution for unqualified names on this machine, unless you also have connection-specific DNS suffixes configured, in which case those suffixes would also be appended during name resolution.

- **Append these DNS suffixes (in order).** You can use this to append specified DNS domain suffixes to host names during name resolution.

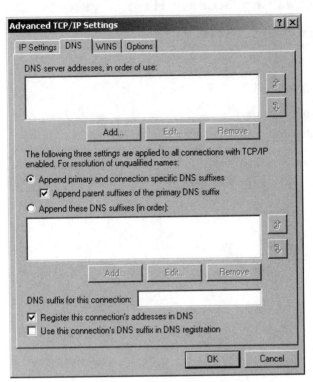

Exhibit 11-4: The Advanced TCP/IP Settings dialog box in Windows Server 2003

Do it!

A-2: Discussing Domain Name System

Questions and answers

1 Which of the following operating systems can take advantage of DNS?

   A   Windows NT/2000/Server 2003/XP

   B   Windows 95/98

   C   Novell NetWare

   D   UNIX-based workstations

   E   All of the above

   F   None of the above

2 List three organizational domains.

3 How does a name server handle a name resolution request?

Topic B: NetBIOS name resolution

This topic covers the following CompTIA Network+ exam objectives:

#	Objective
2.13	Identify the purpose of network services and protocols (For example: • WINS (Windows Internet Name Service)
4.6	Given a scenario, determine the impact of modifying, adding or removing network services for network resources and users. (For example: • WINS (Windows Internet Name Service)

The role of NetBIOS

Explanation

NetBIOS, as shown in Exhibit 11-5, is an application layer (OSI Model Session layer) interface between the network operating system and lower-level functions.

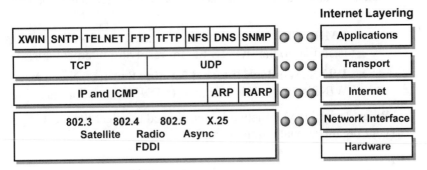

Exhibit 11-5: The NetBIOS

NetBIOS is implemented across most popular network protocols, including NetBEUI, IPX/SPX, and TCP/IP. The NetBIOS implementation that operates over TCP/IP is called *NBT*. NWLINK, Microsoft's implementation of IPX/SPX, supports NetBIOS names through *NWNBLink*. NetBIOS support is provided with the following operating systems:

- Microsoft LAN Manager
- Windows NT/2000/XP/Server 2003
- Windows for Workgroups
- Windows 95/98
- IBM PC LAN and LAN Server
- DEC Pathworks
- HP LM/X

In addition to these, NetBIOS support is included with most other popular network operating systems, including Novell NetWare.

NetBIOS names

NetBIOS is a relatively easy-to-use interface. A full range of session-based datagram and broadcast services are provided for identifying destinations through NetBIOS names. This is done with eighteen simple commands.

All NetBIOS activity is based on NetBIOS names. Each network device supporting NetBIOS communications must have a unique NetBIOS name, up to 15 characters long. These include:

- Computers
- Windows NT/2000/Server 2003 Domains
- Workgroups
- User names

Note that Windows 2000 and Windows 2003 domain names are based on DNS, but these domains also have a NetBIOS name to ensure backward compatibility. Often the leftmost part of the DNS name is the NetBIOS name, but you can specify a different NetBIOS name.

In an internetwork TCP/IP environment, it is necessary to support resolution between NetBIOS names and IP addresses. Microsoft provides two methods of supporting this name resolution:

- **LMHOSTS.** Name resolution is based on a locally stored ASCII text file. This is similar to the HOSTS file for resolving Internet names.
- **WINS (Windows Internet Naming Service).** Name resolution is based on WINS servers. This is similar to DNS servers for resolving Internet names.

When designing your network, you'll need to select the most appropriate method for your organizational requirements.

Do it!   **B-1: Discussing NetBIOS**

Questions and answers

1 Which of the following items have a NetBIOS name?

   A   Windows NT/2000/Server 2003 domains

   B   Windows 98 workstations

   C   NetWare servers

   D   Windows 95 workgroups

   E   All of the above

2 What is NBT?

3 State the difference between the two methods of supporting name resolution provided by Microsoft.

The LMHOSTS file

Explanation

The LMHOSTS file is stored in the \WINDOWS\SYSTEM32\DRIVERS\ETC directory on a Windows Server 2003/XP computer and in \WINNT\SYSTEM32\DRIVERS\ETC on a Windows NT/2000 computer. It is stored in the \WINDOWS directory on a Windows 9x computer. It is in the same location as the HOSTS file. A sample file named LMHOSTS.SAM is placed in the directory during installation of TCP/IP. The actual file should be renamed LMHOSTS without the .SAM extension. The LMHOSTS file can contain both local and remote subnet entries. Below is a sample LMHOSTS file:

#This is the standard LMHOSTS file for WAVE Technologies UK Ltd.

```
150.200.100.2 STL-DC01 #DOM:STLOUIS #Admin Server & BBS
150.200.101.1 RST-DC01 #DOM:RESTON #Development Server
150.200.101.56 RST-WEB1 #WWW Server in Reston
#INCLUDE \\UK-DC-01\PUBLIC\LMHOST #Standard UK LMHOSTS file
#BEGIN_ALTERNATE
#INCLUDE \\EUR-DC01\PUBLIC\LMHOST #European LMHOSTS file
#INCLUDE \\USA-DC01\PUBLIC\LMHOSTS #US LMHOSTS file
#END_ALTERNATE
150.200.200.1 EUR-DC01 #DOM:EUROPE #PRE
150.200.200.2 UK-DC-01 #DOM:UK #PRE
150.200.100.1 USA-DC01 #DOM:USA #PRE
```

The file format is similar to that used with the HOSTS file. It does, however, support some special keyword values.

LMHOSTS keywords

Some entries in the LMHOSTS file are preceded by a pound sign (#). In most cases, this indicates a comment line. In some cases, it is used to identify special keywords.

Item	Description
#PRE	This is an entry that should be preloaded into the cache at system startup. Place these entries near the end of the file. They are only used during TCP/IP initialization.
#DOM:domain	This is used to identify domain controller entries. The entry is the domain controller for the specified domain.
#INCLUDE:filename	An #INCLUDE statement permits you to use a remote, centrally managed LMHOSTS file. The file is treated as if it were a local LMHOSTS file. Use the #PRE statement to preload the servers containing LMHOSTS files into the cache.
#BEGIN_ALTERNATE/ #END_ALTERNATE	A list of LMHOSTS files will be bracketed between these statements. They are used to identify alternate LMHOSTS files. Alternate files are read only if the entry is not found in the cache or any of the preceding entries.

Your station must be configured for LMHOSTS support if using LMHOSTS files for address resolution.

LMHOSTS example

When the system initially launches, all #PRE entries are added to the LMHOSTS cache as permanent entries. Next, the system issues a broadcast name query.

When name resolution is attempted and the name is not local or in the cache, the LMHOSTS file is checked. Entries in the file are parsed in order. That is why the #PRE entries are the last entries in the file, so they are not encountered every time the file is checked.

The IP address entries are checked first. Since the #DOM keyword is used to identify a domain controller, older types of systems, such as IBM LAN Server, will ignore the #DOM in the entry, treating it as a remark.

Next, any #INCLUDE entries are checked. In the example, the IP address for the #INCLUDE entry is in the LMHOSTS file so that the system can be located. If still unable to locate the name and address, any entries between #BEGIN_ALTERNATE and #END_ALTERNATE are checked. LMHOSTS file entries, unlike their HOSTS file counterparts, are not case sensitive. Also, alias entries, that is, multiple names for one IP address, are not supported.

In Windows 2000/XP/Server 2003, access the WINS tab of a Local Area Connection's TCP/IP properties to enable and configure LMHOSTS lookup, using the following options:

- **Enable LMHOSTS Lookup.** When checked, LMHOSTS support is permitted. This is the default selection.
- **Import LMHOSTS.** Click Import LMHOSTS to specify the directory path to the LMHOSTS file you want to use.

Introducing WINS

Windows Internet Name Service, or WINS, is an automated way of supporting NetBIOS address resolution. It is analogous to DNS in that it does away with the necessity of maintaining static LMHOSTS files on each Windows-based machine on the network.

As each WINS client system starts up, it registers itself with a WINS server. In this way, a database of IP addresses and NetBIOS names is created for all future name resolutions.

When a client issues a command to a NetBIOS name, the client will try the following:
- Check to see if the name is on the local machine
- Check the local cache of remote NetBIOS names
- Query the WINS server for address resolution
- Issue a local name query broadcast
- Parse the LMHOSTS file, if LMHOSTS support is configured at the client
- Parse the HOSTS file, if one exists
- Query DNS, if supported

Each of the above will be attempted until address resolution occurs.

The WINS client configuration

You can configure Windows 2000/XP/Server 2003 WINS clients by accessing the Advanced TCP/IP Settings of a LAN connection, and activating the WINS tab, as shown in Exhibit 11-6. Click Add to enter WINS Server IP addresses, in the order in which you want them to be used.

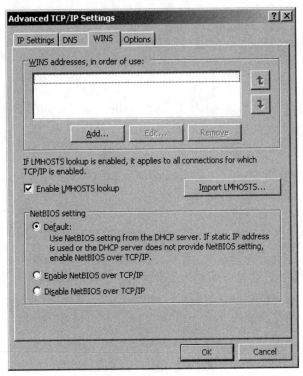

Exhibit 11-6: The Advanced TCP/IP Settings dialog box with the WINS Configuration tab activated in Windows Server 2003

Do it!

B-2:   Discussing the LMHOSTS file and WINS

Questions and answers

1 What is the significance of an LMHOSTS file entry with a comment beginning with #PRE?

2 Assuming that Windows XP was installed in the C:\WINDOWS directory, where should you place an LMHOSTS file?

3 You want to edit your LMHOSTS file and add some #PRE statements. Where in the file should you place these entries?

   A   At the top of the file

   B   Immediately after any #LOAD statements

   C   At the bottom of the file

   D   Prior to any #DOM statements

   E   LMHOSTS does not support the use of the #PRE keyword

4 On a Windows Server-2003-based system, on which tab do you configure LMHOSTS support?

5 What is the purpose of WINS?

6 How does a WINS server learn about WINS clients?

Unit summary: Name resolution

Topic A   In this topic, you learned about **HOSTS files**. You also learned about **HOST name resolution**. You learned about the **Domain Name System (DNS)**. You learned that DNS is an alternative to using HOSTS files for name resolution. You also learned about **DNS domains**, **DNS name resolution**, and **DNS client configuration**.

Topic B   In this topic, you learned about **NETBIOS**. You learned that NETBIOS is an application layer (OSI Model Session layer) interface between the network operating system and lower-level functions. You also learned about the role of **NETBIOS**, the **NETBIOS names**, and the **name resolution methods**. Then you learned about the **LMHOSTS file**. You also learned about **LMHOSTS keywords** and **LMHOSTS configuration**. Finally, you learned about **WINS** and **WINS client configuration**.

Review questions

1 Consider this excerpt from a configuration file. In which file might you find this sort of entry?

```
193.121.98.65 mainserver.wavetech.com
193.121.98.78 wavesite WAVESITE wavesite.wavetech.com
#194.150.30.30 oldserver.wavetech.com OLDSERVER
oldserver
```

2 You want to access a Web site that is located in France. The site that you need is in the company.fr domain. Your host belongs to the company.us domain. In what order will the domain name be resolved?

A COMPANY.US, COMPANY.FR, US, FR

B US, FR, COMPANY.FR

C COMPANY.US, FR, US, COMPANY.FR

D COMPANY.US, US, FR, COMPANY.FR

E COMPANY.US, US, COM, FR, COMPANY.FR

3 How do you enable a Windows XP workstation to use an LMHOSTS file?

4 Consider this excerpt from a configuration file. In which file might you find this sort of entry?

```
175.202.200.25 PDC-01 #DOM:WONDERLAND #PDC
175.201.101.87 BDC-02 #DOM:WAVE
```

5 You want to configure a client as a WINS client. What information do you have to provide on the WINS tab about the WINS server?

Unit 12

Firewalls and proxies

Unit time: 30 minutes

Complete this unit, and you'll know how to:

A Discuss the purpose of a firewall.

B Discuss the functionality of a proxy server.

Topic A: Firewalls

This topic covers the following CompTIA Network+ exam objectives:

#	Objective
1.6	Identify the purposes, features and functions of the following network components: • Firewalls
3.5	Identify the purpose, benefits and characteristics of using a firewall.
3.9	Identify the main characteristics and purpose of extranets and intranets.

An introduction to firewalls

Explanation

As more and more private networks are connected in one way or another with public networks, such as the Internet, the need for security has grown. One way to prevent unauthorized access to your private intranet is to set up a firewall between the public network and your private systems.

A *firewall* is a mechanism for controlling access between networks. Typically, firewalls are placed between a publicly trafficked network, such as the Internet, and a private network. Firewalls provide an extra layer of security to protect private organizational systems from external intruders and can be hardware- or software-based.

Prior to implementation of any firewall, an organization needs to define a security policy to access other networks and access internal resources by the external network. Failure to create this policy is a common cause of internal security breaches.

Typically, firewalls are implemented within the router that connects the private network with the public network. For example, when a user accesses a site on the Internet, the source IP address can be read by anyone tracking the Web. Activating firewall software at the router provides a filter for both outgoing and incoming transmissions. Hackers trying to invade internal organizational systems can track IP addresses to the firewall, but without proper authorization, they can't get beyond it.

It's also possible for a firewall to filter and deny access to Web sites that are considered inappropriate. For example, since Internet access is a corporate resource, management's decision to restrict access to pornographic Web sites or to multi-session games isn't necessarily denial of free speech.

Managing a firewall can become complicated if multiple protocols and various filters are involved. Managing secure Internet connectivity needs dedicated supervision. Firewall management is the center point of intranet and extranet architectural designs.

There are three types of firewalls. They are:

- Packet filters
- Bastion hosts
- Proxy servers

Packet filtering

Packet filtering is the technique of examining each datagram as it passes through a router. If the contents of the datagram agree with the criteria defined by the security administrator and stored on the router, then the datagram is passed on to its destination. If the contents don't agree with the criteria, the packet is discarded. This mechanism is typically implemented within routers.

For example, the security administrator helps SMTP requests from an external server at the specified address 205.192.2.2 to be passed to the internal SMTP server at IP address 192.168.200.100. If an inbound datagram containing SMTP information is sent from host 205.192.2.2 to the internal network, that datagram is forwarded by the router to the internal network upon inspection. Conversely, if SMTP traffic from any other host is directed to the internal network, the packets are discarded.

In another example, the security administrator might want to prevent the internal host at IP address 128.5.2.50 from browsing the World Wide Web. When the user at this workstation opens his or her Web browser and enters a Web site, the router intercepts the datagrams sent by the host and discards them. Thus, the user at that host is unable to browse the Internet.

Bastion hosts

A *bastion host* is a heavily fortified server on the network through which all external traffic must pass. A typical network server provides file, login, print, and other services, including access to various servers. On the bastion host, all services but those absolutely essential to running the system are eliminated. In this way, even if an intruder were to break into the system, damage would be limited.

A bastion host sits inside the firewall and is the main point of contact between the intranet and the Internet. By having an isolated, heavily defended server as the main point of contact, the rest of the intranet resources can be shielded from attacks originating from the Internet. Exhibit 12-1 shows an example of bastion host topology.

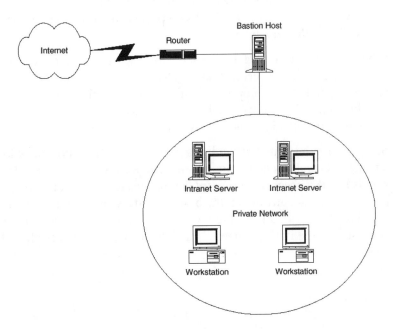

Exhibit 12-1: An example of bastion host topology

Bastion host configuration

Bastion hosts are built so that every network service possible is disabled. The only service that the server performs is providing specified Internet access. For example, there shouldn't be any user accounts on a bastion server. This policy ensures that no one can log into the bastion server, take control of it, and then gain access to the intranet.

In a Windows 2000 network, even the Network File System (NFS), which helps a system to access files across a network on a remote system, should be disabled so that intruders can't gain access to the bastion host and subsequently to resources on the intranet. The safest way to use bastion hosts is to put them on their own subnetwork as part of an intranet firewall. By putting them on their own network, if they're broken into, no other intranet resources are compromised.

Tracking bastion host activity

Bastion hosts typically log all activity so that intranet administrators can tell if the intranet has been attacked. They often keep two copies of system logs for security reasons. In case one log is destroyed or tampered with, the other log is always available as a backup. One way to keep a secure copy of the log is to connect the bastion server via a serial port to a dedicated computer, whose only purpose is to keep track of the security backup log.

Automated monitors are even more sophisticated programs than auditing software. Automated monitors regularly check the bastion server's system logs and send an alarm if they find a suspicious pattern. For example, an alarm might be sent if someone attempted more than three unsuccessful logins.

Sometimes, a bastion host can be used as a victim machine. A victim machine is a server that's stripped bare of almost all services except one specific Internet service. Victim machines can be used to provide Internet services that are difficult to support by using a proxy or a filtering router or whose security concerns aren't yet known. The services are put on the victim machine instead of a bastion host with other services. That way, if the server is broken into, other bastion hosts aren't affected.

Placing a filtering router between the bastion host and the intranet provides additional security. The filtering router checks all packets between the Internet and the intranet and drops all unauthorized traffic.

When a bastion host receives a request for a service, such as sending a Web page or delivering e-mail, the server doesn't handle the request itself. Instead, it sends the request along to the appropriate intranet server. The intranet server handles the request and then sends the information back to the bastion host. The bastion host now sends the requested information to the requester on the Internet.

Some bastion hosts include auditing programs that actively check to see whether an attack has been launched against them. There's a variety of ways to do auditing. One way is to use a checksum program that checks to see whether an unauthorized person has changed any software on the bastion host. A checksum program calculates a number based on the size of an executable program on the server. It then regularly calculates the checksum to see if it's changed. If it's changed, someone has altered the software, which could signal an attack.

Do it!   **A-1:   Discussing firewalls**

Questions and answers
1   What is a firewall?
2   Describe packet filtering.
3   Describe the purpose of a bastion host.

Topic B: Proxy servers

This topic covers the following CompTIA Network+ exam objectives:

#	Objective
2.13	Identify the purpose of network services and protocols (For example: • NAT (Network Address Translation)
3.6	Identify the purpose, benefits and characteristics of using a proxy service.

Introducing proxy servers

Explanation

Another type of firewall that you might encounter is a proxy server, sometimes called an IP proxy. The IP proxy masks the IP address of internal hosts and represents itself instead. Several types of proxy servers exist. These include:

- Winsock proxy
- Web proxy
- SOCKS proxy
- Network Address Translation

Winsock proxy

The Winsock proxy that's used in the Windows arena is frequently implemented through the use of Microsoft's proxy server. This is primarily an IP proxy. All Internet applications, from Archie to WWW, that are sent from the private network are represented by the IP address of the proxy server. When the application is launched, the proxy server determines whether the user has rights to request the action. If the rights exist, the proxy issues the request to the external network and responds to the internal host. In order for the client to have access to the external network, Proxy Server client software must be installed.

Web proxy

The Web proxy is identical to the Winsock proxy, except that the proxy server processes only WWW requests. Additionally, the Web proxy can be used to cache commonly used Web pages, making Internet access appear to be faster. Certain incompatibilities exist between certain Web browsers and Web proxy applications. It's important to investigate your specific requirements prior to implementing a Web proxy server.

SOCKS proxy

SOCKS is a UNIX-based IP proxy server. In concept, it parallels the Winsock proxy server in its functionality. However, no additional client software is needed to access this type of proxy.

Network Address Translation

Network Address Translation (NAT) is a feature implemented on many routers that provide Internet access. NAT simply strips the IP address of the internal host from each datagram and replaces it with the IP address of the router. It doesn't provide any additional firewall capabilities other than masking all internal hosts from the external network.

Do it!

B-1:   Discussing proxy servers

Questions and answers
1 What's the purpose of a proxy server?
2 What's essential on a Windows 95 system to use Microsoft's Winsock Proxy?
3 What's the advantage of Web proxy over Winsock proxy?
4 What's the advantage of SOCKS proxy over Winsock proxy?
5 Which of the following is the technology used on routers to strip the internal IP address and replace it with that of the router?   A   SOCKS proxy   B   Web proxy   C   Winsock Proxy   D   NAT

Unit summary: Firewalls and proxies

Topic A

In this topic, you learned about **firewalls**. You learned that a firewall is a mechanism for controlling access between networks. You also learned about **packet filters**, **bastion hosts**, and **packet filtering**.

Topic B

In this topic, you learned about **proxies**, which are another type of firewall. You also learned about **Winsock proxy**, **Web proxy**, and **SOCKS proxy**. You learned that **Network Address Translation** is a feature implemented on many routers that provide Internet access.

Review questions

1 What's the benefit of implementing a proxy instead of a firewall?

2 What's the most important component of any firewall strategy?

3 How are the Internet applications that are sent from the private network represented?

Unit 13

Troubleshooting network connectivity

Unit time: 90 minutes

Complete this unit, and you'll know how to:

A Identify TCP/IP troubleshooting tools.

B Discuss the Telnet utility and its functions.

C Discuss the functions of the File Transfer Protocol (FTP) utility.

D Diagnose a problem and choose the appropriate troubleshooting tools.

Topic A: TCP/IP troubleshooting tools

This topic covers the following CompTIA Network+ exam objectives:

#	Objective
4.1	Given a troubleshooting scenario, select the appropriate network utility from the following: • Tracert / traceroute • Ping • Arp • Netstat • Nbtstat • Ipconfig / Ifconfig • Winipcfg • Nslookup / dig
4.2	Given output from a network diagnostic utility (For example: those utilities listed in objective 4.1), identify the utility and interpret the output.

Introducing TCP/IP troubleshooting tools

Explanation

More than any other local or wide area network protocol, TCP/IP provides the network administrator with great capabilities to troubleshoot problems. Some of the TCP/IP troubleshooting tools are ARP, NBTSTAT, NETSTAT, PING, HOSTNAME, NSLOOKUP, DIG, TRACERT, IPCONFIG, WINIPCFG, IFCONFIG, and ROUTE.

In Windows, these commands are typically run from a command prompt, with the exception of WINIPCFG, which opens a GUI dialog box.

ARP

The platforms supported by ARP are all TCP/IP clients.

Description

ARP, or Address Resolution Protocol, helps a host to find the MAC address of another host on the same internetwork, given the host's IP address. To reduce the amount of ARP-related traffic on a network, each host caches IP-to-MAC address resolutions. The ARP command helps you to display or modify the address translation tables that are stored in the cache of the host.

Syntax

```
ARP -a [-g] [inet_addr] [-N if_addr]
ARP -s inet_addr eth_addr [if_addr]
ARP -d inet_addr [if_addr]
```

Where:

- **inet_addr** is the Internet address in the X.X.X.X format.
- **eth_addr** is the Ethernet address (or MAC address).
- **if_addr** is the interface address. If provided, this specifies the IP address of the interface whose address translation table should be modified. If not provided, the first applicable interface is used.
- **-a** queries TCP/IP and displays current ARP cache contents. Include inet_addr to display the IP and MAC addresses for that specified computer only.
- **-g** is the same as -a.
- **-N [if_addr]** can be used in combination with the -a option. It limits the display to the network adapter specified by if_addr.
- **-s** creates a permanent entry, mapping the IP address (in_addr) to the MAC address (ether_addr) specified. If a local adapter address is provided (if_addr), the entry is changed for that adapter only.
- **-d** deletes the ARP entry for the IP address specified as in_addr. You must include an IP address with this option. If a MAC address is supplied, only the entry for that network adapter is deleted.

HOSTNAME

All TCP/IP clients are supported by HOSTNAME.

Description

This utility can be used to determine the local machine's host name.

Syntax

```
HOSTNAME
```

This utility doesn't have any optional switches.

IPCONFIG

The platforms supported by IPCONFIG are Windows 98 and Windows NT/2000/XP/Server 2003.

Description

This utility displays the current IP settings for the system. IPCONFIG can also be used to renew or release IP addresses assigned by a DHCP server.

Syntax

```
IPCONFIG [/? /all | /renew [adapter] | /release [adapter]]
```

Where:

- **?** displays a help message describing IPCONFIG usage.
- **All** displays full configuration information. When IPCONFIG is run without this option, only the IP address, subnet mask, and default gateway are shown.
- **renew [adapter]** renews the IP address for the specified adapter. You can use this option only if the computer obtains its address from a DHCP server. If you want to renew the address for a specific adapter, use the adapter name displayed by IPCONFIG.
- **release [adapter]** releases the IP address for the specified adapter. You can use this option only if the computer obtains its address from a DHCP server. If you want to renew the address for a specific adapter, use the adapter name displayed by IPCONFIG.

WINIPCFG

The platforms for WINIPCFG are Windows 95 and Windows 98.

Description

WINIPCFG helps you to obtain information about the system's TCP/IP configuration. This is an especially useful tool if you're obtaining your TCP/IP settings through DHCP or obtaining an address through autoconfiguration.

Syntax

```
WINIPCFG
```

This utility has no optional command switches.

Example

An IP configuration that was assigned through autoconfiguration is shown in Exhibit 13-1.

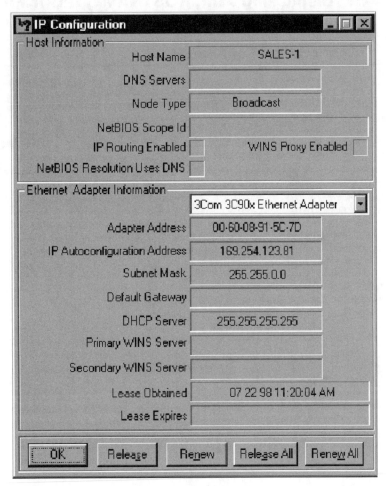

Exhibit 13-1: An example of WINIPCFG

Do it!

A-1: Discussing ARP, HOSTNAME, IPCONFIG, and WINIPCFG

Questions and answers

1 Which TCP/IP troubleshooting tool helps a host to find the MAC address of another host on the same internetwork?

   A   Address Resolution Protocol (ARP)

   B   HOSTNAME

   C   IPCONFIG

2 Which utility is used by all TCP/IP clients to determine the machine's host name?

3 Which utility is used to renew or release IP addresses assigned by a DHCP server?

4 Which utility is used by Windows 95 and Windows 98 clients to view their current TCP/IP configuration?

   A   HOSTNAME

   B   IPCONFIG

   C   WINIPCFG

IFCONFIG

Explanation   The platform for IFCONFIG is UNIX.

Description

IFCONFIG displays the current network interface setting for the system. Running IFCONFIG without any options displays the settings on all current network interfaces.

Example

IFCONFIG can also be used to set the IP address on the specified interface.

NBTSTAT

Windows 95/98 and Windows NT/2000/XP/Server 2003 are the platforms for NBTSTAT.

Description

NBTSTAT is a diagnostic utility that helps you to view and manage NetBIOS name cache information.

Syntax

```
nbtstat [-a remote] [-A IP_address] [-c] [-n] [-R] [-r] [-S]
[-s] [interval]
```

Where:

- **-a remote** helps you to specify a remote computer's name and list its name table.

- **-A IP_address** helps you to specify a remote computer by its IP address and lists the computer's name table.

- **-c** lists the contents of the NetBIOS name cache. The listing includes the IP address for each name.

- **-n** lists the local NetBIOS names and whether registered by B-node broadcast or WINS.

- **-R** purges all names from the NetBIOS name cache and reloads the LMHOSTS file.

- **-r** lists name resolution statistics.

- **-S** lists client and server sessions. Remote hosts are listed by IP address.

- **-s** lists client and server sessions. When possible, the HOSTS file is used to convert remote IP addresses to names.

- **Interval** sets the interval, in seconds, for repeating the information. If this term isn't specified, the information appears once.

Example

```
C:\>nbtstat -n
Node IpAddress: [200.200.200.19] Scope Id: []
```

Here's an example of a NetBIOS Local Name table:

Name	Type		Status
40SERVER	<20>	UNIQUE	Registered
40SERVER	<00>	UNIQUE	Registered
WONDERLAND	<00>	GROUP	Registered
WONDERLAND	<1C>	GROUP	Registered
WONDERLAND	<1B>	UNIQUE	Registered
40SERVER	<03>	UNIQUE	Registered
ADMIN	<03>	UNIQUE	Registered
WONDERLAND	<1E>	GROUP	Registered

In a sample nbtstat -n, a Windows system tracks several NetBIOS names. In this example, this includes the computer name 40SERVER and a domain name of WONDERLAND. There's also a user named Admin logged on at the server. Along with each of these, there's a hexadecimal value indicating a process running on the computer and attached to that NetBIOS name.

NETSTAT

All TCP/IP clients are supported by NETSTAT.

Description

This utility displays protocol statistics and current TCP/IP network connections.

Syntax

```
netstat [-a] [-e][-n][-s] [-p protocol] [-r] [interval]
```

Where:

- **-a** shows all connections and listening ports.
- **-e** shows Ethernet statistics.
- **-n** shows addresses and ports in numerical order.
- **-s** displays statistics per protocol.
- **-p protocol** shows the connections for either UDP or TCP. Replace the word protocol with either UDP or TCP to display the respective connections.
- **-r** causes the routing table to be printed before connection information.
- **interval** sets the interval, in seconds, for repeating the information. If this term isn't specified, the information is printed once.

Example

An example of NETSTAT is shown in Exhibit 13-2.

```
G:\>netstat

Active Connections

  Proto  Local Address          Foreign Address         State
  TCP    mark:1026              localhost:1027          ESTABLISHED
  TCP    mark:1027              localhost:1026          ESTABLISHED
  TCP    mark:1025              HATTER:nbsession        ESTABLISHED
  TCP    mark:1028              TIM:nbsession           ESTABLISHED
  TCP    mark:1029              POOBAH:nbsession        ESTABLISHED
  TCP    mark:1031              HATTER:1745             TIME_WAIT

G:\>
```

Exhibit 13-2: An example of NETSTAT

Do it!

A-2: Discussing **IFCONFIG, NBTSTAT, and NETSTAT**

Questions and answers

1 How can you view the settings on all current network interfaces on a UNIX client?

2 Which utility is used by Windows 95/98 and Windows NT/2000/XP/Server 2003 computers to view and manage NetBIOS name cache information?

3 Which of the following utilities is used by all TCP/IP clients to display protocol statistics?

A IFCONFIG

B NETSTAT

C NBTSTAT

NSLOOKUP

Explanation

NSLOOKUP supports all TCP/IP clients.

Description

NSLOOKUP helps you to retrieve information stored by the DNS server. This utility is an industry standard used for obtaining information from a DNS server.

Syntax

```
nslookup [-option . . . ] [hostname | - [server]]
```

Nslookup can function in two modes:

- **Interactive.** In this mode, an application shell is entered, in which various commands can be issued to retrieve information from the DNS server.
- **Command Line.** This mode helps for the query parameters to be specified after the NSLOOKUP command. This doesn't force the user to enter an interactive application shell.

DIG

DIG used to support only UNIX clients but has now been ported to the Windows platform as well.

Description

Like NSLOOKUP, DIG lets you retrieve information stored by the DNS server. DIG doesn't come with Windows. You have to download and install the files appropriate for the OS you're running. Doing a search on dig Windows 2000 should give you links to the downloadable files and instructions on how to install dig. The site we used was http://pigtail.net/LRP/dig/; however, keep in mind that Web sites change all the time.

Syntax

```
dig [@global-server] [domain] [q-type] [q-class] <q-opt>
<global-d-opt> host [@local-server] <local-d-opt> [host
[@local-server] <local-d-opt> [...]]
```

The available switches for this command are extensive. Exhibit 13-3 shows sample output from the dig command without switches.

```
C:\WINDOWS\System32\command.com                                    _ □ ×

C:\DIG>dig

; <<>> DiG 9.2.3 <<>>
;; global options:  printcmd
;; Got answer:
;; ->>HEADER<<- opcode: QUERY, status: NOERROR, id: 41
;; flags: qr rd ra; QUERY: 1, ANSWER: 13, AUTHORITY: 0, ADDITIONAL: 13

;; QUESTION SECTION:
;.                              IN      NS

;; ANSWER SECTION:
.                     255145   IN      NS      L.ROOT-SERVERS.NET.
.                     255145   IN      NS      M.ROOT-SERVERS.NET.
.                     255145   IN      NS      A.ROOT-SERVERS.NET.
.                     255145   IN      NS      B.ROOT-SERVERS.NET.
.                     255145   IN      NS      C.ROOT-SERVERS.NET.
.                     255145   IN      NS      D.ROOT-SERVERS.NET.
.                     255145   IN      NS      E.ROOT-SERVERS.NET.
.                     255145   IN      NS      F.ROOT-SERVERS.NET.
.                     255145   IN      NS      G.ROOT-SERVERS.NET.
.                     255145   IN      NS      H.ROOT-SERVERS.NET.
.                     255145   IN      NS      I.ROOT-SERVERS.NET.
.                     255145   IN      NS      J.ROOT-SERVERS.NET.
.                     255145   IN      NS      K.ROOT-SERVERS.NET.

;; ADDITIONAL SECTION:
A.ROOT-SERVERS.NET.   94364    IN      A       198.41.0.4
B.ROOT-SERVERS.NET.   94364    IN      A       192.228.79.201
C.ROOT-SERVERS.NET.   588158   IN      A       192.33.4.12
D.ROOT-SERVERS.NET.   588158   IN      A       128.8.10.90
E.ROOT-SERVERS.NET.   529626   IN      A       192.203.230.10
F.ROOT-SERVERS.NET.   588158   IN      A       192.5.5.241
G.ROOT-SERVERS.NET.   92427    IN      A       192.112.36.4
H.ROOT-SERVERS.NET.   94364    IN      A       128.63.2.53
I.ROOT-SERVERS.NET.   588158   IN      A       192.36.148.17
J.ROOT-SERVERS.NET.   94364    IN      A       192.58.128.30
K.ROOT-SERVERS.NET.   588158   IN      A       193.0.14.129
L.ROOT-SERVERS.NET.   588158   IN      A       198.32.64.12
M.ROOT-SERVERS.NET.   588158   IN      A       202.12.27.33

;; Query time: 15 msec
;; SERVER: 24.93.1.118#53(24.93.1.118)
;; WHEN: Wed Nov 10 11:43:44 2004
;; MSG SIZE  rcvd: 436

C:\DIG>
```

Exhibit 13-3: Sample output from the dig command.

PING

All TCP/IP clients are supported by PING.

Description

This utility verifies connections to one or more remote computers.

Syntax

```
PING [-t] [-a] [-n count] [-l length] [-f] [-i ttl] [-v tos]
[-r count] [-s count] [[-j host-list] | [-k host-list]]
[-w timeout] destination-list
```

Where:

- **-t** continues to ping the host until explicitly interrupted.
- **-a** resolves IP addresses to host names.
- **-n count** specifies how many packets to send. The default is four.
- **-l length** sets the amount of data to send. The default is 64 bytes and the maximum is 8,192 bytes.
- **-f** prevents gateways from fragmenting packets.
- **-i ttl** forces the time to live to the time specified by ttl.
- **-v tos** sets the type of service, which treats high precedence traffic as more important on networks that support this feature.
- **-r count** records the route of packet, both outbound and inbound. The count parameter records the number of hosts, where the minimum is 1 and maximum is 9.
- **-s count** displays the timestamp for the number of hops specified by count.
- **-j host-list** specifies the route by which the packets are to be routed. You can specify up to 9 hosts. The hosts can be separated by gateways along the route. This is known as *loose-source routed*.
- **-k host-list** specifies the route by which the packets are to be routed. You can specify up to 9 hosts. The hosts can't be separated by gateways along the route. This is known as *strict-source routed*.
- **-w timeout** specifies the timeout period in milliseconds.
- **destination-list** specifies the remote hosts to ping.

TRACERT

All TCP/IP clients are supported by TRACERT.

Description

This utility is used to trace the route that a packet takes to reach the destination. It does so by sending packets to the destination with varying time-to-live (TTL). Each router along the path is needed to decrement the TTL value by one before forwarding it. Therefore, the TTL effectively counts the number of hops to the destination.

To determine the route, TRACERT sends the first packet with a ttl of one and then increments successive packets by one until the destination responds or until maximum TTL size is achieved. The route is determined by examining ICMP Time Exceeded messages sent back by the intermediate routers.

Syntax

```
tracert [-d] [-h maximum_hops] [-j host_list] [-w timeout]
target_name
```

Where:

- **-d** prevents addresses from being resolved to host names.
- **-h maximum_hops** specifies the maximum number of hops to reach the destination.
- **-j host-list** specifies the hosts that can be separated by intermediate routers (loose-source routing).
- **-w timeout** specifies the number of milliseconds to wait for a reply.
- **target_name** is the name of the target host.

Example

An example of TRACERT is shown in Exhibit 13-4.

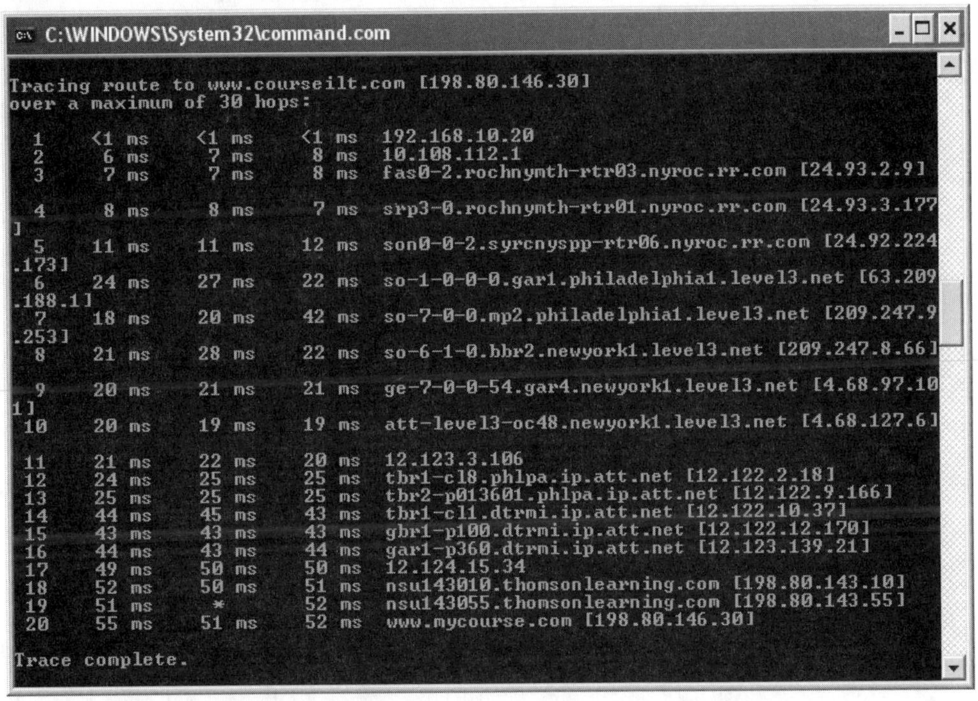

Exhibit 13-4: An example of TRACERT

ROUTE

ROUTE supports all TCP/IP clients.

Description

This utility is used to manage static routing tables.

Syntax

```
route [-f -p] [command [destination] [MASK netmask] [gateway]
[METRIC metric]]
```

Where:

- **-f** clears all routing tables of gateway entries.
- **-p** makes the added route persistent across restarts of the computer. By default, routes aren't preserved between computer restarts. This switch can also be used with the print command to display the list of registered persistent routes.
- **command** can be one of four commands:
  - **Print** is used to print the route
  - **Add** is used to add the route
  - **Delete** is used to delete the route
  - **Change** is used to modify an existing route.
- **destination** specifies the host to which the command is being sent.
- **MASK netmask** signifies that the netmask parameter is the subnet mask to use.
- **gateway** specifies the gateway.
- **METRIC** helps you to specify the number of hops to the destination when using that route.

Example

Every system needs a routing table to determine the path to the destination. ROUTE PRINT displays the contents of this table.

Here's an example of a routing table:

Network address	Netmask	Gateway address	Interface	Metric
0.0.0.0	0.0.0.0	199.34.157.65	199.34.157.78	1
127.0.0.0	255.0.0.0	127.0.0.1	127.0.0.1	1
199.34.157.64	255.255.255.192	199.34.157.78	199.34.157.78	1
199.34.157.78	255.255.255.255	127.0.0.1	127.0.0.1	1
199.34.157.255	255.255.255.255	199.34.157.78	199.34.157.78	1
224.0.0.0	224.0.0.0	199.34.157.78	199.34.157.78	1
255.255.255.255	255.255.255.255	199.34.157.78	0.0.0.0	1

The routing table on a system with only one network adapter has seven rows of information, listing the most frequent route to the most generic. The order is:

1 Default route

2 Loopback address

3 Local subnet

4 Network card address

5 Subnet broadcast address

6 Multicast address

7 Limited broadcast address

Do it!

A-3: Discussing NSLOOKUP, DIG, TRACERT, PING, and ROUTE

Questions and answers

1 How do you verify current entries in DNS?

2 How does the TRACERT utility trace the route that a packet takes to reach the destination?

3 Aside from NSLOOKUP, which utility can you use to obtain DNS server information?

4 Which tool can be used to manipulate the routing table on a host?

Topic B: Telnet

This topic covers the following CompTIA Network+ exam objective:

#	Objective
2.10	Define the purpose, function and use of the following protocols used in the TCP / IP (Transmission Control Protocol / Internet Protocol) suite: • Telnet

Working with Telnet

Explanation

Telnet supports dumb terminal connection and emulation with remote servers. This connection is necessary to support some applications. Telnet provides access, through terminal emulation, to any host running a Telnet daemon service. This includes most UNIX hosts, as well as DEC and IBM mainframes running TCP/IP. It's also commonly used for remote configuration of hubs and routers. However, you can't log on interactively to Windows or Novell NetWare through Telnet.

There are several variants of Telnet. This variation enables versions configured in a manner appropriate to the host with which it's designed to communicate. Some versions have special terminal facilities, such as VT220 or VT320 support. Others have the ability to handle special data streams, such as providing 3270 or 5350 support for communication with IBM mainframes and minicomputers.

When activating a Telnet session, you specify both an IP address and a port/socket address. The port address defaults to 23 for the Telnet daemon process.

Telnet utility on Windows NT/2000/XP/Server 2003

When TCP/IP is installed on a Windows NT/2000/XP/Server 2003 workstation, Telnet is added to the system. You can run Telnet from a command prompt. This is a basic Telnet utility providing VT52, VT100, and TTY terminal emulation. None of these terminal emulation utilities provides a Telnet daemon.

In Windows NT, when the Telnet window is open, from the Connect menu, choose Remote System. You're prompted to identify the destination host, either by host name or IP address. You can also specify the terminal emulation type, defaulting to VT100, and port ID, defaulting to Telnet. There are additional port options supported, matching the simple TCP/IP services provided by Windows. You can connect to any service port by manually entering the port number.

In Windows 2000/XP/Server 2003, you have to use the command line interface to use Telnet.

Syntax

```
telnet[host[port]]
```

Where host is the IP address or host name of the computer to which you want to connect and port is the port number or the name of the service.

Troubleshooting with Telnet

Telnet is also a powerful diagnostic tool. Telnet provides a way of sending commands directly to a server process and viewing the results when higher-level protocols or applications appear to be failing.

For example, you can use Telnet to check the status of an SMTP server. In Windows NT, from the Telnet menu, select Connect. Enter the name of the server that you want to check and change the port to 25, which is the default port for SMTP. In Windows 2000/XP/Server 2003, use the Telnet command line interface to specify the name of the server and the port.

After you connect to the server, you get a message describing the status of the mail server.

In this case, the SMTP server is up and running. In the same manner, you can check the status of an FTP server by using Telnet and port 21. In this case, FTP.NOVELL.COM is up and running.

Do it!

B-1: Discussing Telnet

Questions and answers

1 How can you use the Telnet utility to check if an SMTP server is functioning?

2 Name the hosts to which Telnet provides access, through terminal emulation?

Topic C: File Transfer Protocol

This topic covers the following CompTIA Network+ exam objective:

#	Objective
2.10	Define the purpose, function and use of the following protocols used in the TCP / IP (Transmission Control Protocol / Internet Protocol) suite: • FTP (File Transfer Protocol)

FTP

Explanation

File Transfer Protocol (FTP) transfers text and binary files between systems, including dissimilar platforms. If necessary, it performs a format and type conversion on the file.

The platforms supported by FTP are all TCP/IP clients.

Description

FTP can be used interactively at the command prompt or in a script (batch) file. The source host must be running the FTP server service (daemon).

Syntax

```
ftp [-v] [-d] [-i] [-n] [-g] [-s:filename] [-a] [-w:windowsize]
```

Where:

- **-v** suppresses the display of remote server responses to the command.
- **-n** suppresses auto-login at initial connection.
- **-i** disables interactive prompting when performing multiple file transfers.
- **-d** enables debugging. When enabled, all FTP commands passed between the client and server are shown.
- **-g** disables filename globbing. When globbing is enabled (the default setting), wildcard characters are supported in local path and filenames.
- **-s:filename** executes a series of FTP commands. Replace filename with the name of a text file containing FTP command strings. When FTP starts, the commands in the file run automatically.
- **-a** specifies that any local interface can be used during data connection binding.
- **-w:windowsize** overrides the default transfer buffer size.

FTP commands

FTP supports a wide range of commands. There are 42 in Microsoft's implementation of the utility. This implementation includes a mix of DOS and UNIX commands. For example, you can use either `dir` or `ls` to list the contents of the current working directory on the remote host. Type `help` at the FTP interactive mode prompt, FTP>, to display a list of supported commands. Commands must be entered in lower case.

Commonly used commands include:

- **help [command]** — Typing `help` without additional input displays a command list. Type `help` followed by a command's name to receive help information specific to that command.
- **quit** or **bye** — Exits FTP interactive mode.
- **ascii** — Converts the file transfer type to ASCII. This is the default setting. A carriage return is added after each line feed found in the file.
- **binary** — Converts the file transfer type to binary.
- **get** — Use this command to transfer a file from a remote FTP server.
- **put** — Use this command to transfer a file to a remote FTP server.

Additionally, it's important to use the appropriate file transfer type. Text files frequently need carriage return (CR) codes appended to the end of each line. In a binary file, there might be values equal to the line feed character. Appending carriage returns would cause file corruption.

Do it!

C-1:   Discussing File Transfer Protocol

Questions and answers

1 How can you get the help information about a specific command?

2 Which command do you use to transfer a file from a remote FTP server?

Topic D: Troubleshooting examples

Explanation

You'll now look at several troubleshooting examples. While there's no replacement for real world experience, these examples might help you better understand the capabilities of the TCP/IP suite of utilities. In addition, this section contains some real world DHCP troubleshooting scenarios.

Example 1: Using PING and TRACERT

You're working at the IS Help Desk at ABC Software Corporation at the home office in Alexandria, Virginia. Your network is a multi-site, routed IP network. You receive a call from Phil, a client on the network located in Cincinnati, that he is unable to access ABC-SERV1 in Terre Haute. You open the command prompt on your computer, type `Ping ABC-SERV1` and press Enter.

You receive an immediate response indicating that the server is running. You ask Phil to do the same. Phil, however, receives the message, "Destination Host Unreachable." Next, you ask Phil to execute the `tracert ABC-SERV1` command and press Enter.

Phil sees a response from three servers, after which he continually receives the message, "Destination Unreachable." The last server seen has IP address 10.2.2.2. Upon examining that router, you discover that it's been improperly configured. You adjust the configuration, and now Phil can access the server.

Example 2: Using NETSTAT

You're the administrator of an IP Network. You obtain a report from both external and internal users that they're unable to send or receive messages. You log on to the e-mail server. At the command prompt, you type `NETSTAT -a`.

You see that the server is no longer listening on port 25. You check the e-mail system and see that SMTP messaging has been disabled.

Example 3: Using ARP

You're the administrator of an IP network. A workstation reports that it can't connect to a host at 202.12.22.33. The local area network topology consists of a single subnet. Your computer, the host, and the workstation are on the same physical network segment. From your system, you can ping the host and the workstation. You then log on to the workstation and attempt to ping the host. You receive numerous "destination unreachable" messages in return. You can, however, ping your workstation and other workstations on the network. At a command prompt, you type `ARP -a`.

You note an entry for the unreachable host. However, the associated MAC address is not the MAC address for the adapter on the host. You then delete the entry by typing

```
ARP -d 202.12.22.33.
```

Then you re-create the entry by typing

```
ARP -a 202.12.22.33 00-a0-c9-b4-5a-b3.
```

Now you can access the host.

Example 4: DHCP and fixed addresses

Joe decides to make the dynamic address assigned to him by the DHCP server into a static address. He opens the Network Control Panel utility and changes the properties of the TCP/IP protocol to use a static address that's the same as his current DHCP-assigned address. What are the possible repercussions of this action?

After the user changes his IP address from DHCP-assigned to static, IP address conflicts occur when another DHCP client logs into the network. After the lease for the original unit expires, the DHCP server helps it to be reused. The DHCP client is unable to obtain a proper IP address, as the IP address exists on the network as a fixed IP address and DHCP is unaware of its existence. It's possible that both clients lose communications as an ARP broadcast of the new system is sent out. On a Windows NT/2000/Server 2003 network, this isn't the case, as the defending system issues an ARP broadcast so that all other systems maintain the proper ARP entries.

Example 5: DHCP address conflicts

You've received a new computer that will be used on your TCP/IP network. Most of the addresses in the network are managed with DHCP. However, instead of having your DHCP server assign an IP address, you decide to assign a static address to this computer. Your current DHCP pool of addresses starts at 192.168.100.10 and ends at 192.168.100.200, so you decide to assign 192.168.100.151 to this computer. What are the repercussions of your actions?

On a Windows NT/2000/Server 2003 network, the system that already has the appropriate IP address continues to function. However, both computers receive an error message. The message on the new computer states that the IP address already exists on the network and that you should assign a different IP address. The message on the existing computer states that there's an IP address conflict with another system and that network operations might be interrupted as a result.

On a Windows NT/2000/Server 2003 network, the defending NT/2000/Server 2003 system issues an ARP broadcast so that other clients maintain the proper IP Address. To resolve the issue, reset the offending system's IP address to act as a DHCP client.

Example 6: DHCP and overlapping scopes

Your network has two DHCP servers for redundancy. The first DHCP server has an address pool, or scope, of 192.168.200.10 through 192.168.200.50. The second DHCP server has a scope of 192.168.200.40 through 192.168.200.80. What are the possible repercussions?

In this case, IP address conflicts will occur. It's important to note that DHCP scopes can't overlap.

Do it!

D-1: Troubleshooting sample problems

Questions and answers

1 You decide to make the dynamic address assigned to you by the DHCP server into a static address. You open the Network and Dial-Up Connections Control Panel utility and change the properties of the TCP/IP protocol of the Local Area Connection to use a static address that's the same as your current DHCP-assigned address. What are the possible repercussions of this action?

2 Your network has two DHCP servers for redundancy. The first DHCP server has an address pool, or scope, of 192.168.200.10 through 192.168.200.50. The second DHCP server has a scope of 192.168.200.40 through 192.168.200.80. You see an IP address conflict. What's the possible reason for this?

Unit summary: Troubleshooting network connectivity

Topic A

In this topic, you learned about several **TCP/IP troubleshooting tools** including, **ARP, HOSTNAME, IPCONFIG, WINIPCFG, IFCONFIG, NBTSTAT, NETSTAT, NSLOOKUP, DIG, PING, TRACERT,** and **ROUTE**.

Topic B

In this topic, you learned about the **Telnet utility**. You learned that Telnet provides access, through terminal emulation, to any host running a Telnet daemon service. You also learned about using Telnet and troubleshooting with Telnet.

Topic C

In this topic, you learned about the **File Transfer Protocol (FTP) utility**. You also learned **FTP commands**. You learned that FTP can be used interactively at the command prompt or in a script (batch) file. Also, FTP supports a wide range of commands.

Topic D

In this topic, you saw some **troubleshooting examples**.

Review questions

1 Which troubleshooting tools can you use to determine a host's IP address?

2 Which tools can you use to query a name server?

3 Telnet provides a way of sending commands directly to a server process. True or False?

4 Which command do you use to transfer a file from a remote FTP server?

5 What are the implications of a user assigning a fixed IP address within the range of the DHCP scope defined by the DHCP server?

Unit 14

Identifying network operating system features

Unit time: 60 minutes

Complete this unit, and you'll know how to:

A Discuss the features of Microsoft Windows NT, Windows 2000, and Windows Server 2003.

B Discuss the features of Novell NetWare.

C Discuss the features of UNIX, Linux, and Mac OS X Server.

D Discuss the features of AppleShare IP.

Topic A: Microsoft Windows

This topic covers the following CompTIA Network+ exam objectives:

#	Objective
3.1	Identify the basic capabilities (For example: client support, interoperability, authentication, file and print services, application support and security) of the following server operating systems to access network resources: • Windows
3.4	Given a remote connectivity scenario comprised of a protocol, an authentication scheme, and physical connectivity, configure the connection. Includes connection to the following servers: • Windows
4.5	Given a troubleshooting scenario between a client and the following server environments, identify the cause of a stated problem: • Windows

Explanation

One of the most popular network operating systems for PC-based LANs is Microsoft Corporation's Windows. Newer versions of Windows – 2000 and XP - are based on Windows NT, with added functionality and updated interfaces. Most of the information on NT also applies to 2000 and XP.

Windows NT

Windows NT is no longer available for sale; however, it's still installed in many network environments. When speaking of Windows NT, it's important to note that this operating system comes in four distinct editions:

Server Bash • **Windows NT Workstation.** A robust desktop operating system designed for high-end business applications.

Directory Bash • **Windows NT Server.** A general-purpose network operating system for small, medium, or large networks.

• **Windows NT Server–Enterprise Edition.** Takes the foundation of Windows NT Server and builds on it to provide a platform for large-scale, mission-critical applications.

• **Windows NT Server–Terminal Server Edition.** Makes it possible for non-PC hardware, such as dumb terminals, to participate on a Windows NT-based network through terminal emulation.

Other server components that extend Windows NT functionality are:

• **Exchange Server.** Provides messaging and collaboration services

• **Proxy Server.** Provides a robust firewall with Web-caching services

• **Internet Information Server.** Provides a platform for Internet and intranet sites

• **Site Server.** Provides advanced management of intranet, Internet, and electronic commerce Web sites

• **Systems Management Server.** Provides a platform for centralized management of computer inventory, network diagnostics, and software distribution

- **SNA Server.** Provides integration of legacy systems and data with more modern network systems
- **SQL Server.** Provides high-performance relational database management

Features of Windows NT

All Windows NT-family products share a number of common features. These include:

- **32-bit operating system.**
- **Hardware platform support.** Windows NT supports x86- and RISC-based platforms.
- **Preemptive multitasking.** The operating system retains control over system activity, sharing available processor time between the processes running.
- **Security.** Windows NT meets C2 security specifications. A valid user name and password is needed for logon and resource access. Permissions can be set on a user-by-user basis or by groups of users.
- **Application support.** In addition to native applications written to the Win32 API set, Windows NT supports a wide variety of 16-bit Windows and MS-DOS applications.
- **Network support.** Windows NT can be used to build a network or as a powerful addition to an existing network environment.
- **Internet/intranet support.** Windows NT includes Microsoft's Internet Explorer and other Internet support tools. These simplify the implementation of a corporate intranet.
- **Microsoft Exchange Client.** Microsoft Exchange Client installs during Windows NT setup. It provides support for both Microsoft Exchange and Internet Mail.

Some features are specific to Windows NT Server products. These include:

- **Microsoft Networking.** Windows NT Server includes a fully integrated network operating system.
- **NetWare support.** Windows NT includes utilities specifically designed to support existing NetWare networks.
- **Advanced fault tolerance.** Windows NT Server provides support for disk mirroring, disk duplexing, and disk striping with parity. This support gives you the ability not only to protect your data but also to keep working when a disk failure occurs.
- **Internet and TCP/IP support.** Windows NT provides support for a DNS server. Microsoft Internet Information Server (IIS) can be installed at the same time as NT Server or after the NT installation. Windows NT Server also includes Microsoft's FrontPage, an easy-to-use HTML page editor.

Facts about Windows NT

Here are some facts about Windows NT:

- Windows NT servers frequently fulfill the role of domain controllers.
- The super user on a Windows NT system is named Administrator by default. The Administrator account has complete control over the NOS.
- Windows NT supports the New Technology File System (NTFS) that has several advantages over the traditional File Allocation Table (FAT) file system, including advanced security capabilities, auditing, and on-the-fly compression.

Do it!

A-1: Discussing Windows NT

Questions and answers

1 Name the Windows NT edition designed for high-end business applications.

2 List the four distinct editions of Windows NT.

3 The super user account on a Windows NT server is:

A Admin

B Supervisor

C Administrator

D Root

4 Additional products can extend the functionality of Windows NT Server. True or False?

Windows 2000

Explanation

Like Windows NT, Windows 2000 comes in several editions:

[handwritten: Server Based]

- **Windows 2000 Professional.** Designed for desktop/workstation use. It has basic services for sharing resources but isn't intended to be a server.

[handwritten: Directory Based (AD)]

- **Windows 2000 Server.** Designed for general server use: file and print services and group mail. Supports up to 4 processors and 4 gigabytes of RAM.
- **Windows 2000 Advanced Server.** Designed for larger business and .com services. Supports up to 8 processors and 8 gigabytes of RAM.
- **Windows 2000 Datacenter Server.** For large-scale business and mission-critical, enterprise applications. Supports clustering and up to 32 processors and 32 gigabytes of RAM.

Windows 2000 updates and improves on NT in several ways. Here are a few of them:

- Windows 2000 can support a lot of RAM and many processors. In addition, clustering allows several servers to be connected and act as one unit, with the load automatically balanced among them.

[handwritten: Microsofts answer to Novells NDS]

- Active Directory, Microsoft's directory service implementation that's used to store information about network objects in Windows 2000 domains and later, also provides a new way to manage network objects.
- Updated and added protocols and improved security, as well as improved integration with other network types.
- New centralized administration tools, such as the Microsoft Management Console (MMC) and the Computer Management tool.
- Updated user interface.
- Integrated Internet services.
- Increased hardware and peripheral support.

Do it!

A-2:   Discussing Windows 2000

Questions and answers
1 What are the versions of Windows 2000?
2 What features make Datacenter Server able to handle the most network load?
3 What's the system for storing information about network objects in Windows 2000?

Windows Server 2003

Explanation

Like Windows NT and Windows 2000, Windows Server 2003 comes in several editions:

- **Windows Server 2003 Standard Edition.** Designed for standard workloads, such as those of a single department.
- **Windows Server 2003 Enterprise Edition** Designed for mission-critical applications and services. Supports up 64-bit processing for up to 8 processors and up to 32 GB of memory.
- **Windows Server 2003 Datacenter edition.** Designed for larger businesses and .com services to provide increased scalability and reliability. Available as a 32-bit and 64-bit version.
- **Windows Server 2003 Web Edition.** Designed to provide dedicated Web services.

Windows 2003 updates and improves on Windows 2000 in several ways. Here are some examples:

- Windows Server 2003 incorporates Microsoft's .NET software technologies that use XML Web services to connect information, people, devices, and systems over the Internet.
- Improved clustering and load-balancing support.
- New and improved security features, such as common language runtime and a new, improved version of Internet Information Services (IIS) 6.0.
- Increased performance and scalability of Active Directory.
- New services to automate management, such as Microsoft Software Update Services (SUS), server configuration wizards, and Group Policy Management Console (GPMC).

Do it!

A-3: Discussing Windows Server 2003

Questions and answers

1 Which Windows Server 2003 is designed for running mission-critical applications?

2 Windows 2003 Data Center Edition is available in what versions?

A 32-bit

B 64-bit

C Both of the above

D Neither of the above

3 Which technologies use XML Web services to connect information, people, devices, and systems over the Internet?

Topic B: Novell NetWare

This topic covers the following CompTIA Network+ exam objectives:

#	Objective
3.1	Identify the basic capabilities (For example: client support, interoperability, authentication, file and print services, application support and security) of the following server operating systems to access network resources: • NetWare
3.4	Given a remote connectivity scenario comprised of a protocol, an authentication scheme, and physical connectivity, configure the connection. Includes connection to the following servers: • NetWare
4.5	Given a troubleshooting scenario between a client and the following server environments, identify the cause of a stated problem: • NetWare

Introducing NetWare

Explanation

Another major network operating system seen on PC-based networks is Novell NetWare.

Novell NetWare is currently in its sixth generation. NetWare 6, released in 2003, provides many new features for improving performance and scalability, designed for both local and global networks.

Some key points to remember about NetWare include:

- Support for NetWare is readily available.
- Many applications are NetWare-compatible.
- NetWare provides straightforward installation.
- NetWare provides multiprotocol support.
- Connectivity to several other platforms is readily available.
- The super user on NetWare is named Admin by default. The Admin account has complete control over the NOS.

Note: The super user on NetWare 3.x and earlier was named Supervisor.

Features of NetWare

Novell's NetWare network operating system provides network administrators and users with several key services, including the following:

- **Application sharing.** Network-based applications reduce the time needed to administer software applications to multiple users.

- **Data file storage and retrieval.** NetWare provides high-speed, reliable access to large quantities of data stored on magnetic and optical disk subsystems.

- **Network printing.** Shared network printing provides users with access to multiple output devices, such as laser printers, ink-jet printers, and plotters.

- **Security.** NetWare provides high levels of network security. Proper implementation of NetWare's security features virtually eliminates unauthorized users from accessing the network.

- **Communications.** NetWare supports several third-party communications and messaging systems, such as Novell's GroupWise, cc:Mail, MHS, SMTP, and mainframe mail gateways.

- **Data backup and archiving.** You can back up and restore specific targets, including the NetWare file system, eDirectory (formerly NDS), and GroupWise, by using Novell's Storage Management Services (SMS).

- **Multiprotocol routing.** The NetWare Multiprotocol Router (MPR) provides all the features necessary to connect your network to public or private networks through several types of data services including T1, frame relay, and ISDN.

- **Novell Directory Services (NDS)/eDirectory.** NDS is a globally accessible, enterprise-wide database of all network resource information. The current version, called eDirectory, is available for NetWare, as well as for a host of other platforms, such as Windows NT 4, Windows 2000, Windows Server 2003, SuSE Linux Enterprise Server, RedHat Linux Advanced Server, Solaris, AIX, and HP-UX.

  - NDS created the first true directory in the PC world.

- **Failure recovery.** Improved recovery from system errors improves stability and increases server uptime.

- **Symmetric Multiprocessing (SMP) support.** Support for industry-standard SMP is bundled with NetWare.

- **File server installation and server migration utilities.** This service supports improved and simplified installation through automatic hardware detection. Multiple utilities are provided for migrating older NetWare servers and non-NetWare servers.

- **File services and storage management services.** The NetWare file system has been improved so that it can have up to 16 million directory entries per volume.

- **Connectivity services.** Native IP is the default protocol of NetWare 5.x/6.x. IPX/SPX was the default protocol in earlier versions and continues to be supported.

- **Print services.** NetWare 4.x, 5.x, and 6.x include NetWare Distributed Print Services (NDPS) that provides improved network printing capabilities.

- **Security services.** NetWare Enhanced Security complies with DoD (United States Department of Defense) Class C2 specifications.

- Improved connectivity to the Internet and other TCP/IP-based networks.

- A wealth of additional features and services, some of which are:
  - Included Web server
  - File Transfer Protocol (FTP) server
  - IPX/IP gateway
  - Dynamic Host Configuration Protocol (DHCP) server
  - Domain Name System (DNS) server and client
  - UNIX-to-NetWare and NetWare-to-UNIX printing services
  - Clustering support through Novell Cluster Services (NCS)
  - Browser-based network and resource management through iManager
  - Client/Server file synchronization through iFolder.
  - Easy user account synchronization and administration in mixed networks through Novell DirXML, now called Novell Nsure Identity Manager. Drivers are available for Windows NT, 2000, XP, 2003, SuSE or Redhat Linux, Solaris, and others.
  - Open source product support, including Apache, MySQL, Perl, PHP, Jakarta Tomkat, all of which are included with NetWare 6.5
  - Internet-enabled printing through iPrint.
  - Easy configuration of specialized servers during the NetWare installation.

Do it!

B-1: Discussing the features of NetWare

Questions and answers

1 The super user account on a NetWare server is:

A Admin

B Supervisor

C Administrator

D Root

2 The default protocol of NetWare 5.x/6.x is:

A IPX/SPX

B TCP/IP

C NetBEUI

D Native IP

3 What service provides user account synchronization in mixed-platform environments?

Topic C: UNIX, Linux, and Mac OS X Server

This topic covers the following CompTIA Network+ exam objectives:

#	Objective
3.1	Identify the basic capabilities (For example: client support, interoperability, authentication, file and print services, application support and security) of the following server operating systems to access network resources: • UNIX / Linux / Mac OS X Server
3.4	Given a remote connectivity scenario comprised of a protocol, an authentication scheme, and physical connectivity, configure the connection. Includes connection to the following servers: • UNIX / Linux / Mac OS X Server
4.5	Given a troubleshooting scenario between a client and the following server environments, identify the cause of a stated problem: • UNIX / Linux / Mac OS X Server

Introducing UNIX

Explanation

The operating system with the most staying power on a LAN or WAN is UNIX. UNIX originated at Bell Labs in the late 1960s and became the first standard operating system. UNIX-based operating systems, such as Linux, from vendors such as Hewlett-Packard, Sun Microsystems, and IBM, continue to be widely implemented.

UNIX comes in several versions and is known by different names. The numerous UNIX vendors that emerged during the 1980s had a choice of two UNIX variants to base their operating system on, AT&T System V or Berkeley BSD4. Most vendors incorporated their own modifications to the basic system and transferred features from other versions of UNIX.

As a result of this parallel development, by the late 1980s there were several variations of UNIX which, while fundamentally the same, had small but significant variations.

Features of UNIX

UNIX's popularity can be attributed to a number of factors. UNIX is available on a wide range of hardware platforms and presents nearly the same interface to users and programmers on each. It's relatively straightforward to migrate an application from one UNIX system to another, even if the underlying hardware is radically different. Users can sit at a new UNIX system and be given the same facilities as at their old system. Therefore, applications can be written to run on a variety of hardware, freeing users from being tied to specific systems due to application availability.

The standard utility commands of UNIX are flexible, and the system provides the ability to combine them into highly sophisticated, custom-built utilities. UNIX was developed primarily to support software development activities. As a result, several of its features support this, and there are several specialized software development utilities that make the developers' roles easier.

Several facilities are available for communicating with other systems, both UNIX and non-UNIX.

The operating-system kernel includes the basic building blocks, and there are several utilities and third-party products that give you connectivity to systems such as VMS, MVS, MS-DOS, NetWare, and NT/2000/Server 2003.

UNIX also has its downfalls. It's a complex operating system to learn. Its commands are case-sensitive and cryptic.

Facts about UNIX

Some facts that you might want to remember about UNIX-based operating systems are these:

- The super user for UNIX is named root by default. The root account has complete control over the OS.
- Major vendors of UNIX server systems include:
  - Pyramid (DC/OSx)
  - SNI (Synix, SCO)
  - HP (HP/UX)
  - IBM (AIX)
  - Sequent (Dynix/PTX)
  - ICL (NTX)
- Major vendors of UNIX workstation systems include:
  - Sun (SunOS, Solaris)
  - HP (HP/UX)
  - IBM (AIX)
  - Silicon Graphics (IRIX)
- Major types of PC UNIX include:
  - SCO UNIX
  - Solaris

Do it!

C-1: Discussing UNIX

Questions and answers

1 The super user account on a UNIX server is:

A Admin

B Supervisor

C Administrator

D Root

2 UNIX commands are case-sensitive and cryptic. True or False?

3 List two types of PC UNIX.

Linux

Explanation

Linux is a UNIX-like operating system originally created by Linus Torvalds at the University of Finland with the assistance of developers around the world. The goal of Linux is to provide the PC with a free or low-cost operating system comparable to high-priced UNIX system software.

Linux conforms to the POSIX standard user and programming interfaces and comes in various versions that can run on Intel-based, PowerPC, Sparc, and Alpha-based computers. It works well both as a workstation and as a server on a LAN.

An unusual aspect of Linux is that the source code, normally closely guarded by operating system developers, is freely available to all. The advantage to this is that anyone can write improvements to the operating system.

Linux is one of the few operating systems that have an official mascot. The Linux Penguin serves as the logo for the operating system and was chosen by Linus Torvalds. You can get more information about Linux, including free downloads of various versions of the operating system, from the following Internet sites:

- www.linux.org
- www.linuxlinks.com
- www.redhat.com
- www.suse.com
- www.debian.org
- www.mandrakesoft.com

Do it!

C-2: Discussing Linux

Questions and answers
1 What is the purpose of Linux?
2 Users can write improvements to the Linux operating system. True or False?

Mac OS X Server

Explanation

Mac OS X Server is Apple Corporation's UNIX-based network operating system. The current release is v10.3, and it provides a variety of features and functionality.

Mac OS X Server is geared at small to medium-sized business. It includes Open Directory 2, the directory services implementation for MAC OS X Server.

Some of the network services provided by Mac OS X Server include the following:

- **File and Print services**. Enables sharing of files and printers among Macintosh, Linux, and Windows clients.
- **Open Directory 2**. Designed to let you host an LDAP-compliant directory service as well as Kerberos authentication services.
- **Mail services**. Users can access their e-mail via POP or IMAP or through a Web interface.
- **Web hosting**. Designed to let you host Web sites with very little effort. Uses Apache Web Server as the Web server platform.
- **Networking and VPN**. Provides a variety of networking services, such as DNS, DHCP, and NAT, and supports a variety of security protocols, such as IPSec, BIND, and IPv6. Also supports VPN for Mac OS X, Windows, and UNIX/Linux clients. Further, Mac OS X Server uses the open source ipfw to provide firewall services.
- **Media streaming**. Lets you broadcast and stream on-demand as well as real-time video and audio.
- **Workstation cloning**. NetBoot enables Macintosh clients to boot from a server hard disk, using a single image for all workstations. Network Install lets you automate workstation application installations.
- **Remote Desktop**. Designed to give you remote control over workstations in the network.

Do it!

C-3: Discussing Mac OS X Server

Questions and answers

1 What's the directory services implementation in Mac OS X Server?

2 What clients does Mac OS X Server support for file and printer sharing?

Topic D: AppleShare IP

This topic covers the following CompTIA Network+ exam objectives:

#	Objective
3.1	Identify the basic capabilities (For example: client support, interoperability, authentication, file and print services, application support and security) of the following server operating systems to access network resources: • Appleshare IP (Internet Protocol)
3.4	Given a remote connectivity scenario comprised of a protocol, an authentication scheme, and physical connectivity, configure the connection. Includes connection to the following servers: • Appleshare IP (Internet Protocol)

Features of AppleShare IP

Explanation

AppleShare IP is Apple Corporation's network operating system that can run over either TCP/IP or AppleTalk. It comes with integrated file and print services and supports Macintosh (Mac OS), AppleTalk, and Windows clients.

AppleShare IP is aimed at small to medium-sized businesses that are familiar with the Macintosh environment and want to set up and maintain a network without a lot of configuration and maintenance concerns. Some of the features provided by AppleShare IP include the following:

- **Multiple Client support**. AppleShare IP supports both Mac and Windows clients. Windows clients can browse for and use AppleShare IP services through Network neighborhood.
- **File transfer capabilities**. AppleShare IP lets Macintosh and Windows clients easily transfer files between each other.
- **User support**. AppleShare IP supports up to 500 simultaneous users.
- **Indexing capabilities**. AppleShare IP lets you index server volumes with the Sherlock utility.
- **FTP support**. AppleShare IP lets you provide FTP services to clients.
- **Web hosting**. AppleShare IP lets you host up to 50 Web sites that can also be indexed with Sherlock.
- **Distributed printing**. AppleShare IP lets you distribute printing needs to up to 10 printers across up to 10 print queues. Printing can occur either over AppleTalk or over IP. Printer access can be password-protected to maintain control over who has access to which printing resources
- **Mail services**. AppleShare IP lets you provide email services to clients using POP and IMAP. Each mail server you configure can support more than 1,000 mail clients. Mail services include spam protection and built-in group mailing lists.

- **Centralized user management**. AppleShare IP lets you centrally manage all groups and user information and supports up to 10,000 users. It also allows you to share users and groups between several AppleShare IP servers.
- **Security features**. AppleShare IP includes firewall services, password protection for file and print, as well as Web server/site access.

Do it!

D-1: Discussing AppleShare IP

Questions and answers
1 AppleShare IP can run over which transport protocols?
2 How many users does AppleShare IP support?
3 How many Web sites can you host with AppleShare IP?

Unit summary: Identifying network operating system features

Topic A
In this topic, you learned about the **Windows** family of server operating systems. You learned that **Windows NT, Windows 2000,** and **Windows Server 2003** are different versions of the Windows server operating system. You also learned about the features and functionalities of each version.

Topic B
In this topic, you learned about **Novell NetWare** and its features. You learned that NetWare 5.x and NetWare 6.x provide features for improving performance, designed for both local and global networks.

Topic C
In this topic, you learned about **UNIX**. You also learned about the features about UNIX. You then learned that **Linux** is a UNIX-like operating system. You also learned that the source code in Linux is freely available to all. Next, you learned about **Mac OS X Server**, the Unix-based network operating system from Apple Corp.

Topic D
In this topic, you learned about **AppleShare IP**. You learned that AppleShare IP can run over **TCP/IP** and **AppleTalk**. You learned that AppleShare IP provides support for **Mac OS** and **Windows** clients. You also learned about the features and services available with AppleShare IP.

Review questions

1 Which of the following are network operating systems?

A Mac OS X Server

B NetWare

C MS-DOS

D Windows Server 2003

E Multiprotocol routing

2 Name the NetWare service that provides all the features necessary to connect your network to public or private networks through several types of data services.

3 List the disadvantages of UNIX.

4 Which standard does Linux comply with?

5 Which Webserver is included with Mac OS X Server

    A Netscape Fasttrack

    B Apache

    C Both of the above

    D Mac OS X Server doesn't include a Web server

6 AppleShare IP supports which mail service protocols?

Unit 15

Network clients

Unit time: 30 minutes

Complete this unit, and you'll know how to:

A Describe the network clients that are
available to connect DOS-, Windows-, and
Macintosh-based computers to a network.

Topic A: Network client review

This topic covers the following CompTIA Network+ exam objectives:

#	Objective
2.13	Identify the purpose of network services and protocols (For example: • SMB (Server Message Block)
3.2	Identify the basic capabilities needed for client workstations to connect to and use network resources (For example: media, network protocols and peer and server services).
3.4	Given a remote connectivity scenario comprised of a protocol, an authentication scheme, and physical connectivity, configure the connection. Includes connection to the following servers: • UNIX / Linux / MAC OS X Server • Windows • NetWare • Appleshare IP (Internet Protocol)

Introducing network clients

Explanation

Network clients provide the connectivity between the server and the individual workstations in any client/server network configuration. Because the choice of client to be used is critical to overall network performance, it's important to know about a variety of individual clients. The choice of which client to use can also be driven by the choice of which operating system is being used.

DOS clients

DOS is an operating system that doesn't provide for network connectivity. As such, a DOS-compatible client must be installed to provide connectivity from the DOS workstation to the server. The network client you use is determined by the network operating system resident on the server.

DOS is limited to having only one real-mode client loaded at a time. This can pose problems in a mixed environment, such as a network that uses both Windows NT/2000/Server 2003 and NetWare servers. DOS-based machines in such an environment are able to attach to and use resources on only one type of server. More advanced desktop operating systems, such as Windows 95/98 and Windows 2000, use both real-mode and protected-mode clients, resulting in much more flexibility in accessing multiple server platforms.

Note: *Protected mode* is an operating mode of the 80286 and higher microprocessors by which the operating system can protect one application from another application running on the computer at the same time.

Windows 3.x clients

Windows 3.x was an improvement over DOS with regards to network capability because Windows 3.x provided an operating environment that's network-aware. However, because Windows 3.x isn't a true operating system, in that it depends on the underlying DOS operating system, many of the limitations seen with DOS-based clients also exist with Windows 3.x clients.

Although no onboard network client software was included with Windows 3.x, the operating system shell can be configured for a wide selection of external clients. Examples of these clients include Artisoft LANtastic, Novell NetWare, Banyan VINES, and the Microsoft Network Client.

As a general rule, when using client software other than the Microsoft Network Client with Windows 3.x, the DOS share.exe program should always be loaded prior to loading Windows. This prevents the two applications from operating on the same data file simultaneously and, subsequently, corrupting it.

Note that only one Windows 3.x network client can be active at a time because Windows 3.x doesn't support protected-mode network clients. Some Windows 3.x clients are:

- **Artisoft LANtastic.** This provides a proprietary client for connectivity within a LANtastic network

- **Novell NetWare.** This provides a network client for Windows 3.x to achieve connectivity to Novell NetWare servers. To make use of the Novell client, the latest versions of the operating shell network files must be used. There are three files that meet this criterion:

  - **NETX.COM.** Loads the network shell in DOS and makes it available to Windows 3.x.

  - **IPX.OBJ.** Makes it possible for the workstation to communicate with the server by using the IPX protocol.

  - **TBMI2.COM.** This is relevant when using Windows 3.x in standard mode. It makes applications work more reliably in standard mode by loading Novell's Task-switched Buffer Manager for IPX.

- **Banyan VINES.** This provides another network client that can be used with Windows 3.x. VINES is a simplistic means of network communication that provides wide area connectivity. Depending on the architecture of the WAN, a user can log in to a VINES network in any office and connect to network resources worldwide.

- **Microsoft Network Client.** This offers connectivity to a Microsoft-based server. Network drive operations under Windows 3.1 don't need the DOS share.exe program. The Microsoft Network automatically checks for multiple processes and doesn't permit more than one access to a given data file at a time.

Windows for Workgroups 3.x clients

Microsoft Windows for Workgroups 3.x (WFW) is a peer-to-peer networking version of Windows 3.x. With WFW, any system can act as a server and share its resources with other users on the network. Additionally, any other system connected to the network and using WFW can use those shared resources as a client. WFW is compatible with existing networks such as Windows NT, Novell NetWare, Artisoft LANtastic, and Banyan VINES.

A WFW improvement over Windows 3.x is the introduction of a protected-mode client for use on Microsoft networks. Due to the presence of the protected-mode client, as well as real-mode client support, WFW users can simultaneously access Microsoft networks by using the protected-mode network client and NetWare networks by using real-mode components.

Some of the network client options available to WFW are:

- Artisoft LANtastic, which is a proprietary client that provides connectivity in a LANtastic network. It can be loaded under Windows for Workgroups.
- Novell NetWare, which provides a network client for Windows for Workgroups that is compatible with Novell NetWare servers. To make use of the Novell client, the newest versions of the operating shell network files must be used with the Windows 3.x client.
- The Banyan VINES client, which can be used with Windows for Workgroups.
- The Microsoft Network Client, which uses the default network driver supplied in Windows for Workgroups. It offers connectivity to a Microsoft-based server. Network drive operation under Windows for Workgroups doesn't need the DOS share command.

Windows 95 clients

Windows 95 supports both the newer, protected-mode network clients and older, real-mode clients. The various clients included with Windows 95 are:

- Banyan VINES DOS/Windows 3.1 client
- FTP Software NFS client (InterDrive 95)
- Microsoft's Client for Microsoft Networks
- Microsoft's Client for NetWare Networks
- Novell NetWare Workstation Shell 3.x (NETX)
- Novell NetWare Workstation Shell 4.0 and above (VLM)
- SunSoft PC-NFS (5.0)

Windows 95 provides two protected-mode clients, Microsoft's Client for NetWare Networks and Client for Microsoft Networks. These clients use protected-mode support files, such as protocols and adapter drivers. An advantage of using these clients is that they use no conventional memory.

By using the Network Control Panel utility, you can install, manage, and remove network components. By using the Configuration tab you can:

- Add client support, adapters, protocols, and services
- Select the primary network logon
- Enable or disable file and printer sharing

By using the additional tabs at the top of the dialog box, you can enter the identification parameters for your workstation and select an access control method for the resources you share with the network.

Installing network components

In the Network dialog box, as shown in Exhibit 15-1, click Add to open the Select Network Component Type dialog box. Select the type of component you want to install and click Add to activate your available selections.

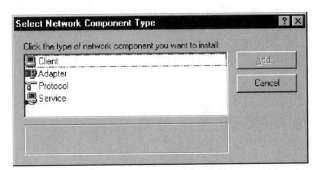

Exhibit 15-1: The Select Network Component Type dialog box

The network driver and shell files already installed on your machine when Windows 95 was installed determine the available selections. Microsoft components are always available.

Select the manufacturer from the list to view the available network clients, adapters, protocols, and services. You might see manufacturers other than those shown in Exhibit 15-2, depending on the client software that was installed on your system when you ran Windows 95 Setup.

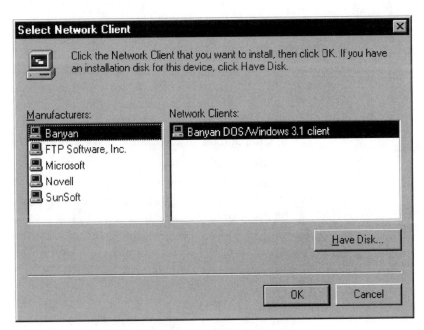

Exhibit 15-2: The Select Network Client dialog box

Note: Only one real-mode client can be installed at any time. An unlimited number of protected-mode clients might be used concurrently.

Windows 98 clients

Windows 98 builds on the networking foundation used in Windows 95 and contains several networking clients. Specifically, Windows 98 includes these protected-mode clients:

- Client for Microsoft Networks
- Client for NetWare Networks
- Microsoft Family Logon

Windows 98 includes these real-mode networking clients:

- Banyan DOS/Windows 3.1 client
- FTP Software NFS Client (InterDrive 95)
- Novell NetWare (Workstation Shell 3.x [NETX])
- Novell NetWare (Workstation Shell 4.0 and above [VLM])

The following protected-mode network clients are supplied by third-party manufacturers and can also be added:

- Artisoft LANtastic 7.0 or above
- Banyan's 32-bit or 16-bit client
- Digital PATHWORKS 32
- IBM Networks Client for Windows 95

The method of adding a networking client on a Windows 98 platform is similar to that of adding a client on a Windows 95 platform. The steps involved are:

1 Close all running applications.
2 From the Control Panel, open the Network utility or right-click the Network Neighborhood icon on the desktop and choose Properties.
3 Click Add.
4 Select Client and double-click or click Add. The Select Network Client dialog box appears, as shown in Exhibit 15-3.
5 If the client is included with Windows 98, select the manufacturer of the client, the client, and then click OK. (The Windows 98 installation source is needed). If it isn't included, insert the manufacturer's disk or CD-ROM, click Have Disk, and select the client.
6 Click OK to complete the installation.
7 Click Yes when prompted to reboot your computer.

Note: As is the case with Windows 95, any combination of 32-bit networking clients can be installed on the system. However, only one real-mode networking client can be installed at the same time.

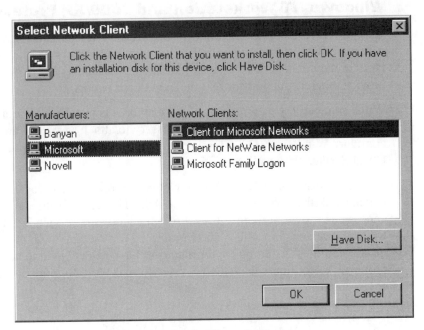

Exhibit 15-3: The Select Network Client dialog box

Windows NT Workstation and 2000/XP Professional clients

Windows NT/2000 provides built-in support for Microsoft and Novell NetWare networks. When compared with Windows 95 or Windows 98, the support for multiple types of networks isn't as robust. Additionally, Windows NT Workstation doesn't provide inherent support for real-mode network clients.

While connectivity to Windows-based networks is installed by default, Windows NT/2000 provides all the software necessary to attach to a NetWare network. To configure Windows NT/2000 to log on to a NetWare network, you must install the Client Service for NetWare service.

To accomplish this on NT, open the Network property sheet located in the Control Panel. Click the Services tab, and click Add. The Select Network Service window appears, as shown in Exhibit 15-4. From the Network Service list, select Client Service for NetWare and click OK. You're prompted for the path to your Windows NT installation files. After the appropriate files have been copied to your computer, you're prompted to configure the Client Service for NetWare for your specific network environment.

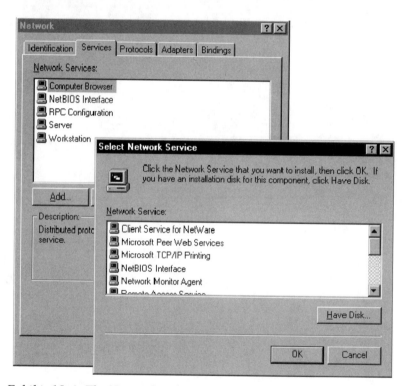

Exhibit 15-4: The Network utility in Windows NT

To add the client service for NetWare in Windows 2000 Professional, double-click Network and Dial-up Connections in the Control Panel, then right-click on Local Area Connection and choose Properties. Click Install, then select Client and click Add, as shown in Exhibit 15-5. From the Select Network Client window, choose Client Service for NetWare and click OK.

Note: The procedure for adding the Client Service for NetWare on a Windows NT/2000 Server follows the same steps.

To add the client service for NetWare in Windows XP Professional, double-click Network Connections in the Control Panel. Then, follow the instructions for Windows 2000 Professional.

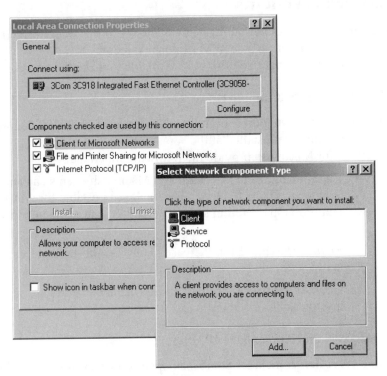

Exhibit 15-5: Adding a client in Windows 2000

Do it!

A-1:   Discussing Windows network clients

Questions and answers

1 What native network client software does DOS support?

2 Where do you go to configure a network client in Windows 95?

3 What determines which client can be used to log in to a network?

4 How many protected-mode network clients can Windows 98 support concurrently?

5 Which clients are included with Windows NT Workstation and Windows 2000/XP Professional?

Macintosh clients

Explanation

In today's network environments, the majority of the Macintosh clients in the business world must also participate in Macintosh, Windows NT/2000 or Novell NetWare environments. Various solutions are available to make this possible.

Windows NT/2000 support

Macintosh client support is built into Windows NT and 2000 Server. Services for Macintosh must be installed at the Windows Server for this support to be active. Services for Macintosh provide the following functionality:

- **File sharing.** Both PC-based and Macintosh clients can access files on the Windows NT/2000 Server. This makes it possible for all users, regardless of their desktop operating system, to collaborate on documents and share information.

- **Printer sharing.** Both PC-based and Macintosh clients can print to all networked printers.

- **Centralized user administration.** Macintosh users are administered in the same fashion as PC-based users.

Mac OS X and AppleShare IP support

Mac OS X Server includes Samba, an open source software suite that uses the Server Message Block (SMB) message format to enable Unix, Linux, and Windows clients to access a Mac OS X Server network and use file and print services on the network.

AppleShare IP provides the AppleShare Client, which enables Mac OS workstations to connect to AppleShare IP and Mac OS X Server servers. AppleShare IP also provides for Windows client connectivity through the AppleShare Client for Windows.

Novell NetWare support

For a Macintosh computer to participate on a NetWare 4.x network, you must install the Novell-supplied NetWare Client for Macintosh on each Mac. In addition, a small program is loaded on the server to support Macintosh connectivity. Features of NetWare Client for Macintosh client include:

- A login menu snaps in to the standard Macintosh menu bar permitting convenient login/logout from Mac workstations.

- Mac users have full access to NetWare file system and printing resources.

- The NetWare Print Chooser utility provides connection to NetWare printing resources.

- The NetWare Volume Mounter utility provides fast access to NetWare file system resources.

- MacIPX makes it possible for Macintosh users to communicate with NetWare servers by using NetWare's native IPX/SPX protocol suite.

- Support for NetWare/IP is provided.

- Supports the built-in Ethernet adapter included on a number of Power Macintosh computers.

Macintosh support in NetWare 5.x and later

Since the release of NetWare 5, Novell no longer provides tools for Macintosh connectivity. However, Prosoft Engineering (http://www.prosofteng.com) develops Macintosh connectivity solutions for NetWare 5.x/6.x networks. Available clients include the NetWare Client for Mac OS X and the NetWare Client for Mac OS. The former connects via IP, the latter via IPX.

Novell NetWare clients

Novell offers a network client that can be installed and configured on a workstation for network connectivity. The Novell Client is a software client that provides 32-bit access to NetWare 2.x, NetWare 3.x, NetWare 4.x, NetWare 5.x and NetWare 6.x servers from Windows 2000/XP, Windows NT Workstation, Windows 95, Windows 98, Windows for Workgroups 3.x, Windows 3.x, and DOS.

The Novell Client for Windows provides a graphical utility to log in from Windows workstations and provides the capability to access network files and printers through Windows dialog boxes. The Novell Clients for Windows 95/98 and Windows NT/2000/XP both offer 32-bit speed and stability, as well as the ability to connect simultaneously to and access resources from multiple Novell Directory Services/eDirectory directories on NetWare servers.

Note: To obtain the latest release of the Novell Client, point your Web browser to http://www.novell.com/download.

Depending on the network environment, better performance might be found by using the Novell-supplied client to access NetWare resources rather than using the Microsoft-supplied clients. Both types of clients on your network need to be tested prior to making a system-wide decision on which client to use as the standard.

Under NetWare 6.x, Windows, Macintosh, and Unix/Linux clients can also access NetWare server resources using their native protocols (CIFS, AFP and NFS respectively) through Novell File Access Pack (NFAP).

Do it!

A-2:   Discussing Macintosh and Novell NetWare clients

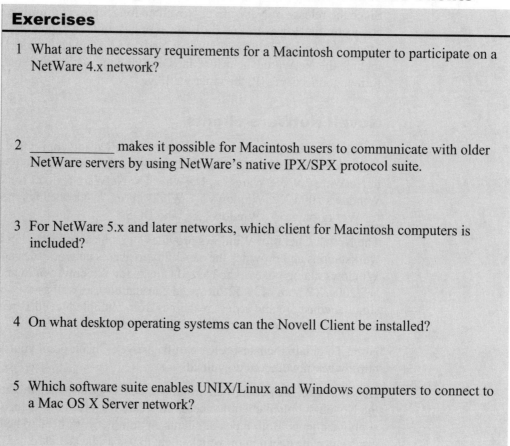

Exercises

1 What are the necessary requirements for a Macintosh computer to participate on a NetWare 4.x network?

2 _____ makes it possible for Macintosh users to communicate with older NetWare servers by using NetWare's native IPX/SPX protocol suite.

3 For NetWare 5.x and later networks, which client for Macintosh computers is included?

4 On what desktop operating systems can the Novell Client be installed?

5 Which software suite enables UNIX/Linux and Windows computers to connect to a Mac OS X Server network?

Unit summary: Network clients

Topic A

In this topic, you learned about **network clients.** You learned that network clients provide the connectivity between the server and the individual workstations in any client/server network configuration. Then you learned about the network clients that are available to **DOS, Windows 3.x, Windows for Workgroups 3.x, Windows 95, Windows 98, Windows NT Workstation, 2000 Professional and XP, Macintosh**, and **Novell NetWare** clients.

Review questions

1 Novell supplies the Novell Client for which operating systems?

2 In a Windows NT network, what must be loaded at the Windows NT server to connect a Macintosh computer to the network?

3 Windows 98 differs from Windows 95 in that it offers three protected modes as opposed to two. What are the three protected-mode network clients native to Windows 98?

4 What two protected-mode clients are native to Windows 95/98 and Windows NT/2000/XP?

5 Which client provides access for Macintosh computer to AppleShare IP and Mac OS X Servers? For Windows computers?

6 How can Linux and Macintosh clients connect natively to a NetWare 6.x server?

Unit 16

Directory services

Unit time: 120 minutes

Complete this unit, and you'll know how to:

A Describe Windows networking concepts.

B Discuss planning of a directory services implementation.

C Describe and install Microsoft's Active Directory.

D Discuss what's new in Active Directory in Windows Server 2003.

E Discuss the Windows NT domain model.

F Explain the design and purpose of Novell Directory Services/eDirectory.

Topic A: Windows networking concepts

This topic covers the following CompTIA Network+ exam objectives:

#	Objective
3.1	Identify the basic capabilities (For example: client support, interoperability, authentication, file and print services, application support and security) of the following server operating systems to access network resources: • Windows
3.7	Given a connectivity scenario, determine the impact on network functionality of a particular security implementation (For example: • Authentication and encryption
4.5	Given a troubleshooting scenario between a client and the following server environments, identify the cause of a stated problem: • Windows

Windows security models and server roles

Explanation

Before looking at directory services in Windows, you need to understand basic Windows networking concepts. The two security models used in Windows network environments are the workgroup and the domain.

The workgroup model is often implemented in small environments. Most midsize and large organizations use the domain model and also implement Active Directory. You should be familiar with both models and the benefits and limitations of each.

When a Windows 2000/Server 2003 system is deployed, it can participate on the network in one of three major roles:

*   Standalone server
*   Member server
*   Domain controller

The role for which you configure a server is a function of the network model in use (workgroup or domain), as well as the types of tasks that the server will handle. In the following sections, you'll learn more about both networking models and both server roles.

Workgroups

A Windows *workgroup* is a logical group of computers characterized by a decentralized security and administration model. In a workgroup, every computer holds its own security database, known as the local *Security Accounts Manager (SAM) database*, as illustrated in Exhibit 16-1. Because workstations don't share a common security database, each workstation or server must authenticate users independently.

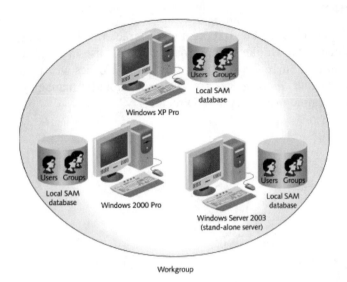

Exhibit 16-1: Workgroup security model

One of the major benefits of the workgroup model is that it's simple and doesn't require a server. Users can share resources directly from their desktop systems. However, workgroups can be difficult to manage. If a user who's logged on to one computer wants to access resources on another computer, that user must have an account on the computer that hosts the resource. If the user name and password with which the user is currently logged on matches the account on the other machine, he or she is authenticated automatically. If not, it's necessary to log on using the right credentials for that machine.

In either event, you must create and manage user accounts on multiple computers. If users want to change their passwords on one system, they must also change their passwords on all the other computers individually. Also, in the workgroup model, individual users effectively manage their own systems, an arrangement which can lead to an increase in support calls and security problems.

Note: Microsoft recommends that a workgroup be no larger than 10 computers, because Windows 2000 Professional and Windows XP Professional have been deliberately limited to allow only 10 network users to connect to the resources that the computer is sharing. Additionally, once the number of computers exceeds 10, it becomes difficult to manage all the machines individually.

Although the workgroup model doesn't require a server, a Windows 2000/Server 2003 system can still be made part of a workgroup. In the workgroup model, a server would be used for traditional purposes, such as storage of user data files or to act as an e-mail server. A Windows 2000/Server 2003 system that's configured as a member of a workgroup is referred to as a *standalone* server.

Domains

A *domain* is a logical group of computers characterized by centralized authentication and administration. Unlike a workgroup, a domain uses a centralized security database, as shown in Exhibit 16-2, that each computer references when a user logs on. Servers known as *domain controllers (DCs)* are responsible for managing the security database and authenticating users in Active Directory.

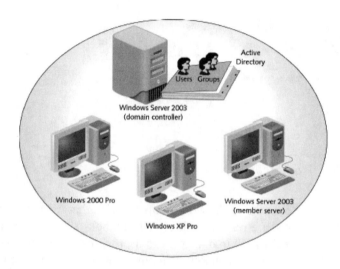

Exhibit 16-2: Domain security model

Once a user has been authenticated in the domain, individual computers, known as *domain members* or *member servers*, can authorize access to a particular resource based on the domain authentication.

Note: Domain member and member server computers still have access to their local security databases in addition to the domain database. User accounts that are stored in the domain database are referred to as *domain accounts*, whereas those stored in the computer's local security database are called *local accounts*. Local accounts are accessible only on the computer they're created on.

The domain model is highly recommended in any environment that consists of more than 10 users or workstations. One drawback of the model is that it requires at least one server to be configured as a domain controller, which means additional expense. In fact, there should be a minimum of two domain controllers in a high-demand environment.

Member servers

A member server is a Windows 2000/Server 2003 system that has a *computer account* in a domain but isn't configured as a domain controller. You use member servers for a wide variety of functions, including file, print, and application services. Member servers also commonly host network services, such as the Domain Name Service (DNS), Dynamic Host Configuration Protocol (DHCP), and others. Each of the four Windows 2000/Server 2003 editions can be configured in the role of a member server in a domain environment.

Domain controllers

In addition to being a member of a domain, a domain controller is configured to store a copy of the Active Directory database and service user authentication requests or queries about domain objects.

While there may be only one Active Directory, you can store it on multiple Domain Controllers. Multiple DC storage is a good idea for several reasons. If one DC crashes, another is running. And two or more can share the load of processing logons and directory requests. In a Windows Server 2003 environment, a domain controller can run Windows Server 2003 or Windows 2000 Server.

Note: A Windows NT Server 4.0 system can also participate as a domain controller. However, because it doesn't actually store a copy of Active Directory, it's limited to performing domain functions, such as user authentication. It can't do anything regarding Active Directory. While you can choose to dedicate domain controllers to that same role, you can also use domain controllers to provide file, print, application, and networking services. When deciding which additional roles a domain controller takes on, you need to look at the current utilization of the server, as well as whether sufficient resources (such as memory) are available to handle those other roles.

Accessing domain resources

Once a computer has joined a domain, users can log on to the computer using a domain user account. When the user provides credentials and selects a domain to log on to, instead of the local computer authenticating the user, the request for authentication is sent to a domain controller.

If the domain controller successfully authenticates the user, the local computer then allows the user to log on to the workstation or server. This method provides a high level of security, as even access to the computer's desktop is governed by authentication. As the user connects to other domain member computers, no further authentication is necessary, because the original authentication is used.

Do it!

A-1: Discussing Windows security models

Questions and answers

1 Which Windows security model uses a decentralized security and administration model?

2 In what way is the workgroup model inefficient?

3 Which Windows security model uses a centralized security and administration model?

   A   Workgroup

   B   Enterprise

   C   Department

   D   Domain

4 What's the difference between a member server and a domain controller in the domain security model in Windows 2000/Windows Server 2003?

Topic B: Directory services planning and implementation

This topic covers the following CompTIA Network+ exam objectives:

#	Objective
3.1	Identify the basic capabilities (For example: client support, interoperability, authentication, file and print services, application support and security) of the following server operating systems to access network resources: • Windows
3.7	Given a connectivity scenario, determine the impact on network functionality of a particular security implementation (For example: • Authentication and encryption
4.5	Given a troubleshooting scenario between a client and the following server environments, identify the cause of a stated problem: • Windows

Active Directory

Explanation

Active Directory is a core service for networks that use Windows 2000/Server 2003 as the *network operating system (NOS)*. Active Directory provides a central repository for information about the users and resources on a network. Active Directory was introduced in the Windows 2000 Server product family and has been improved in Windows Server 2003. The improvements include additional performance, scalability, and management features that make it easier to manage complicated network environments. Windows Server 2003 also offers greater flexibility in designing, deploying, and managing an organization's directory, which is an increasingly significant feature as more directory-enabled applications are developed.

Directory service

A *directory service (DS)* is a network service that allows users or computers to look up information about users or the location of network resources. The name of the Microsoft directory service is Active Directory.

To understand further what a directory service is, think of the directory assistance service offered by telephone companies. If you don't know the phone number of a person you want to contact, you can ask the directory operator to look up the person's number for you. The directory service for a NOS is very similar. Its first function is to provide information about objects in the directory, including users and resources such as file shares, printers, and e-mail addresses.

Active Directory is more important than a directory assistance service, however, because the information it contains is crucial for the correct and secure operation of the network. The security information includes user accounts, which identify users; and groups, which represent a collection of user accounts that require access to the same resources. Active Directory also defines security policies that include how passwords are handled and when data should be encrypted.

Planning and implementing an infrastructure

The most crucial step in any deployment is planning. A poorly designed Active Directory can slow an otherwise high-performance network to a crawl. You have to consider factors such as network bandwidth, location of users and resources, and the types of operations being performed by the network. These are all things that can influence your design. In many cases, a pre-existing network must be taken into consideration when performing a migration.

Managing and maintaining an infrastructure

Once Active Directory has been deployed, you often have to make small changes to optimize the performance of the network. Regular maintenance helps insure that data is secure and that performance doesn't degrade over time. Also, problems may arise after the deployment that require troubleshooting to identify the malfunction.

Planning and implementing user, computer, and group strategies

Security is one of your highest concerns as a NOS administrator. The first step in securing a network is *authentication*, which is the process of identifying users and making sure the users are who they say they are. In Active Directory, the user account contains the identification of the person and the information needed to authenticate the user. The level of security required by the organization is the primary factor when planning a user account strategy. Password length and complexity and account use time limits are issues you should address when defining user account policies.

Besides controlling logins, Active Directory helps you control access to network resources, such as file shares and printers. This process of allowing or denying access to resources is referred to as *authorization*. Once the network knows who a particular user is, authorization controls what the user can and can't do. To make user access management easier, you can add users to groups, which are in turn given access to resources. Designing a group strategy is a complex task, and such factors as resource control and user account location have an affect on the strategy.

Planning and implementing Group Policy

Group Policy is used to manage the way workstations, servers, and user environments behave. You can implement policies that require all communication between clients and servers to be encrypted, that control user desktop appearance, that perform maintenance tasks, and much more. Group Policy can also be used to deploy applications to computers or users. User requirements, corporate policies, the network design, and management policies are all factors that influence a Group Policy design.

Managing and Maintaining Group Policy

Once a Group Policy design is implemented, you'll probably have to make changes to policies and troubleshoot unintended results. Also, applications are often updated, and these updates must be applied to computers and users that had the application installed by Group Policy.

Do it!

B-1: Planning and implementing directory services

Questions and answers

1 List the factors that can influence an Active Directory design.

2 The management of users and resources on a network is provided by _____.

   A   an operating system

   B   a network operating system

   C   a network service

   D   an authentication policy

3 Active Directory is the directory service for Windows Server 2003 networks. True or False?

4 _____ policy is used to manage the way workstations, servers, and user environments behave.

Topic C: Introduction to Active Directory

This topic covers the following CompTIA Network+ exam objectives:

#	Objective
3.1	Identify the basic capabilities (For example: client support, interoperability, authentication, file and print services, application support and security) of the following server operating systems to access network resources: • Windows
4.5	Given a troubleshooting scenario between a client and the following server environments, identify the cause of a stated problem: • Windows

Active Directory (AD)

Explanation

Active Directory (AD)is the native directory service included with Windows 2000/Server 2003 operating systems. Active Directory provides the following services and features to the network environment:

- A central point for storing, organizing, managing, and controlling network objects, such as users, computers, and groups
- A single point of administration of objects, such as users, groups, computers, and Active Directory-published resources, such as printers or shared folders
- Logon and authentication services for users
- Delegation of administration to allow for decentralized administration of Active Directory objects, such as users and groups

The Active Directory database is stored on any Windows 2000/Server 2003 server that has been promoted to the role of domain controller. Each domain controller on the network has a writeable copy of the directory database. This means that you can make Active Directory changes to any domain controller within your network, and those changes are replicated to all of the other domain controllers. This process is called *multi-master replication* and provides a form of fault tolerance. If a single server fails, Active Directory doesn't fail, because replicated copies of the database are available from other servers within the network.

Active Directory uses the *Domain Name Service (DNS)* to maintain domain-naming structures and locate network resources. What this means to a network designer is that all Active Directory names must follow standard DNS naming conventions. An example of a standard DNS naming convention is Dovercorp.net. A child domain of Dovercorp.net would add its name as a prefix, such as Europe.Dovercorp.net.

Active Directory objects

Active Directory stores a variety of objects within the directory database. An *object* represents network resources, such as users, groups, computers, and printers. When an object is created in Active Directory, various attributes are assigned to it to provide information about the object. For example, Exhibit 16-3 shows the New Object – User dialog box for creating a new user object and the ability to add various attributes, such as First name, Last name, and User logon name.

If you need to locate information about an object from Active Directory, you can perform a search on specific attributes relating to the object. For example, Exhibit 16-4 shows the Properties box in which you can find the e-mail address of a user object after searching for the specific user name in Active Directory. You can also view this Properties box by right-clicking a user object and choosing Properties.

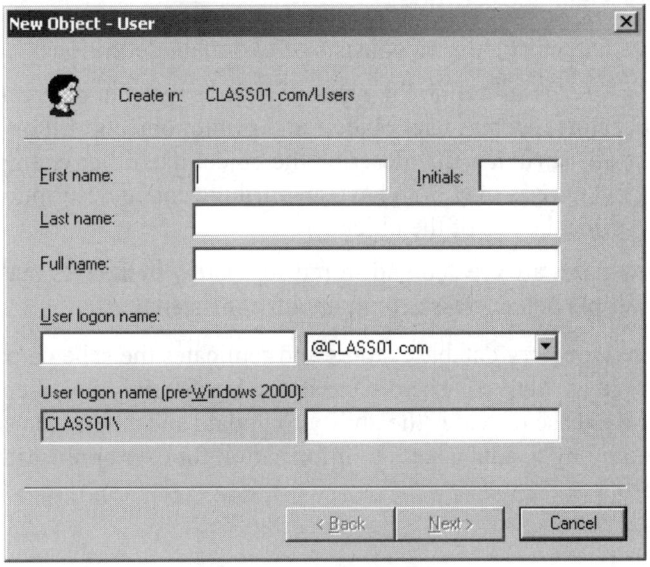

Exhibit 16-3: Creating a new user object

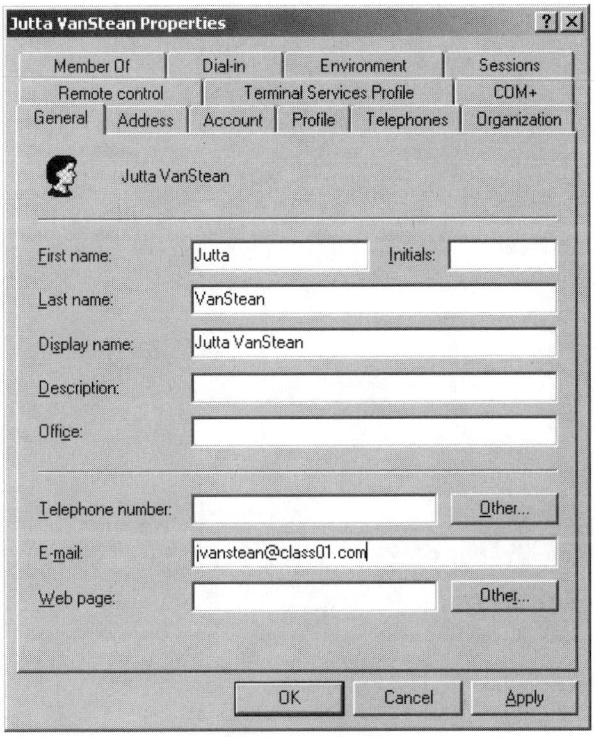

Exhibit 16-4: Viewing user object properties in Windows Server 2003

Active Directory schema

All of the objects and attributes that are available in Active Directory are defined in the *Active Directory schema*. In Windows 2000/Server 2003, the schema defines the objects for the entire Active Directory structure. This means that there's only one schema for a given Active Directory implementation, and this schema is replicated among all domain controllers within the network.

The Active Directory schema consists of two main definitions:

- *Object classes* define the types of objects that can be created within Active Directory, such as user objects and printer objects. All object classes consist of various attributes that describe the object itself. For example, the user and printer object classes may both have an attribute called description, which is used to describe the use of the object.

- *Attributes* are created and stored separately in the schema and can be used with multiple object classes to maintain consistency.

The Active Directory database stores and replicates the schema partition to all domain controllers in an Active Directory environment. Storing the schema within the Active Directory database provides the ability to update and extend the schema dynamically, as well as providing instant access to information for user applications that need to read the schema properties.

Do it!

C-1:   Discussing Active Directory

Questions and answers

1 Active Directory allows a single point of _____ of objects.

2 Objects in an Active Directory can include:

 A   Users

 B   Printers

 C   Groups

 D   All the above

3 Multi-master replication is a form of _____ _____ .

4 To locate network resources, the Active Directory uses:

 A   NetBIOS

 B   A database

 C   Active Directory Directory

 D   Domain Name Service

5 An Active Directory implementation can have only one schema. True or false?

Active Directory logical structure and components

Explanation

Active Directory is made of several components that provide you with a way to design and administer the hierarchical, logical structure of the network. The logical components that make up an Active Directory structure include:

- Domains and organizational units
- Trees and forests
- A global catalog

To ensure efficient maintenance and troubleshooting within Active Directory, it's essential that you understand these logical components. The next few sections discuss each component in greater detail.

Domains and organizational units

A Windows 2000/Server 2003 domain is a logically structured organization of objects, including users, computers, groups, and printers that are part of a network and share a common directory database. Each domain has a unique name and is organized in levels and administered as a unit with common rules and procedures.

Windows 2000/Server 2003 domains provide a number of administrative benefits, including the ability to configure unique security settings, decentralize administration (if necessary), and control replication traffic. By default, members of the Administrators group are allowed to manage only the objects within their own domain. All domain controllers within a single domain store a copy of the Active Directory database, and domain-specific information is replicated only among the domain controllers of the same domain.

An *organizational unit (OU)* is a logical container used to organize objects within a single domain. Objects, such as users, groups, computers, and other OUs, can be stored in an OU container. For example, you may want to organize your users based upon the department in which they work. You could create a Sales OU to store all your sales department users and objects. You might also create a Marketing OU to store all your marketing department users and objects. Not only does this make it easier to locate and manage Active Directory objects, but it also allows you to apply *Group Policy* settings to define more advanced features, such as software deployment or desktop restrictions based upon department, job function, or geographic location. Exhibit 16-5 shows an example of a domain with several OUs.

Another main advantage of using an OU structure is the ability to delegate administrative control over OUs. For example, you may want to give a set of users the right to add or remove new users within the Sales OU. You don't have to provide the group with full administrative rights to accomplish this task, because Active Directory allows you to delegate very specific tasks, if necessary.

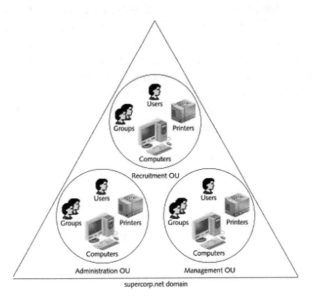

Exhibit 16-5: An Active Directory domain and OU structure

Trees and forests

When designing a Windows 2000/Server 2003 network infrastructure, the nature of the organization might require you to create multiple domains within an organization. Multiple domains are created in a structure called trees and forests. Some of the reasons for doing so include the following:

- Divisions within the company may be administered on a geographic basis. To make administration easier, a separate domain is created for each division.

- Different password policies are needed among divisions within an organization.

- A very large number of objects need to be defined.

- Replication performance needs to be improved.

The first Active Directory domain created in an organization is called the *forest root domain*. When multiple domains are needed, they're connected to the forest root to form either a single tree or multiple trees, depending upon the design of the domain name structure. A *tree* is a hierarchical collection of domains that share a contiguous DNS namespace. For example, Dover Leasing has its head office in Boston with a forest root domain called Dovercorp.net. Dover has two divisions, one located in London and the other in Hong Kong. Because of geographic and administrative differences, you might decide to create a distinct domain for each division. Two child domains can be created off of the forest root domain. The London domain can be named Europe.Dovercorp.net, which follows the contiguous DNS namespace design. Similarly, the Hong Kong domain can be called Asia.Dovercorp.net. Exhibit 16-6 is an example of this structure.

Whenever a child domain is created, a two-way, transitive trust relationship is automatically created between the child and parent domains. A *transitive trust* means that all other trusted domains implicitly trust one another. For example, because Europe.Dovercorp.net trusts the Dovercorp.net forest root domain, Europe also implicitly trusts the Asia.Dovercorp.net domain via the Dovercorp.net domain. These two-way, transitive trusts allow for resource access anywhere throughout the Active Directory structure. Windows 2000/Server 2003 also allows explicit trusts to be created between domains in the same forest, as well as between forests, if necessary.

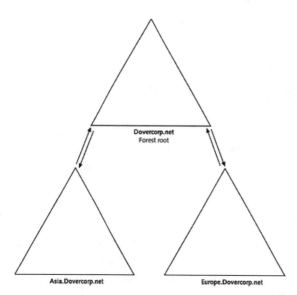

Exhibit 16-6: The Dovercorp.net domain tree

A *forest* can consist of a collection of trees, a single tree, or a single domain that doesn't share a contiguous DNS naming structure. Although the term "forest" implies a number of trees, an Active Directory forest might consist of only a single domain. For example, Dover Leasing purchases a large international company called Seven Acres Property Management. It may not make sense to make the Seven Acres domain a child of Dovercorp.net because of the renaming required to maintain a contiguous naming convention based on Dovercorp.net. Instead, you could create a new tree and allow Seven Acres to start its own contiguous naming hierarchy. Both trees make up an Active Directory forest, as shown in Exhibit 16-7. Domains in a forest also have a two-way, transitive trust relationship.

Even though the trees within a forest don't share a common namespace, they do share a single Active Directory schema, which ensures that all object classes and attributes are consistent throughout the entire structure. A special group called Enterprise Admins is also created, which allows members to manage objects throughout the entire forest. The Enterprise Admins group is created within the initial forest root domain and has a scope throughout the entire forest. Another component that's shared throughout the forest is a global catalog.

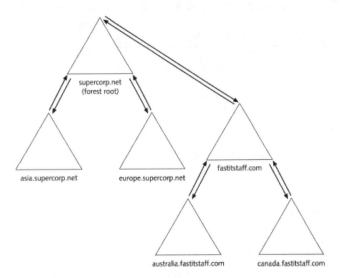

Exhibit 16-7: An Active Directory forest

Global catalog

A *global catalog* is an index and partial replica of the objects and attributes most frequently used in the Active Directory structure. Some of the common attributes that are stored in a global catalog include a user's first and last names, logon name, or e-mail address. A global catalog is replicated to any server within the forest that's configured to be a global catalog server. A global catalog is used primarily for four main functions:

- To enable users to find Active Directory information from anywhere in the forest.

- To provide universal group membership information to facilitate logging on to the network. During the logon process in a multiple-domain environment, a global catalog server is contacted to provide universal group membership information.

- To supply authentication services when a user from another domain logs on using a *user principal name (UPN)* (A UPN is a representation of a user's logon credentials in the form user@domain.com. When a UPN is used, a domain name doesn't need to be specified explicitly in the Log on to dropdown box.)

- To respond to directory lookup requests from Exchange 2000 and other applications. Global catalog servers also host the Exchange 2000 Global Address List (GAL).

The first domain controller in the forest root domain automatically becomes a global catalog server. To provide redundancy, you can configure additional domain controllers to be global catalog servers. Multiple global catalogs can improve user query and logon authentication performance, especially in Active Directory environments that include geographically distant sites. Microsoft recommends that each Active Directory site be configured with at least one domain controller acting as a global catalog server.

In cases where placing a global catalog in a specific site isn't practical (possibly because of slow WAN links between locations), Windows Server 2003 Active Directory provides a new feature known as universal group caching. Universal group caching allows the domain controllers within a particular site to query a global catalog server in another location for a user's universal group membership information, and then cache that information locally for use in subsequent logons.

Do it!

C-2: Discussing components of Active Directory

Questions and answers

1 In Windows 2000/Server 2003, a two-way, transitive trust relationship is maintained between which of the following?

   A   Child and parent forests

   B   Child and parent groups

   C   Child and parent domains

   D   None of the above

2 On which of the following systems is the global address list (GAL) stored for Exchange 2000 e-mail systems?

   A   All domain controllers

   B   All member servers

   C   All desktop systems

   D   Global catalog server

3 Which group exists within the forest root domain only but has administrative privileges in all forest domains by default?

   A   Administrators

   B   Enterprise Admins

   C   Domain Admins

   D   Forest Admins

4 Which of the following domain controllers become global catalog servers by default?

   A   First domain controller in all domains

   B   All domain controllers in the forest root domain

   C   First domain controller in the forest root domain

   D   None

5 Which of the following logical Active Directory components is created mainly for the delegation of administrative authority and the implementation of group policy settings?

   A   Tree

   B   Domain

   C   Forest

   D   Organizational unit

6 Which of the following statements best describes an Active Directory forest?

   A   A collection of domains that share a common schema

   B   A collection of organizational units

   C   A collection of trees with different schemas

   D   A collection of users with common settings

Installing Active Directory

Explanation

Active Directory isn't installed by default. In Windows Server 2003, you can install it using the Manage your server tool in your server's Administrative Tools. You can access Administrative Tools either from the Start menu or through the Control Panel.

Do it!

C-3: Installing Active Directory

Here's how	Here's why
1 At your Windows Server 2003 computer, choose **Start**, **Manage Your Server**	To open the Windows Server 2003 Manage Your Server dialog box.
2 Click **Add or remove a role**	To start the Configure Your Server wizard.
3 In the Preliminary Steps dialog box, read the information and click **Next**	
4 In the Configuration Options dialog box, select **Custom Configuration**	If necessary.
5 In the list of server roles, select **Domain Controller (Active Directory)**	To specify that you want this server to be a domain controller, which means Active Directory will be installed on the server.
6 Click **Next**	
7 Click **Next**	To start the Active Directory Installation Wizard.
8 In the Welcome dialog box, click **Next**	
9 In the Operating System Compatibility dialog box, read the information	Because of Windows Server 2003 security settings, Windows 95 and Windows NT 4.0 SP3 or earlier machines cannot log on to a Windows Server 2003 domain or access domain resources.
10 Click **Next**	
11 In the Domain Controller Type dialog box, verify that Domain Controller for a new domain is selected	This will be the first domain controller in the network.
12 Click **Next**	
13 Verify that Domain in a new forest is selected	No forest exists yet.
14 Click **Next**	

15	In the Full DNS name for new domain box, enter **CLASS##.com** Click **Next**	Where ## is the number assigned to your Windows Server 2003 student computer.
16	Click **Next**	To accept the default domain NetBIOS name.
17	Click **Next**	To accept the default database and log locations.
18	Click **Next**	To accept the default Sysvol folder location.
19	Click **Next**	To install and configure DNS on this computer.
20	Verify that Permissions compatible only with Windows 2000 or Windows Server 2003 operating systems is selected and click **Next**	
21	Enter **password** in the Restore Mode Password and Confirm Password boxes Click **Next**	To assign a password to the Administrator account.
22	Click **Next**	To start the installation. The installation process takes a while to complete.
23	If prompted, insert the Windows Server 2003 CD into the CD-ROM drive and click **OK**	
24	Click **Cancel**	To close the dialog box asking you if you want to perform an action.
25	Click **Finish**	Active Directory is now installed on your computer.
26	Click **Restart Now**	The computer has to be rebooted before changes take effect.
27	When the computer has rebooted, log in as Administrator	
28	When prompted, click **Finish** to complete the Active Directory installation	
29	Close the Manage Your Server dialog box	

Active Directory naming standards

Explanation
Active Directory uses the DNS naming standard for host name resolution and for providing information on the location of network services and resources. For example, if you need to locate a server called database.Dovercorp.net, your workstation first queries a DNS server to resolve the IP address of the database server. Once the IP address is known, a direct communication session can take place.

The same process occurs when you need to log on to the domain. Your workstation queries DNS to find a domain controller to perform authentication. Once the location of a domain controller is known, the authentication process can take place.

When users need to access Active Directory, the *Lightweight Directory Access Protocol (LDAP)* is used to query or update the Active Directory database directly. Just as a DNS name contains a specific naming convention (e.g., Dovercorp.net), LDAP also follows a specific naming convention. LDAP naming paths are used when referring to objects stored within the Active Directory. Two main components of the naming paths include:

- **Distinguished name.** Every object in Active Directory has a unique *distinguished name (DN)*. For example, the Dovercorp.net domain component (DC) has a user object with a common name (CN) of Moira Cowan that's stored within the Marketing OU. The distinguished name for the object would be CN=Moira Cowan, OU=Marketing, DC=Dovercorp, DC=Net.

- **Relative distinguished name.** A portion of the distinguished name that uniquely identifies the object within the container is referred to as the *relative distinguished name (RDN)*. For example, the distinguished name OU=Marketing, DC=Dovercorp, DC=Net would have a relative distinguished name of OU=Marketing. For the distinguished name CN=Moira Cowan, OU=Marketing, DC=Dovercorp, DC=Net, the relative distinguished name would be CN=Moira Cowan.

Active Directory physical structure

The Active Directory physical structure relates to the actual connectivity of the physical network itself. Because the Active Directory database is stored on multiple servers, you need to make sure that any modification to the database is replicated as quickly as possible between domain controllers. You must also design your topology so that replication doesn't saturate the available network bandwidth. One replication problem that you may encounter is when domain controllers are separated over a slow WAN connection. In this scenario, you likely want to control the frequency and the time that replication takes place.

In addition to replication, you may also want to control logon traffic. Referring back to the previous scenario, you generally don't want any user authentication requests to have to cross over slow WAN links during the logon process. Optimally, users should authenticate to a domain controller on their side of the WAN connection.

Note: Keep in mind that the physical structure of Active Directory is totally separate from the logical structure. The logical structure is used to organize your network resources, whereas the physical structure is used to control network traffic.

You can control Active Directory replication and authentication traffic by configuring sites and site links. An Active Directory site is a combination of one or more Internet Protocol (IP) subnets connected by a high-speed connection. It's assumed that domain controllers that belong to the same site all have a common network connection. It's also assumed that any connection between sites that aren't reliable at all times must have replication controlled through replication schedules and frequency intervals.

A *site link* is a configurable object that represents a connection between sites. Site links created using the Active Directory Sites and Services snap-in are the core of Active Directory replication. The site links can be adjusted for replication availability, bandwidth costs, and replication frequency. Windows 2000/Server 2003 uses this information to generate the replication topology for the sites, including the schedule for replication. Exhibit 16-8 shows an example of a site structure within a domain. Each site contains domain controllers that share a high-speed connection. Because of a slower WAN connection between Boston, Hong Kong, and London, sites and site links have been defined better to control replication and logon traffic.

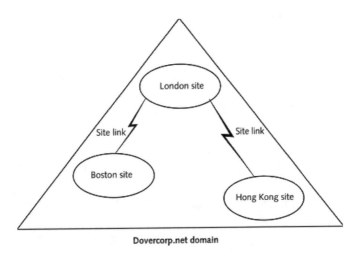

Exhibit 16-8: The site structure of Dovercorp.net

Replication within a site takes place based on a change notification process. If any change is made within Active Directory, the server waits 15 seconds and then announces the changes to another domain controller. In cases where a domain controller has multiple replication partners within a site, changes are sent out to additional domain controllers at three-se-cond intervals. Replication between sites is initially set at every three hours by default but can easily be changed by editing the properties of the site link object.

Do it!

C-4: Discussing Active Directory naming standards and physical structure

Questions and answers

1 Assuming a user name of John Doe with a user account located in the Marketing OU of the domain supercorp.net, what would be the object's distinguished name?

   A   CN=John Doe

   B   OU=Marketing, CN=John Doe

   C   DC=net, DC=supercorp, OU= Marketing, CN=John Doe

   D   CN=John Doe, OU=Marketing, DC= supercorp, DC=net

2 Assuming the same user name and account location, what would be the object's relative distinguished name?

   A   CN=John Doe

   B   OU=Marketing, CN=John Doe

   C   DC=net, DC=supercorp, OU= Marketing, CN=John Doe

   D   CN=John Doe, OU=Marketing, DC= supercorp, DC=net

3 The physical structure of Active Directory is totally separate from the logical structure. True or false?

4 By default, how often does Active Directory replication take place between sites?

   A   Every hour

   B   Every 2 hours

   C   Every 3 hours

   D   Never

5 The two main components of the LDAP naming paths include:

   A   Distinguished name

   B   DNS name

   C   Relative distinguished name

   D   Common name

6 Replication between domain controllers within a site is triggered by a change notification process initiated how many seconds after the change occurs?

   A   10

   B   20

   C   15

   D   5

Topic D: New Active Directory features in Windows Server 2003

This topic covers the following CompTIA Network+ exam objectives:

#	Objective
3.1	Identify the basic capabilities (For example: client support, interoperability, authentication, file and print services, application support and security) of the following server operating systems to access network resources: • Windows
4.5	Given a troubleshooting scenario between a client and the following server environments, identify the cause of a stated problem: • Windows

Active Directory and Windows Server 2003

Explanation

Although Active Directory isn't new, Windows Server 2003 offers new features and capabilities in the areas of deployment, management, security, performance, and dependability. These enhancements make Active Directory more flexible and lower the total cost of ownership (TCO). The following sections describe some of the new features of Active Directory in Windows Server 2003.

Deployment and management

In very large enterprises with multiple forests, domains, and sites, Windows Server 2003 makes configuring and managing Active Directory easier. For easier deployment, Windows Server 2003 allows you to rename domains and has improved tools for migrating from earlier versions of Windows. After Active Directory is deployed, new management features, such as multi-object selection, better drag-and-drop capabilities, and improvements in Group Policy, help you to be more productive. Security is also enhanced and simplified by implementing Cross-forest trusts and a Credential Manager.

Active Directory Migration Tool (ADMT) 2.0

The second major release of the Active Directory Migration Tool (ADMT) 2.0 makes it easier migrating to Active Directory by allowing passwords to be migrated from Windows NT 4.0 to Windows 2000 and Windows Server 2003 domains.

Domain renaming

Once a domain was created in Windows 2000, no method existed for renaming it other than removing the domain and recreating it. Windows Server 2003 adds support for renaming both the Domain Name System (DNS) and NetBIOS names of existing domains. This new feature makes administration much easier, because decisions that were once final are now reversible. Organizations that are restructuring or merging can now redesign their Active Directory deployment, completely recreating the environment.

Schema redefinition

The Active Directory schema has been made more flexible by adding the ability to deactivate class definitions and attributes. If a class or attribute definition contains an error, it can now be redefined to correct the error.

Cross-forest trust

A cross-forest trust is a trust created between the root domains of two forests. It allows for secure access to resources when the user account and computer account aren't in the same forest. While still keeping the benefits of easier administration and single sign-on, a cross-forest trust allows a user to be authenticated securely in another forest. Additionally, a cross-forest trust makes authorization easier for administrators by allowing selection of users and groups in a trusted forest when setting permissions on resources or setting group memberships.

Credential Manager

The Credential Manager increases the usefulness of single sign-on by providing secure storage of passwords and certificates. The first time users attempt to access a business application that requires authentication, they're prompted to provide the credentials. After the first logon, the credentials are stored and associated with the requesting application, and any requests for authentication by the same application use the saved credentials instead of prompting the user again.

Software Restriction Policies

Software Restriction Policies now allow you to restrict what software can run on a system. By restricting the use of unknown or distrusted software, you can better protect the network. Policies can be set up that either allow or disallow unknown software to run, with additional rules added that make exceptions for individual applications.

Do it!

D-1: Discussing deployment and management

Questions and answers

1 Why would you need to change a domain's name? Choose all that apply.

    A   If an organization restructures

    B   If two organizations merge

    C   If a server fails

    D   For security

2 A cross-forest trust manages what relationship?

    A   Between a forest and trees

    B   Between a forest and another forest's trees

    C   Between the root domains of two forests

3 A Credential Manager simplifies access to applications. True or False?

4 Software Restriction Policies define only what software can't be run on a domain system. True or False?

Performance and dependability

Explanation

With improvements in replication and synchronization, Windows Server 2003 is more efficient at propagating updates. It offers better control over the types of information that domain controllers replicate within a domain or among multiple domains. Also, by replicating only the changes to groups rather than to the entire group membership list, network bandwidth and processor usage are decreased.

Universal group caching

In Windows Server 2003, branch offices with only a Windows Server 2003 domain controller can now use cached credentials to log on users without having to contact a global catalog server. Caching user credentials improves reliability, because the loss of a WAN link between a branch office and global catalog no longer affects a user's ability to log on. Also, not having to wait for a global catalog to respond improves logon performance while lowering WAN bandwidth utilization.

Application directory partitions

Some information stored in Active Directory doesn't need to be available on all domain controllers across the entire forest. Application directory partitions allow you to configure the location of replicas and the scope of replication. This, in turn, allows information for applications to be stored where it's needed while impacting the network performance as little as possible. The DNS Server in Windows Server 2003 is one of the first applications/services to take advantage of this new feature.

Install replication from media

When you create a new domain controller in an existing domain or forest, one of the most network-intensive steps is the initial replication, where existing information is copied to the new DC. A new feature in Windows Server 2003 allows initial replication to be sourced from the backup of an existing domain controller or global catalog. This method saves network bandwidth, because only changes from the time the backup was made must be replicated. Also, for branch offices with slow links, sourcing from media can save a considerable amount of time in creating a domain controller.

Do it!

D-2: Discussing performance and dependability

Questions and answers

1 How has Active Directory schema been made more flexible?

2 When creating a new domain controller in an existing domain or forest, one of the most network-intensive steps is the _____, where existing Active Directory information is copied to the new domain controller.

Topic E: Windows NT domains

This topic covers the following CompTIA Network+ exam objectives:

#	Objective
3.1	Identify the basic capabilities (For example: client support, interoperability, authentication, file and print services, application support and security) of the following server operating systems to access network resources: • Windows
4.5	Given a troubleshooting scenario between a client and the following server environments, identify the cause of a stated problem: • Windows

Legacy systems

Explanation

As a system administrator, you may also encounter legacy systems such as Windows NT servers and networks, so it's helpful to understand the Windows NT networking model. Windows NT organizes resources on a network and makes these resources available to users. Windows NT Directory Services provide one important benefit to administrators, the concept of a domain and primary and backup domain controllers.

A domain is a logical entity built around a client/server model. In Windows NT, one Windows NT Server acts as the *Primary Domain Controller* (PDC), providing centralized management of resources, user accounts, group accounts, permissions, and rights. Normally, the domain includes at least one *backup domain controller (BDC)* to provide additional resources to the domain and assist with logon verification. A backup domain controller can also be promoted to primary domain controller should the primary domain controller become unavailable.

On Windows 2000/Server 2003, primary and backup domain controllers are replaced by multiple domain controllers of equal status. In the NT model, user accounts cannot be modified if the primary domain controller is down. In 2000's "multi-master" model, all domain controllers replicate directory services databases with each other. This provides for fault tolerance in case a domain controller becomes unavailable.

You can support and manage a large number of users and workstations by using Domains. User accounts, group accounts, resources, and security are all centrally managed.

In Windows NT, user account and security information are contained in the Security Accounts Manager (SAM) database. A master copy of SAM exists in the registry on the primary domain controller and is replicated to the backup domain controllers on a regular basis. In Windows 2000, user account and security information is contained in the Active Directory.

The Windows NT domain model

Windows NT supports various types of domain models. The flexibility of these models is one of the advantages of using Windows NT Server. Rather than forcing an organization to fit into a specific design dictated by the network operating system, you can design the network to meet your specific needs.

As your organizational needs evolve, you can evolve your domain model to match them. These models are guidelines but not the only possible models you can develop.

Trust relationships

Trust relationships are an important part of Windows NT Server domain management and security. They provide a way of combining domains into a single management unit. A *trust relationship* is a logical link implemented between two domains by the domain administrators.

Trust relationships:

- **Provide flexibility in network planning and design.** Domains can be combined in various ways to meet operational needs.

- **Simplify administrative overhead for multiple domains.** Multiple domains can be managed from a central point. A single-user database can be maintained and applied across multiple domains.

- **Simplify network access for end users.** End users need to remember only one global user account name and password to be able to access all necessary network resources.

- **Permit domains to share resources easily.** Domain boundaries don't have to act as barriers to resource access.

About trust relationships

Each trust relationship is established between two domains: a trusting domain and a trusted domain, as shown in Exhibit 16-9. After the relationship is established, users and groups in the trusted domain can be assigned rights and permissions in the trusting domain. It's important to note that users and groups in the trusted domain don't automatically receive any rights or permissions.

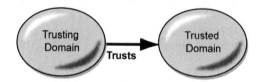

Exhibit 16-9: The trusting domain and trusted domain in a trust relationship

One-way trusts

A one-way trust is the basic type of trust relationship. An example is shown in Exhibit 16-10. More elaborate relationships are built through multiple one-way trusts between domains.

Exhibit 16-10: A one-way trust

Two-way trusts

The other basic type of trust is a two-way trust. A two-way trust is two separate one-way trust relationships established between a pair of domains, as shown in Exhibit 16-11.

Exhibit 16-11: An example of two-way trust

Do it!

E-1:   Discussing Windows NT and trust relationships

Questions and answers

1 The Windows NT server that provides centralized management of resources, user accounts, group accounts, permissions, and rights is called the _____ .

2 A _____ is a logical link implemented between two domains by the domain administrators.

3 What's a two-way trust?

Single domain model

Explanation

In the single NT domain model, you have a single primary domain controller containing the account information for the user, workstations, and other servers in the domain. You might also have backup domain controllers to assist in logon authentication and additional (member) servers to provide resources.

Master domain model

The master domain model combines both domain independence and centralized administration.

It works well in environments where departments want to retain control over resources, with a central management department available to handle user administration.

- **Master domain.** The master domain acts as the logon domain. User accounts and global group accounts are created and managed in the master domain.
- **Resource domains.** Each resource domain has a one-way trust relationship with the master domain. There's normally no trust relationship established between the resource domains. Local group accounts are created and managed on the resource domains.

This model is well suited to both local and wide area networks. When implemented in a WAN, it's suggested that a backup domain controller for the master domain be placed at each remote location.

Multiple master domain model

The master domain model is neither large nor flexible enough to meet the needs of all networks. The multiple master domain uses this model but builds it out further. Again, user accounts and network resources are managed separately. The difference is that the master accounts are spread across multiple domains.

This model is used in the same organizational environment as the master domain model but where the number of accounts has grown beyond what a single master domain can support. It's also an expansion path for a single domain that's grown too large to manage easily.

Complete trust model

In the complete trust model, each domain can act both as a master domain and as a resource domain. Usually, each domain is managed separately, with access to other domains granted through two-way trust relationships.

The complete trust model is a mix of:

- **Independence.** Each domain has its own users and groups. Each domain sets its own access, rights, and permission policies. Each domain administrator is responsible for his or her domain and must be trusted to manage that domain properly.

- **Interdependence.** Unless there's a need to share resources between domains, there's no reason for setting up a complete trust model. Domain administrators must work together to provide resource access while ensuring that security isn't compromised.

This model is appropriate to organizations that don't have a central MIS department available to manage master domains. It fits well into organizations made up of independent departments or divisions.

Do it!

E-2: Discussing Windows NT domains

Questions and answers
1 Which two network design situations are supported by a single domain?
2 The four Microsoft Windows NT domain models are _____, _____, _____, and _____.
3 Explain the functions of resource domains in a master domain model.
4 In a _____, each domain can act both as a master domain and a as resource domain.

Topic F: Novell Directory Services/eDirectory

This topic covers the following CompTIA Network+ exam objectives:

#	Objective
3.1	Identify the basic capabilities (For example: client support, interoperability, authentication, file and print services, application support and security) of the following server operating systems to access network resources: • NetWare
4.5	Given a troubleshooting scenario between a client and the following server environments, identify the cause of a stated problem: • NetWare

Managing network objects

Explanation

Novell NetWare and Novell Directory Services provide the network administrator with robust administration capabilities. Older versions of NetWare (NetWare 2.x/NetWare 3.x) used three files, called the bindery, to store information about network users and groups. Newer versions of NetWare use Novell Directory Service, now renamed eDirectory, to manage network objects.

Bindery files

In the earlier versions of NetWare, such as 2.x and 3.x, bindery files were used to store information about users, groups, file servers, and other logical and physical entities on the network. Network information, such as passwords, account balances, and trustee assignments, were also kept in the bindery files. The bindery files (NET$OBJ.SYS, NET$PROP.SYS and NET$VAL.SYS) were system files and didn't appear in a normal directory search.

Because each NetWare server kept its own set of bindery files, users who wanted access to more than one server had to have separate accounts created on each server. This caused a lot of administrative overhead, especially in large networks.

It was confusing for the users needing to access resources on multiple servers, because they had to log in to their primary file server and then attach to each additional server.

Novell Directory Services/eDirectory

Novell Directory Services/eDirectory (NDS) replaces the bindery files used in previous versions of NetWare. Commonly referred to as the Directory tree, Novell Directory Services/eDirectory can be organized the way your organization is structured. Therefore, the design of a NetWare 4.x, 5.x or 6.x network is different from the design of older NetWare networks.

NDS/eDirectory database logical structure

The NDS/eDirectory database is an enterprise-wide database containing information about network objects (resources), such as NetWare servers, users, groups, print queues, printers, applications, and so on, as well as associated properties. eDirectory can run on many platforms in addition to NetWare, such as Windows NT/2000/Server 2003, SuSE LINUX Enterprise Server 8 or 9, Red Hat Linux and Red Hat Linux Advanced Server and so on.

Note: The primary tool for managing NDS/eDirectory used to be NetWare Administrator. This tool can still be used in older NetWare networks but is no longer distributed or developed further by Novell. ConsoleOne and iManager are now the primary NDS/eDirectory management tools.

Each object has properties, which are related to the object. Properties might be single or multi-valued. The properties of an object vary depending on the object type. One property of a user object is titled Home Directory. The value of this property is the path to the user's home directory in the NetWare file system. A print queue object doesn't have a Home Directory property, because a print queue doesn't log in to the network and use the file system.

NDS/eDirectory objects

NDS/eDirectory objects represent items that are defined in the NDS/eDirectory database. Because NDS/eDirectory is an enterprise-wide database, the pre-NetWare 4.x concept of printers, servers, and users being associated with a specific server is no longer true. NDS/eDirectory maintains these objects globally for the entire network and not on a per-server basis.

Each server on the network looks to the global NDS/eDirectory for information on objects. Therefore, all servers and clients have access to the same information. When a network administrator makes any change to NDS/eDirectory, it's made one time only, and all servers see the new information.

NDS/eDirectory object classes

The three classes of objects are root, container, and leaf. These object classes make up the NDS/eDirectory directory database. The logical organization of the NDS/eDirectory database is depicted as an inverted tree, as shown in Exhibit 16-12. At the top of each Directory tree is the [Root] object, created at the time of installation.

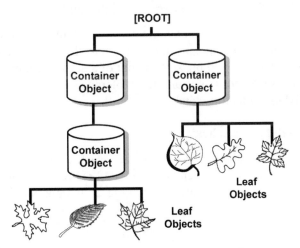

Exhibit 16-12: The three classes of NDS/eDirectory objects

Only one [Root] object exists per NDS/eDirectory directory tree. When referring to the [Root] object, brackets are used. Because the [Root] contains all objects, it's considered to be a Container object. The [Root] object can't be deleted or renamed.

Container objects are used to organize the NDS database hierarchically and can contain other objects. Leaf objects are resources found in a container object, such as users, servers, or printers.

Container objects

The NDS/eDirectory structure supports three types of container objects:

- **Country (C=).** Identifies the name of the country. Many companies have multiple countries identified for WANs. This container object might contain Organization and Alias objects only. Country is a two-character field. The Country object is identified by the attribute type C=.

- **Organization (O=).** Identifies the name of the company, a division within a company, or a department. The [Root] of the NDS/eDirectory tree needs a minimum of one Organization object. Organization objects might contain Organizational Unit objects and Leaf objects. The Organization object can be up to 64 characters and is identified by the attribute type O=.

- **Organizational Unit (OU=).** Identifies various divisions or departments within the company. The OU is a sublevel of Organization. The Organizational Unit objects are optional within the Directory tree. The Organizational Unit can be up to 64 characters and is identified by the attribute type OU=.

Leaf objects

Leaf objects represent physical resources on the network, such as servers, printers, and users. Leaf objects cannot contain other objects.

All NDS/eDirectory leaf objects have a common name (CN), which identifies the object in the directory. The attribute type for a leaf object's common name is specified as CN=.

NDS/eDirectory database physical structure

The NDS/eDirectory database is stored in a hidden directory on the SYS: volume of a NetWare 4.x, 5.x, or 6.x server. The design of NDS/eDirectory permits the database to reside entirely, or in part, on NetWare servers throughout the network. This distributed design makes NDS/eDirectory an extremely flexible and scalable directory service.

The NDS/eDirectory database can be logically divided into partitions. By default, the entire database resides in a single partition known as the Root partition. Depending on the NDS/eDirectory design and physical layout of a network, it might be necessary to partition the database. Performance and fault tolerance are the primary reasons for partitioning an NDS/eDirectory database.

NDS/eDirectory database schema

The objects known to an NDS/eDirectory database comprise its schema. To provide a mechanism for third-party enhancements, the NDS/eDirectory schema is extensible. Developers can define new NDS/eDirectory objects by updating the schema of a database.

Bindery emulation in NDS/eDirectory

The NDS/eDirectory directory database replaces the bindery files used in previous versions of NetWare. Many applications and devices have been designed to operate on bindery versions of NetWare, that is, versions 3.12 and earlier. To provide backward compatibility with NetWare bindery applications and third-party bindery products, NetWare 4.x, 5.x, and 6.x provide bindery emulation.

The NetWare 3.x bindery consists of three files:

- NET$OBJ.SYS
- NET$PROP.SYS
- NET$VAL.SYS

These files contain the objects, properties, and values known to the server. NetWare 3.x servers don't share bindery information. Separate bindery files are maintained and stored on each individual file server. Newer versions of NetWare emulate these files through software, but the servers themselves don't have bindery files. Bindery emulation permits clients in NetWare 3.x environments to access network resources managed by the NDS in newer NetWare networks.

Do it!

F-1: Discussing NDS/eDirectory

Questions and answers

1 Explain the difference between the NetWare bindery files and Novell Directory Services/eDirectory.

2 List the types of container objects supported by the NDS/eDirectory structure.

3 _____ represent physical resources on the network, such as servers, printers, and users.

   A Roots

   B Containers

   C Leaf objects

   D All the above

4 Briefly describe the difference in NDS/eDirectory between a container object and a leaf object.

5 Explain the significance of bindery emulation.

Unit summary: Directory services

Topic A   In this topic, you learned about Windows networking concepts, including the concepts of **workgroups** and **domains**. You also learned about accessing domain resources.

Topic B   In this topic, you learned about **directory services planning** and **implementation**. You learned what a directory service is and how to plan, implement, manage and maintain an **infrastructure**, user, computer and group **strategies**, and **group policy**.

Topic C   In this topic, you learned about **Active Directory (AD)**. You learned about Active Directory **objects** and the Active Directory **schema**. Next, you learned about the **logical structure** and components of Active Directory. You learned about the **global catalog** and about **naming standards** and the **physical structure** of Active Directory. You also learned how to install Active Directory on a Windows Server 2003 server.

Topic D   In this topic, you learned about the **new** Active Directory **features** in **Windows Server 2003**. You learned about new features in the areas of deployment, management, performance, and dependability.

Topic E   In this topic, you learned about the functions of **Windows NT Directory Services**, including the role of **Windows NT domains**. Then, you learned about the purpose and function of Windows NT Directory Services, **domains**, **logical configuration of single domain**, **master domain**, **multiple master domain**, and **complete trust.**

Topic F   In this topic, you identified the differences between the **Novell bindery files** and **Novell Directory Services/eDirectory**. You learned that older versions of NetWare used bindery files to store information about network users and groups, while newer versions of NetWare use the Novell Directory Services (NDS/eDirectory) to manage network objects. Then you learned about the purpose of **Novell Directory Services/eDirectory**, the significance of **NDS/eDirectory objects**, and **bindery emulation**.

Review questions

1 What's a workgroup?

2 What's the main difference between a workgroup and a domain?

3 Describe the term Directory Service.

4 What naming conventions must Active Directory objects follow?

5 Which of the following isn't a valid Active Directory component?

   A Tree

   B Forest

   C Domain

   D Country

6 A Windows Server 2003 Active Directory domain can't be renamed. True or false?

7 Dover Leasing Corporation has recently implemented Windows Server 2003 and Active Directory. Dover's network consists of three main locations with offices in Boston, Hong Kong, and London. The Boston location is the head office and connects to London via a dedicated T1 WAN link, whereas the Hong Kong location connects to London via a 256-Kbps Frame Relay link. Dover had recently considered opening a new office in San Francisco, which would connect via WAN links to both the Boston and Hong Kong offices. Different password policies need to be implemented in the Boston, Hong Kong, and London locations. Ultimately, the San Francisco office will become the administrative responsibility of IT staff in Boston. Based on what you know of Windows Server 2003 thus far and given the information provided above, the IT manager has asked you to assess Dover Leasing's Active Directory design by answering the following questions.

   a Of the factors listed in the scenario, which would influence the logical design of Dover Leasing's Active Directory implementation?

   b What type of domain structure would you suggest for Dover Leasing?

   c Based on Dover Leasing's current and future locations, what would be the best naming strategy for its Active Directory domain structure?

   d How many sites would likely be configured as part of Dover Leasing's Active Directory implementation once the San Francisco office opens, and how many site links would be required?

    e Once the San Francisco office is opened, how many global catalog servers should be implemented on the network to ensure adequate performance?

8 Which of the following are Microsoft NT domain models?

    A Single

    B Master

    C Multiple master

    D Primary

    E All of the above

9 A Microsoft NT trust relationship is established between two domains: a _____ domain and a _____ domain.

    A Primary, backup

    B Single, master

    C Local, global

    D Trusting, trusted

10 You're the sole network administrator for a small organization with fewer than thirty employees. All of the employees are located at one site and you're the only one responsible for network management. Based on this information, which of the following Microsoft Windows NT domain models would you select?

    A Single domain

    B Master domain

    C Multiple Master domain

    D Local domain

11 List the three classes of NDS/eDirectory objects.

12 Which of the following is at the top of the NDS/eDirectory hierarchy?

    A Top-level OU

    B Admin leaf object

    C Country container

    D [Root]

Unit 17

Accessing and managing resources in a Windows network

Unit time: 90 minutes

Complete this unit, and you'll know how to:

A Create and manage Active Directory user accounts.

B Discuss group accounts in Active Directory.

C Discuss the NTFS file system and permissions.

D Discuss shared folder concepts.

E Discuss Windows 2000/Server 2003 printing concepts.

Topic A: Creating and managing Active Directory user accounts

This topic covers the following CompTIA Network+ exam objectives:

#	Objective
2.18	Identify authentication protocols: • Kerberos
3.1	Identify the basic capabilities (For example: client support, interoperability, authentication, file and print services, application support and security) of the following server operating systems to access network resources: • Windows
3.7	Given a connectivity scenario, determine the impact on network functionality of a particular security implementation (For example: • Authentication and encryption
4.5	Given a troubleshooting scenario between a client and the following server environments, identify the cause of a stated problem: • Windows

Active Directory Users and Computers

Explanation

Every user who needs access to a Windows 2000/Server 2003 network requires a unique user account. In an Active Directory environment, user accounts are created and stored on domain controllers in the Active Directory database. The standard tool with which to do this is Active Directory Users and Computers. Note that, in Windows Server 2003, there are also a number of command line tools and utilities you can choose to add, delete, modify, import, and export user accounts.

The primary tool used to create and manage user accounts in an Active Directory environment is Active Directory Users and Computers. Available from the Administrative Tools menu, it can also be added to a custom Microsoft Management Console (MMC) or opened directly from the Run command by entering its filename, dsa.msc. This graphical tool makes it easy for administrators to add, modify, move, and delete user accounts. Because Active Directory implementations can scale to very large sizes with thousands of user objects, this tool can search for user objects based on various settings or criteria.

The version of Active Directory Users and Computers supplied with Windows Server 2003 is functionally very similar to the Windows 2000 version. However, the newer version has been enhanced to include some additional features, such as the ability to move objects between containers, such as the Users container and an OU, for example, using common Windows techniques like drag and drop. Another new feature is the inclusion of a node called Saved Queries, which allows an administrator to search for user accounts quickly based on specific settings, such as all users with a particular manager or all accounts that have been disabled. The Active Directory Users and Computers interface is shown in Exhibit 17-1.

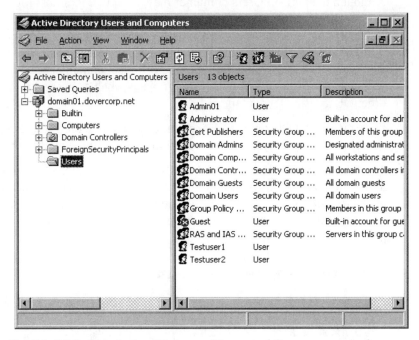

Exhibit 17-1: The Active Directory Users and Computers interface

Creating user accounts in Active Directory Users and Computers is as simple as right-clicking on a particular container, such as Users, selecting New, and then clicking User. This opens the New Object – User dialog box, as shown in Exhibit 17-2.

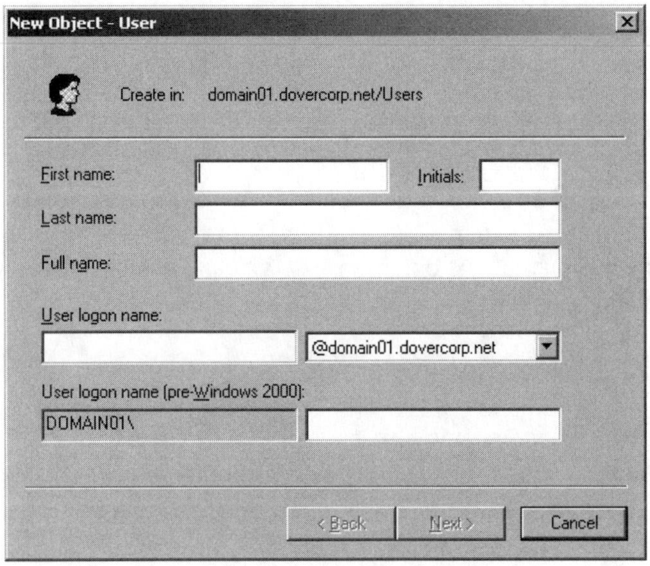

Exhibit 17-2: The New Object - User dialog box

Although the built-in Users container may seem like the most logical place to create new user objects, it isn't the only place they can be created or located. In larger Active Directory implementations, administrators typically create additional organizational unit (OU) objects to organize users for administration and *Group Policy* application. Remember that an organizational unit is a logical container used to organize objects within a single domain. You can store objects, such as users, groups, computers, and other OUs, in an OU container.

For example, an OU named Marketing might contain all of the user, computer, and group accounts associated with users in the Marketing department.

The settings configured as part of creating a new user object in Active Directory Users and Computers are fairly limited. Once a new user object has been created, additional attribute settings are configured from the properties of the account. From the properties of a user object, an administrator can easily add a user to various groups, configure profile settings, and so forth.

Do it!

A-1: Creating user accounts

Here's how	Here's why
1 Choose **Start**, **Administrative Tools**, **Active Directory Users and Computers**	You'll use Active Directory Users and Computers to create user accounts.
2 Expand **CLASS##.com**	If necessary. To display the contents of the domain.
3 Right-click **Users**	
Choose **New**, **User**	To open the New Object – User dialog box.
4 In the First name box, enter **John**	
5 Press ⎡TAB⎤ twice	
In the Last name box, enter **Smith**	Notice that the Full name box is populated automatically.
6 Press ⎡TAB⎤ twice	
In the User logon name box, enter **jsmith**	To specify the user's logon name.
Click **Next**	
7 In the Password box, enter **Password##&**	For ##, use the numbers assigned to your Student ID here. For example, for Student01, enter Password01.
Press ⎡TAB⎤	
8 In the Confirm password box, enter **Password##&**	

9 Click **Next**

10 Click **Finish**

11 Right-click **Domain Controllers**

12 Choose **Properties**

13 Activate the **Group Policy** tab

14 Verify that Default Domain Controllers Policy is selected

15 Click **Edit**   The Group Policy Object Editor window appears.

    Next to Computer Configuration, Windows Settings, click the plus sign (+)   To expand it.

    Click the plus sign next to Security Settings

    Expand Local Policies

16 Click **User Rights Assignment**

17 Double-click **Allow log on locally**

18 Click **Add User or Group...**

19 Click **Browse**

20 In the text box, enter **John Smith**   To specify the object name to select.

21 Click **OK**   To find the user.

22 Click **OK**   To add the user to the list of users that are allowed to log on locally.

23 Click **OK**   To close the Allow Log on locally Properties dialog box.

24 Close the Group Policy Object Editor window

25 Click **OK**   To close the Domain Controllers Properties dialog box.

26 Close Active Directory Users and Computers

User account configuration and troubleshooting

Explanation

Although creating and configuring user accounts is a relatively straightforward process, a number of issues can impact a user's ability to log on to a Windows 2000/Server 2003 Active Directory network. Some of these issues are directly related to the configuration of a user account, such as an account being locked out. In other cases, various policy settings may prohibit a user from being successfully authenticated, either interactively or over the network. In the following sections, you'll learn about some of the key policy settings that can impact the user authentication process, methods of gathering more information about authentication issues, and solutions to common authentication problems.

Account Policies

A variety of configuration settings can and do impact the user authentication process in an Active Directory domain environment. Some of the most important settings to consider are those configured in the Account Policies node of Group Policy objects applied at the domain level.

Windows 2000/Server 2003 creates a default Group Policy object at the domain level. This object is called the Default Domain Policy. Although you can configure this object with a wide variety of settings, the domain level is the only level at which account lockout, password, and Kerberos settings can be configured for all domain users. Kerberos v5 is the authentication protocol supported by both Windows 2000 and Windows Server 2003.

The Default Domain Policy can be accessed from Active Directory Users and Computers by right-clicking the domain object, clicking Properties, and then activating the Group Policy tab. The Windows Server 2003 Group Policy tab, which looks almost identical in Windows 2000, is shown in Exhibit 17-3.

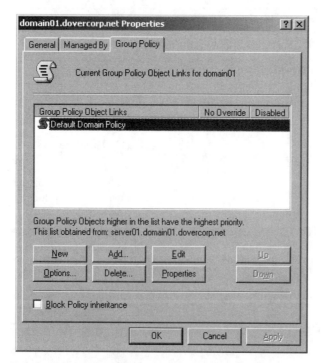

Exhibit 17-3: The Windows Server 2003 Group Policy tab

Clicking the Edit button opens the Group Policy Object Editor window. The Account Policies node is found in the Computer Configuration section, under Windows Settings—Security Settings—Account Policies, as shown in Exhibit 17-4.

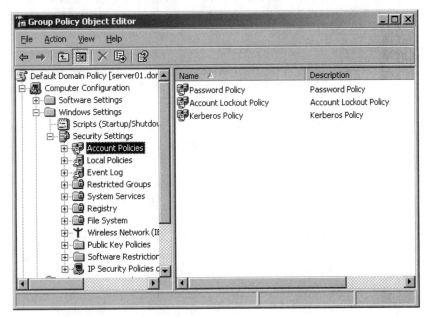

Exhibit 17-4: The Account Policies node

In the following sections, you'll learn more about each of the three main Account Policies nodes, namely:

- Password Policy
- Account Lockout Policy
- Kerberos Policy

In learning about each node and its configurable settings, pay particular attention to the impact it can have on authentication-related issues.

Password Policy

The Password Policy node contains configuration settings that refer to the required history, age, length, and complexity of user passwords. Settings found in this section don't usually impact a user's ability to authenticate, if they know and submit their current and correct password, but they do impact how often a user must change his or her password, when the password expires, and so forth. The following list outlines each individual policy item, its default setting, and its intended purpose:

- **Enforce password history.** Defines the number of passwords that have to be unique before a user can reuse an old password. The default configuration setting is 24 passwords remembered.

- **Maximum password age.** Defines the number of days that a password can be used before the user is required to change it. The default configuration setting is 42 days.

- **Minimum password age.** Defines the number of days that a password must be used before a user is allowed to change it. The default configuration setting is 1 day.

- **Minimum password length.** Defines the least number of characters required in a password. Values can be from 1 to 14 characters. If no password is required, set the value to 0. The default configuration setting is 7 characters.

- **Passwords must meet complexity requirements.** Increases password complexity by enforcing rules that passwords must meet. This setting is enabled by default. A complex password can't include any portion of the user's account name, must be at least 6 characters in length, and must include 3 of the 4 elements below:
  - English uppercase letters
  - English lowercase letters
  - Numbers
  - Non-alphanumeric characters (e.g., !, $, #)

- **Store passwords using reversible encryption.** This setting is the same as storing passwords in clear text. It provides support for applications using protocols that need the passwords in clear text for authentication purposes. This setting is disabled by default.

Account Lockout Policy

The Account Lockout Policy node contains configuration settings that refer to the password lockout thresholds and durations, as well as to reset options. Settings configured in this section may impact the user authentication process by locking out user accounts after a specified number of incorrect logon attempts, such as when a user enters an incorrect user name and password combination. The policy items are:

- **Account lockout duration.** Defines the number of failed logon attempts after which the user account is locked. This setting isn't defined by default.

- **Account lockout threshold.** Defines the number of incorrect logon attempts that must occur before an account is locked out. The default value is 0, meaning that accounts are never locked out.

- **Reset account lockout counter after.** Determines the number of minutes that must elapse after a single failed logon attempt before the bad logon counter is reset to 0. This setting isn't configured by default.

Kerberos Policy

The Kerberos Policy node contains configuration settings that refer to the Kerberos ticket-granting ticket (TGT), session ticket lifetimes, and timestamp settings. Settings configured in this section may impact both a user's ability to log on to the network and to access network resources. For example, Kerberos relies upon timestamped tickets in order to ensure that old tickets can't be reused. If the clock on a user desktop is greatly out of sync with the KDC (a domain controller), the user isn't allowed to log on to the network. The policy items are:

- **Enforce user logon restrictions.** Requires the Key Distribution Center (KDC), a service of Kerberos V5, to validate every request for a session ticket against the user rights policy of the target computer. If enforced, there may be performance degradation on network access. This setting is enabled by default.

- **Maximum lifetime for service ticket.** Determines the maximum amount of time, in minutes, that a service ticket is valid to access a resource. The default is 600 minutes (10 hours).

- **Maximum lifetime for user ticket.** Determines the maximum amount of time, in hours, that a TGT may be used. The default is 10 hours.

- **Maximum lifetime for user ticket renewal.** Determines the amount of time, in days, that a user's TGT may be renewed. The default is seven days.

- **Maximum tolerance for computer clock synchronization.** Determines the amount of time difference, in minutes, that Kerberos tolerates between the client machine's clock and the time on the server's clock. The default is five minutes.

Do it!

A-2: Using Account Policies

Questions and answers

1 The Windows 2000/Server 2003 Default Domain Policy specifies that a user password must be how long by default?

 A 5 characters

 B 6 characters

 C 7 characters

 D 8 characters

2 Which of the following isn't a required element in a complex password?

 A Must include English uppercase letters

 B Maximum of 6 characters

 C Can't include the user name

 D Must include numbers

3 After how many days must a Windows domain user change his or her password by default?

 A 30

 B 10

 C 42

 D 34

4 Active Directory user accounts are configured to lockout after 3 incorrect logon attempts. True or false?

5 How many user passwords are remembered by a domain controller as part of password history setting by default?

 A 6

 B 8

 C 16

 D 24

Resolving logon issues

Explanation

In an Active Directory environment, users may not be able to log on to the domain for a variety of reasons. In some cases, the problem can be as simple as the user forgetting or mistyping his or her user name or password, while in others, network settings may be to blame.

The list below outlines some of the more common logon issues that may occur in an Active Directory environment and how they can be resolved.

- **Incorrect user name or password.** A user simply forgetting or mistyping his or her user name or password is among the most common reasons for not being able to authenticate. The obvious solution to this problem is to reset the user's domain password using an administrative tool such as Active Directory Users and Computers or the user's local password using a Reset Disk.

- **Account lockout.** After multiple incorrect logon attempts, a user's account may be locked out, depending on the Account lockout policy settings configured in the domain. User accounts can be unlocked manually from the Account tab in the properties of a user account.

- **Account disabled.** Users are unable to logon unless their account has been enabled. In some cases, such as when a new user is created based on a template account, their account may not have been enabled. Use Active Directory Users or Computers or the DSMOD USER command line utility to enable the user's account.

- **Logon hour restrictions.** If users are having trouble logging on at certain times during the day, check to ensure that no logon hour restrictions are configured for their accounts. If users need access after normal business hours, ensure that the logon hour restrictions for their accounts are configured appropriately.

- **Workstation restrictions.** If users aren't able to log on from certain workstations only, check to ensure that workstation restrictions haven't been configured in the properties of their user accounts. Permit their accounts to log on to additional workstations or all workstations, if necessary.

- **Domain controllers.** If workstations running Windows XP/2000/2003 seem not to be able to contact a domain controller, check to ensure that their configured DNS settings are correct. The operating systems query DNS to find the IP address of a domain controller, and incorrect settings may prohibit them from doing so.

- **Client time settings.** If users can't log on to Windows XP, 2000, or 2003 workstations or member servers, check to ensure that their clocks are less than 5 minutes out of sync with the domain controller. Synchronization settings more than 5 minutes apart prohibit users from logging on due to default Kerberos policy settings. Time zone differences account for many clock sync problems.

- **Down-level client issues.** If down-level clients, such as workstations running Windows 95/98 and Windows NT, are experiencing logon issues, consider installing the Active Directory Client Extensions software on their systems. The AD Client is provided on the Windows Server 2003 installation CD.

- **UPN logon issues.** If users can't log on using their UPN in a multiple-domain environment, ensure that a Global Catalog server is configured and accessible. Global Catalog servers must be available when a user attempts logon using a UPN.

- **Users unable to log on locally.** If users need to log on locally to specific servers or domain controllers, you need to grant them that right in the policy settings on those servers or DCs. The default Domain Controller Policy doesn't grant logon rights to non-privileged accounts.

- **Remote access logon issues.** If users can't log on via a dial-up or VPN connection, be sure that their accounts are configured to allow access on the Dial-up tab in the properties of their user accounts.

- **Terminal Services logon issues.** If users can't log on to a Terminal Server in the domain, ensure that the Allow logon to terminal server checkbox is checked on the Terminal Services Profile tabs in the properties of their user accounts.

Do it!

A-3: Resolving logon issues

Questions and answers

1 How can you resolve the issue of workstations running Windows XP/2000/2003 not able to contact a domain controller?

2 How can you resolve the logon issue of down-level clients, such as workstations running Windows 95/98 and Windows NT?

Topic B: Introduction to group accounts

This topic covers the following CompTIA Network+ exam objectives:

#	Objective
3.1	Identify the basic capabilities (For example: client support, interoperability, authentication, file and print services, application support and security) of the following server operating systems to access network resources: • Windows
4.5	Given a troubleshooting scenario between a client and the following server environments, identify the cause of a stated problem: • Windows

Working with group accounts

Explanation

Although user accounts represent the primary method used to identify users on a network, trying to configure permissions or rights for multiple users within their individual accounts can quickly become unmanageable, especially in large environments. For this reason, most network operating systems, including Windows 2000/Server 2003, include the ability to aggregate user accounts into entities known as groups.

Grouping together users with common needs makes it easier to assign rights and permissions. For example, you can create a group to represent all users in the marketing department or all users who work in a particular location. When a new user requires these rights or permissions, you can add them to the group to which an appropriate level of access is granted. And when you wish to change the permissions for a department or location, you can make the change to the group and have it apply automatically to all the users in the group.

As with user accounts, Active Directory Users and Computers is the primary tool you use to create and manage group accounts in an Active Directory environment.

A Windows 2000/Server 2003 *group* organizes users, computers, contacts, or other groups into a single directory object. A group sounds similar to an organizational unit (OU), in that both organize other objects into logical containers. The main differences between an OU and a group are as follows:

- OUs aren't security principals and, as such, can't be used to define permissions on resources or be assigned rights. Active Directory security groups are security principals that can be assigned both permissions and rights.
- OUs can contain objects only from their parent domains. Some groups can contain objects from any domain within the forest.

In the following sections you'll learn more about the various group types and scopes available in a Windows 2000/Server 2003 Active Directory environment, as well as the various membership rules that apply to those groups.

Group types

A group's type is used to define how a group can be used within an Active Directory domain or forest. Windows 2000/Server 2003 supports two types of groups:

- Security groups
- Distribution groups

The distinction between each type of group is important, because each is created for a different purpose and has different characteristics.

Security groups

Security groups are the most popular type of group in an Active Directory environment. As the name suggests, *security groups* are group objects that can be secured by having rights and permissions defined. In a manner similar to a user account, security groups have a Security Identifier (SID) that allows them to be assigned permissions for resources in *discretionary access control lists (DACLs)*, as well as rights to perform various tasks.

When trying to determine whether to create a security group or a distribution group, you need to consider how that group will be used. If you need to control permissions and rights in the group, it must be a security group, because permissions and rights can't be assigned to distribution groups.

Although the assignment of permissions and rights is the primary function of security groups, these groups can also be used as e-mail entities. Sending an e-mail message to an e-mail-enabled Active Directory security group, when Microsoft Exchange 2000 is installed, sends the message to all of the members of that group.

Distribution groups

Unlike security groups, distribution groups don't have an associated SID and, therefore, can't be used to assign permissions or rights to members. The primary purpose of a *distribution group* is for use with e-mail applications, such as Microsoft Exchange 2000, where sending an e-mail message to the distribution group sends the message to all members of that group.

While distribution groups may not seem useful in light of the fact that e-mail messages can also be sent to security groups, they differentiate themselves in an important way. Because distribution groups don't have an SID associated with them, they don't impact the user authentication process unnecessarily with excess information not required for security purposes. For this reason, if a group will never be used for security purposes, its type should be configured as a distribution group rather than a security group.

Do it! **B-1:   Exploring group types**

Questions and answers

1 Which of the following are considered group types?

   A   Global

   B   Domain local

   C   Security

   D   Distribution

2 Rights and permissions can be assigned to both distribution and security groups. True or false?

3 When creating a group for users of sensitive information that must be protected from unwanted changes, you'd create a _____ group.

Group scopes

A group's *scope* refers to the logical boundary within which a group can be assigned permissions to a specific resource. Security and distribution groups in Active Directory can be assigned one of three possible scopes:

- Global
- Domain local
- Universal

Global groups

Global groups are created for the purpose of logically organizing users, computers, and potentially other groups that exist within the same domain in an Active Directory forest. For example, a global group created in a Domain A can include objects, such as users, from Domain A but not objects from Domain B.

You usually create a global group to organize objects that have a common geographic location or job function. You can then assign rights to the group and have those rights apply to all the objects contained in the group.

The type of objects you can add to a global group is directly related to the configured functional level of a domain. Windows 2000/Server 2003 supports three main *domain functional levels* in environments that include various combinations of Windows 2000 Server and Windows Server 2003 domain controllers. These include:

- **Windows 2000 mixed.** This domain functional level is the default when Windows Server 2003 Active Directory is installed. This level supports a combination of Windows NT Server 4.0, Windows 2000 Server, and Windows Server 2003 domain controllers. Because each type of domain controller is supported, this level follows many of the group membership rules associated with Windows NT 4.0 domain environments, which aren't as extensive as the newer environments.

- **Windows 2000 native.** This domain functional level supports a combination of Windows 2000 Server and Windows Server 2003 domain controllers only. At this level, a domain can support a variety of advanced group membership features.

- **Windows Server 2003.** This domain functional level supports Windows Server 2003 domain controllers only. This level supports the same group membership features as the Windows 2000 native function level.

As you can see, the functional level that a domain supports is directly related to the types of domain controllers in the domain. A company that gradually upgrades an existing Windows NT 4.0 domain needs to run at the Windows 2000 mixed level for some period of time. Once all the domain controllers have been upgraded to at least Windows 2000 Server, the domain functional level can be raised to Windows 2000 native. If all domain controllers are upgraded to Windows Server 2003, the functional level can be upgraded again. Ultimately, the functional level of a domain impacts much more than group membership rules.

Note: For more information on the various capabilities of various Windows Server 2003 domain functional levels, see the Domain and forest functionality: Active Directory topic in Help and Support Center.

When a domain is configured to the Windows 2000 mixed domain functional level, the following rules apply to global groups within an Active Directory forest:

- Can contain user accounts from the same domain
- Can't be added to universal groups in the forest, since universal groups don't exist at the Windows 2000 mixed domain functional level
- Can be added to local groups or domain local groups in any domain

When a domain is configured to the Windows 2000 native or Windows Server 2003 domain functional levels, the following rules apply to global groups within an Active Directory forest:

- Can contain user accounts or other global groups from the same domain
- Can be added to universal groups created in any domain
- Can be added to local groups or domain local groups in any domain

Domain local groups

Domain local groups are typically created for the purpose of assigning rights and permissions to groups of users in an Active Directory environment. Created on domain controllers, a domain local group can be assigned rights and permissions to any resource within the same domain only. However, domain local groups can contain not only users, but also groups from other domains.

For example, you might create a domain local group named Marketing on a domain controller in Domain A. This domain local group could then be assigned permissions to a folder on a server in Domain A. Then, instead of assigning permissions on this folder for multiple groups, global groups from Domain A, as well as other trusted domains, could be added to the Marketing domain local group. This would ultimately grant users in those global groups the permissions associated with the Marketing domain local group.

In much the same way that the functional level of a domain impacts the membership rules for global groups, the same is true of domain local groups. When an Active Directory domain is configured to the Windows 2000 mixed domain functional level, the following rules apply to domain local groups within an Active Directory forest:

- Can contain user accounts from any domain
- Can contain global groups from any domain

When a domain is configured to the Windows 2000 native or Windows Server 2003 domain functional levels, the following rules apply to domain local groups:

- Can contain user accounts from any domain
- Can contain global groups from any domain
- Can contain universal groups
- Can contain other domain local groups from the same domain

Note: Groups created on Windows 2000/Server 2003 member servers or Windows XP Professional clients are called *local groups*. Local groups can be assigned permissions only to a resource available on the local machine on which it's created.

Universal groups

Universal groups are typically created for the purpose of aggregating users or groups in different domains throughout an Active Directory forest. Stored on domain controllers configured as global catalog servers, a *universal group* can be assigned rights and permissions to any resource within a forest. Universal groups can contain not only users and global groups from any domain, but also other universal groups.

For example, a universal group named Enterprise Marketing might be configured in a large organization with multiple domains. Then, the Marketing Users global groups from various domains, which contain individual marketing user accounts, could be added to the Enterprise Marketing universal group, forming a single group that encompasses all of the marketing users within an organization across domain boundaries. Then, when rights or permissions need to be assigned to all marketing users in the forest, they could be assigned once to the Enterprise Marketing universal group, rather than individual Marketing Users groups from each domain.

Unlike global and domain local groups, which can exist at the Windows 2000 mixed domain functional level, universal groups can be created only once a domain is configured to the Windows 2000 native or Windows Server 2003 domain functional level. The following rules apply to universal groups:

- Can contain user accounts from any trusted domain
- Can contain global group accounts from any trusted domain
- Can contain other universal groups

Use universal groups with caution. All universal groups, along with their memberships, are listed in the global catalog. When there's any change to any member of a universal group, this change must be replicated to every global catalog in the forest. Global and domain local groups are also listed in the global catalog but don't have their memberships listed. A best practice is to place individual members within the global groups and then place the global groups within universal groups.

The following table provides a summary of each group type, its use, and its membership options within an Active Directory forest:

Group scope	Usage	Windows 2000 mixed domain functional level membership options	Windows 2000 Native/Windows Server 2003 domain functional level membership options
Local	Used to assign permissions to resources on the local computer only	User accounts from any domain, global groups from any domain	User accounts from any domain, global groups from any domain
Domain local	Assigned to resources within local domain	User accounts from any domain, global groups from any domain	User accounts, global groups, and universal groups from any domain; domain local groups from the same domain
Global	Used to aggregate individual objects such as user accounts within a domain	User accounts from the same domain only	User accounts and global groups from the same domain only
Universal	Used to aggregate individual objects, such as users or global groups, from any domain in a forest	Not available	User accounts, global groups, and universal groups from any domain

Do it!   **B-2:   Exploring group scopes**

Questions and answers

1   Which of the following are considered group scopes?

   A   Global

   B   Universal

   C   Domain local

   D   Distribution

2   A local group can be used to assign permissions for resources on a local computer only. True or false?

3   Permissions can be granted only to resources within the same domain when creating:

   A   Global groups

   B   Local groups

   C   Domain local groups

   D   Universal groups

Topic C: The NTFS file system and permissions

This topic covers the following CompTIA Network+ exam objectives:

#	Objective
3.1	Identify the basic capabilities (For example: client support, interoperability, authentication, file and print services, application support and security) of the following server operating systems to access network resources: • Windows
4.5	Given a troubleshooting scenario between a client and the following server environments, identify the cause of a stated problem: • Windows

Allowing access to shared resources

Explanation

The main reason for implementing a network is to allow users to access shared resources. Examples of shared resources include files, folders, and printers. While keeping resources available is a primary goal, the resources also need to be secured properly to ensure that they're made available only to those users who require access. Furthermore, the level of access that users need for a particular resource also needs to be considered, since it's likely to be different for different users and groups.

Resources are secured on a Windows 2000/Server 2003 network through the use of permissions. By configuring various permissions on a particular resource, you can grant a certain group of users the ability to read files only, while granting another group the ability to change or delete files. The ability to configure permissions in a very specific fashion gives you a high degree of control over how resources are used. But these permissions must be managed carefully. An understanding of how permissions apply in a Windows 2000/Server 2003 environment is critical for all network administration staff.

Windows 2000/Server 2003 supports two main types of permissions in order to secure file and folder resources.

- **NTFS permissions** can be applied to resources that are stored on partitions or volumes formatted with the NTFS file system.
- **Shared folder permissions** can be applied to any folder that has been shared to allow access from network workstations.

The combination of NTFS and shared folder permissions can be the source of a lot of trouble for users and administrators. It's important to understand how permissions are applied to ensure that clients obtain appropriate access to resources.

Windows 2000/Server 2003 support three main file systems:

- **File Allocation Table (FAT)**
- **FAT32**
- **NTFS**

FAT

FAT is a file system used by MS-DOS and supported in all the versions of Windows created since. Although traditionally limited to partitions up to 2 GB in size, the version of FAT included with Windows Server 2003 supports partitions up to 4 GB. The two biggest limitations of FAT are the relatively small supported partition sizes and the fact that FAT provides no file system security features, such as those available with NTFS. Also, FAT uses disk space inefficiently compared to FAT32 and NTFS. For these reasons, most administrators avoid using FAT on Windows 2000/Server 2003 systems.

FAT32

A derivative of FAT, *FAT32* was originally introduced in Windows 95 OSR2. The main advantage of FAT32 is its support of much larger partition sizes, up to 2 TB. However, like FAT, FAT32 doesn't provide any advanced security features.

NTFS

Beginning with Windows NT, Microsoft introduced a new file system known as *NTFS*. The current version of NTFS is version 5, which is supported by systems running Windows NT 4.0 (SP5 or later), Windows 2000, Windows XP, and Windows Server 2003. The NTFS file system theoretically supports much larger partition sizes, since it's capable of addressing up to 16 Exabytes (EB) of disk space. In practice, however, the maximum NTFS partition sizes range from 2 TB up to approximately 16 TB, depending on the disk type and cluster size used.

NTFS is the preferred file system for all partitions and volumes on a Windows 2000/Server 2003 system. Some of the advantages of NTFS include:

- Greater scalability for large disks and better performance than FAT-based systems on larger partitions.

- Support for Active Directory on systems configured as domain controllers. All domain controllers must have at least one NTFS partition or volume available to hold the Sysvol folder.

- Ability to configure security permissions on individual files and folders stored on an NTFS partition or volume.

- Built-in support for both compression and encryption.

- Ability to configure disk space quotas for individual users.

- Support for Remote Storage, the ability to extend disk space using removable media.

- Recovery logging of disk activities, which allows information relating to NTFS partitions or volumes to be recovered quickly in the event of system problems.

The choice of file system for a particular partition or volume is usually a function of how the system will be used, whether multiple operating systems are installed on the same system, and the security requirements for the system. For example, if Windows 2000/Server 2003 is installed on a system in a lab environment, it might be configured in a dual-boot configuration with another operating system, such as Windows 98. Because Windows 98 supports only the FAT and FAT32 file systems, you might not format any partitions or volumes using NTFS, because Windows 98 can't access this file system locally.

On a production server, however, a dual-boot configuration is exceptionally rare. Because of the security features provided by NTFS, this file system is highly recommended for all partitions on a Windows 2000/Server 2003 system, with very few exceptions.

Do it!

C-1: Identifying file system types

Questions and answers

1 Match the following file systems with their descriptions given below: FAT, FAT32, NTFS.

A file system supported by systems running Windows NT 4.0 (SP5 or later), Windows 2000, Windows XP, and Windows Server 2003

A file system used by MS-DOS and supported in all versions of Windows created since

A file system introduced in Windows 95 OSR2 and that supports partition sizes up to 2 TB

2 List the advantages of NTFS.

NTFS permission concepts

Explanation

Files and folders located on NTFS partitions or volumes can be secured through the use of NTFS permissions. It's important to understand the various NTFS file and directory permissions that are available, as well as how they're applied. Remember that NTFS permissions can be applied only to files and folders that exist on partitions formatted with the NTFS file system. As such, NTFS permissions can't be applied to files or folders that reside on partitions formatted using the FAT or FAT32 file systems.

- NTFS permissions are configured via the Security tab, which is accessed by right-clicking any file or folder and clicking Properties.

- NTFS permissions are cumulative. If a user is a member of multiple groups that have different permissions, the final permission is the sum of all permissions.

- Permissions that are explicitly denied always override those that are allowed. For example, if the Mark Manore user account is explicitly denied Full Control on a folder through an individual or group permission assignment, this overrides any permissions that Mark may have been allowed via other group memberships.

- NTFS folder permissions are inherited by child folders and files, unless otherwise specified. Clearing the Allow inheritable permissions from the parent to propagate to this object and all child objects check box in the Advanced section of the Security property sheet can prevent the inheritance of NTFS permissions.

- NTFS permissions can be set at a file level, as well as at a folder level.

- When a new access control entry is added to an NTFS file or folder, the default permissions allow the user or group both the Read and the Read and Execute permissions for files, along with the List Folder Contents permission for folders.

- Windows 2000/Server 2003 has a set of standard NTFS permissions, as well as special permissions.

Exhibit 17-5 shows the standard NTFS permissions available for a folder.

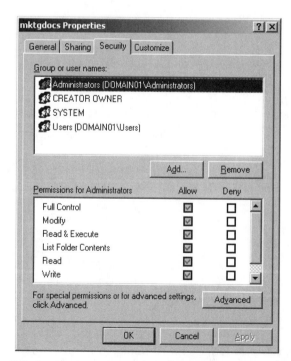

Exhibit 17-5: Standard NTFS permissions for a folder

The following table lists the standard NTFS permissions in Windows 2000/Server 2003:

NTFS permission	Capabilities
Full Control	Allows the user to make any changes to the file or folder.
Modify	Gives full permissions except the permission to delete subfolders and files, change permissions, and take ownership.
Read and Execute	Gives permissions to traverse folders, list folders, read attributes and extended attributes, read permissions, and synchronize; these permissions are inherited by both files and folders.
List Folder Contents	Same as Read and Execute permissions, except that the permissions are inherited only by folders and not by files; visible only on folders.
Read	Same as Read and Execute, except without the permission to traverse folder; inherited by files and folders.
Write	Gives permissions to create files and folders, write attributes and extended attributes, read permissions, and synchronize.
Special Permissions	Designates that a user has been allowed or denied one or more of the more granular special permissions configured in the Advanced section of the security settings.

Note: When assigning shared folder or NTFS permissions to users and groups, never grant them a higher level of access than they actually require. For example, if users need to be able only to read but not change files, the Read permission would be sufficient. Granting users too liberal a level of access can result in files being accidentally or purposely deleted, changed, and so forth.

Do it!

C-2:   Discussing NTFS permissions

Questions and answers

1 A user has been given the Modify right to the folder, Marketing. When trying to delete the folder Marketing\Presentations, she's unable to do so. Why?

2 You can assign NTFS permissions at which level(s)?

   A   Folder only

   B   File and folder

   C   File only

   D   None of the above

3 You need to configure NTFS permissions for a user. Where do you perform this action?

Topic D: Working with shared folders

This topic covers the following CompTIA Network+ exam objectives:

#	Objective
3.1	Identify the basic capabilities (For example: client support, interoperability, authentication, file and print services, application support and security) of the following server operating systems to access network resources: • Windows
4.5	Given a troubleshooting scenario between a client and the following server environments, identify the cause of a stated problem: • Windows

Shared folders

Explanation

To permit users to access data from a location on the network, you have to configure shared folders with the proper access-control permissions. A *shared folder* is a data resource that's been made available to authorized network clients. These clients can then view or modify the contents of the folder, depending upon the level of permissions granted. These permissions can be either for the user or for the group of which the user is a member.

To create shared folders, you must have the appropriate rights. If you're a member of the Administrators or Server Operators groups, you can create shared folders within a domain. Members of the Power Users group can also configure shared folders on Windows 2000/Server 2003 systems that aren't configured as domain controllers.

There are several ways to create shared folders. Two of the more popular methods include using the Windows Explorer interface and the Computer Management console. Beyond simply allowing you to create new shared folders, the Computer Management console also allows you to monitor the use of shared folders.

Using Windows Explorer

Windows Explorer is the standard method used to create and share folders for all versions of Windows since Windows 95. It can be used to create, maintain, and share folders on any drive connected to the computer. There are many ways to open Windows Explorer. For example, you can click the Windows Explorer icon on the Accessories menu, or you can right-click almost any drive-related object and click the Explore command on the shortcut menu.

Folders are shared in Windows 2000/Server 2003 by accessing the Sharing tab of a folder's properties, as shown in Exhibit 17-6.

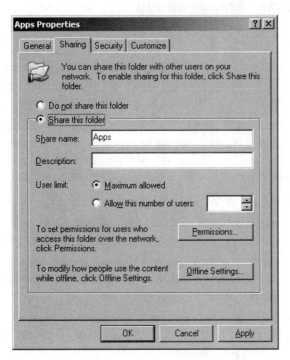

Exhibit 17-6: The Sharing tab in the properties of a folder

There may be times when you want to create a shared folder but don't have it listed in My Network Places or Network Neighborhood. To hide a shared folder, place a dollar sign ($) after its name. For example, if you create a shared folder called "Salary," you can hide it by giving it the share name "Salary$." To map or connect to a hidden share, a user needs manually to type the share name, including the dollar sign.

Using Computer Management

Another popular method for creating and managing shared folders in Windows 2000/Server 2003 is through the use of the *Computer Management console*, shown in Exhibit 17-7. Computer Management is a predefined Microsoft Management Console (MMC) application that allows you to perform a variety of administrative tasks, such as sharing and monitoring folders for both local and remote computers.

Shared folders are created in the Shared Folders section of Computer Management using the Share a Folder Wizard. Besides allowing you to create new shared folders, this wizard also helps you configure shared folder permissions. Three of the choices are pre-configured, whereas the fourth allows custom permissions to be specified.

Permission options found in the wizard include:

- **All users have read-only access.** Grants the Read permission to the Everyone group.

- **Administrators have full access; other users have read-only access.** Grants Full Control to the local Administrators group and Read permission to the Everyone group.

- **Administrators have full access; other users have read and write access.** Grants Full Control to the local Administrators group and both Read and Change access to the Everyone group.

- **Use custom share and folder permissions.** Allows you to define both share and NTFS permissions manually.

If you want to stop sharing a folder, the easiest way to do so is via the Shares node in the Computer Management console. The list of shares appears in the details pane of the console. To stop sharing a particular folder, you simply right-click the share that's to be discontinued and click Stop Sharing on the shortcut menu.

A third method sometimes used to share folders on a Windows Server 2003 system is the NET SHARE command. This command can be used to share an existing folder from the command line. For example, to share the folder C:\testfolder with a share name of test, the correct syntax for the command would be:

```
net share test="C:\testfolder"
```

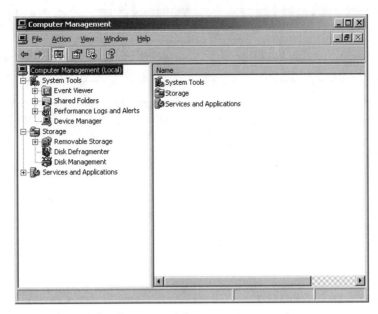

Exhibit 17-7: The Computer Management console

Do it!

D-1: Discussing shared folders

Questions and answers

1 Which group membership(s) automatically give(s) you the right to share files and folders in a domain?

   A   Administrators

   B   Admins

   C   Power Operator

   D   Server Operator

2 How can you hide a shared folder?

3 Which tool would you use if you want to create a shared folder and also configure shared folder permissions at the same time?

Topic E: Introduction to printing concepts

This topic covers the following CompTIA Network+ exam objectives:

#	Objective
3.1	Identify the basic capabilities (For example: client support, interoperability, authentication, file and print services, application support and security) of the following server operating systems to access network resources: • Windows
4.5	Given a troubleshooting scenario between a client and the following server environments, identify the cause of a stated problem: • Windows

Network printing

Explanation

Sharing file resources is still the most common reason to implement a network; sharing access to printers is a close second. Windows 2000/Server 2003 includes the ability to act as a *print server*, allowing both locally attached and network-interface print devices to be shared among network users.

When you've created and shared file and print resources on your network, users may need a simple and effective way to search for these objects. Publishing resources into Active Directory allows any Active Directory-aware client to perform a simple search on the network.

To configure and troubleshoot Windows 2000/Server 2003 printing successfully, you should be aware of specific terms used to define the components of the print system. The following list defines these terms:

- **Print device.** The actual hardware device that produces the printed document. There are two main types of print devices: a *local print device* and a *network print device*. Local print devices are connected directly to a port on the print server or workstation. A network print device connects to a print server through its own network adapter and connection to the network.

- **Printer.** A configuration object in Windows 2000/Server 2003, which controls the connection to the print device.

- **Print driver.** Files that contain information that Windows 2000/Server 2003 uses to convert raw print commands to a language that the printer understands, a specific *print driver* is needed for each print device model used and for each type of operating system.

- **Print server.** The computer in which the printers and print drivers are located. This is usually where you set up and configure the shared printing system.

- **Print client.** The computer from which a particular print job originates.

To set up an efficient printing environment, it's important to make sure your network meets the following hardware requirements:

- **One or more computers to act as print servers.** Windows 2000/Server 2003 and Windows XP Professional can be used as print servers, Windows XP Professional supports a maximum of only 10 simultaneous client connections. This makes XP an inappropriate choice as a print server in all but the smallest network environments.

- **Sufficient space on the hard drive for the print server.** This is important because Windows 2000/Server 2003 uses space on the hard drive to queue and buffer documents as they're directed to the print device.

- **Sufficient RAM beyond that of the minimum Windows 2000/Server 2003 requirements.** This is critical if you expect to have a large number of print jobs and still require acceptable performance.

Understanding network printing

When a user sends a print job to a locally attached printer, the job is spooled on the local machine and ultimately directed to a particular port, such as LPT1. When a user attempts to print a document to a network printer, the process is more involved. Both the print client and the print server run specific processes to deliver a print job to a network printer. The following steps outline the network printing process:

1 The first stage in the process is when the software application at the client generates a print file.

2 As it creates the print file, the application communicates with the Windows *graphics device interface (GDI)*. The GDI integrates information about the print file—such as word-processing codes for fonts, colors, and embedded graphic objects—with information obtained from the printer driver installed at the client for the target printer, in a process that Microsoft calls *rendering*.

3 When the GDI is finished, the print file is formatted with control codes to implement the special graphics, font, and color characteristics of the file. At the same time, the software application places the print file in the client's spooler by writing the file, called the spool file, to a subfolder used for spooling. In the Windows 95, 98, NT, 2000, XP, and 2003 operating systems, a *spooler* is a group of DLLs, information files, and programs that process print jobs.

4 The remote print provider at the client makes a remote procedure call to the network print server to which the print file is targeted, such as a Windows 2000/2003 server. If the print server is responding and ready to accept the print file, the remote printer transmits that file from the client's spooler folder to the Server service on Windows 2000/Server 2003.

5 The network print server uses four processes to receive and process a print file: router, print provider, print processor, and print monitor. The router, print provider, and print processor are all pieces of the network print server's spooler.

6 Once contacted by the remote print provider on the client, the Server service calls its router, the Print Spooler service. The router directs the print file to the print provider, which stores it in a spool file until it can be sent to the printer. You can configure and start/restart the Print Spooler service on a Windows 2000/2003 Server through the Computer Management console.

7 While the file is spooled, the print provider works with the print processor to ensure that the file is formatted to use the right data type, such as *TEXT* or *RAW*.

8 When the spool file is fully formatted for transmission to the printer, the print monitor pulls it from the spooler's disk storage and sends it to the printer.

The final step in the printing process should result in the print device producing and outputting the intended file.

Publishing printers in Active Directory

To help users find network printer resources, you can publish shared printers into Active Directory. Any Windows Server 2003- or Windows 2000-compatible printer that's installed on a domain print server is automatically *published* into Active Directory during installation. Published printer objects are hidden in the Active Directory Users and Computers interface by default.

To view the published printers in Active Directory Users and Computers, click View on the menu bar, and click Users, Groups, and Computers as containers. This option modifies the view to show objects that are associated with a user, group, or a computer object. Printer objects are associated with the computer object that acts as their print server. When the container in which the print server is located is expanded, computer objects can also be expanded to view the printer objects associated with them, as shown in Exhibit 17-8.

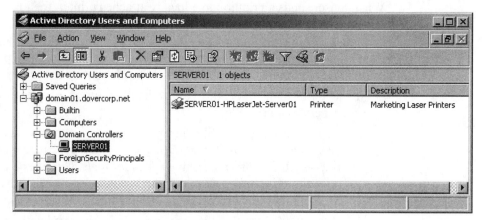

Exhibit 17-8: Viewing published printers in Active Directory Users and Computers

Printer shares that are created on pre-Windows 2000 print servers aren't published into Active Directory by default. These printers can be added manually to the directory by creating new published printer objects in Active Directory Users and Computers. Like shared folder objects, these printers can be published in whichever container makes the most sense, based on your environment and administrative goals.

Do it!

E-1: Discussing Windows 2000/Server 2003 printing concepts

Questions and answers

1 What's the difference between a local print device and a network print device?

2 What's a print client?

3 When a print job is ready to send to the print server, it's stored in the client's
_____.

A CDI

B Print Spooler service

C spooler

D RAM

4 In a Windows 2000/Server 2003 system, a printer is defined as:

A a spooling device

B a hardware device

C a network device

D a configuration object that controls the connection to a print device

5 What can you do to make printers easy to find for users in a Windows 2000/Server 2003 network?

6 Which interface can you use to view published printers in Active Directory?

Common printing problems

Explanation
Printers installed on a Windows 2000/Server 2003 system include a wide variety of configurable options and settings, problems eventually can and probably will occur.

The most common printing problems you're likely to encounter, and appropriate solutions, include:

- **Print jobs won't print.** Print jobs may not physically print from a particular print device for a variety of reasons, but some of the most common include that the print device is offline, not enough hard disk space is available to spool the job, or the print device is simply out of paper. To fix these problems, ensure that the print device is online, consider moving the spool folder to another location or free up disk space on the current volume, or add more paper to the device.

- **Printer output appears garbled.** Printed output may appear garbled or incomplete. In such cases, the usual source of the problem is that an incorrect driver for the device is installed. Download the correct driver from the manufacturer's Web site for the appropriate platforms and then reinstall these drivers on the print server.

- **Users receive an Access Denied message when attempting to print.** This message usually indicates incorrectly configured permissions. Review and correct permissions for the printer from the Security tab in the printer's properties to solve the problem.

- **Users can't find a printer when searching Active Directory.** Begin by ensuring that the printer is still published. If it's a Windows 2000 or later printer, it's published in Active Directory automatically. Right-click the printer and choose Properties. Activate the Sharing tab and make sure Share this printer is selected and List in the directory is checked. For pre-Windows 2000 shared printers, publish the printer manually using Active Directory Users and Computers or the PUBPRN.VBS script.

- **Printer works only at certain times of the day.** Windows 2000/Server 2003 allows schedules to be configured to control printer availability by the time of day. Either change the availability from the Advanced tab of the printer's properties or direct the user towards another configured printer that allows printing at those times.

- **Windows 95/98/ME users can't connect to a printer.** When a printer is installed on a Windows 2000/Server 2003 system, drivers for Windows 95/98/ME aren't installed by default. If users on these platforms require access to the printer, make the required drivers available from the Sharing tab of the printer's properties.

- **Print jobs become stuck in the print queue.** Some documents may appear in the print queue, but they don't print, and they can't be deleted. To fix this problem, open the Services console on the Administrative Tools menu on the print server, right-click the Print Spooler service, and then click Restart. Notice that any print jobs that are in the queue are deleted.

- **Failure of a print device.** A print device may fail because of a paper jam, hardware failure, or a stuck print job. Any documents that are behind the current document in the queue can be redirected to a new print device that uses the same print driver. To redirect the print jobs, access the properties of the printer that's connected to the failed print device. Click the Ports tab and then click the port to another printer assigned on the print server. If you need to redirect to another print server, click the Add Port button to add a local port that's directed to the IP address and share name of the other print server.

Do it!

E-2:   Working with the Print Spooler service

Here's how	Here's why
1 Choose **Start**	
Right click **My Computer**	
Choose **Manage**	The Computer Management window appears.
2 Next to the Services and Applications node, click the plus sign	
3 Click the **Services** node	To view its contents.
4 Scroll through the list of services until you find the Print Spooler service	
5 Double-click **Print Spooler**	The service is configured to start automatically when Windows 2000/Server 2003 starts.
6 Click the **Log On** tab	The Print Spooler service is enabled.
7 Click the **Recovery** tab	Notice that when the service fails, it's configured to restart automatically.
8 Click the **Dependencies** tab	Notice the services upon which the Print Spooler service depends in order to function correctly. In this case, if the Remote Procedure Call isn't running, the Print Spooler service can't function.
9 Click **OK**	To close the properties dialog box of the Print Spooler service.
10 In the list of services, right-click the **Print Spooler** service	
Choose **Restart**	A dialog box appears indicating that the service is restarting.
11 Close Computer Management	

Unit summary: Accessing and managing resources in a Windows network

Topic A   In this topic, you learned that the primary tool used to create and manage user accounts is **Active Directory Users and Computers**. You also learned how to troubleshoot user account and authentication issues, as well as the various settings and policies that can cause logons to fail.

Topic B   In this topic, you learned that the primary purpose of **groups** in a network environment is to ease the administrative burden associated with assigning rights and permissions with individual user accounts. Next, you learned that Windows 2000/Server 2003 supports two group types, known as **security groups** and **distribution groups**. You also learned that Windows 2000/Server 2003 supports three different **group scopes**: **global**, **domain local**, and **universal**.

Topic C   In this topic, you learned that Windows 2000/Server 2003 supports the **FAT**, **FAT32**, and **NTFS** file systems. Only the NTFS file system allows local security permissions to be configured. You also learned that Windows 2000/Server 2003 supports both standard and special **NTFS permissions**. Special NTFS permissions give an administrator a more granular level of control over how permissions are applied. You learned that NTFS permissions are cumulative.

Topic D   In this topic, you learned that, to create a shared folder, you need the appropriate rights. The primary tools used to create shared folders are Windows Explorer, Computer Management, and the **NET SHARE** command-line utility.

Topic E   In this topic, you learned that **printing** in a Windows 2000/Server 2003 environment has its own unique terminology, an understanding of which is critical towards understanding how the printing system functions. You also learned that **printer publishing** allows users to query Active Directory for a list of available printers. Finally, you learned how to troubleshoot common printing problems.

Review questions

1 New Active Directory users must be created in which folder?

   A Users

   B Builtin

   C Computers

   D User accounts don't have to be created in any particular folder

2 Where can you configure additional user account settings after creating a user account in Active Directory?

3 Which of the following objects can be added to a global group when a domain is configured to the Windows Server 2003 domain functional level?

A Users

B Global groups

C Domain local groups

D Universal groups

4 Which of the following objects can be added to a domain local group when a domain is configured to the Windows 2000 mixed domain functional level?

A Users

B Global groups

C Domain local groups

D Universal groups

5 Which of the following group types can't be created when a domain is configured to the Windows 2000 mixed domain functional level?

A Global groups

B Domain local groups

C Universal groups

6 Which of the following are NTFS folder permissions? (Choose all that apply.)

A Read & Execute

B List Folder Contents

C Read

D Change

7 Which of the following are NTFS file permissions? (Choose all that apply.)

A Read & Execute

B List Folder Contents

C Read

D Modify

8 Which of the following shared folders would be hidden in My Network Places?

A Documents

B Documents$

C $Documents

D Documents%

9 Which of the following file systems support local security?

A NTFS

B FAT

C FAT32

10 Which of the following NTFS permissions allow a user to change the permissions associated with a file?

A Full Control

B Modify

C Read & Execute

D Write

11 Which of the following tools can be used to create shared folders on a Windows Server 2003 system? (Choose all that apply.)

A Computer Management

B Windows Explorer

C Internet Explorer

D The NET SHARE command

12 Printers installed on a Windows Server 2003 system are published to Active Directory by default. True or false?

13 When a new printer is installed, drivers are made available for which of the following operating systems by default? (Choose all that apply.)

A Windows 2000

B Windows Server 2003

C Windows 95

D Windows 98

14 When documents appear to be stuck in the print queue, which of the following services should be restarted?

A Print Spooler

B Server

C Workstation

D Plug and Play

Unit 18

Monitoring and troubleshooting a Windows server

Unit time: 60 minutes

Complete this unit, and you'll know how to:

A Use Task Manager to monitor server performance and resource usage.

B Use Event Viewer to identify and troubleshoot problems.

C Discuss the Performance console with System Monitor and Performance Logs and Alerts.

Topic A: Introduction to server monitoring

This topic covers the following CompTIA Network+ exam objective:

#	Objective
4.5	Given a troubleshooting scenario between a client and the following server environments, identify the cause of a stated problem: • Windows

Introducing server health monitoring

Explanation

One of the more important reasons for monitoring the health of your server is that it can help alert you to problems before they occur or become more serious. Over time, networks change, and the demands placed on a server can vary or increase. Monitoring server performance can help you determine what normal behavior is for your server under the current demands and alert you to any performance issues that may occur if the normal behavior changes. This normal behavior is known as *baseline* performance.

Windows 2000/Server 2003 comes with several built-in tools that can be used to monitor server health and performance, including:

- Task Manager
- Event Viewer
- Performance console

The following sections introduce you to these tools, providing you with a description of how they can be used to monitor your server.

Task Manager

Task Manager gives you a snapshot of current overall CPU and memory usage, as well as the CPU and the memory usage of each process. While this real-time performance information can be valuable, it's rather limited in scope for troubleshooting. Task Manager is generally used as a starting point, before other tools and utilities, to gather additional information.

You can access Task Manager in several ways:

- Press the Ctrl+Shift+Esc key combination
- Right-click the Windows taskbar and choose Task Manager
- Press the Ctrl+Alt+Delete key combination and click the Task Manager button in the Windows Security dialog box

Once opened, Windows Task Manager displays five main tabs:

- Applications
- Processes
- Performance
- Networking
- Users

Monitoring and managing applications

The Applications tab presents a list of all foreground software applications (as opposed to background processes) that are running, as shown in Exhibit 18-1. To stop an application, select it from the displayed list and click the End Task button. If an application is listed as Not Responding (no longer responding to user input), you can select that application and press End Task to stop the program. The Switch To button brings the highlighted application to the foreground, and the New Task button enables you to start another application at the console, in a manner similar to the Run command.

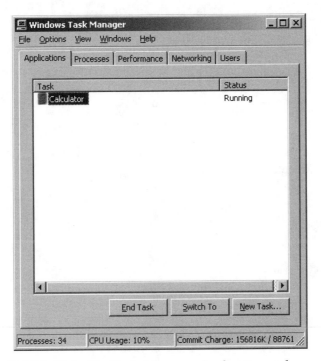

Exhibit 18-1: The Task Manager Applications tab

If you right-click a particular task, several options appear in a shortcut menu:

- **Switch To.** Takes you into the highlighted program
- **Bring To Front.** Brings the highlighted program to the foreground, but leaves the focus on Task Manager
- **Minimize.** Causes the program to be minimized
- **Maximize.** Causes the program to be maximized, but leaves you in Task Manager
- **End Task.** Stops the highlighted program
- **Go To Process.** Takes you to the Processes tab and highlights the main process associated with the program

Do it!

A-1: Using Task Manager to control applications

Questions and answers

1 Which of the following methods can be used to access the Task Manager utility? (Choose all that apply.)

   A   Press Ctrl+Alt+Delete, then click Task Manager

   B   Press Ctrl+T

   C   Right-click on the taskbar, click Task Manager

   D   Click Start, click Task Manager

2 Task Manager gives you a view of system activity over a long period of time. True or False?

3 Which of the following Task Manager tabs can be used to view the current status of a foreground program?

   A   Processes

   B   Applications

   C   Users

   D   Networking

Monitoring and managing processes

Explanation

The Task Manager Processes tab, as shown in Exhibit 18-2, lists all of the processes in use by applications and system services, including those running in the background. Besides allowing you to right-click on a process to end it, this tab also displays important information about each running process:

Process information	Description
Image Name	The process name, such as winword.exe for Microsoft Word
User Name	The user account under which the process is running
CPU	The percentage of CPU resources currently used by the process
Mem Usage	The amount of memory currently used by the process

In addition to showing how resources are being used, the Processes tab also allows you to configure the priority associated with a process. Most processes run under *Normal priority* by default, meaning that all running processes are granted the same level of access to system CPU resources. In some cases, you might want to grant certain processes a higher or lower level of access to these resources, based on their importance or for performance-tuning purposes. For example, for a time-critical application, you might choose to run the associated process at a higher priority to ensure that it gains immediate access to the processor.

To change the priority of a process, right-click on it in the Image Name column, select Set Priority, and then click the priority level required for the process.

Use the Realtime priority with caution. If assigned to a process, that process may completely monopolize the server's CPU resources, preventing access by any other processes.

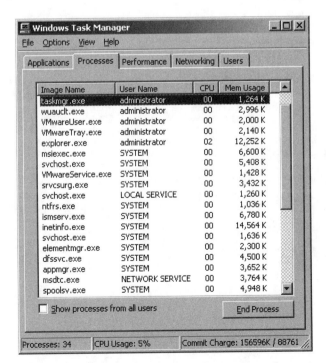

Exhibit 18-2: The Task Manager Processes tab

Do it!

A-2: Using Task Manager to manage applications and processes

Here's how	Here's why
1 Press CTRL + ALT + DELETE	To start the process of accessing Task Manager
On the Windows Server 2003 computer only, click **Task Manager** in the Windows Security dialog box	
2 Click **Applications**	(If necessary.) Assuming that you have no foreground applications running, this tab should not currently list any running tasks.
3 Choose **Start**, **Run...**	
In the Open box, type **calc.exe**	
Click **OK**	This opens the Calculator program, which is now listed on the Applications tab with a status of Running.
4 On the Applications tab, select **Calculator**	To select it.
Click **Switch To**	This minimizes Task Manager and brings the Calculator program to the foreground.
5 On the taskbar, click **Windows Task Manager**	To restore it.
6 On the Applications tab, right-click **Calculator**	To view the items available on the shortcut menu that appears.
Choose **Go To Process**	Notice that this action switches focus to the Processes tab, with the process calc.exe highlighted.
Verify the User Name, CPU, and Mem Usage columns associated with the process	
7 Right-click **calc.exe**	To view the items available on the shortcut menu that appears.
Choose **End Process**	

8 In the Task Manager Warning
   message box, observe the message

   Click **Yes**   Notice that the Calculator window closes, and
                                              the calc.exe process no longer appears on the
                                              Processes tab.

9 Click the **Applications** tab

   Verify that the Calculator task is
   no longer present

10 Close the Windows Task Manager
   window

Monitoring network performance

Explanation

New in Windows Server 2003 and Windows XP, Task Manager's Networking tab, shown in Exhibit 18-3, allows you to monitor the performance of the network cards installed on the system. The graphical interface on this tab displays total network utilization information, which is roughly the percentage of the network bandwidth in use.

The lower portion of the Networking tab displays network performance data for each network card. It lists the name of the adapter (or connection), the network utilization detected by the adapter (from 0% to 100%), the speed of the network link, such as 10 Mbps, and the operational state of the adapter. This information can be valuable if you suspect there's a problem with a NIC in the server and you want to determine if it's working. The information can also be an initial warning that something is causing prolonged high network utilization—80% to 100%, for instance.

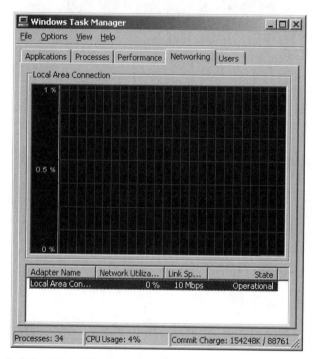

Exhibit 18-3: The Task Manager Networking tab

Monitoring users

Also new in Windows Server 2003 and Windows XP, the Users tab provides a listing of the users currently logged on to a system, including network clients with connections to the system. You can log off a user by selecting user and clicking the Logoff button, thus ensuring that any open files are closed before the user is logged off, or select the Disconnect option to disconnect a user's session, usually if that session is hung or can't be logged off. Other options include the ability to send a network message to a user or to connect to another user's session. The Windows Task Manager Users tab is shown in Exhibit 18-4.

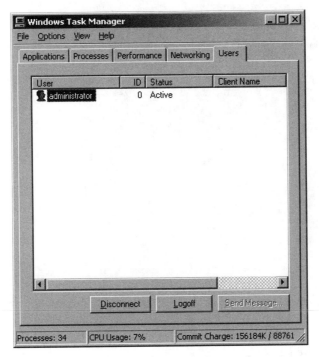

Exhibit 18-4: The Task Manager Users tab

Monitoring real-time performance

The Performance tab shows CPU and memory performance information through bar charts, line graphs, and performance statistics, as shown in Exhibit 18-5. The CPU Usage and PF Usage bars show current usage. To the right of each bar is a graph showing recent history statistics.

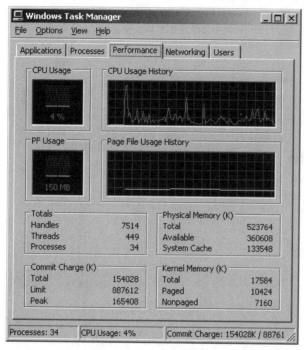

Exhibit 18-5: The Task Manager Performance tab

The bottom of the Performance tab shows more detailed statistics, which are described in the following table:

Performance information	Description
Totals	Displays the total number of handles, threads, and processes
Physical Memory	Displays the total amount of memory, how much is available, and the amount of memory used for the system cache
Commit Charge	Displays the amount of memory that's been committed to all applications currently running
Kernel Memory	Displays the amount of memory that's been allocated to kernel functions, the amount of memory that could be paged to disk, and the amount of nonpaged memory

You use the Performance tab to gain a quick look at the current performance of a system and then use a tool like System Monitor to gather more detailed information.

Do it!

A-3:   Using Task Manager to monitor performance

Here's how	Here's why
1 Press (CTRL) + (ALT) + (DELETE)	You'll use Task Manager to monitor server performance.
At the Windows Server 2003 computer only, click **Task Manager** in the Windows Security dialog box	
2 Click the **Performance** tab	
Observe the information provided on the Performance tab	The tab provides information such as CPU Usage, CPU Usage History, PF Usage, and Page File Usage History.
3 With the Windows Task Manager window open, choose **Start, Run...**	
In the Open box, enter **write.exe**	
Click **OK**	
Observe the CPU Usage History graph on the Performance tab	Spikes should be visible at the point when WordPad was opened.
4 Click the **Applications** tab	
From the Task list, select **Document - WordPad**	
Click **End Task**	To close WordPad.
5 Open additional applications and activate the Performance tab	To view the impact on both CPU and Page File usage.
6 Close all open windows, including the Windows Task Manager window	

Topic B: Troubleshooting with Event Viewer

This topic covers the following CompTIA Network+ exam objective:

#	Objective
4.5	Given a troubleshooting scenario between a client and the following server environments, identify the cause of a stated problem: • Windows

Event Viewer

Explanation

The most common and effective monitoring and troubleshooting tool in Windows 2000/Server 2003 is *Event Viewer*. You can use Event Viewer to gather information to troubleshoot software, hardware, and system problems. Exhibit 18-6 shows the Event Viewer console.

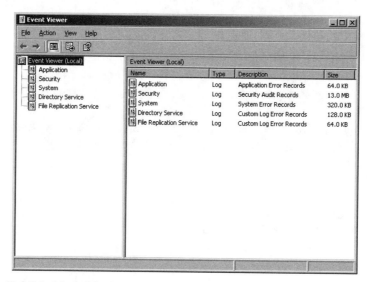

Exhibit 18-6: The Event Viewer console

Events that occur on a system are tracked and recorded in various log files. You can use Event Viewer to view the contents of the log files. For example, you can use Event Viewer to view the contents of the *System log* to determine when and possibly why a specific service failed to start.

Whenever you're troubleshooting a problem with a server, one of the first places to look to gather information about the cause is Event Viewer. Entries in the log files can alert you to warnings and errors that are occurring, the component or application that's generating the message, and possibly why the problem is happening. Most entries also include an event ID that you can research on Microsoft's Support Web site (or the vendor's Web site, in the case of third-party products) to gather more detailed information on the problem and find a solution.

Events are typically written to one of three log files:

- **Application log.** Records information, warnings, and errors generated by programs.
- **Security log.** Records events pertaining to audit policy. For example, if the audit policy is tracking failed logon attempts, an event is written to the security log each time a user is unsuccessful in logging on. By default, security logging is disabled until an audit policy is configured.
- **System log.** Records information, warnings, and errors generated by Windows 2000/Server 2003 system components, such as drivers and services.

A domain controller has two additional logs:

- **Directory Service log.** Records events logged by Active Directory
- **File Replication Service log**. Records file replication events

A server that has the DNS service installed also includes:

- **DNS Server log**. Records events related to the DNS server service

Any user can view the contents of the application and system log, by default. The security log can be viewed only by administrators and by those users who've been assigned the Manage Auditing and Security Log right.

The system and application logs display the following types of events:

- **Information.** Indicates that a component or application successfully performs an operation. Information events are identified by an "i" icon.
- **Warning.** Indicates that an event occurs that may not be a problem at the current time but might become a problem in the future. An exclamation point (!) icon indicates warnings.
- **Error.** Indicates that a significant event has occurred, such as a service failing to start or a device driver failing to load. An "x" icon indicates errors.

Notice that two other types of events are logged based on the configuration of an audit policy. These are successes and failures of actions that are performed on the network.

Interpreting events

When you click a log file in Event Viewer, the details pane lists all the events that have occurred and provides general information about each one, such as:

- Type of event (information, warning, or error)
- The date and time that the event occurred
- The source of the event (the component or application that logged the event)
- The category and event ID
- The computer on which the event occurred

An example of an event message is shown in Exhibit 18-7.

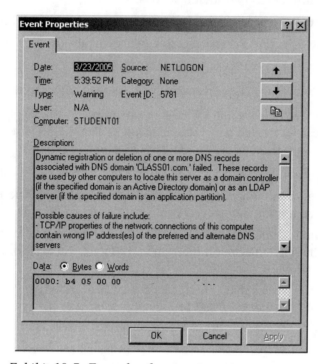

Exhibit 18-7: Example of an event message

The header for an event provides the same information listed above. The event description tells you what occurred and why the event is significant, which is usually the most useful information.

Notice that the data field of an event displays information that is generated by the program or component. It contains binary data that can be used by application support technicians to troubleshoot the problem.

Do it!

B-1: Viewing Event Viewer application and system log events

Here's how	Here's why
1 At the Windows Server 2003 computer, choose **Start**, **Administrative Tools**, **Event Viewer**	You'll view events in the Event Viewer system and application logs.
At the Windows XP computer, choose **Start**, **Control Panel**, then double-click **Administrative Tools** and open Event Viewer	Double-click Event Viewer to open it.
2 In the left pane, click the **Application** icon	To view the contents of the application log.
3 Double-click the first Information event found in the list	To view its properties. The Event Properties dialog box opens.
4 Observe the information contained in the event header and Description fields	
Click the down-arrow	To display the next event in the application log.
5 Click **Cancel**	To close the Event Properties dialog box.
6 Click the **System** icon	To view the contents of the system log.
7 Double-click the first Error event found in list	To view its properties. (You may need to scroll down.)
Observe the details of the event header and Description fields	
8 Close all open windows and dialog boxes	

Topic C: Working with the Performance console

This topic covers the following CompTIA Network+ exam objective:

#	Objective
4.5	Given a troubleshooting scenario between a client and the following server environments, identify the cause of a stated problem: • Windows

Performance console

Explanation

Although Task Manager provides administrators with an easy way to gauge server performance quickly, Windows 2000/Server 2003 also includes an administrative tool known as the *Performance console* that allows more detailed information to be gathered.

The Performance console consists of two distinct tools:

- **System Monitor**. Displays data gathered from a wide variety of counter objects in real time, usually with a graphical representation of the data.
- **Performance Logs and Alerts**. Logs data to a file, which can be imported into other applications, such as Microsoft Excel or SQL Server, or used to generate alerts when specified thresholds are met.

The Performance console is displayed in Exhibit 18-8.

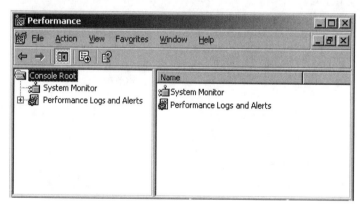

Exhibit 18-8: The Performance console

The processes that the Performance console monitors are called objects. The specific performance aspect that's measured is determined by what's called a counter, which is assigned to the object. Objects and counters can be added and customized to help you gather the data you need.

System Monitor

System Monitor is one of the most useful tools for collecting data on real-time server performance. As part of the Windows 2000/Server 2003 Performance MMC, this tool allows you to track how system resources are being used and how they're behaving under the current workload.

System Monitor collects data that you can use for the following tasks:

- **Server performance.** If you use System Monitor on a regular basis, it can help you understand how the server performs under the current workload.
- **Problem diagnosis.** Helps you diagnose server components that may not be working right.
- **Capacity planning.** Lets you see how server usage is changing over time and helps you plan for future upgrades.
- **Testing.** If configuration changes are made, you can use the data to observe the impact that the changes have on the server.

System Monitor allows you to define the system components you want to monitor and the type of data you want to collect. It can gather data from the local computer or from a network computer.

System Monitor includes a number of performance objects and counters for processes that are common targets for monitoring, by default. Other objects and counters are added when various services and applications are added to a server, such as DNS or Microsoft SQL Server.

Using System Monitor

When you first open the Performance tool, System Monitor in Windows Server 2003 automatically begins displaying performance data. In Windows 2000, you first need to add counters before data is being displayed. In Windows Server 2003, the tool by default displays data related to the memory, processor, and physical disk objects for the local computer, as displayed in Exhibit 18-9.

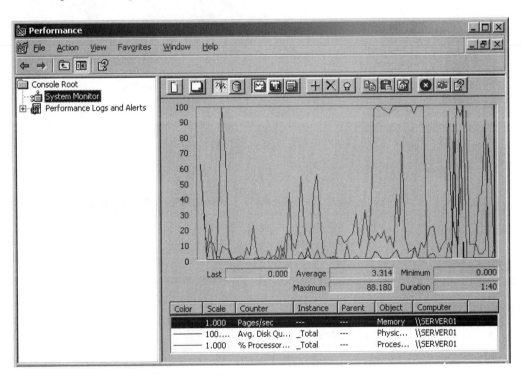

Exhibit 18-9: The default display of System Monitor

The information that System Monitor captures can be displayed in one of three views:

- **Graph.** Displays counter information as a continuous graph that's updated in real time

- **Histogram.** Displays counter information as a histogram, updated in real time. An example is shown in Exhibit 18-10.

- **Report.** Displays a text-based report view of counters, updated in real time

The System Monitor interface provides a number of options for viewing performance data:

- **Add** additional performance counters

- **Switch** between display views

- **Highlight** a selected counter

- **Copy** and **paste** selected information

- **Freeze** the display for analysis

The System Monitor toolbar, found at the top of the details pane in System Monitor, allows you to control these functions easily.

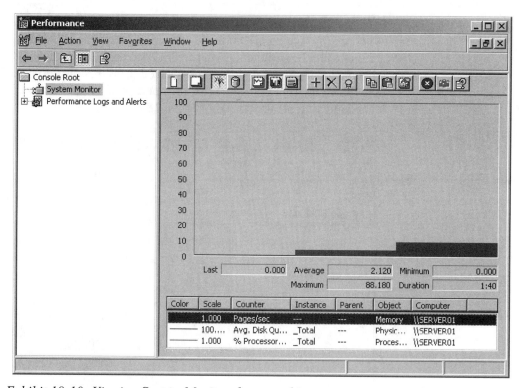

Exhibit 18-10: Viewing System Monitor data as a histogram

Performance objects and counters

Monitoring the performance of your server should be a regular maintenance task. The information you gather can help establish a baseline of performance and identify what's considered normal performance under typical operating conditions. As you continue to monitor the server over time, you can compare the data against the baseline to identify how performance is changing as the network changes or workloads increase. This allows you to pinpoint bottlenecks, such as components, that may be hindering performance, before they become serious problems.

Any time you upgrade or add a component to a system, whether it's a hardware or software component, you should run System Monitor to determine the effect the change has on performance.

When monitoring server performance, there are a few performance objects that should be included, as well as specific performance counters associated with each one.

- **% Processor Time.** This processor counter measures the percentage of time that the processor is executing a non-idle thread. If the value is consistently at or over 80%, a CPU upgrade may be required.

- **% Interrupt Time.** This processor counter measures hardware interrupts. If you experience a combination of Processor Time exceeding 90% and % Interrupt Time exceeding 15%, check for malfunctioning hardware or device drivers.

- **Pages/Second.** This memory counter measures the number of pages read in or out to disk to resolve hard page faults. If this number exceeds 20 or more page faults per second, add more RAM to the computer.

- **Page Faults/Second.** This memory counter measures the number of hard and soft page faults per second. A hard page fault refers to a request that required hard disk access, whereas a soft page fault refers to a request found in another part of memory.

- **% Disk Time.** This physical and logical disk counter measures the percentage of elapsed time that the selected disk drive is busy. If above 90%, try moving the page file to another physical drive or upgrade the hard drive.

- **Avg. Disk Queue Length.** This physical and logical disk counter measures the average number of requests currently outstanding for a volume or partition. If averaging over two, then drive access may be a bottleneck. You may want to upgrade the drive or hard drive controller. Implementing a Stripe Set with multiple drives may also fix this problem.

Notice that in Windows NT, all disk counters were turned off by default. In Windows 2000, the physical disk object is turned on by default and the logical disk object is turned off by default. In Windows Server 2003, all disk counters are enabled by default. Disk counters can be turned on or off by using the DISKPERF –Y and DISKPERF –N commands respectively.

Saving System Monitor data

Gathering data with a tool like System Monitor is the easy part. It's more difficult to interpret the information to determine what component is affecting performance. The difficulty lies in the fact that the performance of some components can affect that of other components. It may appear from the data that one component is performing poorly when this performance can be the result of another component's poor performance. It may even be caused by another component's performing too well.

For example, if you determine that your processor is running over 80%, your first instinct might be to upgrade the processor. Through further analysis, however, you may find that a lack of memory is the bottleneck that's causing excess paging. You would have discovered this by monitoring the Pages/Second Memory counter. Monitoring multiple components on a regular basis should give you an idea of how they perform together and make performance troubleshooting that much easier.

The System Monitor tool provides a number of alternatives for saving or viewing historical performance data. One particularly interesting feature is the ability to save System Monitor data to an HTML file. This allows you to post performance data on a Web server so that it can be easily viewed and retrieved. When System Monitor data is saved in this format, many of the control functions of the tool are available through the Web interface. In other words, the data is presented not in a simple graphics file, but rather an interactive interface, as seen in Exhibit 18-11.

The System Monitor tool is also capable of displaying older data that may have been saved to a log file or database using the *Performance Logs and Alerts* tool. This tool will be looked at in more detail in the next section.

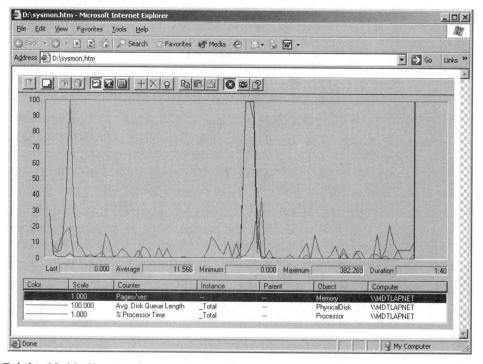

Exhibit 18-11: Viewing System Monitor data in a Web browser

Performance Logs and Alerts

Another tool available within the Performance console is Performance Logs and Alerts. This tool allows you to collect data automatically on the local computer or from another computer on the network and then to view it using System Monitor or another program, such as Microsoft Excel or a relational database such as Microsoft SQL Server.

Performance Logs and Alerts allows you to perform the following tasks:

- Collect data in a binary, comma-separated, tab-separated format, or SQL Server database format. The binary versions of the log files can be read with System Monitor, but comma- and tab-separated data can easily be imported into another program for analysis.
- View data while it's being collected and after it's been collected.
- Configure parameters, such as start and stop times for log generation, file names, and file size.
- Configure and manage multiple logging sessions from a single console window
- Set up alerts so that a message is sent, a program is run, or a log file is started when a specific counter exceeds or drops below a configured value.

You can access Performance Logs and Alerts through the Performance console. There are three options available:

- **Counter logs**. Take the information that you view using System Monitor and save it to a log file. One of the main advantages of using counter logs is that you can configure logging to start and stop at different intervals.
- **Trace logs**. Similar to counter logs but triggered to start when an event occurs.
- **Alerts**. Allow you to configure an event to occur when a counter meets a predefined value. For example, you can choose to run a specific program or utility automatically when a threshold is reached or to send a message to a network administrator.

Configuring Alerts

Logging does increase overhead on a server, so it's generally not something you want to have running all the time. You should set up a regular schedule for collecting data and then review this data regularly as part of a proactive server monitoring strategy. Rather than running logs all the time, alerts can be set up to notify you of a potential problem. For example, you can configure an alert to monitor the LogicalDisk object for %FreeDiskSpace < 20%. If the %FreeDiskSpace is below 20%, an alert notifies you of the problem.

The following table summarizes the options that can be set for generating alerts.

Action	Description
Log an entry in the application event log	An entry is added to the application log when the event is triggered.
Send a network message to	Messenger service sends a message to the specified computer when the alert is triggered.
Start performance data log	Counter log is run when the alert is triggered.
Run this program	Specified program is run when the alert is triggered. For example, a paging program or an e-mail utility.
Command line arguments	Specified command line arguments are copied when the Run this program option is used.

Do it!

C-1: Discussing System Monitor and Performance Logs and Alerts

Questions and answers

1 What type of information does the Histogram view of System Monitor show?

2 You're experiencing a combination of Processor Time of 95% and % Interrupt Time of 20%. What type of problem might be causing these numbers?

3 Which of the following counters measures the percentage of elapsed time that the selected disk drive is busy?

   A % Disk Time

   B Page Faults/Second

   C % Processor Time

   D Avg. Disk Queue Length

4 When do trace logs start?

5 You should have logging enabled at all times. True or false? Please explain your answer.

Unit summary: Monitoring and troubleshooting a Windows server

Topic A   In this topic, you learned that the **Task Manager** utility can be used to view and control running applications and processes, obtain basic **performance information**, view **network utilization** information, and view **connected users**.

Topic B   In this topic, you learned that the **Event Viewer** tool displays **information**, **warning**, and **error** events relating to the operating system and applications. You also learned that all Windows 2000/Server 2003 systems include **System**, **Security**, and **Application logs,** and that additional logs may also be present based on the role of the server.

Topic C   In this topic, you learned that **Performance console** is the primary server monitoring utility. It consists of two main tools, **System Monitor** and **Performance Logs and Alerts**. You learned that System Monitor is a performance monitoring utility that displays data in a **graph**, **histogram**, or **report**. Finally, you learned that data can be collected for analysis using Performance Logs and Alerts.

Review questions

1 Which of the following Task Manager tabs allows the priority of a running process to be configured?

   A Applications

   B Processes

   C Performance

   D Users

2 Which of the following are logs found in Event Viewer on a Windows Server 2003 system? (Choose all that apply.)

   A System log

   B Application log

   C Security log

   D Program log

3 Operating system events are always written to the Application log in Event Viewer. True or false?

4 Which of the following tools are included in the Performance console? (Choose all that apply.)

A System Monitor

B Task Manager.

C Performance Logs and Alerts

D Computer Management

5 Which of the following aren't actions associated with an alert?

A Send a network message to

B Start performance data log

C Run this program

D Disable a service

6 Which of the following counters are displayed by default in the System Monitor display when the Performance console is opened? (Choose all that apply.)

A Pages/sec

B Avg. Disk Queue Length

C % Memory Time

D % Processor Time

7 System Monitor can be used to monitor performance information on a remote computer. True or false?

8 Disk performance counters are enabled by default on a Windows Server 2003 system. True or false?

9 Which command is used to enable or disable disk counters on a Windows Server 2003 system?

A Diskperf

B Diskpart

C Diskpark

D Diskslot

10 Which of the following isn't a type of event stored in the System log in Event Viewer?

A Information

B Warning

C Error

D Success

11 The data displayed on the Task Manager performance tab can be exported to a text file. True or false?

12 Which of the following are valid Recovery actions in the event of a service failure? (Choose all that apply.)

A Take No Action

B Restart the Service

C Run a Program

D Stop the Service

13 Which of the following are available views in the System Monitor tool? (Choose all that apply.)

A Report

B Histogram

C Graph

D Pie Chart

14 The CPU column on the Task Manager processes tab displays current CPU usage information. True or false?

15 Which of the following are valid performance objects in System Monitor on a Windows Server 2003 system? (Choose all that apply.)

A Memory

B Processor

C Server

D System

16 It isn't possible to monitor objects on more than one server at the same time using System Monitor. True or false?

17 You're responsible for the administration of three Dover Leasing servers. You've recently installed a new service on your server. The service is set to start automatically and runs continuously to service user requests. Your manager is concerned about server performance after the service is installed, and you assure him that performance shouldn't suffer. Answer the following questions based on the scenario.

   a After you install the service, what is one of the first things you should do?

   b During peak hours, your manager stops in to see how the server is performing under the added workload. What tool can you use to show your manager quickly the current processor usage on the server?

   c You have a slight concern that the service may indeed have an impact on the amount of time the processor is utilized. The % utilization was running at times near 50% before the service was installed. You would like to be notified if the processor utilization goes above 60%. Explain how this can be done. What other actions can you configure if this occurs?

18 The IT manager at Dover Leasing is looking for a quick way for junior administrators to monitor the performance of Windows Server 2003 systems on the network from any internal desktop system. Given that desktops are running a range of operating systems, including Windows 98, Windows 2000, and Windows XP, what would be the best way to accomplish this?

19 The development staff at Dover Leasing is in the process of developing an SQL Server-based application for the purpose of monitoring historical server performance and baseline data. Which Windows Server 2003 tool and specific data-gathering option would be best suited to obtaining this information?

Unit 19

Managing and troubleshooting NetWare network resources

Unit time: 90 minutes

Complete this unit, and you'll know how to:

A Discuss user and group management.

B Identify the methods for implementing file system security.

C Discuss user account restrictions.

D Discuss NDS context.

E Describe NetWare log files.

F Identify NetWare monitoring and management tools.

Topic A: User and group management

This topic covers the following CompTIA Network+ exam objectives:

#	Objective
3.1	Identify the basic capabilities (For example: client support, interoperability, authentication, file and print services, application support and security) of the following server operating systems to access network resources: • NetWare
4.5	Given a troubleshooting scenario between a client and the following server environments, identify the cause of a stated problem: • NetWare

Creating users with ConsoleOne

Explanation

Managing users is quite possibly the most important and time-consuming task of a network administrator. In older versions of NetWare, such as NetWare 4.x, you used the NetWare Administrator utility to create, delete, rename, and manage user objects in an NDS/eDirectory directory tree. This utility still exists but isn't being developed any further by Novell. User and other resource/NDS management is now performed through ConsoleOne, which you can run from a workstation, at the server console, or through iManager, Novell's Web-based management tool.

The creation of user accounts is one of the fundamental tasks of network administration. The following procedure describes this process using ConsoleOne:

1. Start ConsoleOne and expand the NDS tree:
2. To create an account for a network user, select the parent container and do one of the following:
   - Choose File, New, User.
   - Right-click the container object and choose New, User.
   - Press Insert, select User, and click OK.
   - Click the New User button on the toolbar.
3. The New User dialog box appears. You must complete the fields, Name and Surname, to create a User object.

You also have several options to configure the User object at this point. You can specify a default login sequence to enable access to other file systems using, for example, Macintosh and Windows Native File Access. You can also specify whether an enhanced or simple password should be assigned to the user, for example, for access to other file systems, and specify basic related password settings. Note that this isn't the NDS/eDirectory password for the user. You're prompted for that password automatically when you actually create the User object. The Unique ID field automatically populates with the text entered in the Name box.

Further, you can specify to use a template that contains standard settings for user objects, and you can specify that you want to define additional properties for the user once the object is created. The final option, Create another User, lets you create another user object without having to perform steps one or two from the previous procedure.

When you've finished making your selections, the New User dialog box looks similar to the one shown in Exhibit 19-1. Click OK to create the user object and, when prompted, enter the NDS/eDirectory password for the user.

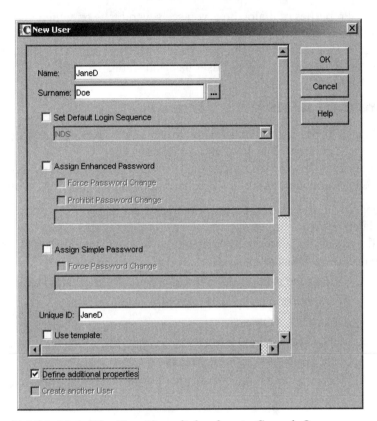

Exhibit 19-1: The New User dialog box in ConsoleOne

Viewing user information

After creating a new user, you can view additional details about the object by using one of the following techniques:

- Double-click the object's icon in the Directory tree in the right pane.
- Right-click the object and choose Properties.
- Click to select the object and choose File, Properties.

In the Properties of dialog box, you see several tabs on which you can configure additional details about the user. Exactly what tabs display and what configuration options are available depend on a variety of items, such as what services are installed on the server, the access rights a user has, and so on.

Creating users with iManager

iManager is the newest addition to Novell's set of NDS/eDirectory management tools. You can access it via a Web browser by entering http://server_IP_address/nps/iManager.html. Using iManager, you can perform many of the same functions, as well as functions additional to the ones available in ConsoleOne.

Supported browsers for iManager include Internet Explorer 6 SP1 or later, Netscape 7.1 or later, and Mozilla 1.4 or later. Note that iManager is optimized for Internet Explorer, and some of the functionality may not work as expected in the other two browsers. To create a User object in iManager:

1 Access the iManager main page (you have to provide credentials to log in).

2 In the left pane, expand eDirectory Administration.

3 Click Create Object.

4 Select User and click OK. You see the pane change to something similar to what's shown in Exhibit 19-2.

2 The following fields are mandatory for creating a User object in iManager:

- Username
- Last Name
- Context

In addition, you can provide other information, such as whether a template should be used, whether to use a password, as well as certain identifying information, such as department, title, and so on. Click OK (you may have to scroll) to create the object.

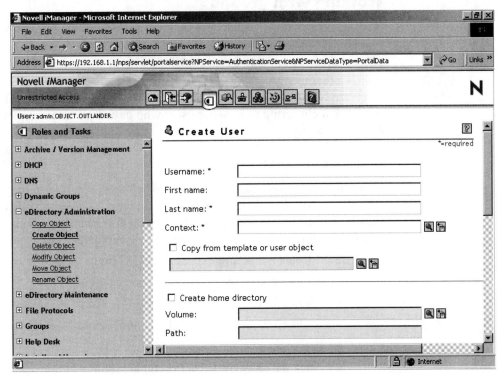

Exhibit 19-2: The Create User pane in iManager

Working with groups

A Group object is generally used for one of two purposes. First, groups are used to configure common login script properties for multiple users who exist in the same NDS/eDirectory context. Conditional tests in the login script are used to determine if the user is a member of a particular group. Second, groups are used as the target of NetWare NDS/eDirectory and file system security assignments. The Group objects represent a clustering of network users who have the same needs for resources in the NDS/eDirectory tree.

Group management

You can use ConsoleOne or iManager to create and manage Group objects in an NDS/eDirectory tree. You can also view and modify a Group object's properties, members, and associated values. The process for creating a Group object is similar to that for creating a User object. To create a Group object using Console One:

1 Start ConsoleOne and expand the NDS tree:

2 Select the parent container and do one of the following:

   - Choose File, New, Group.

   - Right-click the container object and choose New, Group.

   - Press Insert, select Group and click OK.

   - Click the New Group button on the toolbar.

3 The New Group window appears. You must assign a name to the group, and you can click Define additional properties to configure the Group object immediately after creation of the object.

Do it!

A-1:   Discussing user and group management

Questions and answers

1   Name the two utilities used to create and manage Group objects in an NDS/eDirectory tree.

2   You want to create a User object in a NetWare 6.5 network. Which utility do you use if you want to create the object at the server console?

   A   NetWare Administrator

   B   iManager

   C   User Manager for eDirectory

   D   ConsoleOne

3   You've been asked to create a User object using iManager. However, you have trouble accessing iManager. What could be the problem?

4   The Group object can be used to configure common login script properties for multiple users who exist in the same NDS/eDirectory context. True or False?

Topic B: Rights and trustee assignments

This topic covers the following CompTIA Network+ exam objectives:

#	Objective
3.1	Identify the basic capabilities (For example: client support, interoperability, authentication, file and print services, application support and security) of the following server operating systems to access network resources: • NetWare
4.5	Given a troubleshooting scenario between a client and the following server environments, identify the cause of a stated problem: • NetWare

File system rights

Explanation

The NetWare file system is one of the most frequently accessed network resources. Therefore, it's critical to understand the methods behind the implementation of a comprehensive file system security plan, which include file and directory access security and trustee assignments.

File system security determines the type of directory and file access available to a user. Users must be granted rights to file system resources before they're able to access directories and files.

The NetWare file system provides eight distinct directory rights. An object's directory rights determine the type of access available to a directory and its contents. Directory rights are annotated as S R W C E M F A (see below). Rights can be assigned and reassigned at any time by users possessing the necessary file system security access, such as the network administrator.

The following is a list of the available NetWare directory trustee rights.

- **Supervisor (S).** Grants all rights to a directory and overrides any restrictions placed on subdirectories or files with an Inherited Rights Filter. A user with the Supervisor right can assign the Supervisor right to another user and can modify disk space restrictions in subdirectories.

- **Read (R).** Grants the right to open and read files in a directory. This permits the user to view file contents or execute a file.

- **Write (W).** Grants the right to open a file and write to or modify the contents of a file.

- **Create (C).** Permits the user to create files or subdirectories. If the Create right is granted, but not the Write right, the user can create a file, open it, and write the initial contents of the file. However, after closing it, the user can't reopen or modify the file contents.

- **Erase (E).** Grants the right to delete a directory, its subdirectories, and files.

- **Modify (M).** Permits the user to change directory and file attributes, including the directory, subdirectory, and file names. This doesn't permit the user to modify the contents of a file.

- **File Scan (F).** Grants the right to see subdirectories and files when the user views directory contents, as with dir or ndir.
- **Access Control (A).** Permits the user to modify trustee rights and the Inherited Rights Filter (IRF) for a directory. All rights, except Supervisor, might be assigned to other users. If someone has this right, he or she can give more rights to someone else than they have themselves.

Trustees and explicit trustee assignments

File system trustees can be assigned at the directory or file level. *Trustee rights* are granted to users, groups, or NDS/eDirectory container objects to give specific access privileges to directories, subdirectories, and files. Admin or any user who possesses sufficient rights in the file system can grant rights.

A user's rights come from assignments made to the user, groups of which the user is a member, parent containers, the [Root] object, and the [Public] object.

Explicit trustee rights are those granted directly to an object at any level of the file system. Rights that are explicitly assigned to an object override rights that would be inherited by that object. For example, when a user is made a trustee of a directory, those rights that are explicitly assigned flow down the directory structure to all children. If a new explicit assignment is made to the user at a lower level in the directory structure, the new assignment overrides any rights inherited by the user. The newly assigned trustee rights are consequently inherited in all child directories and files.

Inherited rights and the Inherited Rights Filter

File system trustee rights flow down through the file system structure from parent to child. File system trustee rights assigned to a directory remain in effect for all children of the directory, including subdirectories and files, unless modified at a lower level or blocked by an Inherited Rights Filter (IRF).

The *Inherited Rights Filter* (IRF) restricts the inheritance of trustee rights to a specific subdirectory or file. It blocks rights that would normally be inherited. IRFs aren't user-specific and affect all users. All directories, subdirectories, and files possess an IRF. By default, all IRFs are nonrestrictive, permitting all rights to be inherited. When an IRF has been altered to block rights inheritance, the filter is referred to as a *restrictive IRF*. To alter an IRF, you must possess the Access Control [A] or Supervisor [S] trustee right to the directory or file whose IRF you need to change.

The Inherited Rights Filter affects only rights that have trickled down from a higher-level directory. It doesn't affect explicit trustee assignments made at the same level or at levels lower than any given NDS object.

The Inherited Rights Filter is summarized as follows:
- Blocks rights inheritance
- Can block all rights inheritance except the Supervisor [S] right
- Needs the Access Control right to modify
- Permits all rights to be inherited by default
- Affects all users

Do it!

B-1:   Discussing file system security

Questions and answers

1 What are the NetWare directory trustee rights?

2 The Inherited Rights Filter helps in the inheritance of trustee rights to a particular subdirectory or file. True or False?

3 _____ are granted to users, groups, or NDS/eDirectory container objects to give specific access privileges to directories, subdirectories, and files.

4 IRFs are user-specific. True or False?

Effective rights

Explanation

Effective rights determine a user's access to any directory, subdirectory, or file. They are a combination of all rights granted through trustee assignments, minus those blocked by Inherited Rights Filters.

Note: A user has no rights in a directory unless assigned through a trustee assignment (user or group).

If a user has been assigned the Supervisor [S] right in a parent directory, he or she possesses all rights to any child subdirectories or files.

If there's an explicit trustee assignment, the user's effective rights are equal to those explicitly assigned, plus any rights inherited from other sources, such as groups, containers, profiles, the [Root] object, and the [Public] object.

If the IRF permits all rights to be inherited and no new explicit assignments have been made, a user's effective rights are equal to its effective rights in the parent directory. If no additional rights have been explicitly assigned, effective rights for any object are equal to the object's effective rights in the parent directory minus those revoked through the IRF.

Minimum rights requirements

A minimum rights level is necessary for many tasks on the network. The following table describes the rights that a user must possess to perform various file system operations:

Right	File system operations
Read from a file	Read, File Scan
Execute a file	Read, File Scan
See a file	File Scan
Search a directory	File Scan
Create and write to a file	Create
Copy files (source)	Read, File Scan
Copy file (destination)	Create, Write, File Scan
Remove an empty subdirectory	Erase
Delete a file	Erase
Change directory and file attributes	Modify
Change file or directory name	Modify
Change Inherited Rights Filter	Access Control
Add or modify trustee assignments	Access Control
Modify disk space assignment	Access Control
Move a file	Read, Erase, and File Scan to source directory, Create and File Scan in destination directory

Trustee rights assignments can be granted or revoked by using the following NetWare utilities:

- ConsoleOne
- iManager

Do it!

B-2:   Discussing rights and trustee assignments

Questions and answers

1 _____ determine(s) a user's access to any directory, subdirectory, or file.

2 A user has no rights in a directory unless assigned through a trustee assignment. True or False?

3 Which of the following rights must a user possess to change the Inherited Rights Filter?

A   Read, File Scan

B   Create

C   Access Control

D   Modify

Topic C: User account restrictions

This topic covers the following CompTIA Network+ exam objectives:

#	Objective
3.1	Identify the basic capabilities (For example: client support, interoperability, authentication, file and print services, application support and security) of the following server operating systems to access network resources: • NetWare
3.7	Given a connectivity scenario, determine the impact on network functionality of a particular security implementation (For example: • Authentication and encryption
4.5	Given a troubleshooting scenario between a client and the following server environments, identify the cause of a stated problem: • NetWare

Authentication

Explanation

Authentication is a part of NetWare's login security that's managed transparently to the user and the network administrator. This process occurs at login time, guaranteeing valid logins and preventing transmission of user passwords across the network.

The process starts at login after the user enters a password. The system responds with a private key, or unique code, that the password deciphers. After decoding the private key, the system deletes the password from memory. The system then combines user information, such as station ID, and creates a credential.

The workstation software combines the private key and the credential into a signature and deletes the private key from memory. A proof is created for the signature values and all messages. The proof is unique for every request and prevents the signature from being transmitted over the network.

Authentication is important, because it ensures that only valid users have access to the network. Yet there might be instances when you want valid users to have access to the network, but with account restrictions. Perhaps they should be permitted access only during business hours or only from certain workstations. This is where user account restrictions play a role in easing user management overhead. You need to know more about the various user account restrictions available under NetWare, all managed from within the NetWare Administrator, to handle things efficiently.

Login restrictions

Login restrictions are used to enable or disable user accounts, set an account expiration date, and limit the number of concurrent connections for a user.

The options available on the Login Restrictions properties page permit the network administrator to disable a user's account, set an expiration date for the account, and limit the number of concurrent network connections available to the user.

The various properties in the Login Restrictions properties page are explained in the following table.

Property	Description
Account disabled	Check this option to disable the account. A disabled account can't be used for logging in to the network.
Account has expiration date	Check this option to activate account expiration and then set the expiration date and time needed.
Limit concurrent connections	Check this option to limit the number of times a user can be simultaneously logged in to the network. Next, set the maximum number of connections.
Last login	Displays the user's last login date and time.

Password restrictions

Password restrictions are used to ensure that users have passwords, to control whether users can change their passwords, set a minimum password length, force periodic password changes, set a password expiration date, make unique passwords, and limit grace logins.

The various options that are provided in the Password Restriction page are listed in the following table. To change a user's password, click Change Password on this page, provide the new password, and click Set Password.

Option	Description
Allow a user to change password	Check this option to permit the user to change his or her own password.
Require a password	Check this option to require a password and set a minimum password length for the user.
Force Periodic password changes	Check this option to make sure the user periodically changes his or her password. Next, type in the number of days between changes. You can also set a password expiration date.
Require unique passwords	Check this option to prevent users from reusing any one of their eight previous passwords when changing their passwords.
Limit grace logins	Check this option to limit the number of times users can ignore system requests to change their passwords.

Address restrictions

The Address Restrictions properties page permits the network administrator to restrict a user's login location to a single PC or to a particular communications protocol. To configure network address restrictions, click Add to enter a network (cabling address), node (MAC–Media Access Control), or socket (IPX) address, and select the appropriate protocol. Click OK when finished.

Intruder detection and lockout

Novell designed the intruder detection and lockout utility to help network administrators determine when an unauthorized individual has tried to access the network. The login process triggers detection and needs both a valid login name and password, where one exists, before the individual can become a network user. You can apply the intruder detection and lockout function at the organization level or organizational unit level.

The Intruder Detection properties page is available only for container objects. The settings applied here apply to all user accounts below the container.

This page contains the following options:

Option	Description
Detect intruders	Check this option to activate intruder detection for the container. Select Intruder Detection Limit to determine when an intruder attempt should be logged. Intruder detection is activated when a user attempts to log in with an invalid name or with a valid username but the wrong password.
Incorrect login attempts	Enter the number of incorrect login attempts permitted before locking an account.
Lock account after detection	Check this option to disable the affected account. Next, set the time needed in days, hours, and minutes to lock the account.
Intruder attempt reset interval	Tells the server how long to wait before the count is reset to zero.
Lock account after detection	Should be set to Yes for your network's best protection.

If a user reaches the set number of Incorrect Login Attempts, NetWare locks the account. The account must then be unlocked by a network administrator.

Note: When activated, this can lock out the network administrator account. Ensure that you leave yourself a back door, that is, an account with Admin equivalence.

Do it!

C-1: Discussing user account restrictions

Questions and answers

1   Where do you set user password restrictions?

2   Where do you configure Intruder Detection?

3   Which of the following is *not* a NetWare user account restriction?

   A   Login Restriction

   B   Address Restriction

   C   Authentication Restriction

   D   Password Restrictions

Topic D: NDS/eDirectory context

This topic covers the following CompTIA Network+ exam objectives:

#	Objective
3.1	Identify the basic capabilities (For example: client support, interoperability, authentication, file and print services, application support and security) of the following server operating systems to access network resources: • NetWare
4.5	Given a troubleshooting scenario between a client and the following server environments, identify the cause of a stated problem: • NetWare

NDS/eDirectory naming conventions

Explanation

To understand the utilities used to navigate the Directory tree clearly, it's important to understand context first. *Context* is the location of an object in the Directory tree. *Current context* is a logical pointer that indicates the object's current position in the NDS/eDirectory tree.

Information about naming conventions used in the NDS/eDirectory tree is important. There are several kinds of names used to represent the flow and hierarchy of objects in the tree.

Distinguished name

The *distinguished name* is the full path to an object's location. All distinguished names begin with a leading period. The path starts with the leaf object and moves toward the root of the tree. Each object is preceded by the attribute type of the object to which it refers. A period separates objects within the name.

The distinguished name for the user Bsmith, as shown in Exhibit 19-3, is:

```
CN=BSmith.OU=IS.OU=HQ-PTLND.O=Apex.
```

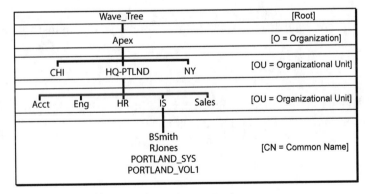

Exhibit 19-3: Example of distinguished name

Relative distinguished name

A relative distinguished name identifies only part of the full name and assumes the current context to be the rest of the name. Using relative distinguished names is easier than using distinguished names. However, users might become confused while looking for an object's exact location in the Directory tree. A relative distinguished name doesn't begin with a leading period.

A relative distinguished name for the user BSmith is:

```
CN=BSmith.OU=IS
```

You can avoid the need to log in with a distinguished name by configuring a default context on the user's workstation. This is accomplished by configuring the Network property page in the Novell Client for Windows 95/98 or Windows NT/2000/XP.

Typeful and typeless names

When NDS/eDirectory attribute type information (C=, O=, OU=, or CN=) is specified, the object name is referred to as a *typeful name*. When NDS attribute type information is not specified, the name is referred to as a *typeless name*.

Here's an example of a typeful distinguished name:

```
.CN=RJones.OU=IS.OU=HQ-PTLND.O=Apex.
```

Here's an example of typeless distinguished name:

```
.RJones.IS.HQ-PTLND.Apex.
```

Do it!

D-1: Discussing NDS/eDirectory context

Questions and answers

1 _____ is a logical pointer that indicates an object's existing position in the NDS/eDirectory tree.

   A   Context

   B   Current context

   C   Distinguished name

   D   All the above

2 Differentiate distinguished name and relative distinguished name.

3 When NDS/eDirectory attribute type information is specified, the object name is referred to as a typeful name. True or False?

Topic E: NetWare log files

This topic covers the following CompTIA Network+ exam objectives:

#	Objective
3.1	Identify the basic capabilities (For example: client support, interoperability, authentication, file and print services, application support and security) of the following server operating systems to access network resources: • NetWare
4.5	Given a troubleshooting scenario between a client and the following server environments, identify the cause of a stated problem: • NetWare

Logging errors

Explanation

One of the ongoing activities of a network administrator is server monitoring. Unless you carefully monitor the server, you might not be aware of network errors and performance issues.

Monitoring the error logs on a regular basis is important to ensure server stability. By routinely checking error log files, you might be able to identify future problems before they occur.

The behavior of many files can be modified with Set commands. Set commands are used to modify the server and network environment. Set commands function similarly to the environmental variables found in an autoexec.bat file, in that the settings must be established each time the server is started. That's why most Set commands are included in the server's startup files (autoexec.ncf and startup.ncf).

SYS$LOG.ERR

The sys$log.err file is automatically created by the server and stored in the SYS:SYSTEM directory. Error and informational messages generated by the server and displayed on the server console are recorded in this log file. For example, this is where volume out of space messages are logged. By routinely checking this log, you can determine if any server console errors were reported that you might have otherwise missed.

The sys$log.err file is limited in size so that it doesn't grow and consume the entire SYS: volume. By default, the size is limited to 4 MB. You can use the following command to change the log length:

```
SET SERVER LOG FILE OVERFLOW SIZE= SIZE IN BYTES
```

When the log reaches its maximum length, the server, by default, deletes the log and starts a new one. You can use the following command to change the default either to do nothing or to rename the log file:

```
SET SERVER LOG FILE STATE = STATE
```

Valid states are:

- **0** — Do nothing.
- **1** — Delete the current log and start a new one (default).
- **2** — Rename the current file and start a new one.

Note: Using state 2 can cause the SYS: volume to fill up as the log files essentially grow without restriction. If you use state 2, check the old log files frequently and delete them regularly.

VOL$LOG.ERR

The server creates one vol$log.err file at the root of each volume. Any errors or informational messages generated by the server are recorded in this log file. By reviewing the log file regularly, you can check for potential problems in the file system. For example, if a volume was dismounted and no longer available to network users, it's recorded in this log.

The vol$log.err file is limited in size so that it doesn't grow and consume the entire volume where it's stored. By default, the size is limited to 4,194,304 bytes (4 MB). Use the following command to change the log length:

```
SET VOLUME LOG FILE OVERFLOW SIZE = SIZE IN BYTES
```

Like the sys$log.err file, the server, by default, deletes the log when it reaches its maximum length and starts a new log. Use the following command to change the default either to do nothing or to rename the log file:

```
SET VOLUME LOG FILE STATE = STATE
```

Valid states are:

- **0** — Do nothing.
- **1** — Delete the current log and start a new one (default).
- **2** — Rename the current file and start a new one.

Note: Using state 2 can cause the volume where the log file resides to fill up, since the log files essentially grow without restriction. If you use state 2, check the old log files frequently and delete them regularly.

Do it!

E-1: Discussing SYS$LOG.ERR and VOL$LOG.ERR

Questions and answers

1 The log file containing error messages generated by the server and displayed on the console is _____ .

2 Which command do you type at the console to increase the maximum size of the volume error log file to 10 MB?

   A   SET VOLUME LOG FILE OVERFLOW SIZE = 10485760

   B   SET VOLUME LOG FILE RESET SIZE = 10485760

   C   SET VOL LOG FILE OVERFLOW SIZE = 10485760

   D   SET VOL$LOG MAX = 10485760

3 Which command do you use to change the log length of a sys$log.err file?

ABEND.LOG

Explanation

An ABEND (ABnormal END) occurs when a server has encountered a critical error. When an ABEND occurs, the server frequently puts the offending process to sleep and sends an alert to the console. In some cases, the offending process can't be isolated and the server reboots to correct the situation.

When the server encounters an ABEND, it initially creates and writes the abend.log file to the DOS partition of the server. The DOS partition is used in the event the offending process is needed to access the NetWare volume. In some instances, the offending process prohibits the writing of any files. In this case, no abend.log file can be generated.

When the server is restarted after an ABEND, the abend.log file is copied from the DOS partition to the SYS:ETC directory, and the DOS file is removed. If there's a previous abend.log file in the SYS:ETC directory, the new ABEND information is appended to the existing file, creating a running record.

The types of information recorded in the abend.log file include:

- The type of ABEND and when it occurred
- The name and memory address of the offending process
- A dump of the registers and stack
- The name and version number of each network module loaded

This information can be of use in determining the cause of an ABEND, especially if the problem is recurring or intermittent.

CONSOLE.LOG

The NetWare server startup process is not interruptible. During the startup process, the system console screen displays configuration information, modules loaded, warnings, and error messages. To capture and log all of the console messages that are generated at the server while booting, you can use the CONLOG utility..

The CONLOG utility writes console system messages to the console.log file located in the SYS:ETC directory.

To load the CONLOG utility, run the following command at the file server console prompt:

```
LOAD CONLOG [SAVE = log_filename] [MAXIMUM = size in KB]
```

This command is typically added to the autoexec.ncf file to record console activity during the startup process.

You can view the console log with any text editor. Before you can view the console.log file, however, you must unload the CONLOG utility from server memory. Each time you restart the server, the old console.log file is deleted and reset. If you want to save the file, you unload CONLOG and rename the console.log before restarting the server or use the SAVE option.

Do it!

E-2: Discussing ABEND.LOG and CONSOLE.LOG

Questions and answers
1 What happens if there's a previous abend.log file in the SYS:ETC directory?
2 Which types of information are recorded in the abend.log file?
3 Where is the console.log file located?

Topic F: Using monitoring and management tools

This topic covers the following CompTIA Network+ exam objective:

#	Objective
3.1	Identify the basic capabilities (For example: client support, interoperability, authentication, file and print services, application support and security) of the following server operating systems to access network resources: • NetWare

Introduction to monitoring and management tools

Explanation

To make sure that everything is running smoothly on each of your servers, NetWare includes a variety of tools you can use to monitor and manage server performance and configuration settings. Some of these tools are run at the server console, while others are web-based utilities.

Using MONITOR.NLM

MONITOR is a very useful utility. Accessible from the server console, this utility provides a wealth of server information you can use to gauge server performance and resource utilization. In addition, the utility provides a screensaver and a password protection function.

To start MONITOR at a NetWare 4.x or earlier server, enter at the server console:

```
LOAD MONITOR [option]
```

To start MONITOR at a NetWare 5.x or later server, enter at the server console:

```
MONITOR [option]
```

The optional switches for the utility are:

- **L** — Immediately locks the server console upon load. You use the Admin user's password to unlock it.
- **M** — Restricts the activation of the screensaver to the monitor screen only. Otherwise, the screensaver becomes active from any currently displayed screen.
- **N** — Disables the screensaver function.
- **Txxx** — Specifies the number of seconds (xxx) of keyboard inactivity before the screensaver is activated. The default is 10 minutes (600 seconds) when the console is unlocked and 1 minute (60 seconds) when the console is locked.

Viewing server statistics with the MONITOR utility

On the MONITOR utility's General Information Screen, you can see information about server up time and utilization, cache buffers, disk requests, service processes, connections, and so on. The screen gives you a quick overview of some of the more important statistics regarding your server's operation.

Do it!

F-1:   Discussing MONITOR.NLM

Questions and answers

1 Which of the following uses the MONITOR utility?

   A   Password protection

   B   Screensaver

   C   Console logging

   D   Resource information

2 What is "xxx" in Txxx?

3 Which screen in MONITOR tells you about server uptime and utilization

Available Options menu

Explanation

The following is a description of the items listed in the MONITOR utility's Available Options menu on a NetWare 6.x server. The options you actually see on a server may vary from the ones listed below, depending on the version of MONITOR.NLM.

- **Connections.** Logical users connected to the server, open files, logical file, record locks, and so on.
- **Storage devices.** Disk statistics.
- **Volumes.** Volume statistics.
- **LAN/WAN drivers.** LAN board statistics.
- **Loaded modules.** Statistics regarding processes running on the file server.
- **File Open/Lock Activity.** File statistics.
- **Disk cache utilization.** Permits you to review how cache memory is being used and check cache-hit statistics.
- **System Resources.** Displays information on available resource types.
- **Virtual memory.** Information on virtual memory address spaces and swap files.
- **Kernel.** Displays information about threads, processors, and interrupts.
- **Server parameters.** Shows server SET parameter information and lets you edit settings.

Do it!

F-2: Discussing the Available Options menu

Questions and answers

1 What does the Connections option display?

2 Which of the following options displays a list of all processes currently running on the server?

A   Virtual memory

B   Kernel

C   Server parameters

D   Loaded modules

3 What does the Disk cache utilization option display?

4 Which option would you use to change the SET parameter settings for a server?

Working with NetWare Remote Manager

Explanation New in more recent versions of NetWare (NetWare 5.1 and later), NetWare Remote Manager (NRM) lets you perform server monitoring and maintenance through a web-based interface.

Using NRM, you can diagnose server problems and manage the server, applications running on the server, server hardware, and eDirectory. To access NRM, enter http://server_name_or_IP_address:8008 in a supported browser. Supported browsers include Netscape 4.5 or later or Internet Explorer 5 or later.

Before you can access NRM, you have to provide authentication information. Once logged in, you see the NRM main page, as shown in Exhibit 19-4. The main page gives you some brief information about the server, such as the volumes mounted on the server, the server name and OS version, up time, and so on.

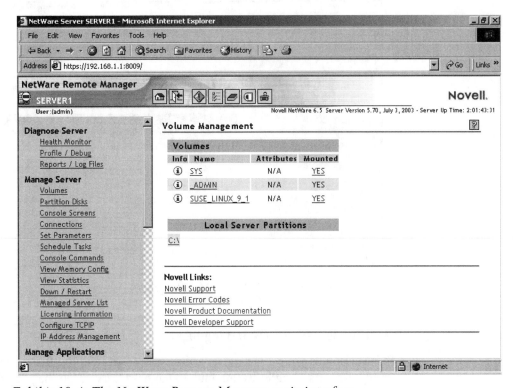

Exhibit 19-4: The NetWare Remote Manager main interface

Monitoring server health

To monitor a server's health, click on the Health Monitor link. On the display page you see information on a variety of items, including server processes, CPU utilization, connections, memory, and so forth, as shown in Exhibit 19-5. A green button in the Status column for an item indicates that that item isn't having any issues. A yellow button indicates a potential problem, and a red button indicates a problem. To see more detailed information on an item, click its link.

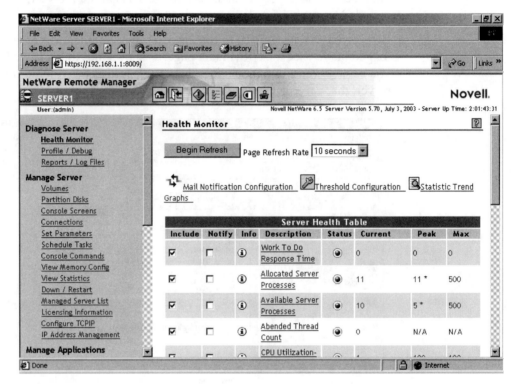

Exhibit 19-5: The NRM Health Monitor page

Viewing server reports and log files

NRM also lets you view a variety of server reports and log files. To access these, click on the Reports / Log Files link under Diagnose Server. On the page that displays, you can then select the report or log file you want to view.

Included reports are the Config Report, which lets you view server configuration information, the Security Report, which lets you view a variety of security-related information, such as trustee and port information, and the Inventory Report, which lets you view information such as how much disk space a user is using, creation and access times for files, and so on.

Included log files are the Server Personal Log Book, where you can make entries yourself about the server for future reference, the System Error Log File (SYS$LOG.ERR), the Abend Log File (ABEND.LOG), and the Server Health Log File (HEALTH.LOG).

Do it!

F-3: Discussing NetWare Remote Manager

Questions and answers

1 What do you enter in the URL field of a browser to access NRM?

2 Your network has been having performance issues lately, with users complaining about slow response times. You suspect that the server might experience high utilization. Where do you go to check into this?

3 Which NRM report provides you with information about the server's current configuration?

The VREPAIR utility

Explanation
Over time, minor problems might occur on your NetWare volumes. This might be due to an improper shutdown or loss of power. The primary File Allocation Table (FAT) or the Directory Entry Table (DET) might become corrupt due to these conditions. For this reason, Novell has included the VREPAIR utility with NetWare. VREPAIR is used with traditional NetWare volumes rather than Novell Storage Services (NSS) volumes.

Volume repair

The NetWare operating system maintains two copies of both the FAT and DET. The VREPAIR utility can be used to compare the primary tables with the mirrored copies. Both sets of tables are checked for errors. If the VREPAIR utility finds any inconsistencies in the primary or secondary FAT or DET, it selects the one that it believes to be intact and corrects the damaged table. Corrections are written directly to the volume's tables. During this process, the VREPAIR utility might have to delete files that have become corrupt.

Typically, a volume doesn't mount if it has sustained even minor damage. Additional problems can occur if the damaged volume is the SYS: volume. A copy of the vrepair.nlm file and all of the name space support modules must exist in both the SYS:SYSTEM directory and the DOS partition.

To repair a traditional NetWare volume by using the VREPAIR utility, the volume must be dismounted. By copying the VREPAIR modules to the server's DOS partition, you can repair a volume even if the SYS: volume is damaged.

Using VREPAIR

To load the VREPAIR utility, type LOAD VREPAIR or just VREPAIR (depending on the server OS version) at the server console prompt, and then press Enter.

When you load VREPAIR, the VREPAIR Options screen appears. You can choose option 1, Repair a volume to use default settings for the repair, or you can use option 2 Set VREPAIR options, to view alternate settings that might be appropriate for your environment.

Note: Run the VREPAIR utility repeatedly until no errors are reported. Vrepair.nlm is used on volumes storing DOS 8.3 name files. If a volume is also storing Macintosh, UNIX NFS, or Windows long file names, you need to run the specialized VREPAIR for each file format: V_MAC, V_NFS, and V_LONG.

Working with NSS volumes

In addition to support for traditional NetWare volumes, more recent versions of NetWare include the ability to take advantage of Novell Storage Services (NSS) volumes. NSS volumes have many advantages over traditional NetWare volumes, such as allowing much larger file sizes, volumes mounting much faster, requiring no additional memory for proper functioning, and so on. NSS has its own management utilities to manage and maintain NSS volumes.

You can manage NSS volumes through a variety of tools, including NRM, ConsoleOne, iManager, and server console commands. Using these tools you can create volumes, verify integrity, rebuild volumes, configure volume settings - such as whether disk space restrictions are enabled and what storage space warning thresholds should be – and perform any other necessary maintenance tasks.

To see a complete list of the available NSS server console commands, along with a brief explanation, enter `nss /help` at the server console prompt.

Do it!

F-4: Discussing the VREPAIR utility and NSS volumes

Questions and answers

1 Explain the purpose of VREPAIR.

2 Your NetWare file server was having volume errors, so you ran VREPAIR. The VREPAIR utility found and corrected three errors. What should you do next?

3 You need to enable disk quotas on an NSS volume. Which command do you enter at the server console to find out which nss command is used to do this?

Unit summary: Managing and troubleshooting NetWare network resources

Topic A In this topic, you learned that you use the **ConsoleOne** and **iManager** utilities to create and manage **User and Group objects**. You also learned how to create a User and Group object using ConsoleOne and iManager.

Topic B In this topic, you learned about **file system rights** and **trustees** and **explicit trustee assignments**. You also learned about **Inherited Rights**, the **Inherited Rights Filter**, and **effective rights.**

Topic C In this topic, you learned about **login restrictions**, **password restrictions**, and **address restrictions**. You also learned about **intruder detection**.

Topic D In this topic, you learned about the **NDS/eDirectory naming conventions** and **context**. You also learned about **distinguished**, **relative**, **typeful** and **typeless** names.

Topic E In this topic, you learned how to use **NetWare log files** such as **SYS$LOG.ERR**, **VOL$LOG.ERR**, **ABEND.LOG**, and **CONSOLE.LOG**.

Topic F In this topic, you learned how to start a **MONITOR** and view **server statistics** with the MONITOR utility. Next, you learned about **NetWare Remote Manager (NRM)** and how to check your server's health. Then, you learned about **Volume repair**. You also learned how to use the **VREPAIR utility** to correct volume errors. Finally, you learned about **NSS** and the utilities used to monitor and manage NSS volumes.

Review questions

1 Which utility lets you create users and groups using a web-based browser interface?

2 What are the minimum rights that a user must have to execute a file?

3 _____ tracks incorrect login attempts over a specified time period.

   A Network Address Restriction

   B Password Restriction

   C The Authentication Process

   D Intruder Detection

4 What information is needed when creating a group object?

5 When a server experiences an ABEND, it attempts to write the abend.log file to which location first?

A SYS:SYSTEM

B SYS:ETC

C DOS partition

D SYS:

6 You're the network administrator for your organization. Joe calls to inform you that he's unable to log in to the NetWare server. You suspect it might be a licensing issue and that you've exceeded the permitted number of network connections. Which Available Option in the MONITOR utility do you use to see the number of current connections?

A LAN/WAN Information

B Resource Utilization

C Connections

D License Utilization

E Active User Information

7 What happens when the VREPAIR utility finds any inconsistencies in the primary or secondary FAT or DET?

8 What are some advantages of NSS volumes over traditional NetWare volumes?

9 How would you access server log files in NRM?

Unit 20

Fault tolerance and disaster recovery

Unit time: 60 minutes

Complete this unit, and you'll know how to:

A Discuss disk configuration.

B Discuss Windows-based replication and NDS/eDirectory partitions and replicas.

C Discuss backups and UPSs.

Topic A: System fault tolerance

This topic covers the following CompTIA Network+ exam objectives:

#	Objective
3.11	Identify the purpose and characteristics of fault tolerance: • Storage • Services
3.12	Identify the purpose and characteristics of disaster recovery: • Hot and cold spares

Disaster planning

Explanation

Fault tolerance solutions are steps taken to ensure minimal network downtime. You can expect problems, such as hardware failures and network crashes. The best thing is to plan for the inevitable, implement as many disaster-avoidance mechanisms as possible, and be ready to react quickly when necessary.

Fault tolerance must be considered when designing any business network. Without disaster planning, loss of time and revenue is an eventuality. With this in mind, a network should be designed to handle failures with minimal impact on users and minimal data loss.

When creating a disaster plan, some key points to be considered include:

- **Plan for the worst.** Look at worst-case scenarios and determine what's necessary for recovery. Identify critical systems, users, and resources. Determine how to get the network working again as quickly as possible. Document disaster plans and distribute them to everyone involved.

- **Implement physical data security.** Protect your data. Whenever possible, set up live redundant copies of data. Back up all data on a regular basis, test backups to verify that they can be read, rotate backups, and keep copies offsite whenever possible.

- **Protect your critical systems.** Implement physical security, keeping critical servers behind locked doors. Install an Uninterruptible Power Supply (UPS) on critical servers and critical user stations.

While these actions can't eliminate every possible disaster, they do help to make disaster recovery significantly easier. It's also recommended that disaster recovery drills be run to prepare fully for emergencies.

RAID

One of the best tools available on a modern network is the implementation of Redundant Array of Independent Disks (RAID) technology. Some documentation might define RAID as Redundant Array of Inexpensive Disks, but because you're working with high-speed, high-capacity disks on the server level, you'll find that they are expensive.

RAID is a set of specifications describing hard disk fault tolerance configurations. These specifications are:

- **RAID Level 0.** Disk striping without parity. Data is distributed across a series of drives. This isn't recommended for file servers, because failure of any drive in a level 0 array leads to the effective loss of all data on the array. This isn't a fault tolerance specification. Its only benefit is that it increases the speed of disk I/O.

- **RAID Level 1.** Mirror sets, including duplexing. Data is mirrored across two disk drives. This can result in better overall performance than other RAID options. Mirroring a pair of disks reduces the total disk storage by one half.

- **RAID Level 2.** Stripe sets with parity. Data is striped across the drives of an array at the bit level with the addition of extra check disks. The data includes an interleaved code used to detect the bit errors. Several check disks are needed due to the amount of information needed for the check bits.

- **RAID Level 3.** Stripe sets with parity. An array of data disks and one disk for parity is used in this configuration. Data is striped across the data disks at the bit level. This type of system works well for workstations needing sequential access to single large files, such as image processing systems. It isn't recommended for transaction processing systems or environments in which most I/O transactions are for small amounts of data.

- **RAID Level 4.** Stripe sets with parity. This is similar to RAID Level 3 except that data is written at the sector level rather than at the bit level. Clusters of data are placed across a series of drives enabling multiple reads. This helps a multitasking operating system to process independent read transactions for each data drive in the array.

- **RAID Level 5.** Stripe sets with parity. Data and parity blocks are spread across all drives in the array. These eliminate the dedicated parity drive and, thereby, you can read and write multiple transactions to be performed in parallel. As more drives are added to the array, performance increases during disk reads.

RAID devices

RAID devices are frequently contained within a separate tower-like unit that connects to the server through a SCSI interface, commonly a high-density 68-pin connector. Other external SCSI connectors include:

- DB25-pin
- High-density 50-pin
- Centronics 50-pin
- High density Centronics 68-pin

For additional information and diagrams on the various types of SCSI connectors, visit one of the leaders in SCSI connectivity, Adaptec, at their Web site, http://www.adaptec.com.

Software-based RAID

In addition to hardware-based RAID devices, network operating systems, such as NetWare and Windows Server, provide the built-in ability to set up and use RAID devices. With these operating systems, you can use multiple controller cards and hard drives to create your own RAID solution. While software-based RAID is less expensive to implement, it suffers from a reduction in performance when compared to hardware-based RAID solutions.

Hot spares

Many RAID implementations (hardware or software) support a feature called *hot spares*. With hot spares, additional drives are attached to the system, but are in standby mode until a drive fails. When this happens, a drive in standby mode can take over for the failed drive.

Disk mirroring

Disk mirroring is an implementation of RAID Level 1. It uses two disk drives configured with equal-sized partitions and connected to the same disk controller, as shown in Exhibit 20-1. During each data write, the same data is written to both disk partitions.

Exhibit 20-1: Disk mirroring

Some facts about disk mirroring include:

- Disk utilization is 50% of the dedicated storage space. That is, if you have two 9-GB drives that are mirrored, you have a total of only 9 GB of available data storage space.
- All-around disk I/O performance is generally better than disk striping with parity.
- A mirrored pair can be split without loss of data.
- The boot partition can be mirrored.
- The active system partition can be mirrored.
- If the disk controller fails, the server is down.

Disk mirroring is designed to keep working, even if there are disk errors or loss of a hard disk. These errors can be:

- **Read error.** If an error occurs during a read, data from the other disk is used.
- **Drive failure.** If one drive fails, the server continues running by using the other drive.

Do it!

A-1: Discussing RAID

Questions and answers
1 What does RAID stand for?
2 Define RAID?
3 Which of the following levels offers the best performance? Explain. A   RAID level 1 B   RAID level 2 C   RAID level 3 D   RAID level 4 E   RAID level 5

Disk duplexing

Explanation

Disk duplexing is an implementation of RAID Level 1 and is similar to disk mirroring. It uses two disk drives configured to have the same logical size and connected to separate disk controllers, as shown in Exhibit 20-2. During each data write, the same data is written to both disk partitions.

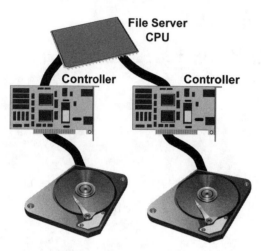

Exhibit 20-2: Disk Duplexing

Disk duplexing features include:

- Disk utilization is 50% of the dedicated storage space
- All-around disk I/O performance is generally better than disk striping with parity and is better than disk mirroring during data reads
- A mirrored pair can be split without loss of data
- The boot partition can be duplexed
- The active system partition can be duplexed
- If one disk controller fails, the server remains up

Disk duplexing is designed to keep working, even when there are disk errors, loss of a hard disk, or loss of a disk controller. Some of these errors might be:

- **Read error.** If an error occurs during a read, data from the other disk is used.
- **Drive failure.** If one drive fails, the server continues running by using the other drive.
- **Controller failure.** If one controller fails, the server continues running by using the other controller.

Using disk mirroring/duplexing

Disk mirroring and disk duplexing are normally used to provide data redundancy on peer-to-peer networks and smaller LANs to protect critical data files. Due to the amount of storage lost through redundancy, disk mirroring and disk duplexing aren't commonly used for data drives on larger LANs. They might, however, be used to mirror the system or boot partition to provide fault tolerance for the operating system.

Use disk mirroring when:

- Data must be protected against drive failures.
- You need to guard against downtime due to the failure of the system or boot drive.
- Hard disk resources are plentiful and continue to be available as system requirements grow.
- Administrative resources are scarce, because the system continues to process read and write requests when a failure occurs.

Disk mirroring protects against the failure of any one drive. Disk duplexing protects against the failure of a drive or disk controller. With either, users can continue to work without interruption.

Do it!

A-2: Discussing disk duplexing

Questions and answers
1 What are the features of disk duplexing?
2 How can you provide data redundancy in peer-to-peer networks and LANs?

Disk striping with parity

Explanation

Disk striping with parity is an implementation of RAID Level 5. Between 3 and 32 disk drives (inclusive) might be included in a stripe set. The disk space used on each drive is approximately the same. Some facts include:

- Disk storage capacity is reduced by the size of one disk drive: That is, if you have three 9-GB drives, you have the total storage capacity of 18 GB. If you have five 9-GB drives, you have the total storage capacity of 36 GB.
- Data and parity information is written across all drives
- Performance is improved on disk reads
- The boot partition can't be included in a stripe set
- The active system partition can't be included in a stripe set

Disk striping with parity is normally used on larger networks where data integrity is a critical concern. While the amount of storage space lost can be significant, the percentage of space lost to parity becomes less as more drives are added. Use disk striping with parity when:

- Multiple hard disks are available
- Optimal read performance is desired
- Data integrity is a critical concern
- You need to maximize storage capacity while providing fault tolerance

With disk striping with parity, you're protected against the failure of any one drive. The failing drive should be replaced as soon as possible. Users can continue working after the failure of any one disk drive. Performance is the same on disk writes but degrades on disk reads.

When performance is the overriding concern and your budget can accommodate it, then you should install a RAID disk subsystem rather than configuring discrete hard disks through disk striping with parity. A RAID disk subsystem, though more expensive, provides significantly better performance.

About disk striping with parity

Data and parity stripes are spread across all of the drives in a stripe set. As data is written, it passes through an algorithm to generate the information for the parity stripe. What might be lost in write performance, however, is made up in read performance and data security.

The way that data clusters are organized, large data files tend to get written across multiple drives. By splitting read requests, the system can give excellent read response.

Possibly more important than the quality of read response is data security. If a drive is lost, the system can recover any missing data by going through its calculations on the remaining data and parity stripes. Of course, read performance suffers when this happens. When the drive is replaced, all of its data can be re-created.

Do it! **A-3:   Discussing disk striping with parity**

Questions and answers

1   When does one use disk stripping with parity?

2   When should you install a RAID disk subsystem?

Other disk configurations

Explanation

You might encounter types of disk configurations on a Windows Server other than fault tolerance disk configurations. These disk configurations aren't fault tolerance methods but do provide unique capabilities that provide the Windows administrator with valuable options.

Volume sets

File space from various hard disks or from different areas on the same hard disk can be combined into one large logical drive by using volume sets, as shown in Exhibit 20-3. Up to 32 drives might be included. However, neither the system partition nor the boot partition can be included in a volume set. A volume set is treated as any other drive. The volume can be formatted with any of the supported file systems. File blocks are assigned normally, filling the first disk area, then working across to the next in sequential writes.

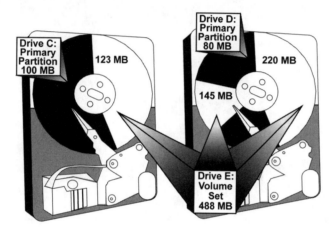

Exhibit 20-3: The combining of file spaces by using volume sets

You can extend an existing volume without data loss. However, if any part of the volume becomes damaged or unavailable, you're unable to access any of the volume.

Use volume sets when you need to expand an existing volume beyond available physical disk space.

Disk striping

As with a volume set, you can use a stripe set, as shown in Exhibit 20-4, to combine disk space from multiple drives into one large logical partition. Between 2 and 32 drives can be placed in one stripe set. Each segment of the set must, however, be about the same size, due to how a stripe set is organized. The segment on each drive is based on the smallest segment selected. After defining, the stripe set can be formatted as FAT or NTFS. As with volume sets, the boot partition and the system partition must be excluded from the stripe set.

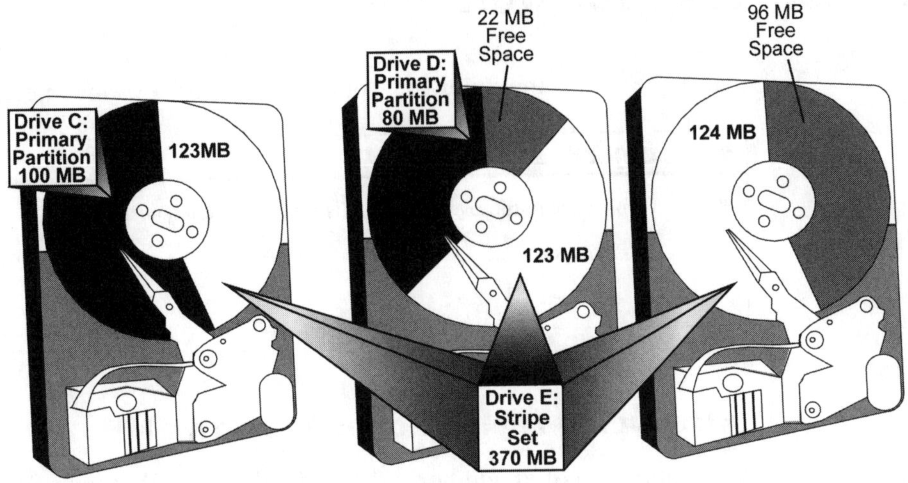

Exhibit 20-4: The combining of disk space by using a stripe set

Stripe sets are based on the same idea as RAID disk configurations and conform to RAID 0, disk striping without the parity. In a stripe set, 64-KB data blocks are set up so that they're spread across all the drives in the stripe set. This arrangement provides better performance, because most disk read and write operations are split across multiple drives rather than having to manage the entire file on one drive.

Because there's no fault tolerance built into this system, if any drive in the stripe set is lost, all of the data in the stripe set is lost. Use disk striping when you need maximum disk input and output performance.

Do it!

A-4:   Managing disk configuration

Questions and answers

1 When would you use a volume set?

2 When would you use disk striping?

Topic B: Replication

This topic covers the following CompTIA Network+ exam objective:

#	Objective
3.11	Identify the purpose and characteristics of fault tolerance: • Storage • Services

Introducing replication in Windows NT

Explanation

Replication can offer additional data redundancy on Windows Server-based networks. With replication, you can specify certain data to be copied from one system to another. To improve operating system efficiency, NetWare provides the capability of segmenting the database into pieces called partitions. These partitions are stored on NetWare servers throughout the network and can be copied, or replicated, to other servers, providing increased performance, fault tolerance, and backward compatibility.

Through *replication*, data is automatically copied from a source system (exporter) to a destination system (importer). This can be a one-to-one relationship, several exporters sending to one importer, or one exporter sending to several importers.

Only Windows NT Servers and LAN Manager 2.x servers might act as exporters. An export directory is specified as the data source. Any numbers of direct subdirectories and up to 32 levels of subdirectories below the export directory are supported.

Windows NT Workstations, Windows Servers, and LAN Manager servers can act as importers. An importer doesn't have to be located in the same domain as the exporter with which it communicates.

Replication occurs when a file is modified, then closed. This gives you a nearly immediate backup of volatile data files, or helps you propagate files as needed between network servers. Replication is a service that defaults to off but can be activated.

Key points about replication

The key points about replication are:

- Replication runs as a background service, invisible to the station's use
- Only subdirectories of the export directory are replicated
- After any changes, files must be closed before they can be replicated
- You can specify to replicate files immediately after a change or have the system wait for a specified time after any changes occur in the subdirectory tree
- Individual subdirectories might be locked, manually preventing replication of that subdirectory
- An exporter can send files to one or more importers
- An importer can receive files from one or more exporters
- The import directory might be locked, manually preventing replication
- A Windows NT Server might act as both an exporter and an importer

The suggested uses for replication include:

- Replication of logon scripts to all domain servers
- Replication of mandatory user profiles
- Replication of files to another location on the same server to provide separate master and working file sets
- Replication of frequently used files across multiple servers to balance server load

As you work with directory replication, you'll find other uses for this tool.

Active Directory

With Active Directory, fault tolerance of directory services information is built into the directory model. Because every domain controller holds a copy of Active Directory, fault tolerance is assured.

Replication in Windows 2000/Server 2003

In Windows 2000/Server 2003, the File Replication Service (FRS) replaces the LAN Manager Replication system used in Windows NT. FRS is used to replicate system policies as well as login scripts. FRS also allows for file replication for the domain-based Distributed File System (DFS).

Do it!

B-1: Discussing replication

Questions and answers
1 What is replication?
2 Name four uses of replication.
3 Which service replicates system policies for Windows 2000/Server 2003 servers with Active Directory installed?

NDS/eDirectory partitions and replicas

Explanation   NDS is used to store information about all of the objects known to the network. Management of the physical NDS database, partitioning, and replication are all important parts of a network administrator's job.

NDS/eDirectory partitions

The NDS database can be logically divided into partitions. During the initial installation of NetWare, the entire database resides in a single partition known as the *root partition*. Depending on the size, application requirements, and physical layout of your network, it might be appropriate to create additional database partitions.

Partitioning is the process of dividing the records stored in the NDS database into logical subsets. Partitioning NDS/eDirectory provides two primary benefits:

- Fault tolerance
- Performance Increase

Partitions are defined around containers. The container closest to the directory tree's root is defined as the *partition root*, as shown inExhibit 20-5. The partition's name is derived from its partition root.

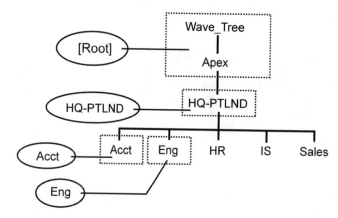

Exhibit 20-5: The NDS directory partitions

A partition that's located immediately above the root of another partition is described as the *parent partition*. Conversely, a partition located below another partition is called the *child partition*. Partitions might have multiple children but only one parent.

A partition's boundary encompasses all objects from the partition root down to the next partition, if any. Therefore, partitions might include more than one container. All of the leaf objects in all of the container objects within the partition are in the same logical partition. An object can't be in more than one partition, and the boundary of a partition can't overlap the boundary of another partition.

Do it!

B-2: Managing NDS/eDirectory partitions

Questions and answers

1 What are the benefits of NDS/eDirectory partitioning?

2 What's the difference between a parent partition and a child partition?

NDS/eDirectory replicas

Explanation

A *replica* is a physical copy of a partition. Each partition has at least one replica. The object data and property values for the containers within the partition are stored in a hidden directory at the root of a NetWare server's SYS: volume. The data stored in replicas is accessed regularly during normal system operation.

From a reliability standpoint, as you increase the number of partition replicas, the NDS/eDirectory database becomes more fault-tolerant. Replicas provide access to the actual data contained in the directory database.

From a performance standpoint, more replicas of a partition mean that a server is more likely to find needed object data more quickly. Directory database information stored on a local server can be accessed more quickly than data that resides on the other side of a WAN link.

Increasing the number of replicas also increases the amount of network traffic. This is due to the exchange of information that must occur between NetWare servers holding database replicas to maintain database synchronization. Changes made to a partition must be forwarded to all servers holding replicas of the data in that partition. This process is called *replica synchronization*.

Effective partitioning schemes attempt to balance the need for database redundancy and fault tolerance with the need to reduce unnecessary network traffic.

To improve network performance, increase access to needed network resources, and improve system fault tolerance, you must understand the various replica types and how to implement them.

NDS/eDirectory replica types

The four types of NDS/eDirectory replicas are:

- **Master replica.** The Master replica is created when a partition is defined. There is one and only one Master replica for each partition. Other replicas might be created from the Master. When a change is made to the Master replica, the change is propagated to all other replicas of the partition throughout the network. You must access the server that contains the Master replica to modify a partition. Modifications include creating new partitions and merging a partition with its parent. NetWare ensures that the Master replica is used to perform only one partitioning operation at a time. While an operation is being performed, all other replicas of the partition are locked to prevent possible database inconsistencies. Master replicas are also used for login authentication.

- **Read/write replica.** A Read/write replica is a copy of another replica. It can be used to update the NDS database and for login authentication but not to perform partitioning operations. Objects can be changed, modified, deleted, or created by accessing a Read/Write replica. When a change is made to the Read/Write replica, the system propagates that change to all other replicas of the partition throughout the network.

- **Read-only replica.** A read-only replica can accept changes from the master and read/write replicas only. It can't be changed directly, nor can it be used for login authentication. It's used to search for and view objects in the database. You can convert a Read-Only replica into a Master or Read/Write replica.

- **Subordinate reference.** A subordinate reference doesn't contain object data as the other types of replicas do. It's used to contact NetWare servers that contain Master, Read/Write, or Read-Only replicas of a partition to retrieve data residing in the partition. This type of replica is automatically created and maintained by NDS/eDirectory. A Subordinate reference is created on a NetWare server that contains a replica of a parent partition but not the partition's child. Subordinate References don't support login authentication, NDS/eDirectory object management, or partition modification.

Note: If the server containing the Master replica becomes unavailable, a Read/Write or Read-Only replica can be made into a Master replica.

Do it!

B-3: Discussing NDS/eDirectory replicas

Questions and answers

1 Which type of replica is created when a partition is defined?

   A   Master replica

   B   Read/write replica

   C   Read only replica

   D   Subordinate reference

2 What's a replica?

3 What's replica synchronization?

Replica ring

Explanation

The servers that hold replicas of a given partition make up the replica ring (replica list) for that partition. Being aware of this list of servers is important, because changes made to any replica must be propagated to all other servers containing the same replica. These servers must be able to communicate with one another to complete the replica synchronization process.

The time it takes for NDS/eDirectory to synchronize depends upon the type of change, the performance of the servers, the available bandwidth, and the speed of the network links. NDS/eDirectory database synchronization time is much greater if the file servers holding the replicas are separated by a slow WAN link.

Documentation of the replica ring might consist of a replica table containing a list of servers, a list of partitions, and the type of replica stored on each server.

Do it!

B-4: Discussing replica rings

Questions and answers

1   What's a replica ring?

2   What are the factors that determine the time for NDS/eDirectory to synchronize?

Topic C: Backup and UPS

This topic covers the following CompTIA Network+ exam objectives:

#	Objective
3.11	Identify the purpose and characteristics of fault tolerance: • Power • Storage
3.12	Identify the purpose and characteristics of disaster recovery: • Backup / restore • Offsite storage • Hot and cold spares • Hot, warm and cold sites

Introduction to data backups

Explanation

You must have a way to back up and recover important data, even though the disk management scheme you implement on your network is good and even if your disk drives are redundant. You can choose from a wide range of storage media including magnetic tape, digital audiotape (DAT), optical disks, or Write Read Many (WORM) drives. But regardless of which media you select, you should perform frequent backups and store a copy of the data off site to protect it in the event of fire, flood, or any other disaster. Another problem that might sometimes turn disastrous is the loss of power. There's hardly anything that power protection devices can do in this regard and this brings the importance of UPS in a networking environment.

Backup schemes

There are essentially three types of backups you can perform:

- **Full backup.** This backs up all the data on the server. File archive bits are reset.
- **Incremental backup.** This backs up any data that has changed after the last full or incremental backup. File archive bits are reset.
- **Differential backup.** This backs up any data that's changed after the last full backup. File archive bits aren't reset.

Backup schedules

When a system backup schedule is being developed, a cost/benefit analysis must be made. The level of restoration capability, that is, the ability to restore data from a previous day, week, month, and so on, must be weighed against the cost of implementing the desired backup schedule.

You should know whether there's a need to restore the server, or the files therein, to the state they were in at the end of a specific day, week, month, or not at all. The system restoration level should be decided on the basis of cost in media, labor, and the various methods used to achieve the level of restoration capability.

After deciding the system restoration level, then the backup plan can be created. For example, if you need to restore files on a server to the state at the end of any specific day, either of the following solutions will work:

- Perform a full system backup daily and save all tapes
- Perform a full backup at the end of each week. Perform incremental backups every other day of the week. On the last day of the week in which the end of the month falls, retain the tape containing the full backup for the first week of the month and all tapes containing incremental backups. Reuse all other tapes.

While both options technically solve the problem, the first costs a large amount of money, as thirty tapes each month need to be purchased. Compare this to the purchase of two tapes, one for full backups and one for incremental backups, using the second method. Operating costs must be a consideration when developing a backup strategy.

Finally, you should always verify your backups and test the actual media from time to time. Just because a backup seems to have worked, doesn't mean it did.

Do it!

C-1: Discussing backup schemes

Questions and answers

1 Your company needs the ability to restore data on the server to a known state at the end of any specific day. However, cost is an issue. Which backup plan would you recommend?

2 Which of the following backs up any data that has changed after the last backup?

A Full backup

B Incremental backup

C Differential backup

Removable media

Explanation

An alternative to tapes is the use of removable media. Tools such as removable hard drives, floptical media, and rewriteable CD-ROMs and DVDs provide a convenient way to archive data. These hardware devices appear as additional drives in the system. As such, they can be used in the same fashion as any fixed media device. Copy the desired data to the device, remove the device, and store it in a secure location.

These types of devices are called *cold spares*, as they are not permanently installed in the computer, but rather stored outside of the system and perhaps even offsite.

While each of these types of devices can be used in place of fixed media devices, it isn't recommended. The access and throughput of removable devices currently don't match the performance of their fixed counterparts.

Do it!

C-2: Discussing removable media

Questions and answers
1 What are removable media?
2 Name three types of removable media.

Backup storage

Explanation

Having a good backup system in place is important but not sufficient for true disaster recovery. For example, the backup you've created and kept in your office will do you no good if the office burns down.

In fact, storing backups in your office isn't a good idea to begin with, since such an unsecured location leaves the backups prone to unauthorized access. For on-site backup storage, you should always keep backups in a secure, access-controlled location that's also preferably temperature controlled to protect the media. In addition, you should have backups stored at offsite locations in the event that your onsite backups are destroyed or if you simply don't have the appropriate space to store your backup media onsite.

Disaster recovery site options

For true disaster recovery, you should create sites at which your data center can be recreated in the event of a disaster. These sites are generally grouped into three types: Cold, Warm, and Hot sites. Without such plans in place, should your headquarters building burn down, for example, your company may well find itself out of business.

Cold sites

A cold site is a site, usually a single room, in which your data center can be recreated in case of disaster. This site can be on site or off site and doesn't actually hold any equipment. All equipment is brought to the site after a disaster. This means that coming back online after a disaster can take quite a bit of time, but this is the least expensive backup site solution.

Warm sites

A warm site can be either on site or off site. It already contains a fair amount of equipment to create a semi-duplicate of your current data center. In the event of a disaster, you need to obtain the latest offsite backups, and perhaps some restoration work needs to be completed before you have your data center up and running again. This type of site can be live in much less time than a cold site. However, it's also more expensive to create and maintain.

Hot sites

At the other end of the spectrum are hot sites, which are typically located off site. A hot site is a complete duplication of your current data center and can be up and running in a matter of hours should disaster strike. The only thing necessary to return to normal operation is getting the most recent backups from your offsite storage facility. Hot sites are very expensive to create and maintain. However, they also provide the best protection in the event of a disaster.

Any of these site types can either be at one of your own facilities or provided by third-party companies that offer disaster recovery solutions. You could also make an arrangement with another company to share their facilities and sites.

Do it!

C-3: Discussing backup storage

Questions and answers

1 Where should you store your backups?

2 Which of the following enables you to come back into full operation within hours of a major disaster?

A   Cold site

B   Warm site

C   Lukewarm site

D   Hot site

Explanation

Uninterruptible Power Supply (UPS)

All of the fault tolerance procedures in the world will not make a difference if the server loses power. While the use of a power protection device cannot guarantee that the electricity will never go out in your organization, it can make sure that the server is gracefully powered down, thereby protecting network data.

UPS basics

An *Uninterruptible Power Supply* (UPS) keeps your system from going down unexpectedly due to line power loss. A UPS should protect both file servers and business-critical workstations. A UPS uses a battery to supply power to the system. The computer is connected directly to the battery, which is connected to the outlet. A UPS also insulates the computer from spikes, surges, and other electrical inconsistencies, thus maintaining a consistent supply of power.

One newer innovation of UPS systems is the addition of a serial port. With a serial port, network operating systems like Novell NetWare and Windows can use a monitoring system that detects a power failure. When one occurs, a graceful shutdown is initiated by the operating system.

Choosing a UPS

When determining whether the backup power of the system is good enough to maintain the computer in the event of a failure, watts and watt-hours need to be examined. The watt rating of the UPS should always be larger than the cumulative number of watts drawn by the equipment that's plugged into the UPS.

Another issue to consider is the length of time that battery power is supplied. To determine maximum time relative to the computer system, check the rating of the batteries it uses. Most batteries are rated in ampere-hours, which describes how much current they can deliver for how long. However, some of this power is consumed for the operation of the device, and the ratings are usually based on new batteries. In most cases, all the devices need to be given several minutes for the computer to shut down gracefully. Five minutes is usually sufficient.

Do it!

C-4: Discussing UPS

Questions and answers
1 What's a UPS?
2 A UPS uses a battery to supply power to the system. True or False?
3 What issues should you consider when determining the backup power for the system?

Unit summary: Fault tolerance and disaster recovery

Topic A   In this topic, you learned about **system fault tolerance** and learned how to plan for handling **disasters**. You also learned about **RAID, disk duplexing,** and **disk striping with parity**. You learned about **disk configurations**, including **volume sets** and disk striping. You learned that disk configuration provides valuable options for a Windows administrator.

Topic B   In this topic, you learned about **replication** and discussed the key points about replication. You learned that replication can offer additional data redundancy on Windows Server-based networks. Next, you learned about **NDS/eDirectory partitions** and **NDS/eDirectory replicas**. You also learned about **replica rings**.

Topic C   In this topic, you learned about **backups** and **removable media**. You learned that removable media provide a convenient way to archive data. Next, you learned about onsite and offsite backup storage, including **cold**, **warm** and **hot sites**. You also learned about **Uninterruptible Power Supply** and about choosing a UPS. You learned that a UPS keeps your system from going down unexpectedly.

Review questions

1 Which RAID Level provides fault tolerance through disk mirroring?

2 What RAID level needs at least three fixed disks and distributes the parity bit across each drive?

A RAID level 1

B RAID level 2

C RAID level 3

D RAID level 5

3 Explain the major difference between disk duplexing and disk mirroring.

4 You've been asked to make a fault tolerance recommendation for your organization. The server stores mission-critical data, spanning four disks. Based on this information, what RAID level would you recommend?

A Level 1

B Level 3

C Level 4

D Level 5

5 A UPS protects your network from data loss due to:

  A A hard disk failure

  B A disk controller failure

  C Unauthorized access

  D Data corruption

  E Line power loss

6 You're setting up an additional server as an application server. You have five SCSI hard disks, 1 GB each. Performance isn't a significant concern. Protecting the database that's stored on this server is critical. The database is projected to grow to nearly 3 GB. How can you configure the system to help proper startup, provide sufficient storage capacity, and protect the database from data loss?

7 You're setting up three domain controllers in remote locations. Storage requirements will be minimal on each of the systems. Because there are no technical people available at the remote locations, you want to keep management to a minimum and provide a way to keep the systems working reliably. How can you configure the systems to minimize downtime and avoid overnight trips and parts shipments?

8 You're setting up a database server that will be used for managing large graphics files. You're told that cost isn't a factor, but that you must provide the best possible access time. How would you configure the system?

9 You want to protect yourself from a disaster, such as a flood or fire. Your budget is limited, but you do have space available at one of your remote facilities. What type of disaster recovery site would you implement?

Unit 21

Routine maintenance

Unit time: 30 minutes

Complete this unit, and you'll know how to:

A Discuss the necessity of keeping NOS software up-to-date.

B Guard against and recover from computer viruses.

Topic A: Keeping NOS software up to date

Explanation

Although software products undergo a period of testing before they're released to the market, some problems aren't detected until a wide user base has used the products. In addition, because technology changes more rapidly than full-fledged product development cycles, improvements to an existing version of an operating system or application sometimes need to be made in an interim update. The purpose of software patches and updates is to address those developments. These provide a convenient way for the manufacturer to refine its product continually, as well as to improve customer satisfaction by providing a vehicle to address industry concerns as they arise. It's a recommended practice to check your software vendor's Web site periodically to ensure that your network stays current.

Support packs, service packs, and updates

Support packs and service packs are traditionally large-scale improvements made to a current version of software. Typically, they contain up-to-the-minute updates in a consolidated package. You can also perform a blanket update without having to research and deploy each individual update separately. Support packs and service packs are basically the same types of update but are for different network environments. Support pack is the term used by Novell, and service pack is the term used by Microsoft. Apple Computer Inc. uses the term update.

Novell support packs

Novell support packs provide improvements to the network operating system and typically update numerous system files. Support packs can be downloaded from the minimum patch list on Novell's Web-based support site (http://support.novell.com/produpdate/patchlist.html) or by downloading or ordering the Consolidated Support Pack (http://support.novell.com/tools/csp/).

Support packs are version- and product-specific. For instance, you don't want to apply a support pack for NetWare 5 to a NetWare 6 server. Likewise, other Novell products, such as GroupWise or Border Manager, need their own specific support packs. Prior to installing any support packs, make sure the server has been backed up and that you've carefully read the installation instructions.

Microsoft Service Packs

Some bugs and issues can cause varying degrees of problems on your network. Typically, it's useful to check the fixes contained within the most recent service pack for possible information about your specific issue. Microsoft releases service packs and makes them available over the Internet at www.microsoft.com/downloads.

Alternatively, in Windows 2000/Server 2003, you can use the Windows Update tool to attach to the Microsoft site. It scans your machine and presents you with a list of critical and suggested updates. You can then choose which service packs and patches to download and install. Microsoft service packs can update servers as well as workstations.

Apple updates

The fixes That Apple provides to its Appleshare IP NOS are called updates and are available from Apple's Appleshare IP Web site at www.apple.com.au/appleshareip. You can also find updates to Apple Oss at www.apple.com/support/downloads.

Hot fixes and patches

Support packs and service packs are considered large-scale updates, because numerous items are corrected and updated at once. *Hot fixes* and patches are generally released to fix one specific problem.

A hot fix or patch for an individual bug fix eventually gets included in a support pack or service pack release. A hot fix or patch is the fastest way to address a specific, critical issue. Hot fixes can be acquired from the software vendor and applied immediately, rather than waiting for the next support or service pack. You can download Novell patches and Microsoft hot fixes from their respective Web sites.

Updating a device driver

From time to time, device drivers are updated. On a Windows computer, you can update drivers through the Device Manager tool.

To update a specific device driver:

1 Launch Device Manager. To do so in Windows 2000, right-click My Computer on the desktop, choose Manage from the shortcut menu, and then double-click Device Manager in the left pane. In Windows XP/Server 2003, the procedure is essentially the same, except that you access My Computer through the Start menu.

2 Expand the device type to display the specific device. Right-click the device and select Properties.

3 Activate the Driver tab.

4 Click Update Driver.

5 Specify whether you want to update the driver automatically or from a list or specific location.

6 Click Next and then follow the prompts to install the new driver and exit the wizard. If a newer driver is not found, the wizard informs you that you already have the most updated driver.

Application updates

Applications also need patches. Like operating systems, applications are released with minor problems that are fixed by patches. Regularly visit the manufacturers' Web sites to check for product updates and fixes.

Common application Web sites include:

- www.novell.com
- www.microsoft.com
- www.adobe.com
- www.symantec.com
- www.lotus.com

Do it!

A-1: Discussing software patches and updates

Questions and answers

1 What's the purpose of service packs and support packs?

2 What type of fix is usually used to correct a single issue in a software program?

Topic B: Virus protection

This topic covers the following CompTIA Network+ exam objective:

#	Objective
3.10	Identify the purpose, benefits and characteristics of using antivirus software.

Introducing virus protection

Explanation

Virus protection is a serious concern on any computer. The concern is exacerbated when the focus is a network or server. Computer viruses can spread easily across a network, infecting every node on the network if left to spread unabated. In today's network environments, it's most prudent to install a network anti-virus suite that protects your workstations, servers, and in most cases, your e-mail and messaging platforms, as well. The importance of up-to-date virus protection on every node of your network can't be stressed enough, especially in today's environment where practically every computer is connected to the Internet. In the past, viruses were usually spread via floppy disks. Today, proliferation through email and other Internet-related means is far more common.

Viruses

A *virus* is a software program that has the ability to reproduce by modifying other programs or duplicating itself. It's a parasitic program written intentionally to enter a computer without the user's permission or knowledge. The word parasitic is used, because a virus attaches to files or boot sectors and replicates itself, thus continuing to spread. Though some viruses do nothing but replicate, others can cause serious damage or affect program and system performance. A virus should never be assumed harmless and left on a system.

Types of viruses

Viruses are classified by the ways in which they infect computer systems:

- **Program.** This type of virus infects executable program files, such as COM, EXE, OVL, DRV, SYS, and BIN files.
- **Boot.** This type of virus infects the boot record, the master boot record, the FAT, and the partition table.
- **Multipartite.** This type of virus has the characteristics of both a program and a boot infector.
- **Specialized.** This type of virus infects a specific program or data file. Examples of a specialized virus are the macro viruses seen with Microsoft Word.

Virus origins

In some cases, apparent virus attacks turn out to be hardware failures or software bugs. However, with the propagation of e-mail and everybody being connected to the Internet all the time, a virus can easily invade your systems and the results can be devastating. Viruses do not just happen. They're written, either by accident or with malicious intent. Either way, they're dangerous if they invade any of your systems.

Viruses enter your systems because you aren't careful to avoid them. They are the result of unsafe computing practices, such as running programs from unknown sources and giving unlimited access invite infection.

Damage

Damage depends upon the virus. Some are benign, but most are destructive. They tend to infect the boot sector and executables, such as COM, EXE, and BAT files. They might corrupt data or program files, corrupt the boot sector, format hard or floppy disks, corrupt the FAT, or just display odd messages on the screen.

Specialized viruses

Recently, there's been a proliferation of specialized viruses that infect Microsoft Word and Microsoft Excel files exclusively. Because these viruses use the macro language of the specific application to spread, they're known as *Macro Viruses*.

The Word macro family of viruses

These viruses use the WordBasic macro language to infect and replicate Microsoft Word documents and templates. Most notably, this family of viruses is platform-independent in that they infect documents and templates on DOS, Macintosh, and Windows operating systems.

After an infected document is opened and the virus launched, generally the virus infects the user's normal.dot template. This template is the basis for the majority of other documents and templates and is globally available to all other MS Word templates on the system. After entrenched in the normal.dot file, the virus spreads to all other documents and templates as they're opened.

By default, the normal.dot file is the template used for the creation of the first document opened when you launch Microsoft Word. This immediately puts the virus in control every time you launch Microsoft Word.

A specific type of Word macro virus, the Concept virus and its variants, forces documents to be saved as Word templates (*.dot), no matter what the name or extension of the document file. Forcing documents to be saved as templates is used as a means of propagation as macros aren't saved in standard DOC files.

With the proliferation of Internet e-mail attachments containing Word documents, this type of virus can quickly spread throughout an enterprise.

The Excel macro family of viruses

These viruses were first discovered in July of 1996 in Africa and Alaska. A virus named XM.Laroux was the first working Excel Macro Virus to be found in general circulation. The actual virus code consists of two macros called Auto_Open and Check_Files, which are stored in a hidden datasheet named laroux.

In infected spreadsheet files, the laroux datasheet isn't readily visible because it's hidden. When an infected spreadsheet is first opened on a system, the Auto_Open macro is automatically run by Excel, which in turn runs the Check_Files macro. This happens each time a worksheet is activated.

The Check_Files macro then copies the worksheet with the virus code into a spreadsheet file stored in the Excel startup directory named personal.xls, which is stored, by default, in the \MSOFFICE\EXCEL\XLSTART directory.

Copying these macros to personal.xls causes the infection of all other spreadsheets opened or created on the infected system in the future.

XM.Laroux contains no deliberately destructive payloads and it exists only to replicate. This virus currently works only under Windows operating systems by using Excel versions 5 and 7. It doesn't work under the Macintosh environment.

CMOS virus

CMOS viruses are destructive, memory-resident viruses. They infect the Master Boot Record (MBR) and can erase the system's CMOS setup information. While these viruses remain in memory, the system's available free memory is typically reduced by about 1,024 bytes. According to virus experts, after a CMOS virus has infected a system, it can erase the setup information approximately one time for every 60 times the system is booted.

To recover from a CMOS virus, boot from an uninfected boot disk and run a current anti-virus program from disk. You can also try to use the SYS C: command to clear the boot sector after booting from the uninfected boot disk.

Do it!

B-1: Discussing viruses

Questions and answers

1 What's a virus?

2 Which of the following types of viruses infects a specific program or data file?

   A   Program

   B   Boot

   C   Multipartite

   D   Specialized

3 What are macro viruses?

4 What are Concept viruses?

5 Pike calls you up with a specific problem. He says that each time he works on a spreadsheet, it gets duplicated. He's working in Excel version 7. What might be the reason for his problem?

Virus protection

Explanation Virus infection can be expensive in terms of time, data loss, and money. While the majority of viruses are nothing more than nuisances, some can be devastating. Viruses can hide in the Master Boot Record, in the DOS boot record, as small files, or attached to executables.

The best way of dealing with viruses is to put measures into place that:

- **Avoid infection.** Review your computing practices to see if you're, in fact, inviting virus infection. Make sure users are informed as to the importance of avoiding viruses.
- **Keep viruses from spreading.** A virus can spread quickly through an organization, infecting a large number of PCs. This is especially true in an unprotected network.

It's less costly in both time and money to avoid infection than to go back and clean up after an infection has occurred.

Prevention

The best way to prevent a virus is never to permit anything to be copied to the system and never to run any unchecked software. If this isn't practical, and it probably isn't, you need to practice safe computing.

Safe computing

Anti-virus programs are a big help, but they can't do the job alone. New viruses are turning up all the time, and it's a constant race to find ways to detect and remove them. Some procedures you can implement to help avoid infection include:

- Don't run software from unknown or unreliable sources.
- Be on the alert for viruses downloaded via Internet e-mail attachments.
- Don't permit employees bring software from home.
- Test software downloaded from bulletin board systems and the Internet on a test system, not on a production system.
- Don't assume that out-of-the-box software is virus-free.
- Don't share a boot disk between computers.
- Don't boot a computer with a startup disk that's been used in another computer.
- Remove disks from drives immediately after use.
- Install anti-virus software on all computers, both clients and servers, throughout your network.
- Make sure the anti-virus software is always running on all machines.
- Make sure that anti-virus signature files are up-to-date.
- Back up data and program files on a regular basis and rotate backup media.
- Accept shareware and public domain software only from known, reputable sources.
- Test all software, including commercial products.
- Keep all original (distribution) copies of software in a safe location.

- Don't permit users to run unauthorized or pirated software on any PC.
- Be diligent about your own materials; maintenance personnel are a major source of infection because they take the same software tool kit from site to site.
- Limit outside access to reduce the risk of accidental or malicious infection across the telephone lines or through the Internet.

Note: Even commercial software, sealed in its original packaging, might be infected with a virus, although this is a rarity.

Anti-virus programs

There are a number of anti-virus programs available. You can classify the programs by their function as maintenance or preventive.

Maintenance (virus scan)

These are programs that can be run periodically to check for virus infection. In some cases, the program might also be able to repair some infected files. The program can be used to check files before they're copied onto the system.

There are some possible problems inherent in this type of program. It doesn't do anything until after an infection is present. Viruses must have a recognizable signature, and the program must look for that signature. In addition, the program needs constant, ongoing updates as new viruses are discovered.

Preventive

The most effective way to avoid losing data due to a virus is to keep the infection from ever happening. Preventive anti-virus programs usually include a virus scan and repair program as part of the application. They might also include other features, such as access monitoring or a lockout feature to keep users from running unauthorized software.

It's important that any policies you set or anti-virus programs you install be easy to follow and use. If it isn't simple or if it needs significant user interaction, it probably won't be used. The more automated the process, the better for you and your users. Any program you install on your network should be able to scan both servers and clients in the network, and regular virus signature updates should be available. Virus signature updates ensure that your anti-virus software is always up to date, which is extremely important given how frequently new viruses appear all the time.

Some vendors of anti-virus programs include:

- Symantec's Norton Anti-Virus (www.symantec.com)
- Network Associates' McAfee Anti-Virus (www.mcafee.com)
- Computer Associates' eTrust (www.ca.com)

Virus recovery

If you determine the type of infection you have, tailor your recovery to the virus type.

- **Boot sector.** Boot from a floppy and try running the SYS command to clear the sector.
- **Executable files.** Boot from a floppy, delete all infected files, and recover from the distribution disks.
- **FAT or directory tables.** Run a low-level format and recover from backups.

Commercial disinfecting utilities are available. In worst-case situations, it's necessary to reinstall applications from the original disks and recover data files from backups. If you're having a problem determining the type of virus you have, there are several sources on the Internet that detail every virus known to date and exactly what they do. Most viruses increase the size of infected files.

Anti-virus software on the network

Anti-virus software is an important element of a comprehensive security program that includes a variety of safety measures, such as regular backup schedules, meaningful password protection, training, and awareness. It's of vital importance to the overall health of your network to institute a package of anti-virus protection.

Three primary providers of network anti-virus support are Symantec, Computer Associates, and McAfee. Each company offers product suites that provide comprehensive network protection. These are only three of a large number of companies that offer such services. A personal evaluation of each product would be a worthwhile task.

In today's age of internetworking and mass communication through a variety of protocols and connectivity devices, the rate of exposure to viral attack is exceedingly high. Many viruses enter through the Internet. A good first line of defense is to implement a network-wide virus protection suite at the server. For improved security, that package should be used in conjunction with virus protection at each individual workstation.

Used in conjunction with a network protection suite, workstation protection provides a high level of resilience against incoming viral attack. Having anti-virus protection at the workstations is important when workstations have access to the Internet.

E-mail protection

It's important to mention that most anti-virus software today integrates itself with the e-mail system on the network. This component scans incoming mail and attachments and stops viruses before they enter your network. This provides an additional layer of security for users who have access to Internet e-mail.

Updating virus signatures

In order for any anti-virus software package to be effective, it's imperative that the virus signatures and definitions be kept up to date. This is accomplished by configuring the software to retrieve and install updates from the manufacturer's Web site automatically. The process can also be done manually by logging in to the Web site and downloading the latest updates to the anti-virus package you're using.

Do it!

B-2:   Discussing virus protection

Questions and answers

1 What's the purpose of anti-virus signature updates?

2 Why is it important to have virus protection at a network level?

3 You have a disk that you frequently use to boot machines prior to conducting
   diagnostics. This disk has contracted a virus. Provide steps to address this
   problem, as well as to prevent it from happening again.

Unit summary: Routine maintenance

Topic A In this topic, you learned about **service packs**, **support packs**, and **updates**, as well as **hot fixes** and **patches**. You also learned about **device driver updates** and **application updates**.

Topic B In this topic, you learned about **viruses** and types of viruses. You also learned about **anti-virus programs**.

Review questions

1 What's the difference between a hot fix and a service pack?

2 NetWare support packs are version-independent. True or False?

3 Differentiate between a service pack, a support pack, and an update.

4 You try to save your Microsoft Word document as myfile.doc, but Word refuses, wanting to save it as myfile.dot. What might be the problem?

5 Emily calls you with a strange problem. She recently received an e-mail that had an attachment. When she opened the attachment, she found it was an executable file that locked her system. She was forced to reboot. Yet when she restarted, her system couldn't find any of her BIOS configuration settings. What's the most likely problem, how would you fix it, and how would you keep this from happening in the future?

Unit 22
Troubleshooting

Unit time: 60 minutes

Complete this unit, and you'll know how to:

A Describe methods to help prioritize network problems.

B List basic troubleshooting steps to be followed when working on a problem.

C Troubleshoot various problems that might occur on the network.

Topic A: Assessing and responding to problems

Explanation

The human being is one of the main components in any network. Without users, the network serves no purpose. When a user reports problems, the network troubleshooting staff needs to listen carefully and prioritize the problems.

The human factor

The IT employee who looks down on the user or coworker when a problem is reported is a destructive force in an organization. This type of behavior is simply unproductive and unprofessional.

Unfortunately, while a good number of IT personnel are technically savvy, there's a big gap in the human factor area. Always remember to listen well and empathize with the user.

Prioritizing problems

If multiple, unrelated problems are occurring on the network simultaneously, the IT professional must have the ability to prioritize them. Typically, address those items that affect the majority of users first, then address the problem that affects the next largest group of people, and so on.

When multiple problems occur, work in the best interest of the company by asking yourself "If all the problems remain unfixed, which will cause the greatest loss of revenue?" Remember to consider personnel costs when evaluating this question.

After the problems have been prioritized, users reporting problems should be kept informed as to when the problem will be addressed.

An example

You're the network administrator at XYZ Company. When you arrive at work on Monday morning, you notice that no system backup was performed on the file server. The log indicates a failure in the SCSI controller to which your tape drive is attached.

Sally, an employee in Accounting, contacts you to report that she can no longer open her Web browser. She states that every time she accesses the application, her system freezes. Several minutes later, Terri in Marketing informs you that she can't access the MARKETING share on the file server. Shortly thereafter, Kim, the VP of the Marketing department, also informs you that she can't access the MARKETING share.

With these three problems, you realize that the inaccessible MARKETING share impacts the productivity of more than one person. This, in addition to the fact that employees are currently attempting to access this share, means that this problem takes highest priority. Because the failed tape drive more than likely means that the file server needs to be taken down, this should be done after hours when the least number of employees are affected. Thus, Sally's Web browser issue should take second highest priority.

Do it!   ## A-1:   Discussing problem prioritization

Questions and answers

1 Why is it important to prioritize problems?

2 You're the network administrator at ABC company. Kate, secretary to the VP of the marketing department, says that she can't access the marketing share on the file server, from which she needs some important information that is time-sensitive. After a few minutes, Sally, an employee in the accounting department, says that she received a message on her Windows 2000 computer indicating that she can't log in to the domain. You're then informed by Betty, who's also in accounting, that she isn't able to print from her Windows XP computer to an HP LaserJet printer.

As network administrator, how would you prioritize these situations?

Topic B: Troubleshooting procedures

This topic covers the following CompTIA CompTIA Network+ exam objective:

#	Objective
4.9	Given a network problem scenario, select an appropriate course of action based on a logical troubleshooting strategy. This strategy can include the following steps: • Identify the symptoms and potential causes • Identify the affected area • Establish what has changed • Select the most probable cause • Implement an action plan and solution including potential effects • Test the result • Identify the results and effects of the solution • Document the solution and process

Introduction to troubleshooting problems

Explanation

Troubleshooting problems can be a daunting experience. To troubleshoot a problem, learn as much as you can about the equipment you support. In addition, approach the situation in a straightforward and logical manner.

Identify the symptoms and possible causes

When a user reports a problem on the network or on his or her system, listen carefully to what's being said. This points you in the right direction. Sometimes, however, the key to identifying the problem is to determine what isn't being said.

Learn to ask open-ended questions. Open-ended questions can't be answered by a simple yes or no. Instead of asking "Are you able to log in to the network?" try "What happens when you try to log in to the network?" Open-ended questions typically encourage the user to provide greater detail about what occurred prior to, during, and after the problem occurred.

Keep in mind that users might flavor their observations with their own interpretations when reporting a problem. These interpretations might not be completely accurate. Error messages, if you don't understand what they're telling you, can be misleading. Learn to recognize the relevant information.

Another problem is that all errors might not be reported. This is especially true if users have reported minor problems in the past and never received any type of response or follow-up. These small difficulties might, however, be leading up to a major failure.

While defining a potential problem, you might realize that there could be a quick solution to the malfunction. Try these quick fixes before proceeding. They might save you time by immediately resolving the problem.

Make sure that you speak to users in a professional manner. Don't become impatient or condescending. Many support professionals work from a script or checklist when speaking with users to remind themselves of pertinent and appropriate areas of inquiry. Make sure that you set expectations with the users, providing them with a timeline for correction.

Identify the affected area

As mentioned before, it's very important to identify who and how many users are affected by a problem. Once you've identified the area that's affected, you can use this information to help you in the troubleshooting process.

Understanding the area that's affected by the problem helps you determine the priority of the issue and whether you may need assistance from other support personnel. It also might give you clues as to the cause of the problem and help you make your questions more specific.

To help with identifying the area that's affected, you can also try to recreate the problem. For example, try the function yourself on the user's workstation to verify that it isn't an operator error. Have the user try to perform the function on another, similar workstation to determine if it's a machine-specific problem. Repeat the factors involved in the original occurrence as closely as possible. Keep variables to a minimum while you're working.

You won't be able to reproduce the problem in all situations. If the problem is physical or data damaging, you don't want to. If it's irregular, you might not be able to. In situations like this, you must depend heavily on intuitive logical processes.

Identify any changes that have occurred

One of the most helpful troubleshooting tools is identifying the changes that have occurred between the time that all was well and the time the problem started. Often, users make changes to their systems and cause unintended problems along the way. Or, the IT department may have made a network environment change that's now causing problems.

Often, when you ask a user about changes they may have made, their first reaction is to deny having made any changes, either because they truly can't remember or because they aren't comfortable admitting that they made changes. Try to get the user to think about it, help him feel ok about any changes he may have made, and ask leading questions that might prompt the user to provide relevant information. The troubleshooting process isn't a good time for admonitions about not making changes.

You can also try to identify changes at the user's workstation yourself if certain standards apply to all workstations or groups of workstations in your organization. Further, think about changes you or other systems administrators have made to the network recently to determine if they could have a part in the problem at hand.

Isolate and select the most likely cause

Next, you need to attempt to isolate and select the most likely source of the problem. A systematic approach to problem solving is generally the best approach. That is, based on the type of problem, determine what parameters should be eliminated first. Upon elimination, check whether the problem still exists. If so, eliminate the next obvious parameter. Repeat the procedure until the problem disappears.

To isolate the cause of failures, you must be familiar with the following components:

- Workstation hardware
- Workstation operating systems
- Workstation applications
- Network operating systems
- Cabling

Complicating the process is the fact that components might work properly when tested separately or fail only in certain specific combinations. In addition, it's seldom possible to isolate all components that you want to test. It's necessary to isolate as much as possible, keeping variables to a minimum.

When isolating the cause, it's helpful to determine its scope on the network. To determine the scope, it's generally best to answer the following questions in order:

- Does the problem exist across the enterprise?
- Is the problem related to the logical arrangement of resources?
- Does the problem exist across a WAN link?
- Does the problem exist in the local area network?
- Does the problem exist at the workstation?

Formulate an action plan and implement a solution

After the problem has been isolated, determine the appropriate course of action to eliminate the cause. Experienced technicians draw on their past experiences to help them formulate a correction. At times, the problem might be large enough to merit a formal plan of correction. If this is the case, you should carefully set forth a plan containing all steps necessary to correct the problem.

Once you've formulated an action plan, it's time to fix the problem. First and foremost, ensure that the operational needs of your business are met. This might mean having the user work at another system while repairs are being made. The first priority is to keep the users productive while you fix the problem.

To make the process of fixing the problem the most efficient, use troubleshooting tools that are at your disposal. These include system logs and monitoring utilities, online or printed documentation, support CDs, telephone support, online knowledge bases, data analyzers, and so forth.

It might also be necessary to bring in a third-party service provider to assist with correcting the problem. You'll find that any background work you've done up to that point helps streamline the process. It also helps reduce costs incurred by implementing the solution.

Test the result

After you've implemented the correction, you must verify that it resolved the issue. This needs ample testing. For example, if the problem is at a user's workstation, test the workstation locally and after it's attached to the network. After you feel certain that the problem is resolved, have the user test it in your presence. The problem's been corrected only when the user feels confident it's been corrected.

Solving the problem doesn't always determine the cause. You need to look at underlying factors, such as system environment, and correct these as well.

Identify the results of the solution and its effects

Once you've tested the results of the solution you implemented, you need to identify its results as well as its effects. This helps with the final step of documenting the problem and solution and with future troubleshooting.

At this point, you should be clear as to what the actual results of your solution are and how it effects the user, the network, and so on. In many cases, this simply means that everything is back to how it was before. In some cases, however, implementing the solution may have created a changed environment for the user or resulted in changes in the network.

Document the problem and the solution

Finally, document the symptoms, cause, and solution, as well as the process you used to arrive at the solution. This becomes a valuable tool when troubleshooting problems in the future. Documentation provides a company with trend information and a knowledge base that can be used to address future issues.

In addition, after you've resolved the problem, make sure that the resolution doesn't create additional problems. Verify the stability of the computing environment through follow-up with the users. Talk to the users. Check whether they're happy with your resolution of the problem.

Continual failure to give feedback to users reporting problems typically results in employee distrust and dissatisfaction with the IT department. This is damaging to the IT department's ability to troubleshoot future issues, not to mention the efficiency of the network.

Do it!

B-1: Discussing troubleshooting procedures

Questions and answers

1 Why is it important to document problems and their resolutions?

2 When identifying a problem, why is it important for the network administrator to ask open-ended questions?

3 What should you do to check if a problem reported to you is machine specific?

Topic C: Troubleshooting scenarios

This topic covers the following CompTIA CompTIA Network+ exam objectives:

#	Objective
4.4	Given a troubleshooting scenario involving a client accessing remote network services, identify the cause of the problem (For example: file services, print services, authentication failure, protocol configuration, physical connectivity and SOHO (Small Office / Home Office) router).
4.5	Given a troubleshooting scenario between a client and the following server environments, identify the cause of a stated problem: • UNIX / Linux / Mac OS X Server
4.6	Given a scenario, determine the impact of modifying, adding or removing network services for network resources and users. (For example: • DHCP (Dynamic Host Configuration Protocol) • DNS (Domain Name Service) • WINS (Windows Internet Name Server)
4.8	Given a troubleshooting scenario involving a network with a particular physical topology (For example: bus, star, mesh or ring) and including a network diagram, identify the network area affected and the cause of the stated failure.

Real-world scenarios

Explanation

The network administrator of an organization is responsible for handling all the problems relating to the network. There are several types of problems relating to the network, and each of them has to be dealt with in a different way.

Inability of a user to access a shared resource

A network administrator can give various types of access rights to users as per the requirements. One common problem is that the user can't access a shared resource.

Do it!

C-1: Troubleshooting the inability of a user to access a shared resource

Questions and answers

Scenario: As a network administrator at ABC Corporation, your sales personnel need access to a file share on the network that contains the data used by the contact management system. You've created the directory and given access to a special group of users called Sales. The Sales group contains user accounts for the members of the Sales team. After providing access to these files, an employee from the Sales department reports that she can't access the resource.

1   What should you do as a part of identifying the exact issue?

2   The other employee reports a failure. What step should be taken to recreate the problem?

3   Both indicate that they saved proposals to the corporate file server within the last several minutes. Now, what should you do to isolate the cause?

4   As part of formulating the correction, you notice that only the Administrators group has been given rights to log in to the contact management system. As the problem has been identified, how can you implement the correction?

5   How can you confirm the correction?

6   You get a positive response. As the network administrator, what should you do after solving the problem?

7   What feedback do you give to the employees?

Preventing illegal attempts to access an account

Explanation

The network administrator can set policies to lock accounts in case of repeated bad login attempts. This procedure is generally followed to prevent illegal attempts to access an account.

Do it!

C-2: Troubleshooting access to an account

Questions and answers

Scenario: You're the network administrator at Mutton, Ewe, and Lamb L.L.P. The law firm network consists of a single NetWare 6 server in a single eDirectory tree. Sally, a secretary to the managing partner, reports that she receives a message on her Windows XP computer indicating that she can't log on to the network. You've also set password restrictions so that users must alter their passwords every 90 days. Passwords must be at least 9 characters in length, and the account is locked out after 5 bad login attempts.

1 To identify the exact issue, what action do you take?

2 In response to your attempt to recreate the problem, she reports that she can't log in at other workstations either. What do you do to isolate the cause?

3 As a part of formulating the correction, you notice that her account is locked out. What do you do to implement the correction and confirm it?

4 This time she's successful. What should you do after solving the problem?

Access permission conflicts in directories and subdirectories

Explanation

Conflicts might arise in accessing directories and subdirectories on a Windows Server 2003 server. A possible cause for such a problem might be access permissions for the directories and subdirectories. You can resolve such problems by checking if the permissions are set properly.

Do it!

C-3: Troubleshooting access permission conflicts in directories and subdirectories

Questions and answers

Scenario: Georgie has just been promoted as branch manager at Big Cluck Nugget Manufacturer. As such, she now has clearance to access various managerial data all located on a Windows Server 2003 server called MANAGANUG in a share on an NTFS partition called MANAGERS. Within this directory is a subdirectory called ROOSTERS that contains information only top-level managers can access. You grant Georgie access to the share \\MANAGANUG\MANAGERS. A week later Georgie reports that she can't open or save any files to the ROOSTERS directory.

1 How do you identify the issue?

2 You get a positive response. What does it indicate?

3 What should you do next?

4 The response is negative. How do you isolate the cause?

5 The directory permissions were set to List, while the file permissions set to Read, Write, Execute, and Delete. How do you implement the correction?

6 How can you test the correction?

7 She reports that now she can. What's next step in troubleshooting?

8 What feedback do you give?

Connectivity issues

Explanation

In a networked environment, connectivity failures might occur due to many factors. Some of the common causes can be:

- Faulty cables
- Hardware failure
- Problems with RAS
- Compatibility issues with other operating systems

Do it!

C-4: Troubleshooting hardware problems

Questions and answers

Scenario: Tim reports that, this morning when attempting to access network resources, he was unable to do so. The network is configured in a Star topology.

1 How can you identify the exact issue?

2 He's able to do so. What does that indicate?

3 How can you recreate the problem?

4 The attempt fails. How do you isolate the cause in this situation?

5 It appears to be connected. What do you check next?

6 You note that it isn't. What do you do next?

7 As part of formulating the correction, when you touched the cable, you noted that the link light on the hub corresponding to Tim's computer flickers. You disconnected and reconnected the cable at the patch panel and at the hub, but the link light doesn't remain on. Wiggling the patch cable causes the link light to flicker. How do you implement the correction?

8 The link light on Tim's network adapter came on and stayed on. How can you test that the problem is solved?

9 He's able to access the network resources. After documenting the problem and the solution, what feedback do you give Tim?

Network problems relating to remote connectivity issues

Explanation

Network problems might occur that are related to remote connectivity issues. Even though the problem is a network problem, the network troubleshooter can't resolve it, because it's a hardware fault in the infrastructure that connects remote sites and is maintained by a remote infrastructure carrier. However, the troubleshooter can detect and expedite the problem resolution by contacting the right people.

Do it!

C-5: Troubleshooting network problems relating to remote connectivity issues

Questions and answers

Scenario: Faht Tso Catering Company has two offices in town. A single Windows Server 2003 domain called CATER1 has been implemented. The network protocol chosen is IP. There's a domain controller at both offices. The company mail server and database server also reside at the main office. A dedicated ISDN connection exists between the main office and the remote facility. Users at the remote site report that they're able to log in to the domain but can no longer send and receive mail at the remote facility.

1 How can you identify the issue?

2 They can. What do you do next?

3 They can do that also. What do you check next?

4 They fail in doing so. What do you do to isolate the cause?

5 The log indicates that the connection is broken. You then establish a serial connection into the router and attempt to force a connection. The connection is established but drops within a few moments. A review of the line quality report from the router indicates that there's a 40% data error rate. How do you implement the correction?

6 Their results indicate that there's a problem with hardware at their end. They immediately replace the faulty equipment. How do you confirm that the problem is resolved?

7 You're now able to send and receive mail from the client workstations at the remote office. Now, after documenting the problem and the solution, what should you do?

Connectivity problems with RAS servers

Explanation

Problems might occur as a result of connectivity issues with a RAS server. You can resolve such a problem by ensuring that the right permissions are set for the RAS server.

Do it!

C-6: Troubleshooting a connectivity issue to a RAS server

Questions and answers

Scenario: ABC Consulting Company has a RAS server that provides employees with remote access to the local network. On the same line internally, a fax server is connected to provide employees with faxing capability. An employee reports that, when attempting to dial in to the RAS server, he's immediately disconnected.

1 Following the troubleshooting procedure, what do you do as the first step?

2 The response is a failure. What do you do next?

3 You find that it's been properly configured. What's your next step based on this inference?

4 The log you review indicates that the connection was dropped at the employee's request. As a part of formulating the correction, you ask another employee to attempt a connection. It also fails. How do you implement the correction?

5 How do you test for the success of the correction?

6 This time the employee is successful. You call the second employee and ask that he or she also attempt a connection, which is also successful. What's the normal procedure you follow after the problem's been solved?

7 What feedback do you give?

A Linux workstation in a Windows Server 2003 network

Explanation

Connectivity issues might occur when there's a Linux workstation in a Windows Server 2003 network. For example, the Linux workstation might have access to the internal network but might not be able to connect to the Internet. In such situations, review the resolv.conf file and ensure that the required information is present in the file.

Do it!

C-7: Troubleshooting a Linux workstation in a Windows Server 2003 network

Questions and answers

Scenario: You've configured a Windows Server 2003 Domain to access the Internet. The router's been configured with Network Address Translation to mask your internal network-addressing scheme from the Internet. The internal IP addressing scheme uses the network of 192.168.20.0. The router's IP address on the LAN side is 192.168.20.1. You recently configured a Linux workstation for Jenny, a new employee in the Engineering department. Linux has been configured to permit Jenny access to the Net BIOS shares on the Windows 2000 network. Several weeks pass, and Jenny's happy with her system. One morning you receive a phone call from Jenny. She's been attempting to browse the Internet from her workstation but has never been able to do so.

1 You attempt to browse the Web and are successful. What do you do to check for the proper functioning of Jenny's workstation IP address and adapter?

2 You receive a successful response. You then log in to Jenny's machine as root to ping the router's IP address (192.168.20.1). You receive a response indicating that the router is functioning properly. How do you isolate the cause?

3 You receive a response that the destination is unreachable. Knowing that name resolution occurs on the Internet by using DNS, you check her resolv.conf file and note that it's empty. How do you implement the correction?

4 How do you test for the success of the correction?

5 You now receive a response. What step do you take after getting a resolution to the problem?

6 What feedback do you give Jenny?

Network problems relating to adding or removing services

Explanation

Problems might occur in a network when services, such as DNS/DHCP and WINS, are added to or removed from the network. Making a change of this sort typically involves updating both the server and client environment and can be a complex task.

Do it!

C-8: Troubleshooting a network problem relating to adding or removing services

Questions and answers

Scenario: Creative Snafus Corp. has seen large growth in the past year. As a result, many new employees have been hired and the number of workstations connected to the network has increased accordingly. Prior to this growth, IP addresses had been assigned manually at the Windows 2000 and Windows XP workstations in the network. Recently, DHCP was added and configured in the network to ease the administrative burden of managing workstation IP addresses. Shortly thereafter, another new employee was hired and a workstation added to the network for him by one of the 1st tier network support people. On his first day, the new employee calls to state that, upon booting his machine, he received a message that an IP address conflict exists and that the local interface has been disabled. Although he's able to access the local workstation, he can't access the network or any network resources.

1 What's the first step in troubleshooting this scenario?

2 You find that an IP address was assigned manually. What do you do next?

3 After changing the setting, what do you do?

4 He's able to do so. What is the next step you take?

5 After correcting the issue, what do you do?

Unit summary: Troubleshooting

Topic A   In this topic, you learned about the human aspects of **troubleshooting** and the importance of **prioritizing problems**. You learned that, if multiple, unrelated problems occur simultaneously on the network, you should address the problem that affects the maximum number of users first.

Topic B   In this topic, you learned about the general procedures followed, which gives you a systematic approach towards troubleshooting network problems. The steps that you learned are identifying the **symptoms** and **exact issue,** identifying the **area affected** by the problem, identifying what **changes** have been made, **isolating the cause,** **formulating** an action plan and **implementing** the solution, **testing the results,** identifying the solution's **results and effects**, and **documenting** the problem, the solution, and the process you followed to arrive at the solution.

Topic C   In this topic, you learned how to **troubleshoot** various **common problems** that might occur on the network. You also learned how to troubleshoot a few scenarios related to **connectivity issues, file and system rights issues, resource access issues,** and **network services issues.**

Review questions

1   What's the most valuable tool in the troubleshooter's toolkit?

2   List the steps in a generic troubleshooting procedure.

Note: Form teams and discuss the following questions. There are no definite answers for these questions.

3 On a Windows Server 2003 peer-to-peer network, Sally has shared the printer on her system and called it MyPrinter. John is attempting to access it but reports he can't see her computer when viewing the Microsoft Windows Network in My Network Places. List the steps to resolve the problem.

4 On an IP network that's connected to the Internet through a router providing network address translation, Jim reports that he can't browse the Internet. List the steps to resolve the problem.

Appendix A
Installing NetWare 6.5

This appendix covers this additional topic:

A A basic NetWare server installation.

Topic A: Basic NetWare Server installation

Explanation

Following are the instructions for a generic default NetWare 6.5 server installation. The installation steps below are basic and are in no way optimized for performance on a production network.

System requirements

The system requirements for NetWare 6.5 are as follows:

- Pentium II or AMD K7 processor
- 512 MB RAM or more
- SVGA display adapter
- 200 MB or larger DOS partition with 200 MB free space available
- 2 GB of available, unpartitioned space in addition to the DOS partition
- CD drive
- NIC

Installation options

NetWare 6.5 can be installed directly from a local CD drive, a CD mounted on an existing file server as a NetWare volume, or from a copy of the CD files that's been uploaded to an existing file server.

The instructions here assume that you're installing from a local, bootable ISO 9660 CD drive that's compatible with the El Torito standard.

NetWare 6.5 default installation

These instructions assume that you've created the 200-MB (or larger) bootable DOS partition and that you have access to the NetWare Operating System CD and the NetWare Products CD.

Note: It's important to watch the keystroke options and prompts displayed at the bottom of the installation utility screen during the non-GUI portion of the installation. Knowing when to press Esc or F10, and so on might not always be clear.

Installation Procedure

1 Insert the Operating System CD into the CD drive and reboot the computer.

2 If prompted, enter I to install a new server.

3 If prompted, enter A three times to auto-detect CD-ROM drivers, restore the floppy drive letter to A, and auto-execute Install.bat.

4 Choose Select This Line To Install English.

5 Review the regional settings and, if they're correct, choose Continue. If you need to make changes, choose Modify and make the necessary changes.

6 Press Page Down to read through the license agreement.

7 Press F10 to accept the license agreement.

8 Verify that Default is selected as the installation type and choose Continue.

9 Choose Continue.

10 If prompted, choose Yes to continue installing the new server. The first file copy starts.

11 After the NetWare GUI starts, select Basic NetWare File Server and click Next.

12 Click Copy Files to start the second file copy.

13 When prompted, insert the NetWare 6.5 Products CD (CD 2) and click OK. The process of copying files may take a while to complete.

14 When prompted, enter a name for the server.

15 Place the license disk into the floppy drive and click Next.

16 In the Protocols dialog box, select the Protocols you want to install. You can choose from IP and IPX. For this installation, we'll select only IP.

17 After selecting IP, a message informs you that the server is being accessed. This process may take a while.

18 When the installation returns to the Protocols dialog box, enter the IP address and Subnet mask in the respective fields and click Next.

19 In the Domain Name Service dialog box, enter a host and domain name. The host name should be the name of a DNS server in the network.

20 In the Name Server 1 field, enter the IP address of the first DNS server. If the server you're installing is a DNS server and is supposed to be the first DNS server queried, enter its IP address in this field. If additional DNS servers are available, enter their respective IP addresses in the Name Server 2 and Name Server 3 text boxes. It's ok if you don't yet have DNS installed and configured in your network; the installation won't fail because of this. However, you won't be able to use services that rely on DNS until you do configure it. If you do have DNS installed and configured, select Verify the DNS information to have the installation verify that the server can communicate with the DNS server you specified.

21 If prompted, click OK to continue.

22 In the Time Zone dialog box, select the correct time zone and then make sure that the default setting for the option Allow system to adjust for Daylight Saving Time is set to your preference. Whether this option is checked or unchecked after you make a time zone selection depends on the time zone you select.

23 Click Next to continue.

24 In the eDriectory Installation dialog box, select Create a new eDirectory tree and click Next.

25 Enter the tree name and context for the server object into their respective fields. Press Tab to auto-populate the Admin Context field. In theory, you can change the admin user name. However, it's recommended to leave it at the default, admin.

26 Enter a password for the admin user in the Password field and reenter the password in the Retype Password field.

27 Click Next to continue.

28 In the eDirectory Summary field, verify the eDirectory information and click Next.

29 When the Licenses dialog box appears, insert the license disk. Then, use the Browse button to browse to and select the appropriate license(s). When the license(s) display(s) in the License(s) to be installed field, click Next. Should you run into a problem installing licenses at this point, remove the licenses, check Install without licenses, and click Next. In this case, after the installation is done, you can use iManager to install the license(s).

30 In the Novell Modular Authentication Services (NMAS) dialog box, click Next to use NDS as the NMAS Login Method. The final configuration and installation process starts. This process might take a while to complete.

31 When prompted, remove disks and CDs from all drives and click Yes to reset/restart the server. When the server is finished rebooting, the installation is complete.

Appendix B

Installing Windows Server 2003

This appendix covers this additional topic:

A Installing Windows Server 2003.

Topic A: Installing Windows Server 2003

Explanation

The following steps walk you through installing Windows Server 2003 as a primary domain controller. This is a basic guideline, and steps might vary based on your computer hardware. Familiarize yourself with the hardware configuration of your system, such as your network adapter settings, before you start.

These instructions assume that you'll install Windows Server 2003 Standard Edition by booting from the Windows Server 2003 CD-ROM. These instructions also assume that Windows Server 2003 will be the only operating system installed on the machine (not a dual-boot setup).

It's strongly suggested that your server be attached to a training network rather than a production network to avoid any chance of interrupting normal operations. If it's necessary to attach to a production network, you should review this exercise carefully with your Network Administrator before proceeding.

1 Boot your system from the Windows Server 2003 CD.

2 When prompted, press any key to boot from the CD ROM.

3 When prompted, press Enter to set up Windows Server 2003 Standard Edition now.

4 When the Licensing Agreement displays, read the agreement, pressing Page Down to move from page to page until you reach the end of the agreement, then press F8 to accept the agreement.

5 If available and unformatted, select drive C: as your destination partition and press Enter. If you have one or more previously formatted partitions, for each partition, select it, press D, press Enter, and then press L to delete the partition. When all partitions have been deleted, you have only unpartitioned space. If you have only unpartitioned space, press Enter to begin installing Windows Server 2003.

6 Press Enter to format the partition using the NTFS file system. Once the formatting is complete, installation files are copied to the computer. This process may take a while to complete. Note that, at some point during this process, the computer will also reboot.

7 Verify the regional settings that display. If the defaults don't apply to your situation, click Customize to change the settings. Click Next to continue.

8 Type in your Name and Organization and click Next.

9 Type in the CD key for your copy of Windows Server 2003, then click Next.

10 Leave the licensing settings at their defaults and click Next.

11 Type in CLASS as your computer name and type in and confirm a password for the Administrator account, then click Next.

Note: If connecting to an existing network, ask your Network Administrator for a unique machine name.

12 Specify the appropriate date and time, as well as time zone, and then click Next. Wait for the network installation process to complete.

13 Leave Typical Settings selected and click Next.

14 Leave the settings for Workgroup or Computer Domain at their defaults and click Next. Wait for the file copy to complete.

15 After the machine reboots, press CTRL+ALT+DEL, enter the Administrator password, and click OK.

16 In the Manage Your Server window, click Add or remove a role.

17 In the Preliminary Steps dialog box, read the informational text and click Next.

18 Wait while the Configure Your Server Wizard detects settings.

19 In the Configuration Options dialog box, select Typical configuration for a first server and click Next.

20 In the Active Directory domain name text box, enter ENTSS.local (or a domain name of your choice) for the new Active Directory domain and click Next.

21 In the NetBIOS Name dialog box, leave the defaults in place and click Next.

22 In the Forwarding DNS Queries dialog box, select No, do not forward queries and click Next.

23 In the Summary of Selections dialog box, review your selections and if satisfied, click Next. To make changes, click Back to step backwards through the configuration process.

24 In the Configure Your Server Wizard dialog box, click OK to acknowledge that the computer will be restarted during the configuration process and that you should close any open programs.

25 The Configure Your Server Wizard now installs and configures the selected services. Note that this process may take a while to complete.

26 After the machine reboots, press CTRL+ALT+DEL, enter the Administrator password and click OK.

27 In the Server Configuration Progress dialog box, review the actions that were performed and click Next.

28 In the This Server is Now Configured dialog box, click Finish.

29 In the Manage Your Server dialog box, check Don't display this page at logon and then Close the Manage Your Server dialog box.

30 Choose Start, Control Panel, Network Connections. Now, right-click Local Area Connection and choose Properties.

31 Select Internet Protocol (TCP/IP) and click Properties.

32 Check the IP address that's been assigned. If it's incorrect, change the IP address to match your environment. If you're in a test environment, type 200.200.200.201 for IP address and 255.255.255.0 for Subnet mask.

33 Click OK twice.

Appendix C
Certification exam objectives map

This appendix provides the following information:

A CompTIA Network+ 2005 exam objectives with references to corresponding coverage in Course ILT courseware.

Topic A: Comprehensive exam objectives

Explanation

The following table lists the CompTIA Network+ 2005 exam objectives and indicates where each objective is covered in conceptual explanations, activities, or both.

Objective	Conceptual information	Supporting activities
1.1 Recognize the following logical or physical network topologies given a diagram, schematic or description:		
Star	Unit 1, Topic C	C-1
Bus	Unit 1, Topic C	C-1
Mesh	Unit 1, Topic C	C-1
Ring	Unit 1, Topic C	C-1
1.2 Specify the main features of 802.2 (Logical Link Control), 802.3 (Ethernet), 802.5 (token ring), 802.11 (wireless), and FDDI (Fiber Distributed Data Interface) networking technologies, including:		
Speed	Unit 4, Topic A Unit 4, Topic B	
Access method (CSMA / CA (Carrier Sense Multiple Access/Collision Avoidance) and CSMA / CD (Carrier Sense Multiple Access / Collision Detection))	Unit 4, Topic A Unit 4, Topic B	B-1
Topology	Unit 1, Topic C Unit 4, Topic A Unit 4, Topic B	B-1, B-2
Media	Unit 4, Topic A Unit 4, Topic B	B-2
1.3 Specify the characteristics (For example: speed, length, topology, and cable type) of the following cable standards:		
10BASE-T and 10BASE-FL	Unit 4, Topic B	
100BASE-TX and 100BASE-FX	Unit 4, Topic B	
1000BASE-TX, 1000BASE-CX, 1000BASE-SX and 1000BASE-LX	Unit 4, Topic B	
10GBASE-SR, 10GBASE-LR and 10GBASE-ER	Unit 4, Topic B	

Objective	Conceptual information	Supporting activities
1.4 Recognize the following media connectors and describe their uses:		
RJ-11 (Registered Jack)	Unit 5, Topic B	
RJ-45 (Registered Jack)	Unit 5, Topic B	B-2
F-Type	Unit 5, Topic C	C-1
ST (Straight Tip)	Unit 5, Topic C	
SC (Standard Connector)	Unit 5, Topic C	
IEEE1394 (FireWire)	Unit 3, Topic A Unit 5, Topic B	B-3
LC (Local Connector)	Unit 5, Topic C	C-2
MTRJ (Mechanical Transfer Registered Jack)	Unit 5, Topic C	C-2
1.5 Recognize the following media types and describe their uses:		
Category 3, 5, 5e, and 6	Unit 5, Topic B	B-1
UTP (Unshielded Twisted Pair)	Unit 5, Topic B	B-1
STP (Shielded Twisted Pair)	Unit 5, Topic B	B-1
Coaxial cable	Unit 5, Topic C	C-2
SMF (Single Mode Fiber) optic cable	Unit 5, Topic C	C-2
MMF (Multimode Fiber) optic cable	Unit 5, Topic C	C-2
1.6 Identify the purposes, features and functions of the following network components:		
Hubs	Unit 5, Topic D	D-1
Switches	Unit 6, Topic B	B-1
Bridges	Unit 6, Topic B	B-1
Routers	Unit 6, Topic B	B-2
Gateways	Unit 4, Topic C	C-1
CSU / DSU (Channel Service Unit / Data Service Unit)	Unit 7, Topic D	
NICs (Network Interface Card)	Unit 3, Topic A	

Objective 1.6 continues on following page…

Objective		Conceptual information	Supporting activities
1.6	(continued) Identify the purposes, features and functions of the following network components:		
	ISDN (Integrated Services Digital Network) adapters	Unit 7, Topic A	A-1
	WAPs (Wireless Access Point)	Unit 4, Topic B	B-3
	Modems	Unit 7, Topic B	B-1
	Transceivers (media converters)	Unit 5, Topic D	D-2
	Firewalls	Unit 12, Topic A	A-1
1.7	Specify the general characteristics (For example: carrier speed, frequency, transmission type and topology) of the following wireless technologies:		
	802.11 (Frequency hopping spread spectrum)	Unit 4, Topic B	
	802.11x (Direct sequence spread spectrum)	Unit 4, Topic B	B-3
	Infrared	Unit 4, Topic B	
	Bluetooth	Unit 4, Topic B	B-3
1.8	Identify factors which affect the range and speed of wireless service. For example:		
	Interference	Unit 4, Topic B	
	Antenna type	Unit 4, Topic B	
	Environmental factors	Unit 4, Topic B	
2.1	Identify a MAC (Media Access Control) address and its parts.	Unit 3, Topic A Unit 6, Topic A	A-1
2.2	Identify the seven layers of the OSI (Open Systems Interconnect) model and their functions.	Unit 2, Topic A	A-1, A-2
2.3	Identify the OSI (Open Systems Interconnect) layers at which the following network components operate:		
	Hubs	Unit 5, Topic D	
	Switches	Unit 6, Topic B	
	Bridges	Unit 6, Topic B	B-1
	Routers	Unit 6, Topic B	B-2
	NICs (Network Interface Card)	Unit 3, Topic A	
	WAPs (Wireless Access Point)	Unit 4, Topic B	

Objective		Conceptual information	Supporting activities
2.4	Differentiate between the following network protocols in terms of routing, addressing schemes, interoperability and naming conventions:		
	IPX / SPX (Internetwork Packet Exchange / Sequence Packet Exchange)	Unit 4, Topic C	C-1
	NetBEUI (Network Basic Input / Output System Extended User Interface)	Unit 4, Topic C	C-1
	AppleTalk / AppleTalk over IP (Internet Protocol)	Unit 4, Topic C	C-1
	TCP / IP (Transmission Control Protocol / Internet Protocol)	Unit 4, Topic C Unit 9, Topic B Unit 10, Topic A Unit 10, Topic B	 A-1, A-2, A-3 B-1, B-2
2.5	Identify the components and structure of IP (Internet Protocol) addresses (IPv4, IPv6) and the required setting for connections across the Internet.	Unit 10, Topic A	A-2, A-3
2.6	Identify classful IP (Internet Protocol) ranges and their subnet masks (For example: Class A, B and C).	Unit 10, Topic A Unit 10, Topic B	A-2 B-1
2.7	Identify the purpose of subnetting.	Unit 10 Topic B	B-1
2.8	Identify the differences between private and public network addressing schemes.	Unit 10, Topic A Unit 10, Topic B	A-3 B-2
2.9	Identify and differentiate between the following IP (Internet Protocol) addressing methods:		
	Static	Unit 10, Topic A	A-3
	Dynamic	Unit 10, Topic A	A-3
	Self-assigned (APIPA (Automatic Private Internet Protocol Addressing))	Unit 10, Topic A	A-3
2.10	Define the purpose, function and use of the following protocols used in the TCP / IP (Transmission Control Protocol / Internet Protocol) suite:		
	TCP (Transmission Control Protocol)	Unit 4, Topic C Unit 9, Topic B	 B-2
	UDP (User Datagram Protocol)	Unit 4, Topic C Unit 9, Topic B	 B-2
	FTP (File Transfer Protocol)	Unit 13, Topic C Unit 9, Topic B	C-1 B-2
	SFTP (Secure File Transfer Protocol)	Unit 9, Topic B	B-2
	TFTP (Trivial File Transfer Protocol)	Unit 9, Topic B	B-2

Objective 2.10 continues on following page…

Objective		Conceptual information	Supporting activities
2.10	(continued) Define the purpose, function and use of the following protocols used in the TCP / IP (Transmission Control Protocol / Internet Protocol) suite:		
	SMTP (Simple Mail Transfer Protocol) HTTP (Hypertext Transfer Protocol)	Unit 9, Topic B	B-2
	HTTPS (Hypertext Transfer Protocol Secure)	Unit 9, Topic B	B-2
	POP3 / IMAP4 (Post Office Protocol version 3 / Internet Message Access Protocol version 4)	Unit 9, Topic B	B-2
	Telnet	Unit 9, Topic B Unit 13, Topic B	B-1 B-1
	SSH (Secure Shell)	Unit 9, Topic B	B-1
	ICMP (Internet Control Message Protocol)	Unit 9, Topic B	B-1
	ARP / RARP (Address Resolution Protocol / Reverse Address Resolution Protocol)	Unit 9, Topic B	B-1
	NTP (Network Time Protocol)	Unit 9, Topic B	B-1
	NNTP (Network News Transport Protocol)	Unit 9, Topic B	B-1
	SCP (Secure Copy Protocol)	Unit 9, Topic B	B-1
	LDAP (Lightweight Directory Access Protocol)	Unit 9, Topic B	B-1
	IGMP (Internet Group Multicast Protocol)	Unit 9, Topic B	B-1
	LPR (Line Printer Remote)	Unit 9, Topic B	B-1
2.11	Define the function of TCP / UDP (Transmission Control Protocol / User Datagram Protocol) ports.	Unit 9, Topic B	B-3
2.12	Identify the well-known ports associated with the following commonly used services and protocols:		
	20 FTP (File Transfer Protocol)	Unit 9, Topic B	B-2
	21 FTP (File Transfer Protocol)	Unit 9, Topic B	B-2
	22 SSH (Secure Shell)	Unit 9, Topic B	B-2
	23 Telnet	Unit 9, Topic B	B-2
	25 SMTP (Simple Mail Transfer Protocol)	Unit 9, Topic B	B-2
	53 DNS (Domain Name Server)	Unit 9, Topic B	B-2
	69 TFTP (Trivial File Transfer Protocol)	Unit 9, Topic B	B-2
	80 HTTP (Hypertext Transfer Protocol)	Unit 9, Topic B	B-2
	110 POP3 (Post Office Protocol version 3)	Unit 9, Topic B	B-2

Objective		Conceptual information	Supporting activities
2.12	(continued) Identify the well-known ports associated with the following commonly used services and protocols:		
	119 NNTP (Network News Transport Protocol)	Unit 9, Topic B	B-2
	123 NTP (Network Time Protocol)	Unit 9, Topic B	B-2
	143 IMAP4 (Internet Message Access Protocol version 4)	Unit 9, Topic B	B-2
	443 HTTPS (Hypertext Transfer Protocol Secure)	Unit 9, Topic B	B-2
2.13	Identify the purpose of network services and protocols (For example:		
	DNS (Domain Name Service)	Unit 11, Topic A	A-2
	NAT (Network Address Translation)	Unit 10, Topic B Unit 12, Topic B	B-2 B-1
	ICS (Internet Connection Sharing)	Unit 7, Topic C	
	WINS (Windows Internet Name Service)	Unit 11, Topic B	B-2
	SNMP (Simple Network Management Protocol)	Unit 9, Topic B	B-2
	NFS (Network File System)	Unit 10, Topic B	B-2
	Zeroconf (Zero configuration)	Unit 9, Topic B	B-2
	SMB (Server Message Block)	Unit 4, Topic C Unit 15, Topic A	
	AFP (Apple File Protocol)	Unit 4, Topic C	
	LPD (Line Printer Daemon)	Unit 9, Topic B	
2.14	Identify the basic characteristics (For example: speed, capacity and media) of the following WAN (Wide Area Networks) technologies:		
	Packet switching	Unit 1, Topic A Unit 7, Topic D	D-1
	Circuit switching	Unit 7, Topic D	
	ISDN (Integrated Services Digital Network)	Unit 7, Topic A	A-1
	FDDI (Fiber Distributed Data Interface)	Unit 4, Topic B	
	T1 (T Carrier level 1) / E1 / J1	Unit 7, Topic D	D-1
	T3 (T Carrier level 3) / E3 / J3	Unit 7, Topic D	D-1
	OCx (Optical Carrier)	Unit 7, Topic D	D-1
	X.25	Unit 7, Topic D	D-1

Objective		Conceptual information	Supporting activities
2.15	Identify the basic characteristics of the following internet access technologies:		
	xDSL (Digital Subscriber Line)	Unit 7, Topic A	A-2
	Broadband Cable (Cable modem)	Unit 7, Topic A	A-2
	POTS / PSTN (Plain Old Telephone Service / Public Switched Telephone Network)	Unit 7, Topic A	A-1
	Satellite	Unit 7, Topic A	A-2
	Wireless	Unit 7, Topic A	A-2
2.16	Define the function of the following remote access protocols and services:		
	RAS (Remote Access Service)	Unit 7, Topic C	C-1
	PPP (Point-to-Point Protocol)	Unit 4, Topic D Unit 7, Topic C	D-1
	SLIP (Serial Line Internet Protocol)	Unit 4, Topic D Unit 7, Topic C	D-1
	PPPoE (Point-to-Point Protocol over Ethernet)	Unit 4, Topic D	D-1
	PPTP (Point-to-Point Tunneling Protocol)	Unit 4, Topic D	D-1
	VPN (Virtual Private Network)	Unit 7, Topic C	C-1
	RDP (Remote Desktop Protocol)	Unit 4, Topic D	D-1
2.17	Identify the following security protocols and describe their purpose and function:		
	IPSec (Internet Protocol Security)	Unit 4, Topic E	E-1
	L2TP (Layer 2 Tunneling Protocol)	Unit 4, Topic E	E-1
	SSL (Secure Sockets Layer)	Unit 4, Topic E	E-1
	WEP (Wired Equivalent Privacy)	Unit 4, Topic E	E-1
	WPA (Wi-Fi Protected Access)	Unit 4, Topic E	E-1
	802.1x	Unit 4, Topic E	E-1

Objective		Conceptual information	Supporting activities
2.18	Identify authentication protocols		
	CHAP (Challenge Handshake Authentication Protocol)	Unit 7, Topic C	
	MS-CHAP (Microsoft Challenge Handshake Authentication Protocol)	Unit 7, Topic C	
	PAP (Password Authentication Protocol)	Unit 7, Topic C	
	RADIUS (Remote Authentication Dial-In User Service)	Unit 7, Topic C	
	Kerberos	Unit 17, Topic A	
	EAP (Extensible Authentication Protocol)	Unit 7, Topic C	
3.1	Identify the basic capabilities (For example: client support, interoperability, authentication, file and print services, application support and security) of the following server operating systems to access network resources:		
	UNIX / Linux / Mac OS X Server	Unit 14, Topic C	C-1
	Netware	Unit 14, Topic B Unit 16, Topic F Unit 19, Topic A Unit 19, Topic B Unit 19, Topic C Unit 19, Topic D Unit 19, Topic E Unit 19, Topic F	B-1 F-1 A-1 B-1, B-2 C-1 D-1 E-1, E-2 F-1, F-2, F-3, F-4
	Windows	Unit 14, Topic A Unit 16, Topic A Unit 16, Topic B Unit 16, Topic C Unit 16, Topic D Unit 16, Topic E Unit 17, Topic A Unit 17, Topic B Unit 17, Topic C Unit 17, Topic D Unit 17, Topic E	A-1, A-2, A-3 A-1 B-1 C-1, C-2, C-3, C-4 D-1, D-2 E-1, E-2 A-1, A-2, A-3 B-1, B-2 C-1, C-2 D-1 E-1, E-2
	Appleshare IP (Internet Protocol)	Unit 14, Topic D	D-1
3.2	Identify the basic capabilities needed for client workstations to connect to and use network resources (For example: media, network protocols and peer and server services).	Unit 1, Topic A Unit 15, Topic A Unit 1, Topic B	A-2 A-1, A-2 B-1, B-2
3.3	Identify the appropriate tool for a given wiring task (For example: wire crimper, media tester / certifier, punch down tool or tone generator).	Unit 5, Topic B Unit 8, Topic B	B-2 B-1

Objective		Conceptual information	Supporting activities
3.4	Given a remote connectivity scenario comprised of a protocol, an authentication scheme, and physical connectivity, configure the connection. Includes connection to the following servers:		
	UNIX / Linux / MAC OS X Server	Unit 14, Topic C Unit 15, Topic A	A-2
	Netware	Unit 14, Topic B Unit 15, Topic A	A-2
	Windows	Unit 7, Topic C Unit 14, Topic A Unit 15, Topic A	C-2 A-2
	Appleshare IP (Internet Protocol)	Unit 14, Topic D Unit 15, Topic A	A-2
3.5	Identify the purpose, benefits and characteristics of using a firewall.	Unit 12, Topic A	A-1
3.6	Identify the purpose, benefits and characteristics of using a proxy service.	Unit 12, Topic B	B-1
3.7	Given a connectivity scenario, determine the impact on network functionality of a particular security implementation (For example:		
	Port blocking / filtering	Unit 10, Topic C	
	Authentication and encryption	Unit 4, Topic E Unit 7, Topic C Unit 16, Topic A Unit 16, Topic B Unit 17, Topic A Unit 19, Topic C	E-1 C-1, C-2
3.8	Identify the main characteristics of VLANs (Virtual Local Area Networks).	Unit 6, Topic B	
3.9	Identify the main characteristics and purpose of extranets and intranets.	Unit 10, Topic B Unit 12, Topic A	B-2
3.10	Identify the purpose, benefits and characteristics of using antivirus software.	Unit 21, Topic B	B-1, B-2

Objective		Conceptual information	Supporting activities
3.11	Identify the purpose and characteristics of fault tolerance:		
	Power	Unit 20, Topic C	C-4
	Link redundancy	Unit 1, Topic C	C-1
	Storage	Unit 20, Topic A	A-1, A-2, A-3
		Unit 20, Topic B	
		Unit 20, Topic C	C-3
	Services	Unit 20, Topic A	A-1, A-2, A-3
		Unit 20, Topic B	B-1, B-2, B-3, B-4
3.12	Identify the purpose and characteristics of disaster recovery:		
	Backup / restore	Unit 20, Topic C	C-1, C-2
	Offsite storage	Unit 20, Topic C	C-3
	Hot and cold spares	Unit 20, Topic A	
		Unit 20, Topic C	
	Hot, warm and cold sites	Unit 20, Topic C	C-3
4.1	Given a troubleshooting scenario, select the appropriate network utility from the following:		
	Tracert / traceroute	Unit 13, Topic A	A-3
	Ping	Unit 13, Topic A	A-3
	Arp	Unit 13, Topic A	A-1
	Netstat	Unit 13, Topic A	A-2
	Nbtstat	Unit 13, Topic A	A-2
	Ipconfig / Ifconfig	Unit 13, Topic A	A-1, A-2
	Winipcfg	Unit 13, Topic A	A-1
	Nslookup / dig	Unit 13, Topic A	A-3
4.2	Given output from a network diagnostic utility (For example: those utilities listed in objective 4.1), identify the utility and interpret the output.	Unit 13, Topic A	A-1, A-2, A-3
4.3	Given a network scenario, interpret visual indicators (For example: link LEDs (Light Emitting Diode) and collision LEDs (Light Emitting Diode)) to determine the nature of a stated problem.	Unit 5, Topic D	D-1, D-2
		Unit 3, Topic B	B-1, B-2
		Unit 22, Topic C	C-4

Objective	Conceptual information	Supporting activities
4.4 Given a troubleshooting scenario involving a client accessing remote network services, identify the cause of the problem (For example: file services, print services, authentication failure, protocol configuration, physical connectivity and SOHO (Small Office / Home Office) router).	Unit 22, Topic C Unit 7, Topic A Unit 7, Topic B Unit 7, Topic C Unit 7, Topic D	C-5, C-6
4.5 Given a troubleshooting scenario between a client and the following server environments, identify the cause of a stated problem:		
UNIX / Linux / Mac OS X Server	Unit 14, Topic C Unit 22, Topic C	 C-7
Netware	Unit 14, Topic B Unit 16, Topic F Unit 19, Topic A Unit 19, Topic B Unit 19, Topic C Unit 19, Topic D Unit 19, Topic E Unit 19, Topic F	B-1 F-1 A-1 B-1, B-2 C-1 D-1 E-1, E-2 F-1, F-2, F-3, F-4
Windows	Unit 14, Topic A Unit 16, Topic A Unit 16, Topic B Unit 16, Topic C Unit 16, Topic D Unit 16, Topic E Unit 17, Topic A Unit 17, Topic B Unit 17, Topic C Unit 17, Topic D Unit 17, Topic E Unit 18, Topic A Unit 18, Topic B Unit 18, Topic C	A-1, A-2, A-3 A-1 B-1 C-1, C-2, C-3, C-4 D-1, D-2 E-1, E-2 A-1, A-2, A-3 B-1, B-2 C-1, C-2 D-1 E-1, E-2 A-1, A-2, A-3 B-1 C-1
Appleshare IP (Internet Protocol)	Unit 14, Topic D	
4.6 Given a scenario, determine the impact of modifying, adding or removing network services for network resources and users. (For example:		
DHCP (Dynamic Host Configuration Protocol)	Unit 10, Topic A Unit 22, Topic C	A-3 C-8
DNS (Domain Name Service)	Unit 10, Topic C Unit 11, Topic A Unit 22, Topic C	 A-2 C-8
WINS (Windows Internet Name Server)	Unit 10, Topic C Unit 11, Topic B Unit 22, Topic C	 B-2 C-8

Objective		Conceptual information	Supporting activities
4.7	Given a troubleshooting scenario involving a network with a particular physical topology (For example: bus, star, mesh or ring) and including a network diagram, identify the network area affected and the cause of the stated failure.	Unit 1, Topic C Unit 22, Topic C	
	Given a network troubleshooting scenario involving an infrastructure (For example: wired or wireless) problem, identify the cause of a stated problem (For example: bad media, interference, network hardware or environment).	Unit 8, Topic A Unit 8, Topic C Unit 22, Topic C	A-1, A-2 C-1, C-2, C-3, C-4
4.9	Given a network problem scenario, select an appropriate course of action based on a logical troubleshooting strategy. This strategy can include the following steps:		
	1 Identify the symptoms and potential causes	Unit 22, Topic B	B-1
	2 Identify the affected area	Unit 22, Topic B	B-1
	3 Establish what has changed	Unit 22, Topic B	B-1
	4 Select the most probable cause	Unit 22, Topic B	B-1
	5 Implement an action plan and solution including potential effects	Unit 22, Topic B	B-1
	6 Test the result	Unit 22, Topic B	B-1
	7 Identify the results and effects of the solution	Unit 22, Topic B	B-1
	8 Document the solution and process	Unit 22, Topic B	B-1

Course summary

This summary contains information to help you bring the course to a successful conclusion. Using this information, you'll be able to:

A Use the summary text to reinforce what you've learned in class.

B Determine the next courses in this series, if any, as well as any other resources that might help you to continue preparing for the CompTIA Network+ certification exam.

Topic A: Course summary

Use the following summary text to reinforce what you've learned in class.

Unit summaries

Unit 1

In this unit, you learned about the role of **network operating systems** and their **advantages** and **pitfalls**. You also learned about **servers** and that a **host** is a network device that has a **TCP/IP address**. You next learned about the various types of networks, such as **legacy**, **peer-to-peer**, and **client/server**. Then, you learned about the various properties and functions of various types of servers, including **fax servers, CD servers, e-mail servers, print servers,** and others. Next, you learned about the characteristics of various **topologies** used in LANs. You learned about **Bus**, **Ring**, **Star**, and **Mesh** topologies and their advantages and disadvantages. Finally, you learned about the importance of planning in network design. You also learned why planning should be an ongoing process.

Unit 2

In this unit, you learned about the **OSI Model**. You learned that the OSI Model acts as a common point of reference for discussing network devices and concepts. Next, you learned about the seven **layers** of the OSI Model: **physical**, **data link**, **network**, **transport**, **session**, **presentation**, and **application** layers.

Unit 3

In this unit, you learned about the properties of **Network Adapter Cards**. You learned about the criteria for the selection of a network adapter and the procedure to install a network adapter. You also learned about **MAC addresses** and **boot PROMs**. You learned about **network adapter configuration** that includes **jumpers**, **switches**, **software configuration**, and **Plug and Play network adapters**. You also learned how to **review and configure networking components** from within a Windows Server 2003 and Windows XP computer. You then learned about the role of network adapter drivers, including the **NDIS** and **ODI** specifications. Next, you learned about the methodology of troubleshooting network adapter problems. Next, you learned about the general troubleshooting tips and discussed the various scenarios that can help your troubleshooting procedures. You also learned about the importance of **diagnostic software** and **hardware** in troubleshooting.

Unit 4

In this unit, you learned about **protocols**. You learned that protocols are the language by which computers interact with each other. You also learned about **access protocols**. You learned that the **data link layer** specifies how devices attached to the network gain access to the network resources. You also compared the **MAC** and **LLC data link sublayers**. You next learned about the characteristics of an **Ethernet network** and a **Token Ring network**. You also identified the differences between popular channel access methods, such as **token passing**, **CSMA/CD**, and **CSMA/CA**. You also learned about the characteristics of **wireless networks** and their channel access methods. Then, you learned about **connectionless** and **connection-oriented protocols**. You learned that a protocol, which supports both connectionless and connection-oriented protocols would help you to have reliable communications with a minimum of overhead traffic. Then, you learned about **transport protocols**. You learned about the **NetBEUI, IPX/SPX , TCP/IP** and **AppleTalk** protocols. You also learned about **gateways**. Next, you learned about **serial protocols**, such as **Point-to-Point Protocol (PPP)** and **Serial Line Internet Protocol (SLIP)**. You also learned about **Point-to-Point Protocol over Ethernet (PPPoE), Point-to-Point Tunneling Protocol (PPTP)**, and **Remote Desktop Protocol (RDP)**. , Finally, you learned about **security protocols**, such as **Internet Protocol Security (IPSec), Layer 2 Tunneling Protocol (L2TP), Secure Sockets Layer (SSL), Wired Equivalent Privacy (WEP), Wi-Fi Protected Access (WPA), and 802.1x**

Unit 5

In this unit, you learned that, when more than one computer is talking on the same cable, there are some rules to be followed and how you are carried out by **broadband, baseband, half-duplex**, and **full-duplex** communication methods. You also learned about **UTP properties, UTP installation**, and **STP**. Then, you learned about **RJ-45**, which is an 8-pin modular plug that is primarily used to terminate UTP and STP cables for both **Ethernet** and **Token Ring** applications. You also learned about **RJ-11** and **RJ-14 twisted pair cable connectors**. Next, you learned about **IEEE 1394**, commonly known as **FireWire.** You also learned about **coaxial cables**, which are composed of two conductors that share the same axis where the center cable is insulated by plastic foam, a second conductor, foil wrap, and an external plastic tube. Then, you learned about **BNC cable connectors**. You also learned about the properties of fiber optic cables, their advantages and disadvantages, and the types of fiber optic cables and connectors. Finally, you learned about the various **Ethernet devices**, such as **passive hubs, active hubs, switching hubs**, and **intelligent hubs** and the various **Token Ring devices**. You learned about the role of **Multistation Access Unit (MSAU)** that helps Token Ring networks to work as a ring. You also learned about the various miscellaneous devices, such as **network patch panels** and **transceivers.**

Unit 6

In this unit, you learned about the various types of **internetworking devices** and about **segments** and **backbones**. You also learned about the role of the **MAC address** in internetworking. You then learned about **repeaters** and their role in internetworking. You also learned that **internetworking** is the technology by which computers communicate across various types of networks. Next, you learned about the functions and types of bridges and switches. You also learned that bridges read the **specific physical address** of a device on one network and **filter information** before passing it on to another network segment. You then learned about **routers**, features of a router, and **brouters**. Further, you compared a bridge with a router and learned that a router opens the **MAC (Media Access Control) layer envelope** and then uses it to make **routing decisions**. You also learned about **routing tables** and the various types of routers. You learned that routers can be **static** or **dynamic**. Finally, you learned how to describe various **routing protocols** and how to configure routing on a Windows 2000/Server 2003 server.

Unit 7

In this unit, you learned that **remote connectivity** means establishing a local connection to the network from a **remote site**. You learned that a **modem** provides connection over a standard phone line and that **Integrated Services Digital Network (ISDN)** provides a moderate-speed connection between stationary remote sites. You also learned that **POTS** stands for Plain Old Telephone Service and is the standard telephone service you subscribe to for making **voice calls**. You learned about the properties, hardware, interfaces, and provisioning related to ISDN. Further, you learned about other remote access options, including **cable modem** access, **xDSL**, **satellite**, and **wireless.** You also learned how to install and configure a modem to be used by a remote access client or a remote access server. Next, you learned how to configure general and specific modem settings. You also learned about the Windows 2000/Server 2003 **Routing and Remote Access Service (RRAS).** You learned that you can configure Windows 2000/Server 2003 as a **dial-in or VPN server**, among others. You then learned that to configure a Windows 2000/Server 2003/XP **remote access client**, you must create a **dial-up connection** using the **New Connection Wizard** in **Network Connections**. You learned that users can create dial-up connections to remote servers, such as ISPs or perhaps a server on a network at work. You also learned that, through a dial-up connection, mobile users have the opportunity to work as if they were connected directly to the remote network. Next, you learned how to create and configure a dial-up connection and how to connect to a remote server. You also learned that the most common **T-carrier** lines are **T1** and **T3**, which have transfer rates of 1.544 Mbps and 44.736 Mbps, respectively. You also learned that a **CSU/DSU** connects a T1 line to a LAN. You learned that **SONET** is the American implementation of **SDH**, and both are a fiber optic standard with very high bandwidth. Finally, you learned about **X.25 packet switched** networks and you also learned about **circuit-switched** networks.

Unit 8

In this unit, you learned about various **environmental factors** that affect the performance, reliability, and longevity of networks. You learned that resolving a network difficulty depends on **troubleshooting, isolating**, and **eliminating** a problem. You also discussed **error messages** and **scenarios** pertaining to physical and logical causes of network trouble. Next, you learned about tools that are used for troubleshooting network problems. You learned that a **crossover cable** refers to a length of network cable that has been wired to provide a connection from one hub to another, or from one network interface card to another. You also learned that a **tone generator** is a device that emits an audible tone to test primarily for continuity and that a **time domain reflectometer** is a sophisticated tool used to find a break in the middle of a cable. Then, you learned that **problem solving** is a process of logically evaluating the symptoms, analyzing possible solutions, and eliminating improbable factors until a resolution is reached. You also looked at **DIReCtional troubleshooting model**. Finally, you learned that documentation forms an essential part of your system troubleshooting and also about various troubleshooting tools.

Unit 9

In this unit, you learned about the history of **TCP/IP** and about **RFCs**, the **Internet**, and **supported systems**. You learned that TCP/IP is the current de facto standard for internetwork communications. Next, you learned about **TCP/IP** and **OSI**. You also learned about the **TCP/IP suite** and **ports and sockets**. Finally, you learned that TCP/IP provides utilities to facilitate communications and information sharing between dissimilar hardware platforms.

Unit 10

In this unit, you learned about **IP addresses**. You also learned how to convert binary to decimal and decimal to binary. You learned that five address classes are supported by TCP/IP: Classes A, B, C, D, and E. You also learned about the concept of **Dynamic Host Configuration Protocol (DHCP)**. Then, you learned how a DHCP server reduces the amount of administration necessary on a TCP/IP-based network. Next, you learned about the role of **subnets** and you learned how **subnetting** works. You also learned about **special addressing** and **private networks**. Then, you learned how to **use TCP/IP**. You learned about the procedures necessary to **configure TCP/IP protocol support** on a Windows Server 2003 and Windows XP computer.

Unit 11

In this unit, you learned about **HOSTS files**. You also learned about **HOST name resolution**. You learned about the **Domain Name System (DNS)**. You also learned that DNS is an alternative to using HOSTS files for name resolution. Then you learned about **DNS domains, DNS name resolution**, and **DNS client configuration**. Next, you learned about **NETBIOS**. You learned that NETBIOS is an application layer (OSI Model Session layer) interface between the network operating system and lower-level functions. You also learned about the role of NETBIOS, the NETBIOS names, and the **name resolution methods**. Then you learned about the **LMHOSTS file**. You also learned about **LMHOSTS keywords** and **LMHOSTS configuration**. Finally, you learned about **WINS** and **WINS client configuration**

Unit 12

In this unit, you learned about **firewalls**. You learned that a firewall is a mechanism for controlling access between networks. You also learned about **packet filters**, **bastion hosts**, and **packet filtering.** Next, you learned about **proxies**, which are another type of firewall. You also learned about **Winsock proxy**, **Web proxy**, and **SOCKS proxy**. Finally, you learned that **Network Address Translation** is a feature implemented on many routers that provide Internet access.

Unit 13

In this unit, you learned about several **TCP/IP troubleshooting tools**, including **ARP, HOSTNAME, IPCONFIG, WINIPCFG, IFCONFIG, NBTSTAT, NETSTAT, NSLOOKUP, DIG, PING, TRACERT**, and **ROUTE**. Next, you learned about **Telnet utility**. You learned that Telnet provides access, through terminal emulation, to any host running a Telnet daemon service. You also learned about using Telnet and troubleshooting with Telnet. Then, you learned about the **File Transfer Protocol (FTP) utility**. You also learned **FTP commands**. You learned that FTP can be used interactively at the command prompt or in a script (batch) file. Also FTP supports a wide range of commands. Finally, you saw various troubleshooting examples.

Unit 14

In this unit, you learned about the **Windows** family of server operating systems. You learned that **Windows NT, Windows 2000 and Windows Server 2003** are different versions of the Windows server operating system. You also learned about the features and functionalities of each version. Next, you learned about **Novell NetWare** and its features. You learned that NetWare 5.x and NetWare 6.x provide features for improving performance, designed for both local and global networks. Then, you learned about **UNIX**. You also learned about the features and facts about UNIX. You then learned that **Linux** is a UNIX-like operating system. You also learned that the source code in Linux is freely available to all. Next, you learned about **Mac OS X Server**, the Unix-based network operating system from Apple Corp. You then learned about **AppleShare IP**. You learned that AppleShare IP can run over **TCP/IP** and **AppleTalk**. You learned that AppleShare IP provides support for **Mac OS** and **Windows** clients. Finally, you learned about the features and services available with AppleShare IP.

Unit 15

In this unit, you learned about **network clients.** You learned that network clients provide the connectivity between the server and the individual workstations in any client/server network configuration. Then you learned about the network clients that are available to **DOS, Windows 3.x, Windows for Workgroups 3.x, Windows 95, Windows 98, Windows NT Workstation, 2000 Professional and XP, Macintosh**, and **Novell NetWare** clients.

Unit 16

In this unit, you learned about general Windows networking concepts, including the concepts of **workgroups** and **domains**. You also learned about accessing domain resources. Next, you learned about **directory services** planning and implementation. You learned what a directory service is, and how to plan, implement, manage and maintain an **infrastructure**, user, computer and group strategies and **group policy.** Then, you learned about **Active Directory (AD)**. You learned about Active Directory **objects** and the Active Directory **schema**. Next, you learned about the **logical structure** and **components** of Active Directory. You then learned about the **global catalog** and about **naming standards** and the **physical structure** of Active Directory. You also learned how to **install** Active Directory on a Windows Server 2003 server. Next, you learned about the **new** Active Directory **features** in **Windows Server 2003**. You learned about new features in the areas of deployment, management, performance and dependability. You also learned about the functions of **Windows NT Directory Services**, including the role of **Windows NT domains**. Then, you learned about the purpose and function of Windows NT Directory Services, **domains, logical configuration of single domain, master domain, multiple master domain**, and **complete trust.** Next, you learned how to identify the differences between the **Novell bindery files** and **Novell Directory Services/eDirectory**. You learned that older versions of NetWare used bindery files to store information about network users and groups while the newer versions of NetWare use the Novell Directory Services (NDS/eDirectory) to manage network objects. Finally, you learned about the purpose of **Novell Directory Services/eDirectory**, the significance of **NDS/eDirectory objects**, and **bindery emulation**.

Unit 17

In this unit, you learned that the primary tool used to create and manage user accounts is **Active Directory Users and Computers**. You also learned how to troubleshoot user account and **authentication** issues and the various settings and policies that can cause logons to fail. Next, you learned that the primary purpose of **groups** in a network environment is to ease the administrative burden associated with assigning rights and permissions with individual user accounts. You also learned that Windows 2000/Server 2003 supports two group types, known as **security groups** and **distribution groups**. You then learned that Windows 2000/Server 2003 supports three different **group scopes**: **global, domain local**, and **universal.** Next, you learned that Windows 2000/Server 2003 supports the **FAT, FAT32**, and **NTFS** file systems. Only the NTFS file system allows local security permissions to be configured. You also learned that Windows 2000/Server 2003 supports both standard and special **NTFS permissions**. Special NTFS permissions give an administrator a more granular level of control over how permissions are applied. You learned that NTFS permissions are cumulative. Then, you learned that, to create a shared folder, you should have the appropriate rights. The primary tools used to create shared folders are Windows Explorer, Computer Management, and the **NET SHARE** command-line utility. You also learned that printing in a Windows 2000/Server 2003 environment has its own unique terminology, an understanding of which is critical towards understanding how the printing system functions. Next, you learned that **printer publishing** allows users to query Active Directory for a list of available printers. Finally, you learned how to troubleshoot common printing problems.

Unit 18

In this unit, you learned that the **Task Manager** utility can be used to view and control running applications and processes, obtain basic performance information, view network utilization information, and view **connected users**. You also learned that the **Event Viewer** tool displays information, warning, and error events relating to the operating system and applications. Next, you learned that all Windows 2000/Server 2003 systems include **System**, **Security**, and **Application logs,** and that additional logs may also be present based on the role of the server. Then, you learned that **Performance console** is the primary server monitoring utility. It consists of two main tools, **System Monitor** and **Performance Logs and Alerts**. You learned that System Monitor is a performance-monitoring utility that displays data in a **graph**, **histogram**, or **report**. Finally, you learned that data could be collected for analysis using Performance Logs and Alerts.

Unit 19

In this unit, you learned that you use the **ConsoleOne** and **iManager** utilities to create and manage **User and Group objects**. You also learned how to create a User and Group object using ConsoleOne and iManager. Next, you learned about **file system rights** and **trustees** and **explicit trustee assignments**. You also learned about **Inherited Rights**, the **Inherited Rights Filter**, as well as **effective rights.** Then, you learned about **login restrictions**, **password restrictions**, and **address restrictions**. You also learned about **intruder detection.** Next, you learned about the **NDS/eDirectory naming conventions** and **context.** You also learned about **distinguished**, **relative**, **typeful** and **typeless** names. You also learned how to use **NetWare log files**, such as **SYS$LOG.ERR, VOL$LOG.ERR, ABEND.LOG,** and **CONSOLE.LOG.** You learned how to start **MONITOR.NLM** and view server statistics with the **MONITOR utility**. Next, you learned about **NetWare Remote Manager (NRM)** and how to check a server's health. Then, you learned about **volume repair**. You also learned how to use the **VREPAIR utility** to correct volume errors. Finally, you learned about **NSS** and the utilities used to monitor and manage NSS volumes.

Unit 20

In this unit, you learned about **system fault tolerance** and learned how to **plan** for handling disasters. You also learned about **RAID, disk duplexing**, and **disk stripping with parity**. You learned about **disk configurations** including **volume sets** and disk stripping. You learned that disk configuration provides valuable options for a Windows administrator. Next, you learned about **replication** and discussed the key points about replication. You learned that replication can offer additional data redundancy on Windows Server-based networks. You then learned about **NDS/eDirectory partition** and **NDS/eDirectory replicas**. You also learned about **replica rings**. Finally, you learned about **backup** and **removable media**. You learned that removable media provide a convenient way to archive data. You also learned about **Uninterruptible Power Supply (UPS)** and about choosing a UPS. You learned that UPS keeps a system from going down unexpectedly.

Unit 21

In this unit, you learned about **service packs**, **support packs**, and **updates**, as well as **hot fixes** and **patches**. You also learned about **device driver updates** and **application updates**. Finally, you learned about **viruses** and types of viruses. You also learned about **anti-virus programs**.

Unit 22

In this unit, you learned about the human aspects of **troubleshooting** and the importance of **prioritizing problems**. You learned that in case multiple, unrelated problems occur simultaneously on the network, you should address the problem that affects the maximum number of users first. You learned about the general procedures followed, giving you a systematic approach towards troubleshooting network problems. The steps that you learned are **identifying the symptoms and exact issue, identifying the area that is affected by the problem, identifying what changes have been made, isolating the cause, formulating an action plan and implementing the solution, testing the results, identifying the solution's results and effects and documenting the problem, the solution, and the process you followed to arrive at the solution**. Next, you learned how to **troubleshoot** various **common problems** that might occur on the network. You also learned how to troubleshoot a few scenarios related to **connectivity issues, file and system rights issues, resource access issues,** and **network services issues.**

Topic B: Continued learning after class

It's impossible to learn to use any technology effectively in a single course. To get the most out of this class, you should begin using your newly acquired skills and knowledge to perform real tasks as soon as possible. Course Technology also offers resources for continued learning.

Next courses in this series

This is the only course in this series.

Other resources

For more information, visit www.course.com

Glossary

Active Directory (AD)

Directory service that provides a central repository for information about the users and resources on a Windows 2000 or later network.

Active Directory Users and Computers

A Windows 2000 and later administrative tool for creating and managing user and computer accounts.

Active hub

Retransmits the data with proper transmission voltage and current.

Address database

An association of a computer's hexadecimal address with its friendly name.

Application errors

Errors relating to application or data files.

Automatic Private Internet Protocol Addressing (APIPA)

IP addressing system in which a client can assign an IP address to itself in the event that a DHCP server isn't available.

Backbone

A high-speed network link connecting only segments.

Backup Domain Controller (BDC)

Windows NT Server having a backup copy of domain security information. The BDC can validate logon and security access.

Baseband

Transmission method that uses the media in such a way that the entire capacity of the cable is taken up by a single transmission. Used in most networks.

Bastion host

A heavily fortified server on the network through which all external traffic must pass. On the bastion host, all services but those absolutely essential to running the system are eliminated. In this way, even if an intruder were to break into the system, damage would be limited.

Beaconing

In Token Ring networks, when a station detects a hard error, it begins to transmit beacon frames. The beacon frame is used to define a failure domain. The failure domain includes the station reporting the failure, its nearest active upstream neighbor (NAUN), and everything in between.

Binary digits (bit)

A computer only knows two states: ON and OFF. Each bit is either a one (1), or zero (0). The Binary Digit 1 represents "ON," while the number 0 represents "OFF." The term "bit" is derived from Binary DigIT. Eight bits make up a byte.

Bindery

Set of files that held user and other resource information in NetWare 3.x and earlier networks.

Binding

The process by which an object's type library is located.

Bluetooth

Allows for the creation of small, short range, wireless networks comprised of computers, keyboards, mice, PDAs, etc., usually within a single room. Bluetooth has a range of 10 meters, speeds of up to 1 Mbps and uses FHSS for its transmission method

Boot PROM chip

An add-on item to a network adapter, which helps a computer to boot entirely from a network server, therefore not using a local hard or floppy drive.

Bridge

Network devices that are more intelligent than repeaters because they can read the specific physical address of devices on one network and filter information before passing it on to another network segment.

Broadband

Transmission method in which the communicators use different frequencies to separate their messages from others by using the same media at the same time.

Brouters

Handle both routable and non-routable features by acting as routers for routable protocols and bridges for non-routable protocols

Bus topology

A network topology that consists of a linear transmission medium that is terminated at both ends.

Cable tester

Performs two functions, namely checking continuity and also the exact wiring order of a piece of cable.

Cabling

The arterial system of any network, which carries within it the data that is the lifeblood of your network.

Cache hits

The number of times the NetWare operating system is able to retrieve information from server RAM, as opposed to reading from a hard disk, which is significantly slower. Higher values indicate better performance.

CD server

Usually a stand-alone device with four or more CD-ROM drives. Can provide the entire enterprise with access to installation media, such as workstation applications, reference media and periodicals, or any other data needed by multiple users.

Campus Area Network (CAN)

Networks in geographically contiguous buildings connected together.

Carrier Sense Multiple Access with Collision Avoidance (CSMA/CD)

Channel access method in which all systems listen for signals from all other systems and all systems have concurrent access to the media. If two systems transmit data at the same time, a collision occurs and data is retransmitted.

Carrier Sense Multiple Access with Collision Detection

Channel access method similar to CSMA/CD, but the goal is to avoid rather than detect collisions. Before actual data is sent, an alert message is sent. Thus, if collisions do occur, they occur with the alert data, not the actual data.

Channel access method

Determines the physical methodology by which data is sent across the transmitting media.

Channel Service Unit/Data Service Unit (CSU/DSU)

Forms the connection point between a T1 line and the customer's internal network.

Child partition

A partition located below another partition.

Client/Server model

The Client/Server Model concerns networking and provides for distributed processing.

Coaxial cable

Cable that is composed of two conductors that share the same axis. The center cable is insulated by plastic foam, then a second conductor, foil wrap, and an external plastic tube. Coaxial cable must always be terminated at both ends and the outer conductor grounded at only one end.

Collision

In some networking schemes, any station might transmit when it senses that the carrier is free. A collision occurs when two stations transmit simultaneously. If a collision is detected, each station will wait for a randomly determined interval before retransmitting the data.

Common Management Information Protocol (CMIP)

The OSI-based protocol expected to provide standard management of network devices in general.

Computer equipment

Refers to the hardware that physically handles data on the network.

ConsoleOne

Administrative utility to create and manage objects in NetWare 5.x and later networks.

Container object

Object in a directory that can hold other objects.

Context

The context points to where you are located in the NDS/eDirectory tree. This serves as a logical pointer to an object, such as a user, printer, or server.

Crossover cable

Refers to a length of network cable that has been wired to provide a connection from one hub to another, or alternatively, from one network interface card to another, alleviating the need of an Ethernet hub.

Crosstalk

The disturbance caused in a circuit by an unwanted transfer of energy from another circuit. Also, interference that occurs when cables are too close to each other, resulting in loss or corruption of data.

Cyclic Redundancy Check

A redundancy check in which the check key is generated by a cyclic algorithm. Also, a system checking or error checking performed at both the sending and receiving station after a block check character has been accumulated.

Data link layer

Specifies how devices attached to the network gain access to the various computing resources.

Dedicated server

A computer that can perform only server functions.

Direct Sequence Spread Spectrum (DSSS)

Wireless transmission technology where the data being transmitted is spread over multiple frequencies, allowing for higher throughput rates. Operates on the 2.4 Ghz band.

Disk duplexing

An implementation of Redundant Arrays of Independent Disks (RAID) Level 1 that is similar to disk mirroring. It uses two disk drives that are configured to have the same logical size. Both drives are connected to separate disk controllers. During each data write, the same data is written to both disks. It is designed to keep a network going in spite of disk errors or the loss of a hard disk. If a read error occurs, data from the other disk is used.

Disk mirroring

An implementation of Redundant Arrays of Independent Disks (RAID) Level 1. It uses two disk drives configured with equal-sized partitions and connected to the same disk controller. During each data write, the same data is written to both disk partitions. It is designed to keep the computer operational in spite of disk errors or loss of a hard disk.

Display filter

Used to eliminate extraneous data and to focus on specific types of data.

Distance vector

Algorithms in which each node maintains the distance from itself to each possible destination.

DoD (Department of Defense) reference model

A four-layer architectural model that TCP/IP is based on.

Domain

A logical grouping for file servers within a network, managed as an integrated whole.

Domain name space

The hierarchical structure identifying domain names.

Domain Name System (DNS)

A hierarchical, distributed method of organizing system and network names on the Internet.

Dotted decimal notation

An IP address represented as four octets or bytes, separated by periods. For example: 195.143.67.2.

Dynamic Host Configuration Protocol (DHCP)

A TCP/IP application-layer protocol that provides dynamic address assignment on a network.

Dynamic router

Automatically configured and updated router. Uses either RIP or OSPF as the routing protocol.

E-mail server

Dedicated server that handles E-mail and other groupware applications exclusively.

Encapsulating mode

The mode in which a bridge packages frames of one format into the format of another.

Ethernet hub

A device that takes the signal transmitted from one computer and propagates it to all the other computers on the network.

Event Viewer

A Windows administrative tool that might be used to monitor peripheral management. You can also see the extent of errors by using the Event Viewer.

Explicit trustee rights

Rights granted directly to an object at any level of the file system in a NetWare network.

Fiber distributed data interface (FDDI)

Uses a double fiber ring and runs at 100 Mbps. It is typically found as the backbone connecting buildings on a campus or wider area.

File Transfer Protocol (FTP)

Used to transfer text and binary files between systems, including dissimilar platforms. If necessary, it will perform a format and type conversion on the file.

Firewall

Used as a security measure between a company's local area network (LAN) and the Internet. The firewall prevents users from accessing certain address Web sites. A firewall also helps to prevent hackers from accessing internal resources on the network. Today, firewalls are commonly used to prevent unauthorized access to a network from the Internet.

FireWire (IEEE 1394)

An external serial bus standard with speeds of up to 400 Mbps. It is most commonly used to connect peripherals to computers, such as external hard drives, video devices, printers, and so on.

Frame

In IEEE (Institute of Electrical and Electronics Engineers) terminology, the unit of data transferred at the OSI (Open Systems Interconnection) data link layer.

Frequency Hopping Spread Spectrum (FHSS)

Wireless transmission technology where data is transmitted on a single frequency at any given time. However, the signal hops from frequency to frequency in a pseudorandom pattern. Operates on the 2.4 Ghz band.

Full-duplex

Communication method where both parties can transmit simultaneously. The computer can receive data while it is transmitting and vice versa.

Gateway

The primary linkage between mixed environments, such as PC-based LANs and host environments, such as SNA.

Global group

A group definition that facilitates permission assignments to local machines or other domains through local group membership of the global group.

Groupware

E-mail packages that provide more functionality than just e-mail. Some examples of popular groupware packages are Microsoft Exchange, Novell GroupWise, and Lotus Notes.

Half-duplex

Communications method where each participant only transmits when the other listens. There is no way for two computers to transmit at the same time.

Hardware loopback test

A diagnostic test that transmits a signal across a medium while the sending device waits for the return of the signal.

Host

A computer that is remotely accessible and provides information or services for users on a network.

Hub

In disk drives, the hub is the central mechanism within the drive that causes the disk to rotate and keeps it centered during the rotation. On floppy diskettes, the hub fits into the hole in the center of the diskette to keep it level and balanced during rotation. In networking, a central connecting point for network wiring.

Hybrid/Partial mesh

Mesh topologies used for interconnecting only the most important sites with multiple links.

iManager

Web-based administrative utility used to create and manage objects in NetWare 5.x and later networks.

Infrared

Wireless technology that allows for wireless connection of devices at very close range. For example, IR technology can be used to connect a keyboard or mouse to a computer. Is line of sight technology with a range of up to 1 meter and speeds from 115 Kbps to 4 Mbps.

Inherited Rights Filter (IRF)

In NetWare 4.x and later, the Inherited Rights Filter (IRF) restricts access privileges to a specific object. The IRF blocks rights that would normally flow down from a parent object. When an IRF has been altered to block rights inheritance, the filter is referred to as a restrictive IRF.

Integrated Services Digital Network (ISDN)

A special kind of telecommunications network designed to handle more than just data. By using existing telephone lines and computer networks, integrated networks can handle video, text, voice, data, facsimile images, and graphics.

Internet Assigned Numbers Authority (IANA)

Responsible for assigning and managing Internet IP addresses and address classes.

Internet gateway

Hardware that provides a LAN connection port, and a connection to the Internet that typically is shared by all computers on the network. Uses a single IP address.

Internetwork Packet Exchange (IPX)

Used with SPX as the resident protocol in NetWare 4.x and earlier. A router with IPX routing can interconnect Local Area Networks (LANs) so that Novell NetWare clients and servers can communicate.

Internetworking

Defined as the technology and devices by which computers can communicate across different types of networks.

IP address

Each host in the network is assigned a unique IP address for each network connection (installed network adapter). The IP address is used to identify packet source and destination hosts. It is a 32-bit address, written as 4 octets (bytes) separated by periods. For example, 195.143.67.2.

IPX/SPX protocol

Consists of Internetwork Packet Exchange (IPX), which runs at the network layer of the OSI Model and Sequenced Packet Exchange (SPX), which runs at the transport layer.

Layer 2 switch or data switch

Generally a more modern term for multiport bridge.

Leaf object

A type of NetWare object that does not contain other objects. Examples are user, printer, or server objects.

Learning bridge

Listens to each of the attached cable segments and creates a table of addresses originating on each segment.

Legacy

The term used to define an existing mainframe or minicomputer environment.

Local Access Transport Areas (LATAs)

Wide area network (WAN) that links networks, which are located in different local calling areas.

Local Area Network (LAN)

A group of computers running specialized communications software and joined through an external data path. A LAN will cover a small geographic area, usually no larger than a single building. A LAN has centralized management of resources and network security.

Local bridge

A bridge that has a LAN link directly attached on each side.

Local group

When discussing Windows Domains, it is a group definition supporting local domain resource management. When discussing Workstations, it is a group definition supporting local management of a Windows NT/2000 workstation.

Logical disk counter

Monitors the activity on logical partitions.

MAC address

The hardware address of a device connected to a channel, such as the address of a terminal connected to an Ethernet.

Macro viruses

Viruses that use the macro language of the specific application to spread.

Member server

A server in a Windows domain that is not a domain controller.

Mesh topology

A configuration that consists of a network in which each device has a point-to-point connection to every other device on the network. This gives the dedicated capacity of a point-to-point link to each device and provides significant fault tolerance.

Metropolitan Area Network (MAN)

A complete communications network set up by a local telephone company. A MAN is larger than a LAN (Local Area Network), but smaller than a WAN (Wide Area Network). It might be made up of several LANs. MANs provide an integrated set of services for real-time voice, data, and image transmission.

Modem

An abbreviation for modulator/demodulator. A modem is a peripheral device that permits a personal computer, microcomputer, or mainframe to receive and transmit data in digital format across voice-oriented communications links, such as telephone lines.

MONITOR

NetWare server console utility that provides a wealth of server information you can use to gauge server performance and resource utilization.

Monolithic drivers

Have a .dsk extension and contain instructions for the controller and drives. NetWare Peripheral Architecture (NPA) drivers consist of two separate drivers. The driver with the .ham extension contains instructions for the controller; the driver with the .cdm extension controls the hard drive itself. NPA drivers are preferred.

Multimeter

Comes in two varieties, analog and digital. Digital versions feature an audible continuity tester while analog versions do not. Can measure resistance.

Multistation Access Unit (MSAU)

Similar in functionality to an Ethernet hub, but for use in Token Ring networks. Even though most Token Ring networks look like a star, they work as a ring. The Multistation Access Unit (MSAU) makes this possible.

Name resolution

The process of converting the friendly name to its IP address. Computers need the IP address to converse with another host.

NetBIOS

Standard programming interface for the development of distributed applications.

NetBIOS Extended User Interface (NetBEUI)

A non-routable transport protocol written to the NetBIOS interface.

NetWare Remote Manager (NRM)

Web-based utility that lets you perform NetWare server monitoring and maintenance.

Network adapter

The card that makes it possible for a computer to interface with the network. Also known as a Network Interface Card (NIC).

Network Address Translation (NAT)

Enables translation of private network addresses into valid Internet addresses.

Network Device Interface Specification (NDIS)

An industry standard for Monolithic Protocol networking model developed by Microsoft and 3Com Corporation

Network fax server

Permits users to send and, in some cases, receive facsimiles at their network workstations. Fax servers manage the re-direction of faxes to the appropriate location. Some fax servers are software-based products that are loaded on a server, while others are separate hardware devices.

Network Interface Card (NIC)

Hardware that lets you connect a workstation computer to the network. Specifically, a NIC provides a communication channel between your computer's motherboard and the network.

Network layer

The OSI layer that is responsible for routing, switching, and accessing the subnetwork across the entire OSI environment.

Network Monitor

Gives administrators the ability to detect and troubleshoot network problems.

Network Neighborhood/Network Places

The focal point for browsing network resources from a Windows 95, 98, NT/2000/XP Workstation.

Network operating system (NOS)

The software running at the server, which provides the network environment for the server and the clients.

New Technology File System (NTFS)

File system used in Windows NT/2000/XP/Windows Server 2003 that brings many advantages over older file systems such as FAT and FAT32. Supports encryption, compression, and file and folder-level security.

Novell Directory Service (NDS)/eDirectory

Directory service that provides a central repository for information about the users and resources on a NetWare 4.x or later network. Is also available for different platforms, such as Windows, Linux, Solaris and others.

nwconfig command

A NetWare 5.x and later utility used at the server console.

Open Datalink Interface (ODI)

NetWare software used in open systems. ODI makes it possible for one network board, LAN driver, and cabling system to support multiple connections to communications protocols, such as AppleTalk, IPX/SPX, and TCP/IP and uses them interchangeably.

Open Systems Interconnection (OSI)

To support international standardization of network terminology and protocols, the International Standards Organization (ISO) proposed a reference model of open systems interconnection. Currently under development, OSI ensures that any open system will communicate with any other OSI-compliant system.

Orthogonal Frequency Division Multiplexing (OFDM)

Wireless transmission technology where the radio signal is split into multiple, smaller signals. These signals are then transmitted at the same time, but at different frequencies. Operates on the 5 Ghz band, which makes it more resistant to interference.

OSI application layer

The layer that provides a series of definitions that are used to provide network-wide system management functions.

OSI layer 1

OSI layer 1 is the Physical layer. It is the lowest of the seven defined layers of the generalized network architecture. It defines the transmission of bits over a communication channel, ensuring that 1s and 0s are recognized as such. The physical layer accepts and transmits a bit stream without recognizing or defining any structure or meaning.

OSI layer 2

OSI layer 2 is the Data link layer. It provides methodologies for transforming the new Physical layer link into a channel that appears free of errors to the network layer (the next higher layer). The Data link layer accomplishes this by splitting the input or data stream provided in the physical layer into data frames that are transmitted sequentially as messages and by processing the acknowledgment (ACK) frames sent back over the channel by the receiver.

OSI layer 3

OSI layer 3 is the Network layer. It accepts messages of data frames from the transmitting host, converts the messages to packets, and routes the packets to their destination.

OSI layer 4

OSI layer 4 is the Transport layer. It accepts data from the Session layer (the next layer up, which is the human user's interface to the network), splits this data into smaller units, passes these units down to the Network layer, and ensures that all the pieces arrive at the destination in the correct order.

OSI layer 5

OSI layer 5 is the Session layer. It is the user's interface into the network through which the user establishes a connection with a process on another distant machine.

OSI layer 6

The Presentation layer protocols format the data to meet the needs of different computers, terminals, or presentation media in the user's end-to-end communications. The protocols at this layer might also provide data encryption for security purposes in transmission over networks or data compression for efficiency and economy.

OSI layer 7

OSI layer 7 is the Application layer. It specifies the protocols for the user's intended interaction with the distant computer, including such applications as database access, document interchange, or financial transactions. Certain industry-specific end-to-end application protocols, such as in banking or airline reservations, enable computers and terminals of connection created by a physical link.

Packet filtering

The technique of examining each datagram as it passes through a router. If the contents of the datagram agree with the criteria defined by the security administrator and stored on the router, then the datagram is passed on to its destination. If the contents do not agree with the criteria, the packet is discarded.

Parent partition

A partition that is located immediately above the root of another partition.

Partition root

The container closest to the directory tree's root. The partition's name is derived from its partition root.

Passive hub

Takes incoming electrical signals on one port and passes them down the cable on its other ports. In this way, all nodes see the signal just as if they were all connected on a physical bus topology.

Peer-to-peer

Communication in which two communications systems communicate as equal partners sharing the processing and control of the exchange, as opposed to host-terminal communication in which the host does most of the processing and controls the exchange.

Performance Monitor

Gives a graphical representation of Windows systems and is used to locate and resolve performance bottlenecks.

Physical layer

The OSI layer that provides the means to activate and use physical connections for bit transmission. In plain terms, the Physical Layer provides the procedures for transferring a single bit across a Physical Media.

Point-to-Point Tunneling Protocol (PPTP)

Provides secure client connections over the Internet.

POTS or Plain Old Telephone Service

The standard telephone service subscribed to for making voice calls.

Presentation layer

Translates data into an appropriate transmission format. One function maintained at this layer is terminal emulation, which helps workstations that use different local data formats to communicate.

Primary Domain Controller (PDC)

Windows NT Server that stores the master copy of domain security information. It is the controlling system for the domain.

Print server

Dedicated or non-dedicated server that provides printing functionality to users in the network. Network-direct printers feature internal network interfaces that provide a direct connection to the network cable system and can also serve as print servers.

Private Internet/Intranet

A network that will not be connecting directly to the Internet.

Promiscuous mode

Makes it possible for a network adapter card to hear all the frames that pass over the network.

Protected mode

The operating mode of the 80286 microprocessor that makes it possible for the operating system to use features that protect one application from another, also called Protect Mode.

Protocol

A set of strict rules (usually developed by a standards committee) that governs the exchange of information between computer devices. Also, a set of semantic and syntactic rules that determine the behavior of hardware and software in achieving communication.

Protocol Data Units (PDU)

The virtual connections between layers of the OSI stack.

Provisioning

A term used by the telecommunication industry to describe the configuration of telephone lines.

Proxy server

Another type of firewall, sometimes called an IP proxy. The IP proxy masks the IP address of internal hosts and represents itself instead.

Redundant Array of Independent Disks (RAID)

Usually referred to as a RAID system. RAID systems are typically expensive. It is composed of multiple hard disks that can either act independently or emulate one large disk. A RAID disk system facilitates increased capacity, speed, and reliability.

Remote Access Service (RAS)

Windows service that provides remote access capabilities to computers. A Windows machine can be configured to be a RAS server or a RAS client.

Remote bridge

A bridge that links a local network across a wide area segment.

Repeaters

Used to extend the physical length of a LAN.

Replica

A physical copy of a partition.

Replica synchronization

The process when changes made to a partition are forwarded to all servers holding replicas of the data in that partition.

Replication

Process whereby data directories are dynamically copied between selected file servers and transactions are applied to copies of database tables.

Request For Comments (RFC)

The name of the result and process for creating a standard on the Internet. New standards are proposed and published on line as a Request For Comments.

Ring topology

Provides a closed-loop transmission medium. Repeaters at each node connection duplicate the signal. This is done to minimize signal degradation.

Router

A connection between two networks that specifies message paths and might perform other functions, such as data compression.

Schema

All of the objects and attributes that are available in a directory service directory such as Active Directory or NDS/eDirectory.

Scope

The range of valid addresses.

Segment

The portion of the network on either side of two network transmission devices, such as a router, bridge, or repeater.

Sequenced Packet Exchange (SPX)

A Novell protocol used as the resident protocol in NetWare, along with IPX.

Serial Line IP (SLIP)

An Internet protocol used to run IP to connect two systems over serial lines such as telephone circuits or RS-232 cables. SLIP is now being replaced by PPP.

Server

A computer or a software package that provides services to client software running on other computers on a network. Possible services include file sharing, printer sharing, or communications services.

Service Data Units (SDUs)

The physical connections between each layer of the OSI stack.

Service packs

Hot fixes combined with additional software fixes to form a minor software upgrade.

Session

The duration of the connection between two applications on different systems.

Session layer

OSI Layer 5 providing means for dialogue control between end systems.

Shared folder

A data resource in a Windows network that has been made available to authorized network clients

Share permissions

Permissions for shared directories. Share permissions can be assigned for directory shares located on a FAT or NTFS partition.

Shielded Twisted Pair (STP)

Includes a protective sheathing around the copper wire. The twisted pair is wrapped in foil to cut down on outside interference and electromagnetic radiation.

Simple Network Management Protocol (SNMP)

A TCP/IP-based management protocol that might be implemented on routers.

Socket creep

The phenomenon in which the sockets creep out of the board due to the difference in the expansion rates.

Star topology

Star/hub networks connect the peripheral devices via point-to-point links to a central location. An Active Hub regenerates signals while Passive Hubs act as a terminating point for the network. Star topologies provide architectural flexibility but might need more cable than traditional bus and ring topologies.

Static router

Manually configured and updated router.

Subnet mask

A filter that separates subnetted addresses into network and local entities. Local systems have subnet masks so they can restrict the broadcast to be received on the local network only.

Switch

See Layer 2 switch.

Switching hub

Builds on the features of an active hub. Each port on a switching hub is isolated from the other ports. When a switching hub is first powered on, it listens to each port and makes a record of the NIC hardware address attached.

System log

Contains error and status messages regarding system devices and services.

Task Manager

Gives a list of the processes and applications that are currently running and also monitors their performance effectively.

The Internet

A collection of diverse networks, each connecting a range of systems together for a distinct purpose.

Time Domain Reflectometer (TDR)

A sophisticated tool used to find a break in the middle of a cable.

Token passing

Channel access method in which a token is passed among the nodes of the network; whichever node is in possession of the token is permitted to transmit. Token Ring uses token passing as its channel access method.

Tone generator

A device that emits an audible tone to test primarily for continuity.

Topology

Defines how the physical media links the network nodes. Examples are bus, star, ring and mesh.

Transceiver

Provides a connection between one media type and another without changing the channel access method.

Translating bridge

Bridges that interconnect different types of networks, such as Ethernet and token ring. One example of this is the IBM model 8209 Ethernet to token ring bridge.

Transmission Control Protocol/Internet Protocol (TCP/IP)

TCP/IP is a protocol that makes communication between the same or different types of computers on a network possible. The Internet Protocol is stream-oriented and breaks data into packets.

Transport layer

OSI Layer 4, which is responsible for reliable end-to-end data transfer between end systems.

Transport protocols

Manages network communication. They determine how data moving up and down through the communications model should be presented to the next layer.

Trust relationships

A one-way or two-way logical relationship established between two Windows Server domains and significant only in a multiple-domain environment.

Trustee rights

Rights granted to users, groups, or NDS container objects to give specific access privileges to directories, subdirectories, and files. Admin or any user who possesses sufficient rights in the file system can grant rights.

Twisted Pair (TP)

Cabling specification that uses two or more pairs of wire, twisted together and housed in a single protective sheath. Often used in star topologies.

Uninterruptible Power Supply (UPS)

Keeps your system from going down unexpectedly due to line power loss.

Unshielded Twisted Pair (UTP)

A set of twisted pairs within a plastic sheath. Common types are Category 3, 5, 5e and 6.

Upgrading

A term used to describe the physical implementation of a new operating system in the place of an older one.

User Manager

A Windows NT user and group administration utility.

User-level security

The option of identifying users through a central security provider.

Virtual LAN (VLAN) features

Advanced filtering techniques implemented by switches to optimize performance.

Virtual Private Network (VPN)

Provides secure remote access to your network via the Internet.

Virus

A software program that has the ability to reproduce by modifying other programs or duplicating itself

Well-known ports

The ports at which an application listens for a request.

Wide Area Networks (WANs)

Expand the basic LAN model by linking LANs and making it possible for them to communicate with each other. By traditional definition, a LAN becomes a WAN when it crosses a public right-of-way, requiring a public carrier for data transmission. More current usage of the term usually includes any situation where a network expands beyond one location/building. A WAN is characterized by low- to high-speed communication links and usually covers a wide geographic area.

Windows Internet Name Service or WINS

An automated way of supporting NetBIOS address resolution. It is analogous to DNS in that it does away with the necessity of maintaining static LMHOSTS files on each Windows-based machine on the network.

Windows sockets or Winsock

A standard application interface defining communications between Windows and the underlying protocol stack.

Wireless

Communication method that enables computers to be connected to each other and peripherals to be connected to computers without the use of cables.

Wireless Access Point (WAP)

Device to which wireless clients connect to in turn get connected to a private network or the Internet.

Workgroup

A logical group of computers characterized by a decentralized security and administration model.

Workstation

Described as a personal computer that is connected to a network, which can perform tasks through applications or utilities.

xDSL

Family of technologies that provide high speed remote access through regular copper telephone lines or over fiber optic cable.

Index

V

Victim machines, 12-4
Viruses, 21-5
  CMOS, 21-7
  Excel, 21-6
  Macro, 21-6
  Protection, 21-5, 21-8
  Recovery, 21-10
  Specialized, 21-6
  Word, 21-6
VLANs, 6-12
VPNs, 4-28, 7-24

W

WANs, 1-6, 7-34
WEP, 4-31
Wi-Fi, 4-31
Windows 2000, 14-5
Windows file systems, 17-21
Windows NT, 14-2
  Complete trust model, 16-33

Domains, 16-29
  Master domain model, 16-32
  Multiple Master domain model, 16-32
  Single domain model, 16-32
  Trust relationships, 16-30
Windows Server 2003, 14-6
WINIPCFG, 13-4
WINS, 10-23, 11-14
  Client configuration, 11-15
Winsock, 9-18
Wireless, 4-15, 7-9
Wireless NICs, 3-3
Workgroups, 16-2
Workstations, 1-9

X

X.25 standard, 7-35
xDSL, 7-8

Z

Zeroconf, 9-14